Sales Promotion and Advertising:
A Legal Guide

AUSTRALIA
The Law Book Company
Brisbane . Sydney . Melbourne . Perth

CANADA
Carswell
Ottawa . Toronto . Calgary . Montreal . Vancouver

Agents:

Steimatzky's Agency Ltd., Tel Aviv;
N.M. Tripathi (Private) Ltd., Bombay;
Eastern Law House (Private) Ltd., Calcutta;
M.P.P. House, Bangalore;
Universal Book Traders, Delhi;
Aditya Books, Delhi;
MacMillan Shuppan KK, Tokyo
Pakistan Law House, Karachi, Lahore

SALES PROMOTION AND ADVERTISING:
A Legal Guide

by

RICHARD BAGEHOT
Solicitor of the Supreme Court,
Partner, Field Fisher Waterhouse

Contributing Author:
NICHOLAS BEECHAM
Solicitor of the Supreme Court,
Partner, Field Fisher Waterhouse

LONDON
SWEET & MAXWELL
1993

Published in 1993 by
Sweet & Maxwell Limited of
South Quay Plaza, 183 Marsh Wall, London E14 9FT
Computerset by York House Typographic Ltd., London W13 8NT
and printed in Great Britain by The Bath Press, Bath, Avon

British Library Cataloguing in Publication Data

A catalogue record for this book is available
from the British Library

ISBN 0-421-7220-0

Set in 10/11pt Plantin Roman

The index was prepared by Robert Spicer

No natural forests were destroyed to make this product; only farmed timber
was used and replanted

Acknowledgments

I would like to thank my patient secretary Pat Allen for all her work on the preparation of this book.

The Author also wishes to thank Her Majesty's Stationery Office who administer the following:

The Copyright, Designs & Patents Act 1988 (Parliamentary Copyright)
The Code of Practice for Traders on Price Indications (Crown Copyright)
H.M. Customs & Excise Materials (Crown Copyright)

Preface

It is not difficult to read all of the legislation, regulations and Codes of Practice which affect sales promotions and product advertising. Deciding how they affect a given promotion or advertisement is another matter. When reviewing a promotion or advertisement for legal clearance it can be difficult to recognise all the danger signals, especially those which are not obvious. Whether there is cause for alarm must involve analysis in the light of any applicable laws and Codes of practice, and a judgment has to be made which will be the basis of the clearance advice.

As promotions and advertisements become more ingenious, the potential for creating legal difficulties also increases. The most troublesome are those circumstances where the legal position is not clear, and a reasoned judgement has to be made on the risk of illegality or Code infringement.

Rather than starting with the law and seeing how it affects promotions and advertising, the author proposes to take common situations and illustrate the major areas of concern in practical, non-legal terms. As all promotions and advertisements are different, it is not possible to cover every conceivable contingency in this book, so the author's intention is to make the practitioner more aware of where danger may lurk.

The author does not intend this to be yet another "how to" book, but inevitably it has to deal with "how to" situations to provide a working context in which the risk in the promotion or advertisement can be identified and explained. This book is only a guide to selected features of promotions and advertisements. It is not an exhaustive or definitive work, and it is not a substitute for detailed legal advice on specific queries.

Richard Bagehot June 1993.

Contents

4   Lotteries, Competitions and Free Prize Draws

5 Consumer Product Advertising

9   Public Relations

Appendices   *page*

1 Promotions—Preliminary Considerations

LEGAL STATUS OF PROMOTIONS

A PROMOTION AS A LEGAL CONTRACT

Promotion participation rights

1.1.1 What legal rights (if any) does a buyer of a product have when he participates in a promotion which is attached to it? Are promotions voluntary and legally unenforceable arrangements, or do they constitute a legal contract between the participant and the manufacturer? If the promotion does not imply some contractual relationship between the manufacturer and the participant, then:

  (a) How can the winner of a valuable prize for a competition obtain his prize if the manufacturer decides not to present it?
  (b) Can the frustrated prizewinner sue the manufacturer for the prize, or can he claim damages instead?
  (c) What rights does a redemption applicant have if he does not receive his promotion gift?

Voluntary contract

1.1.2 The first question to consider is whether the parties intend that there should be a legally enforceable contract. Under the principle which was established by cases such as *Carlill* v. *The Carbolic Smoke Ball Company* [1893] 1 Q.B. 256 the promoted product carries an "open offer" to any person who is eligible under the rules to participate in the promotion. That open offer will be accepted by the buyer making his redemption application or his competition entry which will be received by the handling house as the agent for the manufacturer, at which time a contract will exist. That offer cannot be withdrawn by the manufacturer, subject to the promotion's closing date. The legal consideration (see para. 1.3) is the purchase by the consumer of the promoted product. The acceptance of the offer by the participant is the act of sending in the proofs of purchase, entry form, or whatever else is required to enable him to participate in the promotion.

Paragraphs 1.4 and 1.5 explore how else a legal contract can be constructed from the chain through which the promoted product passes, but it is very clumsy and not necessarily logical.

Effect of promotion illegality on consumer

1.1.3 Is the contract between the manufacturer and the participant nullified because the promotion happens to be, for example, an unlawful lottery? If the manufacturer refused to give the winner the star prize, could he sue the manufacturer for it? The illegality is not in the construction of the contract with the participant, it relates only to the manner in which the manufacturer has constructed the promotion, and therefore the winner could sue for the prize.

What is the position where the promotion mechanic is a "best" or a "reduced" price, such as a "buy now for £10—it will never be this cheap again". If a week later that advertiser is advertising and selling the same product for £5, does the purchaser at £10 have any remedy against the advertiser? Clearly the £10 advertisement has become misleading due to the subsequent £5 price reduction. The £10 advertisement amounts to a representation by the advertiser which induced the consumer to buy the product at that apparently attractive price. There was no misrepresentation by the advertiser at the time the £10 advertisement was published, unless the consumer can prove that the advertiser already intended to drop the price subsequently. That fundamental misrepresentation would enable the consumer to claim £5 damages against the advertiser. If the advertiser could show that it had no such intention when making the £10 sale, the consumer would have no remedy. This would be the case if the £5 reduction is made a long time after the £10 sale, despite the "never again" representation.

Would the position be any different if the advertisement stated "Buy now at £10, it will never be this price again"? The statement is correct as it is written, but the general consumer perception of it would be that any subsequent price would be higher. If the next price was £5 one week later, on balance the £10 price would be found to have been misleading; but providing a contractual misrepresentation would be difficult.

EXPECTATIONS OF PARTICIPANTS

Products must be bought

1.2.1 The benefit of a promotion to the manufacturer is that it provides an inducement to consumers to purchase the promoted product as (with certain exceptions) they have no other means of participating in the promotion. With the exception of free prize draws, all participants in consumer product promotions have to submit proofs of purchase of a specified number of items of the product to comply with the promotion rules.

Intended legal status

1.2.2 A purchaser of a product who participates in the promotion expects the manufacturer to be legally bound to give him whatever he has become entitled to receive as a result of his participation. If the purchaser has fulfilled his commitments under the promotion rules, such as sending in a gift redemption application or a competition entry form plus proofs of purchase of the promoted product, the manufacturer must honour its advertised promotion commitments to that purchaser. Although they may not be conscious of it, both purchasers and manufacturers therefore expect a promotion to be a legal contract which can be sued upon. Unlike other forms of contract, while the participant has good grounds to sue the promoter, there is nothing for which the promoter can sue the participant unless he is in breach of contract where the promoter suffers a loss worth suing for. For example, the participant may have fraudulently obtained a valuable main prize in a competition. Non-compliance with the rules by the participant would be a breach of contract, such as where a substantially excessive number of redemption applications for gifts has been made by the same person, and have been honoured by the handling house in error. In theory the manufacturer could sue the participant for any loss it sustains as a result of that breach, as the promotion constitutes a contract between them. Despite the legal status of the promotion, the likelihood of the promoter suing any participant who has breached the rules is extremely remote, and would only happen in exceptional circumstances.

WHAT CONSTITUTES A CONTRACT?

Necessary elements

1.3 For a legally binding contract to exist, the following elements must be present:

(a) *an unconditional offer* (in this case) by the manufacturer of the product;
(b) *an unconditional acceptance* of that offer by (in this case) a buyer of the product who participates in the promotion;
(c) *consideration* paid by the participant;
(d) an intention between the parties *to create a contractual relationship*;
(e) *the terms of the contract must be fixed* when the contract is concluded;
(f) *the contractual parties must be aware of, and must agree to, the contract terms*. These terms are the rules of the promotion and the mechanic instructions.

OFFER AND ACCEPTANCE

Subject to promotion rules

1.4.1 The manufacturer supplies the products, and the promotion offer is that if the buyer purchases the product, and if he complies with the promotion rules, he will be entitled to participate in the promotion and obtain the promotion benefit. The offer is conditional upon the buyer providing the required number of proofs of purchase of that product, and making a valid competition entry or redemption application.

Selective offer

1.4.2 The offer is only made by the manufacturer to the buyers of the promoted product who may be eligible to participate in the promotion as stated in the rules. For example, the rules may state that persons under 18, or those people who are involved in the creation and management of the promotion, are not entitled to participate in the promotion. If anyone who is ineligible to participate in a promotion does so, they are not entitled to receive the promotion benefits. However, the chances of ineligible participants being discovered and disqualified are remote except where a data base is maintained containing the details of all participants. This will be done for limited entry or application promotions.

Acceptance of offer

1.4.3 The acceptance of the offer is the act of participating in the promotion, such as entering the competition or applying for the voucher or the gift, in accordance with the promotion rules. This is the point at which the contract is made between the manufacturer and the buyer. Purchasing the product only entitles the purchaser to participate in the promotion if he decides to do so, but he has no obligation to do so. In most cases the product purchase does not automatically make the buyer a participant in the promotion. An exception is where, for example, the opening of a tin of cat food automatically gives the purchaser the chance of winning a valuable prize.

LEGAL CONSIDERATION

Benefit to manufacturer

1.5.1 For a contract to become legally effective, some adequate consideration has to pass (in this case) from the participant to the manufacturer, as it is the manufacturer, and not the retailer from whom the product is purchased, who is providing the promotion benefit to the participant. The two possible "considerations" are:

(a) the payment of money to the manufacturer for the purchase of the product. The awkward nature of this alternative is explained below.

(b) The direct connection between the buyer and the manufacturer. This happens only where the buyer becomes an active participant in the promotion by sending in to the manufacturer, via its handling house representative, whatever form of application or cntry is required under the promotion rules. In this alternative the manufacturer has already had its real benefit, *i.e.*, the sale price of the product. The buyer's participation in the promotion is not a benefit to the manufacturer, as honouring any form of redemption or prize represents an economic cost to the manufacturer each time. However, this application or entry is the only connection the buyer has with the manufacturer, and if it is not treated as consideration for the promotion contract, the argument under (a) above would have to prevail.

Who pays consideration?

1.5.2 In the context of a promotion the consideration element is curious, as the participating consumer does not buy the product direct from the manufacturer. As the promotion package of the product contains the promotion and the contract terms, and as the wholesaler has paid the manufacturer for the product which includes the proof of purchase, the wholesaler appears on the face of it to be the party entitled to enter into the promotion contract. Wholesalers are not excluded from participation in the promotion unless there is a rule which states that eligibility is limited to people who "purchase the product for bona fide home consumption", or a rule which excludes them in some other way.

Privity of contract

1.5.3 The consumer, at whom the promotion is aimed, buys the product from a retailer, who is two payment transactions (*i.e.* from manufacturer to wholesaler to retailer) away from the manufacturer who is making the promotion offer. Where is the contractual link between the manufacturer and the buyer? As the buyer cannot buy the product from the manufacturer directly, to create a contractual position, the retailer would have to be considered to be the agent of the manufacturer to pass on the promotion to the buyer, and to collect from him the "consideration" purchase price.

Satisfaction of consideration

1.5.4 On a practical level it is accepted by manufacturers that whoever is eligible to participate in the promotion is entitled to exercise the contractual right to do so. This is so whether it is on the basis that the consideration element for a binding contract has been satisfied, or whether it is the binding acceptance of a voluntary offer contract. This universal custom of the sales promotion industry would be a material factor should the enforceability of a promotion as a legal contract be considered by the courts.

WHAT ARE THE CONTRACT TERMS?

Mechanic instructions and promotion rules

1.6 The mechanic instructions ("the mechanic", see definition in para. 2.1.4) and the promotion rules between them constitute the terms of the promotion, and therefore they also constitute the contract terms. The mechanic instructions represent the commercial terms and the rules represent the administrative terms. A buyer should always make sure that he understands the promotion terms, so that he does not invalidate his competition entry or his redemption application by being too late or by otherwise being in breach of the rules. Buyers seldom read all (or any) of the terms of the promotion on the package before buying the product, and they may not do so afterwards if the promotion mechanic is a familiar one. For that reason if the promotion has any unusual and important rules they should be highlighted prominently on the product package. Section 5.8 of the ASA Sales Promotion Code of Practice gives examples of those rules which must be easily visible on the product container, so that the buyer is aware of them from the outset.

LEGAL CLEARANCE OF PROMOTIONS

LEGAL CLEARANCE

Risk assessment

1.7.1 Legal clearance is desirable because the statement of the relevant law may be clear, but its application to the promotion which is being examined may not be clear. The risk of illegality then becomes a matter of interpretation and judgment. If a manufacturer, having obtained legal advice on the promotion, decides for commercial reasons to proceed with a risky or a plainly illegal promotion, the legal clearance procedure will at least have given it an assessment of:

(a) what makes the promotion illegal;
(b) the likelihood of discovery and legal action being taken by the authorities; and
(c) the potential consequences of a successful prosecution.

An example is the lottery style of promotion which has built in to it a "saving grace" rule of free entry, *i.e.*, without having to buy the promoted product. It is not certain whether such a promotion is illegal under the present law, although a strong indication was given in December 1991 by the Crown Prosecution Service (see Chapter 4, paragraph 21). Ultimately only a test prosecution or an amendment of section 14 of the Lotteries and Amusements Act 1976 will settle the uncertainty. It appears that the Crown Prosecution Service would not be willing to bring any major prosecution against a manufacturer for running an allegedly illegal promotion unless doing so would be clearly in the public interest, and a conviction would be likely. This does not apply to prosecutions brought in magistrates courts by Trading Standards Officers.

Agency implied good faith obligation

1.7.2 Even if there is no reference to the point in the advertising agency's contract with its manufacturer client, one of the implied good faith obligations of an advertising agency is to present to the manufacturer, for approval, promotions which are legal and which comply with the Codes of Practice. If the illegality of the promotion is discovered by the agency or by the manufacturer at a late stage of development of the promotion, or even after its public launch, there are great pressures on the manufacturer to run with it despite the known risk. The manufacturer should query any clause in the agency contract to the effect that it will be the sole responsibility of the manufacturer client to approve for legality and code of practice compliance all material which is created and presented to it by the agency. The only exception should be where the manufacturer insists upon using a specific and potentially risky mechanic for the promotion, or where it provides quotations or other promotion text material to the agency. To avoid any misunderstanding, the party which is to take the ultimate responsibility for an illegal promotion and the consequences of it being legally challenged successfully must be clearly defined in the agency agreement.

Clearance initiation and follow-up

1.7.3 The legal clearance procedure should first be instigated when the promotion is a gleam in the eye of the agency executive. A phone call to the clearance expert to ask if the basic outline of the proposed promotion prompts any immediate alarm bells or useful suggestions can save a lot of wasted time and inconvenience at a later date. This can also incur a cost, and the agency agreement should clarify the circumstances in which the agency or the client will pay it. Clearance of the text and artwork of the promotion should be repeated at each major development stage, as significant modifications to already cleared material can change it to something which is illegal or misleading. This clearance procedure will enable the agency to make the necessary modifications without any interruption in the time schedule for developing, submitting and launching the promotion.

Commercial reasons for legal clearance

Successful clearance saves money

1.8 There are three major reasons why any agency, or a manufacturer's marketing department, should take expert advice on the legality and efficiency of each promotion, however simple it may appear:

(a) If there is no problem in the wording and in the construction of the promotion, then the time which is spent and the cost which is incurred by having the promotion legally checked is small.

(b) If a problem is identified and resolved, the cost of doing so is still modest when compared with the losses and expenses which can be incurred by the manufacturer as a result of being caught operating an illegal promotion.

(c) It should be a regular feature of the agency's service to its clients, because it serves as an independent check on potentially dangerous material caused through carelessness, ignorance or an excess of creative zeal.

Promotion interpretation

Clearance viewpoint

1.9.1 The person who is doing the legal review and clearance of any promotion should assume that he is in the shoes of a pedantic person who is trying to find any fault or error in the promotion, however trivial it may be. The wording and the meaning of the mechanic and the rules of the promotion should be analysed to see whether they can be interpreted so as to be unlawful, misleading, inconclusive or contrary to the relevant Code of Practice. For example, the meaning of the text may be at variance with an indication given by the illustrative artwork.

Does it mean what it says?

1.9.2 Complaints can be made about promotions where the interpretation or the deception which is alleged to exist is well outside what an ordinary consumer would understand by the wording in dispute. The English language is not always used precisely in promotion text, either because the text has to be kept short, or because it has been made to sound exciting and trendy. The same words or phrases can have different meanings when they are put into different contexts. It can be difficult to put a simple message into a foolproof, short form of wording. If the statement is ambiguous it must be amended accordingly.

Is the promotion really a free prize draw?

1.9.3 Free prize draws (see Chapter 4) are popular because they are easy to set up and to run, and no effort is needed by a participant other than completing the entry form. Designing hybrid free prize draws provides a fertile area for the legal pitfalls that can lie in the path of the unwary. Points to watch are whether there are:

(a) any conditions in the promotion rules which have to be performed to enable the participant to enter the draw which would nullify the "free" claim;

(b) any proof of purchase requirements; or

(c) any other form of direct or indirect contribution or consideration which is required from the participant which could constitute a form of entry fee.

If the answer is "yes" to any of these questions it could well be that it is not, in law, a free prize draw at all, and one must then go on to examine the points below to determine if it may be illegal.

Can it be construed as an illegal lottery?

1.9.4 If entry to the promotion is conditional upon some contribution from the entrant, does the promotion mechanic allow the winner to succeed only by chance? If it does, then the promotion will be an illegal lottery, subject to the promotion containing the uncertain benefit of a "saving grace" provision (see Chapter 4, paragraph 4.21.2). Where the promotion has an unusual mechanic it can be difficult to decide whether or not a contribution of skill is being made by participants.

Is it a truly skilful competition?

1.9.5 Is the means of getting the right answer to the competition question achievable by the exercise of skill, where adequate information and instructions are given in the mechanic? The skill, which is supposed to be exercised in obtaining the correct answer to the competition, may be wholly illusory, such as where the question is ridiculously easy. In such a case what is intended to be a lawful competition might be deemed in practice to be an unlawful lottery. Where there is no readily available information to which logic or skill can be applied in order to get a correct answer to the question, the entrant can only guess at what the answer may be—so again there is no possible skill alternative to the application of pure chance. The effect again will be the risk of it being an illegal lottery. If the proper exercise of skill will provide the correct answer to the competition, but instead it is arrived at by a wild guess of the entrant, that fact does not invalidate the competition entry and it does not make the competition into an illegal lottery.

9

Skilful elimination stages

1.9.6 Where there are many correct entries to a skilful competition, it is vital to establish in a legal manner how the winners of the main prize, and the secondary prizes, are to be ascertained from all of the potential winners. The elimination process has to be subject to an exercise of skill, and must not be dependent upon chance. It should be run as a legal mini-competition within the main promotion competition, and it is therefore subject to the same legal restraints. Elimination is usually achieved through using a panel of judges, or a tie-breaker, whichever is appropriate (see Chapter 4, paragraph 4.46).

Is the promotion clear?

1.9.7 A badly constructed promotion, particularly where it has inadequate rules, may have unexpected consequences. It can be both a nuisance and expensive for the manufacturer to be running a badly drafted promotion which might, for example, oblige it to provide more prizes than it had intended. This could happen where the rules of the promotion omit any means of reducing the number of successful participants down to the point at which only one of them is identified as the winner of the major prize. If that happens all of the apparent "winners" will claim the major prize, or its equivalent. The right of the manufacturer to be repaid its excess costs of providing additional prizes will depend on which of them is liable under the agency contract for legal approval.

Are the major promotion details visible on the product package?

1.9.8 The size and the design of the package will limit the space upon it for the promotion's mechanic and rules. The agency must check that the on-package details contain all the essential information relating to the promotion. To comply with section 5.8 of the Code of Sales Promotion Practice, everything by way of information or instruction which has to be visible on the promotion package must be capable of being seen without an exhaustive search. It must also be capable of being read without the necessity of a magnifying glass, and without having to interfere with the packaging.

Define proofs of purchase

1.9.9 If the product is cans of soup, and the manufacturer sells a line of four different flavours of soup, it would make sense to promote them all. If the rules of the promotion require the participant to provide as proofs of purchase a label from a can of each flavour, or from any combination of flavours, as opposed to four labels from a can of only one flavour, that condition must be made clear. Otherwise participants may make assumptions about the proof of purchase requirements which are not in accordance with the rules.

Is anything in the promotion text untrue or misleading?

1.9.10   In the case of a gift redemption promotion where there is a cash balance to be paid, is there a "value" attributed to the gift in the promotion text? Statements like "worth £x" may not be legal and have to comply with the requirements of the 1988 Price Indications Order which is set out in the DTI Code of Practice (see Appendix 2), but "Can be bought at Acme Stores for £x" is acceptable if that is true. The gift can be claimed to be "free" if no cash balance is involved, and if there is no other undeclared payment requirement (such as postage and packing). If the average retail cost of the gift item is £10, and if the cash balance payable on redemption is £5, it is not necessarily correct to claim a £5 saving for the gift. Some shops will charge more, and some less, to arrive at the average retail cost. Any price or value comparison or statement in the promotion text must be fair, accurate and readily checkable from reliable sources. See Chapter 3 for a discussion of "free gifts".

Is any statement misleading?

1.9.11   Helpful statements in the promotion's text are prone to being misleading unless they are worded carefully. For example, where the coupon from only one four-pack of beer will enable the buyer to obtain by mail a money-off voucher to be used against the price of the next product purchase, the manufacturer may be helpful by stating on the pack "only this purchase necessary". This example was queried by the Trading Standards Officer because a member of the public complained that he thought that he should get an immediate reduction from the four-pack he had purchased, despite the prominently placed and clear wording on the packaging that the promotion benefit is achieved through obtaining a voucher by mail to be used against the price of the "next purchase". The complaint revolved around the meaning of "only this purchase necessary", and it was found to be misleading in that context.

Avoid deception

1.9.12   Part of the legal vetting procedure should be to check whether there is any other statement of opinion or fact in the promotion text which needs qualifying or verifying. The question is whether there should be any additional explanatory information in the promotion material to prevent a purchaser of the product from being misled in respect of any statement or inference which affects any material aspect of the promotion.

Effect of clearance

1.9.13   If it is being prosecuted for an offence, the manufacturer should be able to show the court that it took reasonable precautions, including obtaining competent legal clearance advice that the promotion was legal prior to launching it, and that it acted responsibly and promptly upon discovery of the illegality. The court ought to take those factors into account when considering the penalty if it finds the manufacturer guilty of an offence. If the court decides that the manufacturer had been reckless, or that it knew of the illegality but ignored it, the penalty could be severe.

COST OF PREMATURE TERMINATION

CATEGORIES OF EXPENSE

1.10.1 If a promotion is found to be illegal after its launch, and if action is taken by the authorities quickly enough so that the manufacturer has to stop the promotion at the point of its maximum market exposure, the following are among the costs which could be incurred by the manufacturer as a result:

(a) withdrawing promotion packages of the product from sales outlets;
(b) cancelling any outstanding arrangements which have been made to run the promotion;
(c) calling in all point of sale or other material which refers to the promotion;
(d) possibly wasting any contents of withdrawn promotion packages which cannot be repackaged;
(e) cancelling any associated advertising;
(f) cancelling or postponing the handling house deal;
(g) cancelling or postponing redemption gift orders;
(h) publicly advertising that the promotion has been terminated and withdrawn, so that holders of proofs of purchase can be told what they should do with them.

Reinstatement costs

1.10.2 If the manufacturer wants to reinstate the promotion on a legal basis later in the year, the cost of doing so will not be less than the original cost of mounting the flawed promotion. Having a major promotion stopped dead in its tracks by a prosecution for illegality is a risk which manufacturers and all concerned with creating promotions must constantly keep in mind. In practice the delay between the relevant authorities becoming aware of the illegality, investigating it, deciding to prosecute the manufacturer for it, and a trial date being fixed will usually be such that all of the promotion packages of product would have been sold, so the question of scrapping it may not arise. Nevertheless, to continue running the promotion once the manufacturer is aware of its illegality could increase the size of any fine imposed by the court upon the manufacturer.

Scrap cost assessment

1.10.3   The cost to the manufacturer of scrapped product and lost profits will include:

(a) the wasted time of the plant in producing it, which is an ascertainable cost;
(b) the cost of the constituents which went into the scrapped product;
(c) the cost of the useless containers, less any scrap value;
(d) the manufacturer's loss profit on not being able to sell the scrapped product;
(e) all the manufacturer's internal and external administrative and other costs, including storage and transportation, which are attributable to the quantity of product which is being scrapped;
(f) wasted advertising and other promotion-related costs; and
(g) the cost of providing and reprinting new containers with the revised legal promotion on it.

RISK ASSESSMENT

COMMON RISKS

Lotteries

1.11.1   A common form of potential illegality is running an illegal lottery which is dressed up as an ostensible free prize draw. Since a lottery mechanic produces a much more exciting promotion, it will appeal to the gambling instincts of consumers. There is a risk of this happening if an agency starts designing the promotion as a free prize draw, changes the concept and (because participation depends on a product purchase) then tries to create a smokescreen of rules and mechanic instructions with the intention of hiding the illegality by what appears to be a lawful competition mechanic. The "free entry" hybrid is dealt with in Chapter 4, paragraph 21.

Risk of discovery

1.11.2   In practical terms the chances are modest that a simple short-term promotion which happens to be a lottery (although it looks like a competition or a free prize draw) will be challenged by the Crown Prosecution Service with the result that the manufacturer is prosecuted for running an illegal promotion. Occasionally there are major prosecutions in respect of promotions which might be construed as being illegal, or which are in a grey area of legality where the particular unusual interpretation of the law as presented by the promotion has not been tested in court. It is much more likely that misleading promotions will be picked up by Trading Standards Officers and the manufacturers prosecuted in a magistrates Court. However trivial-sounding the technical offence may be, if a manufacturer is successfully prosecuted over an illegal aspect of the promotion with the attendant publicity, hindsight will indicate that it was ridiculous for the manufacturer not to have had the promotion checked for legal clearance, or (as the case may be) not to have accepted and complied with legal advice which had been given that it was illegal. The question for the manufacturer is whether it is worth the risk of running an exciting but possibly illegal promotion to get greater advertising benefits and sales for the promoted product.

CONSEQUENCES OF PROSECUTION

High cost

1.12 The administrative problems for the manufacturer would be immense if a court were to make an order that an illegally promoted product had to be withdrawn from all wholesale and retail outlets at the height of a promotion in store. Some further consequences of a successful prosecution are that:

(a) The manufacturer will receive adverse publicity as the prosecution will be picked up by the local, and possibly the national press.

(b) The agency may be criticised by the manufacturer for having got the design or the wording of the promotion wrong. This will depend on whether the illegality was spotted before the launch of the promotion, and who took the decision to run with it in the light of that knowledge.

(c) There will be confusion among wholesalers and retail outlets until they receive an explanation and clear instructions on what to do with the stock.

(d) There is a criminal conviction recorded against the manufacturer. Rightly, manufacturers are sensitive about being found to be running an illegal promotion, however minor the offence.

(e) The manufacturer has to pay a fine and the legal costs of dealing with the prosecution.

(f) It is also possible that the retail outlet which sold the illegally promoted product will be prosecuted for doing so, and (a), (d) and (e) will apply equally well to them. Should that happen, the retail outlet would undoubtedly look to the manufacturer for an indemnity and re-imbursement of its expenses and losses.

(g) The manufacturer would have to accept the return of the banned stock which is removed from the shelves of retailers and wholesalers and give the retailer the appropriate credit.

PRIOR CONSULTATION WITH AUTHORITIES

PRELIMINARY ADVICE

Industry assistance

1.13.1 If there is any doubt as to whether a promotion may be illegal, misleading or in contravention of a Code of Practice, the Advertising Standards Authority, the Institute of Sales Promotion and the local Trading Standards Officer can be consulted for their opinions. A relatively simple point can be dealt with over the telephone, but if requested a copy of the text or artwork should be provided for them. Their initial opinion will provide experienced and practical guidance, but more detailed advice can be obtained if necessary. The fact of the manufacturer having taken the precaution to consult them would not affect the court's judgment on the illegality of the promotion, but it may influence the level of penalty. The advice which is given by the ASA, the ISP or a Trading Standards Officer to the manufacturer or to the agency is for guidance only. It is not intended to be a substitute for legal advice in the context of a client/solicitor relationship, with the responsibility which that entails if the advice is found to be incorrect, and the cause of a prosecution.

Provide the right information with the enquiry

1.13.2 The answer or the advice which an enquirer receives will depend on the accuracy and completeness of the question which is asked. If the enquirer has not correctly identified the real problem faced, he may be asking for advice on something which will not resolve the real problem. For this reason it is essential for an enquirer to disclose all the relevant factors surrounding the question, to ensure that the person who is advising upon it can do so in the right context. The answer to a point of detail, without the adviser being aware of the context in which that detail fits, may be misleading, incomplete or inaccurate in that context, although it sounds correct insofar as it goes.

Grey area judgments

1.13.3 In the case of a complex or grey area promotion when a legal principle is being examined, it is possible that different Trading Standards Officers may have different opinions, depending on how bullish or how cautious they are. What the law says, and how it is applied, are two different things. Its application to specific circumstances can often be a matter of perception and common sense whereas the strict letter of the law is only a statement of principle. In theory it would be possible for each Trading Standards Department around England independently to prosecute the manufacturer if the illegal promotion is being run in their local authority area, but that never seems to happen.

KEEPING ADEQUATE RECORDS

Promotion development records

1.14.1   The agency should keep a comprehensive file for each competition or other major promotion until some time after the promotion closing date. This file should contain the source material for the justification of any part of the promotion which may become contentious, together with all information and instructions relating to the promotion which is received by the agency from the client manufacturer. It should also contain all independent copyright, trade mark or other clearance requests and the responses, and a note of all legal clearance advice which has been given for the promotion.

Promotion substantiation

1.14.2   The substantiation file should be made readily available for examination by the ASA or by a Trading Standards Authority if a complaint is made about the promotion. The existence of the file also demonstrates that the justifying material has not been hastily put together after the complaint has been made. Justification of the promotion by the subsequent collection of satisfactory back-up and confirmation material can be done provided that it is genuine, and provided that it is not "doctored" to make the back-up material misleading or deceptive.

DEALING WITH COMPLAINTS

COMPLAINTS PROCEDURE

Assessing validity of complaints

1.15.1   Frivolous complaints, and those which are cynically made by members of the public in a deliberate or fraudulent attempt to get a greater benefit from the promotion than they are entitled to, are an inevitable risk of any promotion. All complaints must be responded to promptly, and the complainant should be kept informed of the progress of any investigations, and of their result. While all complaints must be taken seriously and investigated thoroughly, any manufacturer which is constantly involved in promotions for its products will come across the odd member of the public who is impossible to please, and who appears to be incapable of understanding even the simplest of explanations and instructions set out in the promotion material.

Unreasonable complainants

1.15.2   There are also those persons whose life's ambition seems to be finding the slightest flaw or ambiguity in the presentation or operation of a promotion. This seems to be irrespective of whether or not they have participated in the promotion and however trivial the point complained of may be. Even if the manufacturer thinks that the complainant is of this sort, he should still initially be treated seriously and with courtesy.

Maintaining good customer relations

1.15.3   Happy customers are a valuable asset and are derived through good business practice. A genuinely dissatisfied customer can cause more damage in adverse comment and bad publicity than a concilliatory gesture is worth to the manufacturer in the first place. The complainant, having written to complain in his private and personal capacity, may turn out to be the chairman of a major cash and carry chain which does a lot of business with the manufacturer. If he is treated in a cavalier fashion by the manufacturer, or by the handling house on the manufacturer's behalf, he could cause a lot of embarrassment and damage to the manufacturer's business. Alternatively, the complaint may be the start of a piece of investigative television or other journalism, such as the compiling of a comparative study of how different manufacturers deal with awkward or complaining customers. The adverse publicity which can be produced by the manufacturer being seen on a consumer affairs T.V. programme to have a less than caring attitude to dissatisfied customers' reasonable complaints can be very damaging to the manufacturer's image and reputation.

COMPLAINTS TO THE ADVERTISING STANDARDS AUTHORITY

Industry guidance

1.16.1   Complaints regarding advertising or promotional material which appears to be dishonest, misleading or in contravention of the relevant Code of Practice can be referred for comment and action to the Advertising Standards Authority (ASA). The ASA does not investigate complaints which are simply critical of the manufacturer or the use of sales promotions, where there is no justifiable cause for complaint under the appropriate Code of Practice. The complaint may be so worded that it is not possible for the manufacturer to give a simple answer to it, in which case the ASA may request the complainant to make himself clear.

ASA reference to manufacturer

1.16.2 If a complaint is received by the ASA in respect of a promotion, it will contact the manufacturer, either referring to or enclosing a copy of the letter which sets out the complaint. The manufacturer will be asked to comment upon or to explain to the ASA why it considers the complaint to be unjustified (if that is the case).

Response by manufacturer

1.16.3 To support its defence to the complaint, the manufacturer should give the ASA as detailed a response as possible, and should also provide the ASA with any independent documentary or other verification which is available to support that response. This may already be in the agency's substantiation file referred to in paragraph 1.14.1. The ASA will make any further investigation it thinks fit, and will respond to the complainant, with a copy to the manufacturer, giving its views on the complaint. The manufacturer should be able to show the ASA that he has approached the complaint in a responsible manner, and that he took reasonable measures to promptly rectify the cause of the complaint upon becoming aware of the problem.

Role of ASA

1.16.4 The ASA is not a punitive body. It does not have the power of a Trading Standards Officer to take proceedings against an errant manufacturer on behalf of a complainant, and it cannot legally force the manufacturer to adopt any recommendations the ASA may make following its review of the complaint. Nevertheless, all reputable manufacturers support the ASA as an independent body, respect its opinions, and make an effort to comply with its recommendations. All manufacturers should be aware of the adverse publicity which may follow from a finding in a complainant's favour and even more so from failure to rectify the cause of the complaint. The ASA monthly reports publicise complaints which it has investigated.

COMPLAINTS TO A TRADING STANDARDS AUTHORITY

Consumer complaints

1.17.1 The Trading Standards Department is the local authority department through which the consumer protection legislation is enforced. If a consumer gets an unsatisfactory response to a complaint from a manufacturer, he can submit his complaint about an alleged illegal or misleading promotion or advertisement to the local Trading Standards Department for the area in which the cause of complaint has arisen. He can complain even if he has not bought the product.

Investigation of offence

1.17.2 Before a summons can be issued, the Trading Standards Officer will investigate the complaint with the manufacturer. The manufacturer should supply the Trading Standards Officer with all the available information relating to the creation and administration of the promotion insofar as it is relevant to the alleged offence, together with an explanation of why the manufacturer believes the complainant to be mistaken. Unless there is a good reason for it not to be, the response to the Trading Standards Officer should be as complete and detailed as the formal defence or plea in mitigation which would be put before the court were a summons to be issued. This gives the Trading Standards Officer ample opportunity to consider all of the merits of the complaint. It is standard procedure for the formal interview with an authorised representative of the manufacturer to be made under caution, and to be tape recorded as evidence in a possible prosecution.

Deciding whether or not to defend a summons

1.17.3 Unless the manufacturer is confident that it has a cast-iron defence to the summons, it has to make a commercial decision as to whether it is more sensible for it to plead guilty and to get the proceedings over with quickly and quietly. A realistic appraisal is even more necessary if the manufacturer believes that the prosecution would be successful. The decision-making process should take the following points into consideration:

(a) Will a spirited defence produce a degree of media newsworthiness which will not be welcome, especially if the defence fails? The question is whether discretion is the better part of valour, and at what point is it commercially not worth defending a principle. That judgment should only be made after seeking legal advice on whether the proposed defence is likely to be successful. The media interest will also depend on where the court hearing the case is to take place.

(b) What is the likely cost of preparing and putting forward a well prepared defence, and how does that cost compare with the cost of a fine should a plea of guilty be made together with a plea in mitigation? The same criteria as in (a) above should be applied. A plea of guilty should not be made unless the manufacturer is advised legally that it has committed the offence. The internal management cost to the manufacturer of diverted executive time and effort put into dealing with all of the points of the summons which have to be covered, and the time which must be put into researching the circumstances of the offence, and in preparing the defence, and in attending the court, would normally exceed the cost of having independent legal representation at the court hearing.

(c) Magistrates' courts, where the case will be heard, are always very busy. While everyone has a right to defend themselves the magistrates will take a dim view if it is clear that the manufacturer's defence is spurious and a waste of the court's time.

Absolute offences

1.17.4 The offence of misleading the public is an absolute one; the court's decision will state whether or not it happened. If it clearly did happen, however unintentionally and despite precautions taken to prevent it from happening, there is no defence to the charge, and the manufacturer can only submit to the court a plea in mitigation. There is no point in trying to defend on commercial grounds a clear-cut instance of an offence, because it does not depend on any element of knowledge or intention on the part of the manufacturer. Such considerations may, however, influence the magistrates as to the size of the fine imposed. In many cases whether or not an offence has been committed depends on the way an ambiguous statement in the promotion text is interpreted by the court. The manufacturer may have to produce evidence of the general public perception of the meaning of the words in its favour in order to support a defence.

Prosecution after promotion has finished

1.17.5 If the promotion was illegal, the fact that it may have been concluded by the time the threat of legal action arises does not prevent a prosecution from being brought against the manufacturer. By that time the manufacturer will have had the whole of any benefit which could be achieved by running the illegal promotion, so there will be no cost or immediate embarrassment caused to it by terminating the promotion, they will only relate to the prosecution itself. If that is the case, a useful piece of evidence for the defence would be that no other complaint or prosecution has been made in respect of the promotion, particularly where the complaint which is being defended relates to alleged misleading wording in the promotion text.

COPYRIGHT IN PROMOTIONS

DIFFERENT APPLICATIONS OF AN IDEA

Protecting originality

1.18.1 A question which is often asked is whether an agency which has an original idea for a promotion can protect it in any way from being copied. The world of sales promotion is so competitive that to have an unusual and original promotional idea which captures the public imagination, and which is applied successfully to a brand of product, gives it a marketing edge over its competitors during the promotion period.

Concept and form

1.18.2   There is a difference in law between a novel concept which is only an idea, and the design of a complete promotion with mechanic instructions and rules, using that idea. The idea which is being examined may itself be based upon an existing marketing feature, but it may be a "first time" form of expression in sales promotion terms. The basic idea may be capable of being used or interpreted within promotions in many different ways. Most original ideas are capable of evolution and refinement into different promotions when the ingenuity of a creative sales promotion agency is applied to them. Many promotions owe their origin, or their ingenious variation, to somebody else's original idea.

NO COPYRIGHT IN A CONCEPT

Concept

1.19.1   In copyright terms it is not possible to protect the *concept* of a promotion, even in the substance of a completely developed and formalised promotion presentation. For example, whoever first thought of the "10 per cent. extra free" form of promotion had an original idea, but could not protect it as an exclusive proprietary right. A formalised concept, such as a written explanation of what the promotion is and how it works, will be an original copyright literary work, but that written explanation does not protect the idea on which it is based. A facsimile copy of the written and illustrated text of a complete original promotion presentation will be a breach of copyright in that precise presentation only. Another agency can use the promotion concept to create a different promotion, provided that its presentation and text are different. The agency would have to ensure that there is no "passing off" of the product subject to the original promotion.

Promotion title

1.19.2   Nor is there any copyright in the title of a promotion, because it is not long enough to represent a literary work. (*Exxon Corporation* v. *Exxon Insurance Consultants International* [1982] Ch.119). If the promotion title contains a brand name or other trade mark to link it with the promoted product, then it is only that part of the title which could not be used in another promotion, because the proprietary right in the trade mark is protected. If the title of a specific promotion format is unusual and distinctive and has become established through long use as being publicly associated only with a specific brand of product, a "copy cat" similar use of the promotion and the title, or possibly even the use of the title alone, might constitute "passing off" in certain circumstances (see Chapter 7, paragraph 7.30).

1.19.3 The application of copyright to advertisements is dealt with in detail in Chapter 5.

2 Promotion Features

INTRODUCTION

SALES PROMOTIONS DEFINED

Product purchase incentive

2.1.1   A sales promotion, or a purchase incentive, is a consumer-orientated marketing strategy on the product's packaging which is designed to promote the product through its brand name, and to encourage consumers to buy it. The encouragement is that by purchasing the promoted product, the consumer can participate in the promotion which is attached to the product. Promotions are a specialised form of point of sale product advertising which is active, as opposed to passive media advertising. This chapter explains some of the usual promotion concepts, and Chapter 4 deals with some specific forms of promotion which are used to sell consumer products. All promotions should comply with the following criteria:

(a) They must have an attractive offer which makes the promotion worth participating in.
(b) The explanation of the mechanic and the rules must be clear and comprehensive.
(c) The promotion must be legal and must comply with the ASA Code of Sales Promotion Practice and any other applicable Code or regulation.

Selected features

2.1.2   The purpose of this chapter and Chapter 4 is not to teach the reader how to create, present or manage promotions. Consequently there are many aspects of promotions which are not referred to at all. Most promotion mechanics and rules are self-explanatory and do not cause any concern from a legal point of view, provided they are thought through and drafted carefully. This chapter examines some promotions which tend to cause concern legally if they are badly constructed or incorrectly drafted, as it can be difficult sometimes to see what the legal problem is with a promotion. To explain how things can go wrong it is useful to look at working examples. These may be exaggerated to demonstrate the point which is being examined.

Drafting and interpretation

2.1.3 It is surprising how different interpretations can be made of what is thought to be a simple statement in clear language. The agency should never underestimate the risk of the average consumer misunderstanding or finding another meaning for something which appears to be straightforward. To minimise this risk, the wording of the promotion rules should be consistent with the promotion mechanic, and they must be complete, clear and logical. When the final wording is being reviewed, each statement has to pass the "what if" test; and if it does not, it should be modified to plug the logic gap which has been found.

Convenient references

2.1.4 For convenience in this book the following words or phrases are used to identify the meanings set against them, although there may be variations depending on the context in which they are used.

An agency means either a sales promotion agency or an advertising agency.

A buyer consumer or purchaser means a member of the public who purchases the promoted product.

A gift means a gift which is advertised as a promotion benefit.

A handling house means a company which administers the redemption of promotion gifts or which accepts and sorts out competition entries. A handling house may also undertake other third party services for the manufacturer.

A mechanic means the activity of the promotion, and its operating instructions. In a sense the mechanic *is* the promotion, so it can be a gift mechanic, a competition mechanic, a money-off voucher mechanic, and so on.

A participant is a buyer who is participating in the promotion.

A product means a product which is subject to the promotion, or which is being advertised.

The promoter or *the advertiser* or *the manufacturer* means the manufacturer of the product which is being promoted or advertised.

The promotion means the product purchase incentive promotion which is being discussed. For the purposes of this book a promotion is any form of gift offer, competition, voucher offer, or other reward or inducement coupled with a product purchase. It can also mean a free prize draw when that is discussed.

A proof of purchase means any coupon, label, entry form or other proof of purchase of the product which has to be sent in with a redemption application for a gift, or with a competition entry.

A redeemer is a person who makes a redemption application for the gift in a promotion.

Redemption means the process whereby a redeemer completes the gift redemption application form on the product label or package, and sends it to the handling house together with the required proofs of purchase, to obtain the gift.

Rules mean the rules governing the operation of the promotion.

A *voucher* means a money-off coupon, or something similar.

THE "10 PER CENT. EXTRA FREE" PROMOTION

BASIS OF THE PROMOTION

Effective price reduction

2.2.1 The "10 per cent. extra free" promotion states that the promotion-flashed packages of the product contain an additional 10 per cent. volume of the product which can be purchased at the same price as the previously available standard volume package. The basis of the promotion is that both before and after those special "added volume" packages of the product have all been sold, only the standard volume package will be available at the ordinary price. If there is an increase in the ordinary price of the product just before ordering a "10 per cent. free" promotion, it would become misleading because that price increase may be deemed to be in respect of the extra product in the promotion packages of the product. The description of the extra volume in the promotion package as being "free" is based upon the assertion that if a standard volume package costs £1 and the promoted 10 per cent. extra volume package also costs £1, there is no additional charge for the added quantity, so it has been provided free of charge.

Standardisation of promotion packages

2.2.2 If the standard-volume package of the product is phased out, and is replaced permanently by what was the extra-quantity promotion package, then the promotion package would ultimately become the standard-volume package. At that point it would be misleading to continue to call it a "10 per cent. extra free" package, as there is no other package of the product for it to be "extra" from. This point is relevant to the question of how long the manufacturer can sell the promotion package in the form in which it is advertised before it ceases to be a promotion. If it is advertised as a promotion for so long that it has effectively become a standard package, that promotional claim will then be false and misleading. There is no fixed period after which a promotion is deemed to have become a permanent feature. For an added-volume package promotion not to become misleading, the product must have a regular standard volume package upon which the advertised "extra" comparison is based.

VALIDITY OF 10 PER CENT. EXTRA FREE CLAIM

Is it free?

2.3 It is submitted that the "10 per cent. extra free" statement is not technically accurate. It is certainly "extra", and with no price increase for the promotion package there is an added value to it which appears to be free of charge. The "free" statement is misleading because the additional volume of product in the promotion package is not free at all. This is because a payment has to be made to acquire the package which contains the extra volume. A more accurate description of an added quantity promotion package would be "10 per cent. extra value". It is apparently accepted by the authorities that a "10 per cent. extra free" offer is not misleading or incorrect provided that it is presented in the right context. This view is based upon the fact that the promotion is used almost universally for consumer perishable products, and no manufacturer or retailer has been prosecuted for it.

"10 PER CENT. OFF" OR "10 PER CENT. FREE"?

2.4 What is the correct description of a promotion where the price of the product is reduced by 10 per cent.? If the "10 per cent. extra free" statement is legal for an additional product promotion, then logically the price reduction promotion could be described as "10 per cent. free". The rationale is that by reducing the price by 10 per cent. there is 10 per cent. of the product which is apparently no longer being charged for. That is not strictly correct; there is still a charge for the total volume of the product in the package, but the overall cost per unit has been reduced. The promotion flash should refer to a price reduction promotion as being "10 per cent. off". The reason is that the promotional adjustment has been made to the price for that package of product, and not to the quantity of the product which is contained in the package. It would be both incorrect and misleading to call a price reduction promotion "10 per cent. extra free".

FLASH REPRESENTATION ON PACKAGE

Flash banding size

2.5.1 Where the statement "10 per cent. extra free" is set inside or is related to a contrasting colour band which is placed horizontally around the top of the package, the size of the contrasting band should appear to be approximately 10 per cent. of the vertical package area. The smaller the product package is, the more difficult this will be to achieve, particularly if the flash wording is to be put inside the band. In these cases it is safer not to have a representational banding around the package.

Flash representative of free quantity

2.5.2 The reason for making the size of the horizontal band containing the "percentage extra free" flash roughly proportional to the amount of the extra volume in the promotion package is that buyers are influenced by what they see. Depending on the package artwork design, buyers may assume that the proportion of the vertical flash banding area to the whole package area is a visual indication of the amount of additional product which is contained in the package, irrespective of the percentage which is stated by the flash wording as being the extra quantity of the product. If the overall visual impression of the package is that a large and prominent banding round the package is an indicator of a relatively small "free" extra quantity of the product, that indication will be misleading.

Diagonal flash

2.5.3 This concern of not having a misleading indication of the extra free product quantity on the package would not apply to the same extent where there is a diagonal flash band across the package, or to any other visual flash representation (such as a star burst) which is not a horizontal band. This is because the size of that band or flash would not normally be considered to be a visual indication of the apparent additional quantity of the product in the package.

PACKAGING DESIGN AND PRICES

REVISED PACKAGE SIZE

Size related to volume

2.6.1 A promotion package which is bigger than a standard package is justified where it is necessary to accommodate a greater quantity of product. If the increased size of the promotion package which is specifically designed to accommodate the extra amount of the product is not reasonably related to the stated extra promotional volume, it may be considered to be misleading. For example, if a "10 per cent. extra free" flash is blazoned across a revised product package, and if the manufacturer has increased the size of the package by 30 per cent., the buyer can still be misled as to the real value of the additional quantity benefit provided by the promotion. The visual impression tends to override the stated percentage increase when the buyer is looking at the promotion package and assessing the added benefit of the promotion. He will not have the benefit of a standard-size package being to hand to compare with the promotional package, but will be familiar with the standard package size.

Misleading price and quantity increase

2.6.2   If the manufacturer increases by a stated percentage the volume of the product which is sold in the revised package, and if it also increases the purchase price by the same percentage, the new greater volume package cannot be advertised as being a "free" promotion. Even where the increased price is acknowledged on the package, the way in which it is advertised can be misleading. For example, it would be misleading if the standard package of 100 units costing £1 were to be increased to a promotion package containing 110 units, which is advertised in large, bold letters as "new larger package, now only £1.10". The statement is factually correct, but if there is no reference to the old price of £1 on the package the use of the words "now only" would tend to mislead a buyer into believing that there has been a price reduction, or that there has been a less than proportional price increase for the additional volume.

REVISED PACKAGING DESIGN

Change in shape

2.7   The same deception may occur if the shape of the package is changed as a long term product image re-vamp. This happens where the new package shape appears to contain a greater volume of the product than the previous package, although in fact it contains exactly the same. The new package shape will be publicised heavily in media advertising to get it recognised. Advertisements for the new shape of package must not give the impression that it contains a greater quantity of the product, so the advertising text referring to the new package design must be drafted carefully so as not to be misleading. There is no way in which buyers can make a true comparison of the quantity of the product contained within the old and new packages, except by comparing the weights or quantities which are stated on the labels. This "small print" will not normally be visible in a TV commercial. By the time the new packages appear the old packages will have been phased out, which will make an on-shelf comparison impossible.

FREE GIFT WITH PURCHASE

Types of gift item

2.8.1   The promotion mechanic may be that by buying the product the purchaser is entitled at the same time to get the promotion offer gift, which is usually attached to the product, or handed over when payment is made for it and which is normally related to the product.

Comparison of value

2.8.2　The product manufacturer or distributor must not make a statement in the promotion text attributing a cash value to the "free" gift unless it can be justified. Any advertisement such as "gift worth £X", or "save £X on the free gift" or "gift equivalent to product price reduction of £X [or X per cent.]" must comply with the provisions of section 20 of the Consumer Protection Act 1987, as now set out in the Price Markings Code of Practice issued by the DTI, the text of which is set out in Appendix 2.

GIFT REDEMPTION PROMOTIONS

PRODUCT PURCHASE BENEFIT

Free gift incentive

2.9.1　Gift redemption promotions offer a benefit to the buyer of a minimum quantity of the promoted product from which he obtains the number of proofs of purchase required by the promotion rules for a valid application for the free gift. The gift is described in the promotion text as being "free", because apart from purchasing the product to obtain the required proofs of purchase, no further payment has to be made by the buyer to obtain the gift (unless it is a special "added cash payment" promotion). The gift represents a discount value to the buyer from the cost of buying that promoted product. The proofs of purchase which are collected for a gift redemption promotion do not give the buyer an instant benefit for that product purchase, as they have no value unless and until they are used for a valid gift redemption application.

Benefit depends on promotion

2.9.2　Depending on the form of the promotion, a collection of the proofs of purchase will enable the product buyer to apply for either:

(a) a voucher giving a discount value off the price of the next purchase of the product. This encourages product purchase and generates more sales of the product while giving the buyer a benefit; or

(b) a free promotion gift. The value of a promotion gift will probably be greater than the face value of a "money-off" voucher obtainable from a single package of the promoted product, so the number of proofs of purchase required for its redemption will be greater.

CASH BALANCE REDEMPTION

2.10 If the gift has a significant monetary value in relation to the cost of obtaining the required number of proofs of purchase, the quantity of the product which would have to be bought to provide them would be unrealistic. That is because the discount cost to the manufacturer per unit has to be economically viable. To reduce the number of proofs of purchase which would otherwise be required for the redemption of a high value gift, a promotion rule will state that a balancing sum of money has to be paid by the redeemer together with fewer proofs of purchase to obtain the gift. The fewer the number of proofs of purchase which are required to redeem the gift, the greater will be the balancing cash cost to the redeemer. Clearly this kind of promotion cannot be called a "free gift" promotion. The amount of balancing cash which is required for the redemption of the gift should not be so high that, however attractive the gift may be, its cash cost to the redeemer sets up a resistance to any potential redemption.

BALANCING THE ADDED CASH ECONOMICS

Net cost of gift is a discount

2.11.1 The cost of the free gift to the manufacturer of the promoted product represents a different kind of discount opportunity to that which is given to the buyer. Instead of an immediate retail price reduction, which gives the buyer an instant discount and which gives the manufacturer an instant cost, a proof of purchase gift promotion attached to a product which is sold at the normal price is only a potential benefit to the buyer (because it may never be used) and therefore it is only a potential discount cost to the manufacturer. If the purchaser of the product does not participate in the promotion, and most will not, the manufacturer has not suffered a redemption cost. There is a consistently low percentage of buyers who make redemption applications.

Cash balances the discount

2.11.2 Where the cost of each redeemed gift to the manufacturer (including handling house charges and excess redemption insurance premiums) exceeds the discount which he can safely give on the quantity of product that has to be purchased to get the necessary proofs of purchase, there has to be a cash value differential on redemption to balance the deficit in that discount. Without the cash balance, the quantity of product required to obtain the proofs of purchase would be sold at a reduced profit (or even at a loss), particularly if the redemption rate were to be higher than anticipated. The discount value of the gift, and therefore the calculated mix of cash and proofs of purchase needed to redeem the gift, is assessed by the manufacturer on the basis of a forecast redemption rate. This will be expressed as a percentage of product sales during the period of the promotion. If the promotion is popular there is always the risk of excess redemption levels, which can be insured against (see paragraphs 2.41.1–2.43.2).

Return of cash

2.11.3   Where the promotion rules require a cash balance to be paid by the redeemer towards the redemption of a gift which is stated to be "subject to availability", any redeemers who are not successful in getting a gift must get their cash balance back promptly after its receipt by the handling house, with an appropriate letter of apology. If a substitute gift is being offered to disappointed applicants, they must be given the choice of having their money back, or accepting the alternative gift. That gift must have a similar value to the original promotion gift, and where possible should be of a similar nature, so that the redeemer gets an equivalent value for the cash balance payment he has made.

PROMOTION PERIOD AND GIFT AVAILABILITY

SCARCITY OF PROOFS OF PURCHASE

No guarantee of availability

2.12.1   All promotions which are based upon a collection of proofs of purchase of the product to redeem the gift suffer from the problem of diminishing availability towards the end of the promotion period as the promotion packages are replaced by standard packages of product, or by those containing a different promotion. Most of the promotion packages may have been sold by half way through the promotion period. Consequently there comes a time when there are not enough promotion packages of the product available for collectors who are short of the required number of proofs of purchase, and who want to apply for the gift. No manufacturer gives a representation in the mechanic instructions or the rules that all collectors of proofs of purchase will be able to find enough of the promoted product at any time during the promotion period to complete their collection.

Transitional period

2.12.2   The greater the number of proofs of purchase which are needed for redemption of the gift, the greater will be the difficulty in finding a complete collection of them as stocks of promotion packages reduce. During the initial intensive period of the promotion a mix of both standard (or previous

31

promotion) packages and newly distributed promotion packages of the product will be available. Ordinary (or subsequent promotion) packages will start appearing on the shelves sometime towards the end of the second half of the promotion period, as the available stock of promotion packages decreases. The reason is that the promotion period, *i.e.* up to the closing date for redemption application, has a built-in excess time from the estimated sell out date of the promotion packages to allow for slow redemption applications.

Cash off voucher not affected

2.12.3 Where the promotion consists of a proof of purchase which is redeemable for a "50p off next product purchase" voucher, there will always be product available on which that voucher can be used. The voucher must also be used before its stated expiry date, and a promotion rule will be that only one voucher can be used against the purchase price of one product item. The "product item" must be defined if it is not a single item of the product. Where a multi-pack of the product is being promoted, the voucher must only be used against the purchase price of a promoted multi-pack. The phrase "off your next purchase of this product" without any qualification of "this product" could be interpreted as entitling a consumer to use the voucher against the price of a single item of the product, where an outlet has split a multi-pack for the convenience of its customers. There may be another rule to the effect that the 50p voucher cannot be redeemed against any purchase of the same product which is subject to a different promotion.

Instant voucher use

2.12.4 Where the promotion packaging contains a money value voucher to be used directly against the next purchase of the product at the store checkout, in the absence of any rule to the contrary, the following could be done. The purchaser takes two product packages to the check out, and requires (for a 25p voucher) that the price of each package be reduced by 25p, using each voucher against the other "next purchase" although the purchases are contemporaneous. As the vouchers have to be handed in to the store so that they can be redeemed for 25p each from the product manufacturer, they must be detachable at the check out. The promotion rules must make it clear that the vouchers have to be handed over to the store at the check out. If the vouchers are not detachable without first decanting the product, they could not be used for a contemporaneous next purchase.

PROMOTION PERIOD

Active promotion period

2.13.1 The number of promotion packages of the product item will depend on the anticipated active promotion period. If the promotion is a "money-off" on pack scheme, so that the product purchase triggers the discount, the number of promotion packages determines the exact cost of the promotion in redemption terms. In any other case the quantity will enable the manufacturer to:

(a) decide upon the number of proofs of purchase which will be required to make a valid redemption application for the gift;

(b) assess the anticipated proportion of buyers who will be redeemers, *i.e.* the redemption rate;

(c) calculate the number of redemption gifts to order and to put on standby; and

(d) calculate the redemption level at which any excess redemption insurance is to take effect.

Shelf life

2.13.2   The promotion period in the rules has no specific connection with the qualitative shelf life of the promotion packages of perishable products, such as their "best before end . . . " date. The rate of sale of the product, and the quantity which is to be distributed in the promotion packaging, as well as the estimated rate of stock turnover, will be taken into account when setting the promotion closing date. The closing date of the promotion should be sufficiently later than the "best before end" date or the likely retail sale date of the last of the promotion packages of the product to be distributed so that:

(a) all of the promotion packages will have been sold by the closing date; and

(b) buyers have enough time after the purchase of their last promotion packages in which to make their redemption applications.

AVAILABILITY AFTER CLOSING DATE

Causes of excess availability

2.14.1   There may be promotion packages of "hard" (non-perishable) products such as DIY equipment which are still available in retail outlets after the promotion closing date. This will not happen in the case of perishable and fast turnover consumer goods where normal stocking procedures are followed. The quantity of promoted product which is to be distributed during the promotion period must be sold before the promotion closing date. If promotional packages of product are available after the promotion closing date, the cause could be, for example:

(a) too short a promotion period for the number of promotional packages, taking the product distribution and sales pattern into account; or

(b) an isolated package of out-of-date product which is found belatedly at the back of a retailer's premises, and which had slipped through the "first in first out" system of stock rotation.

Manufacturer's liability to buyer

2.14.2   The manufacturer has no liability to buyers in respect of the promotion offer if promotion packages of the product are still available in retail outlets after the promotion's expiry date. That expiry date only affects the promotion, not the product itself. It is not like a "sell by" date for perishable goods. Although it may not be a matter of deception, most buyers would assume that availability of the product in its promotion package means that the promotion period is still running. Even if buyers purchase the product only because they like the look of the promotion, most of them will not take the precaution of checking the closing date for the promotion on the package before they buy it.

Obligations of retailer to buyer

2.14.3   A retailer who sells a promotion package of the product after the closing date of the promotion will have no compensatory liability to the buyer if the latter claims that, because the promotion is no longer running, he does not have the opportunity to enter the competition, or to redeem the gift. There is no "lost opportunity" head of claim, as the buyer would have found out that the promotion had expired if he had taken the trouble to inspect the package and read its rules before buying the product. The retailer may have a liability under the misleading advertising legislation if he was actively advertising the promotion at the date of the purchase, for instance by leaving up the original promotion point-of-sale material beyond the promotion's closing date. The purchaser might have a claim for the return of the product to the retailer and a refund of the purchase price where he can prove that the retailer positively knew that he was purchasing the product to participate in the promotion, and did not tell him that the promotion had ended.

Misleading advertisement

2.14.4   An on-pack promotion is a form of advertisement for the product to which it is attached. Therefore it could be argued that the display on shelf of any product which has a time expired prominently featured on-pack promotion is a form of misleading advertising for that product by the retail outlet. The "misleading" will normally be of a member of the public, who buys the product in the belief that the promotion is still open at that date. If such a charge is made successfully by a Trading Standards Officer, the retailer would be responsible for publishing a misleading advertisement, not the product manufacturer.

"Free can" promotions

2.14.5 While the "free can" style of promotion is an obvious bulk retail purchase incentive to consumers, different presentations have different legal effects as stocks of product carrying that promotion reduce at the tail end of the promotion. The two following examples illustrate the difference:

(a) Four for the price of three.

Where the can itself is not in promotional "get-up" it may be sold in bulk or in single cans. Any bulk package, such as a four can pack, may have attached to it a discount promotion such as "four for the price of three". The prominent text of the promotion must make it clear that the promotion only applies to the cans contained in the specially marked bulk packages. The promotion is an instant price reduction at the check-out when those bulk packages are bought, and the promotion will not extend to the multiple purchase of single cans. That is because the manufacturer has calculated the cost to it of the promotion discount by the number of multi-packs of the product it has distributed. As those promoted bulk packages clear from the shelves and are replaced by, say, "10 per cent. extra free" single cans of that product, there should be no confusion between the two promotions.

(b) Buy three get one free.

This promotion is based upon the same concept as "four for the price of three", but it works differently if in the first promotion four cans had to be bought in a specially promoted bulk package whereas in this promotion only three individual cans have to be bought. Consequently the promotion title without any qualification can cause the promotion to be misleading for the following reason.

(i)   The statement "buy three and get one free" is an absolute offer, but what does it mean? The promotion would be on-shelf and applicable to standard cans, but could it apply to any other can of that product which is also available on the shelf? Suppose that as the promotion winds up the standard "buy three get one free" cans are being replaced by "10 per cent. extra free" cans, could one of those be claimed as the "free" can?

(ii) If the "buy three get one free" promotion is an on-can instant price discount for the free can at the check out, and not a voucher reimbursement promotion, the outlet will have received a limited equivalent discount from the manufacturer when it bought the product. When the discount limit has been reached, the on-shelf promotion material must be removed immediately, at which point the promotion has been terminated. To the extent that those cans are only bought in one's or two's by consumers, the outlet makes an additional profit on the "free" cans it does not give away.

(iii) As the outlet buys all its "10 per cent. extra free" cans at the appropriate price, it cannot afford to give one of them away free to a

35

consumer who, prior to the promotion termination, buys the last three standard "buy three get one free" cans on the shelf. The consumer will demand his "free" can, and the outlet will refuse to provide him with a "10 per cent. extra free" one in the absence of an available fourth standard can. At that point the unqualified "get one free" statement is misleading and illegal.

(iv) Therefore, as the "free" can of "buy three get one free" has to be a standard can, that fact will have to be clearly and prominently stated on the on-shelf promotion material. For the retailer's safety the on-shelf promotion material should make it "subject to availability" of the promotion cans.

PROMOTION CLOSING DATE

PROMOTION DATES

Control the promotion

2.15.1 Every promotion, whether it is a prize competition or a gift redemption, must have a closing date by which the competition entries must be submitted, or by which all gift redemption applications must be made, in order to be valid under the promotion rules. Promotions have two effective dates which have to be considered when calculating their advertised running time.

(a) The first date is the date by which the manufacturer estimates the whole of the production run of promotion packages of the product will have been bought by consumers. This date is not relevant to consumers, and is not referred to in the promotion text or supporting advertisements.

(b) The second date is that by which all competition entries or all redemption applications plus the proofs of purchase have to be received by the handling house in order to be valid. This is the promotion closing date, which must be prominently visible in the rules on the package. For consumer perishable products the closing date should be well after the "best before end . . ." date of those products.

A "while stocks last" gift redemption promotion will effectively be terminated before the stated closing date when all of the limited stock of gifts has been redeemed.

Omission of closing date

2.15.2 If the rules of a promotion do not contain any reference to the closing date, the manufacturer would have to publicise as widely as possible and well in advance in the press and elsewhere that a promotion closing date has been set. The date should be chosen so that all the retail stocks of the promotion packages of the product should have been sold, plus a reasonable period for participation in the promotion by late buyers.

DEFINE THE CLOSING DATE

Clarity of rule

2.16.1   The wording of the promotion rules must be clear as to precisely by when a redemption application or a competition entry must be received by the handling house for it to be valid. For convenience promotions have an end-of-month date as the closing date for receipt by the handling house of the last competition entries or applications for the redemption of gifts. What happens when the last day of that month is a Sunday, or any other day when the handling house will not be working? The rule should state that they must be "received" by the handling house "on or before" the closing date. Any wording such as "must be sent by [the closing date]" can mean that if the redemption application is posted on the closing date it will have to be accepted, even if it is received by the handling house after the closing date. The ambiguity arises because the emphasis in the wording of the rule is on the date by which the redemption application can be sent, and is not on the date by which it must be received. Many people assume that "sent by" and "received by" have the same meaning, but obviously they do not.

Posting prior to closing date

2.16.2   If the gift application or the competition entry is posted in good time but is received by the handling house after the closing date, it will still be a valid application or entry if the wording of the rule is "sent by", but it will not be valid if the wording of the rule is "received by". The promotion should have a rule which states that the handling house will not accept any applications or entries which are lost or delayed in the post so that they miss the closing date, even though they can be proved to have been posted in good time.

Discretion for late redemption applications

2.16.3   Subject to the remarks in paragraph 2.16.5 below, a relaxed view may be taken by the manufacturer if redemption applications for the promotion gift come in shortly after the closing date, provided that there are still stocks of the gift at the handling house, as there is nothing competitive in the promotion. By accepting a late redemption application, although it is not strictly valid and it would be a breach of the promotion rules, the manufacturer is not prejudicing or depriving any other valid applicant.

No discretion for late competition entries

2.16.4 Strict compliance with the closing date rule of the promotion is essential in the case of a competition. If any competition entry is received by the handling house after the closing date for whatever reason, it has to be disqualified as being invalid.

Late redemption and insurance

2.16.5 If the manufacturer has taken out excess redemption insurance for the promotion, it must not create or extend the obligations of the insurer to compensate it for the cost of fulfilling excess redemption applications as defined in the insurance policy, such as by accepting late and invalid applications. The whole insurance policy would be nullified if the manufacturer accepted late applications and attempted to claim upon the insurance policy to recover the expense of redeeming them. The manufacturer would not be acting in good faith, and any such claim would be fraudulent (see paragraph 2.41 on redemption insurance).

REDEMPTION APPLICATIONS

REDEMPTION INSTRUCTIONS

Guidance for participant

2.17 In a gift redemption promotion the on-pack directions to the buyer of the product must specify what he has to send to the handling house in order to get the gift. The instructions for redemption will deal with the following items:

(a) The completion of the redemption application form. There should be a rule to the effect that incomplete, illegible, incorrectly completed or mutilated redemption application forms will be deemed to be invalid. This rule is to screen out any applications which look suspicious, or which are in breach of the rules.

(b) What the proof of purchase consists of, and how many proofs of purchase are necessary for a valid redemption application. The redemption application form may also be the proof of purchase taken from the promotion package for convenience.

(c) What cash balance (if any) is required as well as the proofs of purchase, and how payment should be made.

(d) The choices which are available to the applicant where there is an alternative redemption cost promotion, such as X proofs of purchase being sufficient for the redemption of the gift, or with the alternative of submitting only one proof of purchase plus £A.

CORRECT PROOFS OF PURCHASE

Too many proofs of purchase

2.18.1 It does not matter if the redeemer sends more proofs of purchase than are necessary for the gift, as long as the minimum number required by the rules is sent in with the redemption application form. The promotion rule to the effect that an incorrect number of proofs of purchase will invalidate the redemption application should not be applied in these circumstances; it is intended to cover a shortfall.

Too few proofs of purchase

2.18.2 If an application is made with not enough proofs of purchase it will be invalid, and will be rejected by the handling house. If the application form has been completed for the redemption of more than one gift where that is allowed by the rules, then provided that the maximum number of applications rule has not been breached, the proofs of purchase sent with the application form will be applied accordingly. Any shortfall in the number of proofs of purchase which are provided with a valid number of applications will be resolved by accepting as valid the number of applications which are covered by the number of proofs of purchase submitted. If three applications are made, and the proofs of purchase cover only two and a half applications, then two applications will be valid and the remaining proofs of purchase will be wasted.

Multi-choice redemption

2.18.3 The promotion may have escalating values stated for the redemption of different gifts, such as send four proofs of purchase to get gift X, or send eight proofs of purchase to get gift Y. If six proofs of purchase are sent with an application for either gift X or gift Y, the applicant gets the gift X, but not the gift Y. The other two proofs of purchase are not effective and have no value. If a number of redemption applications are made together, the proofs of purchase can be aggregated towards the requirements for each application. In the absence of any indication to the contrary, the handling house should allocate the maximum benefit which can be achieved for the wrong number of proofs of purchase which are submitted with the redemption applications.

RESTRICTIONS ON APPLICATIONS

Restrictions apply to gift redemptions

2.19.1 Despite the fact that promotions are designed to encourage buyers to purchase the products, and despite the fact that redemption application rates are generally low, many promotions have a rule which limits the number of redemption applications which may be made for promotion gifts or for "extra free" product vouchers.

No restrictions for competitions

2.19.2 Entry limits will not be set where the promotion is a lawful competition, as the entry does not create any direct and instant price discount cost to the manufacturer on the purchase of the "proof of purchase" number of products by the entrant. The costs of running the competition and of providing the competition prizes are not directly related to the number of competition entries, and may not be significant on a per unit basis for the product which is distributed in promotion packages.

Limitation per household

2.19.3 The limitation is usually related to a number of applications which can be made "per person" or "per household". The rules never define what a "household" is for the purposes of the promotion, but the alarm bells ring at the handling house when an excessive number of applications from different named individuals come in from the same address. The "per household" rule may seem to be arbitrary, as different independent sections of one family living in one large house will be deemed to be one household within the promotion rules. These restrictions are not foolproof, as they do not prevent other people with different addresses from making the applications on a redeemer's behalf, providing they each keep to the promotion application limit. If the same name appears on several applications from different addresses, are they valid if the limit is "per household"? If the applicant is not a bona fide member of each of those households, the applications should be invalid. If the courts were to decide that a "household" for these purposes means only a postal address, without reference to who purports to be there, such multi-applications would be valid. This could also be done by several people making applications from the same address if the limitation is "per person", as there could be several persons living in one household. Therefore the "per household" rule is more restrictive.

PURPOSE OF RESTRICTIONS

Ordinary buyer

2.20.1 Restricting redemption applications for a promotion gift may seem to be contrary to the concept of the manufacturer advertising the gifts as a product purchase incentive. The restrictions limit the buyer's right to take excessive advantage of the "free value" benefits which are obtainable by participation in the promotion. The restriction does not affect an ordinary buyer, because it is not likely that he would want more than, say, three items of the gift for his own use or enjoyment, however much of the promoted product he buys. The promotion packages of a rapid turnover product may only be available for four to six weeks calculated on average retail sales. In the ordinary course of household replenishment few people would buy such a quantity of the product, with the exception of drinks, as will enable them to make a significant number of redemption applications.

Trade promotions

2.20.2 Gift redemption promotions are intended to be for the benefit of ordinary buyers of the promoted product through retail outlets. They are not intended to be a bulk discount bonanza opportunity for commercial enterprises, such as catering companies, or even for an individual who runs a market stall. Manufacturers run separate product purchase incentives for the benefit of bona fide traders. Trade promotions are normally for extra free product or money off vouchers, and have terms which are more appropriate to bulk buyers of the product. These promotions will have strict redemption application limits.

LIMIT ON TRADE REDEMPTIONS

Discount risk

2.21 Any additional trade interest which can be generated by the promotion will benefit the manufacturer, but only up to a point. Trade promotions help the profitability of the trader when he sells "free products" on to his customers, and so encourage the trader to buy more of it from the manufacturer while the promotion lasts. Unlimited bulk trade redemptions are an unacceptable risk for the manufacturer while the promotion lasts because:

(a) The per unit discount cost to the manufacturer of an excessively high redemption rate will wipe out the benefit to it of running the promotion.
(b) A limit on the number of redemption applications which can be made by a trader will be a condition of excess redemption insurance (the same condition will be applied to consumer redemption gift promotions).
(c) If there were no redemption limit an assessment of likely trade redemptions would be difficult to make. This affects proof of purchase requirements, as they are calculated on a projected rate of valid redemptions and the cost of the gift.

APPLICATION LIMITATIONS

Escalating gift values

2.22.1   The promotion may have two different value gifts, each of which has a different number of proofs of purchase which are required for its redemption. The purpose of the differential is to encourage the purchase of more product in order to apply for the higher value gift, or a higher value "money-off" voucher. Where there are limits on what can be chosen from the different gifts on making a redemption application, the rules must be clear. A producer of alcoholic drinks must comply with Section C.XII of the Code of Advertising Practice, and not encourage excessive drinking. Encouraging economical and reasonable bulk purchase is not the same thing, but the promotion presentation should not give the impression of encouraging alcoholic excess.

Limits on choice of gifts

2.22.2   Do the rules of the promotion require the redeemer to choose only one of the alternative gifts, or can his redemption application be for a mix of each of them? The promotion may be that a redemption application can be made for gift A by sending four proofs of purchase, or it may be made for gift B by sending eight proofs of purchase. The rules must state whether the choice has to be one or the other of gift A or gift B, or whether for twelve proofs of purchase the redeemer can get both of gifts A and B.

Define total redemption limit

2.22.3   If the promotion rules allow a maximum of three redemption applications to be made, without any further qualification, they could mean that each application limit will be treated independently in respect of the choices of A or B gifts. On that basis three of each gift could be redeemed. If the rule states that "no more than three applications for any gift will be allowed", it is ambiguous as to whether "any" could be construed as "either" or "both". The redemption possibilities are:

(a) Three only of either gift A or gift B.
(b) Three A gifts and three B gifts.
(c) Three gifts, being a mixture of A gifts and B gifts.

From the above it can be seen that the wording of the applications limit rule must be drafted with care, making sure that it sets the intended limit without any ambiguity.

REGISTERED RETAIL TRADERS

Definition

2.23.1   One target for trade promotions is those retail traders who regularly do business with the wholesalers which are supplied by the manufacturer. They are known as "registered traders", because they register with the wholesalers to become eligible as genuine retail traders to purchase bulk quantities of products at wholesale prices. There is no other precise definition of a registered trader, so the eligibility statement in the rules must be clear on who exactly may participate in the promotion. For a registered trader promotion the proofs of purchase are normally contained on the promotion bulk packaging of the product. The redemption will be for vouchers which are available from the handling house, in exchange for which the registered trader will get the product benefit which is advertised in the promotion, such as "Get five cases for the price of four".

Bona fide traders

2.23.2   Whether or not the wholesaler carries out a stringent check to verify the bona fides of an applicant for trader registration status is not within the control of the manufacturer, but if a potentially ineligible "trader" comes to its notice as a result of suspect redemption applications, it may investigate the position. Hotels, restaurants and other regular purchasers of bulk products, which are not for ordinary retail sale, will come within the scope of a wholesaler's concept of a valued customer, and may well be registered with that wholesaler. They are not specifically excluded from the definition of a registered trader by normal trade promotion rules.

MULTIPLE RETAIL OUTLETS

Single outlet

2.24.1   A single shop retailer, who is registered as a trader with his local wholesaler, will be an eligible redeemer under the rules of the trade promotion. What happens if there is a chain of connected retailers, each of which is registered individually with a wholesaler, but not necessarily with the same one? Unless the promotion rules specify otherwise, each of them is an eligible applicant, and therefore each of them could make up to the limit of redemption applications under the promotion rules.

Unregistered branches

2.24.2   A difficulty arises where a registered trader has a number of branches, none of which is a registered trader in its own right. If the different branches are not each validly registered traders, within the rules of the promotion they would not be eligible participants, so they cannot individually make redemption applications for the promotion benefit. If the promotion is only open to "registered traders", only the registered trader's "head office" will be entitled to make redemption applications, and it will be subject to the stated limit.

Agency not permitted

2.24.3   Under normal promotion rules the eligible registered trader's "head office" cannot claim that its branches are retailers which are operating independently under the "registered trader" status of the "head office", so that the "head office" can make the maximum number of applications for each of them as their agent. If that structure is allowed, then each of those branches would become entitled to participate in the promotion as if they were bona fide registered traders in their own right.

Control of abuse

2.24.4   Such a loose style of eligibility would leave the genuine incentive promotion wide open to abuse. The redemption application limitation rule must be complied with strictly for trade promotions, so the answer is for each of such branches to become registered traders with recognised wholesalers, and to make their own redemption applications. The fact that all the branches may be authorised for convenience to buy goods from the wholesaler on the "head office" registration does not affect the issue.

ADDED CASH REDEMPTIONS

Incorrectly made out cheques

2.25.1   Where a cash balance has to be sent with the proofs of purchase and the application form in order to redeem a significant value gift, there should be an express direction not to send cash, but to send a crossed cheque or postal order made out to the handling house. Assuming that the cheque does not bounce, any problem with it will be because the cheque is unsigned, or it is dated last year, or the payee details are wrong, or the amounts stated on the cheque do not match in words and figures; or they may match, but they may not be the correct amount. A cheque for an excessive amount where everything else is correct can be cashed and the balance can be returned to the applicant when the redemption gift is sent to him. If there is anything else wrong with the cheque it should be returned to the redeemer to be corrected.

Bounced cheques

2.25.2   A bounced cheque can be re-presented at the bank, or returned to the redeemer, who should be informed that the handling house will treat the application as being initially invalid, and that it will not be processed until the original or a replacement cheque clears. The same will apply to a cheque which is returned to the redeemer for correction. Two questions arise:

(a) What is the position where, before payment of the cheque is finally cleared, there is a risk that the stock of gifts in a "while stocks last" promotion will be exhausted? If the application is accepted and is only suspended, a gift should be set aside by the handling house for the redeemer pending payment being made. If the application is treated as not being validly made until payment is received, then the gift need not be set aside for him and the redeemer takes the risk that when proper payment is made and the application is accepted the stock of gifts may have been exhausted. Strictly the application is not valid, as payment has not been made in accordance with the promotion rules.

(b) What happens when payment of the bounced cheque is received by the handling house after the closing date of the promotion, although the original application was received and accepted by it in good time? If the original invalid application is suspended as an act of goodwill by the handling house until payment is received, then it is deemed to be valid when it is "reinstated" upon the payment being received. In any other case it will be an invalid application.

INCORRECT ENTRIES AND APPLICATIONS

Invalidity

2.26.1 The redemption application form which has to be completed by the redeemer will carry the minimum requirement of necessary information. Provided that the form is correctly completed, and that all of the other redemption requirements have been fulfilled according to the rules, the application will be valid and the gift will be sent to the redeemer at the address on the application form. There should be a promotion rule which states that application forms will be deemed to be invalid where they are incorrectly or illegibly completed, or where they are mutilated or incomplete.

Invalid competition entries

2.26.2 The "mutilated" rule applies particularly to competition entries, where for example an entry form has had two or more answers put upon it with scratching out of all but one of them. The entrant may also not complete the entry form properly, or may not complete the tie-breaker correctly, for instance by using more than the maximum permitted number of words. With valuable prize competitions, the entry rules must be observed strictly in order to be fair to all entrants and to prevent any cheating.

INVALID REDEMPTION APPLICATIONS

Breach of rules

2.27.1 Participants in the promotion can get the redemption procedure or the proof of purchase requirements wrong through human error. Should any error or omission which is a breach of the promotion rules be overlooked by the handling house, and the invalid redemption application honoured? What represents an incomplete application form should be judged sensibly. If the postcode is omitted from the applicant's address, that should not invalidate the application. If he writes neatly and legibly in script instead of following an instruction to complete the application form in capital letters, that should not invalidate the application either.

Strict interpretation of rule

2.27.2 A standard rule in all promotions is that any redemption application or competition entry which does not comply strictly with the promotion rules will be deemed to be invalid and will not be accepted. A defective application may be made by an *agent provocateur*, such as an executive of a competitor of the manufacturer in his private capacity, to see how fair or strict the promotion managers are being in interpreting and enforcing the promotion rules. The handling house should not accept a defective application which does not comply with the promotion rules. If it were to do so, the handling house would be in breach of its own obligation to the manufacturer to manage the promotion according to its rules. Would a lax system be worth the adverse publicity which would ensue if the *agent provocateur* was from a Sunday tabloid newspaper investigative team?

Keep a record of invalid applications

2.27.3 The handling house should keep a complete record of all rejected invalid redemption applications, together with the original application forms and their enclosures, pending any possible query by the hopeful redeemer, and because of the need to respond promptly to him or to any investigation or analysis of the promotion's invalid applications. Where there is obvious cheating in a trade sector promotion, the manufacturer should also consider what further action should be taken by it against the offending trader.

PROMOTION GIFTS

"FREE" GIFTS

No additional payment

2.28.1 Where a promotion gift redeemable by application is described as being "free", it will have to be provided in a proof of purchase only promotion, with no additional cash payment or promoted product price loading or any other indirect cost which is attributable to the gift. Where the "free" gift is attached to the promoted product at the point of sale, it can still be described as "free" although the redeemer has had to purchase the product to which the gift is linked.

Postage and packing charges

2.28.2 Under paragraph 6 of the ASA Code of Sales Promotion Practice a charge which is made in accordance with the promotion rules to cover the proper cost of the postage and packing of the gift for transmission to the redeemer will not prevent it from being described as "free". If however there is no reference to those costs in the promotion rules, but the redeemer is charged them at any subsequent stage, then the promotion gift is not "free" and any such claim is misleading. An arbitrary and excessive charge for packing and postage nullifies the claim of "free", even though it is stated in the rules as being a reasonable cost. The reason is that the excess will be considered to be a hidden contribution towards the cost of the gift. An unattributed "handling charge" stated in the rules as an extra charge will have the same result if it is excessive.

CONTEXT IN WHICH A GIFT IS "FREE"

The Imperial Tobacco case

2.29.1 This interpretation of what can be called "free" is in contrast to the decision in *Imperial Tobacco* v. *Att.- Gen.* [1981] A.C. 718; [1980] 1 All E.R. 866, where what was advertised as a free prize draw promotion was found by the House of Lords to be an illegal lottery. Part of the decision in the case was that the purchase of a combination of a packet of cigarettes and a scratchcard did not mean that the scratchcard had been acquired "free" by the purchaser of the cigarettes. The House of Lords decided that the purchase price was paid in respect of the combined purchase of the cigarettes and the card, and therefore the purchase price was attributed to them both together. On that basis something had been paid for the inclusion of the card in the cigarette packet. As a result that promotion was a lottery, and not the free prize draw as it had been promoted. (For the distinction between lotteries and free prize draws see Chapter 4.)

Application of the case

2.29.2 For "free gift" redemption promotions the context is different, but the distinction is rather fine. When the buyer purchases the product, he also purchases with it the proof of purchase which has to be submitted to the handling house for the gift redemption to be valid under the promotion rules. The proof of purchase cannot be obtained from the product manufacturer free of cost separately from the promoted product with which it is bought. This is in contrast to lottery style free prize draws (see the "saving grace" provisions for free draws, Chapter 4 paragraph 4.21.2). According to the principle established in the *Imperial Tobacco* case, for free gift promotions, there is a combined purchase of the product and the proof of purchase, and therefore as the proof of purchase is exchanged for the gift, that gift is not free, although there is no specific value or cost attributed to it out of the combined purchase price. It is the same as if the gift were handed over together with the purchased promoted packages of the product, rather than the gift being exchanged for their proofs of purchase. The purchase price of the quantity of product which will produce the relevant proofs of purchase (which represent the right to claim the gift) is a combined purchase price; so the redeemer is in fact paying for the gift as a combined purchase cost.

COMBINATION FREE GIFT PROMOTIONS

Misleading statements

2.30.1 It is fairly common to have a combination promotion, where the buyer is given a choice of how he would like to apply for redemption of the gift. The mechanic may be, "Send five proofs of purchase, or alternatively send one proof of purchase plus £5, to get the *free* gift." The second part of that statement is clearly incorrect, because if the buyer has to send £5, the promotion gift cannot be free. A correct statement would be, "Send five proofs of purchase to obtain the free gift. Alternatively, it can be purchased by sending one proof of purchase plus £5."

Validity of "free" claim

2.30.2 Would it be correct to advertise the promotion in the above example by way of a package flash or on the point-of-sale material, as being a "free gift" promotion? It is possible to get a free promotion gift by collecting five proofs of purchase, but there is a short-cut alternative which enables the redeemer to buy the gift for one proof of purchase plus £5. The existence of the alternative purchase facility does not contradict the promotion claim that a free gift is available, but the wording of any package flash, and the promotion terms, must not be misleading in their overall description of the promotion.

MISLEADING VALUE COMPARISONS

Cash balance redemptions

2.31.1   For promotions where there is a cash balance to be paid for redeeming a significant value gift as well as the required number of proofs of purchase, the promotion material should not describe the cash element in the form of a comparative value for the gift in a manner which does not comply with the Code of Practice on Price Indications (see Appendix 4). A description of the gift in the promotion text such as "worth £X" or "half of its retail purchase price" is not correct and is misleading, even where the cash balance is approximately half of the average retail price of that item in most shops.

Cost of product purchase

2.31.2   The balancing cash payment for the gift under the promotion may have been 50 per cent. of the ordinary cost of the gift in most retail outlets. If there had been no cash balance the gift could have been described as being "free". On a comparative value basis the buyer has to purchase the required quantity of the product to obtain the necessary proofs of purchase for redemption of the gift together with the cash payment. So it could equally well be argued that, if the gift was the sole objective for the redeemer, the cost of getting it is the cash plus the cost of the product purchase—probably altogether rather more than half of the retail price of the gift.

Promotion values

2.31.3   In the case of a promotion which has an alternative cash contribution choice for the gift redemption, the redeemer may know the average retail price of the gift. He can then assess whether one proof of purchase plus £5 makes the acquisition of the gift a bargain, focussing on the £5 and disregarding the purchase price of the product. He then looks at what the proof of purchase redemption requirements are to get the gift "free", and he can compare the different total costs to him of obtaining the same gift. In doing so he must not forget to take account of the value of the product which he purchases.

Purpose of product purchase

2.31.4   The value-for-money perception of the redeemer depends on whether he looks upon the free gift as a bonus for using the product which he buys, or whether he is only buying the minimum amount of product in order to redeem the gift. If the overall expense of one proof of purchase plus £5 is cheaper in cash terms than the product purchase cost of getting five proofs of purchase which are required to get the gift free, in the buyer's mind there may be an unfair discrepancy in the gift acquisition cost. That does not of itself make the promotion misleading. If one unit of the product costs £2, then obtaining five proofs of purchase would mean an outlay of £10. On that basis the buyer would spend £3 more just to get the "free" gift than if he chose the cash alternative method, as the £2 cost of one item of product for its proof of purchase plus £5 cash means an outlay of only £7.

FREE GIFTS AND PRICE INCREASES

Check promotion and price schedules

2.32.1 A misleading price problem under section 20 of the Consumer Protection Act 1987 and the DTI Code of Practice (see Appendix 2) could arise where the wholesale and therefore the ordinary retail price of the product is due to be increased by the manufacturer in the normal course of business from a given date. The validity of a "free" gift promotion may be questioned when that price increase becomes effective during the promotion period, and particularly in its early stages.

Contemporaneous increase

2.32.2 Irrespective of the manufacturer's normal scheduling of price increases, what the buyer sees is that a product which currently costs £1 per unit launches a promotion for a "free gift", and more or less contemporaneously the retail price of the promoted product goes up to £1.25. The buyer may conclude, not unreasonably, that the increase in the product price is a consequence of the launch of the promotion, and is to cover the additional cost to the manufacturer of providing the "free" gifts.

Price increase justification

2.32.3 The basis of what constitutes a misleading promotion is whether a reasonable buyer could be misled, and not what the manufacturer intended. If challenged on the point, the manufacturer will have to satisfy the Trading Standards authorities and the ASA that the increase in the product price at the time when the promotion was launched was not for the purpose of financing the promotion, since that would be misleading the public as to the "free" element of the gift. He would have to prove that the price increase had been scheduled as part of a long-term corporate strategy, and was not connected in any way with the promotion. Even so, it could still be considered to be a misleading advertisement or promotion.

Planning promotions and price increases

2.32.4 The timetable for planning promotions must take into account scheduled price increase dates for the products, and any other relevant corporate product development plans. Advertising campaigns, sales promotions and other marketing proposals should be co-ordinated to maximise their combined effect, and to minimise any obvious legal risks relating to any of them. This is particularly relevant for "money-off" promotions, as there has to be a valid base for determining what the "off" refers to. If a continuously promoted product does not appear to have a "regular price" from which the money off amount can be verified independently, there is a risk of any such advertising or promotion being misleading.

"UNIQUE" GIFTS

Defining "unique"

2.33.1 As promotion material is a form of advertisement, a standard readily available category of gift should not be described as "unique" in the promotion, nor should the gift be given any other description which is not strictly correct. The word "unique" implies that the gift does not exist elsewhere and thus that the only means of obtaining the gift is by participating in the promotion. If the gift or another article identical with it is, or may become, available from other sources, then it cannot be unique. In its usual context "unique" is a description for the only known example of that item. Some buyers may consider that the word "unique" should apply only to a gift available in very limited quantities; others may consider that "unique" can apply solely to a once-only source of supply, irrespective of the substantial number of the gifts which are available for the promotion from that source.

Technical definition

2.33.2 Strictly speaking, "unique" should not apply to a vast quantity of the gift, even if it is only available through the promotion, although that is how the word is used frequently to describe promotion gifts. To avoid being a technically misleading description therefore, the word "unique" must truly apply to the gift. The Oxford Dictionary definition of unique is "being the only one of its kind, unequalled", and that definition should be applied to the gift description of "unique". If the promotion is a competition, the first prize for which is an original painting or sculpture, or something else which is not duplicated in its original state, it could be described as unique. In the case of a brand-personalised quality sweatshirt, the assumption for the promotion terms is that only that particular combination of the product's brand name on the sweatshirt is unique, because that combination at that time cannot be obtained elsewhere. As that make of sweatshirt may be a favourite item for many different brand-personalised item promotions run by different manufacturers, is that a reasonable use of the word "unique"? It could be argued by the manufacturer of the promoted product that no buyer would be so naïve as to believe that the ordinary sweatshirt itself, as the promotion gift, is unique in the sense of the dictionary definition, and that therefore the buyer will not be misled by such a statement referring to a supply source for a distinctive but unlimited-quantity gift.

Unique of unusual

2.33.3 If the gift is an ordinary item, such as a sports bag or a sweatshirt, which has no distinctive "add-on" characteristic which is not generally available elsewhere, it cannot be described as unique. If the attraction of the promotion to the buyer is to obtain a gift which has the logo and the brand name of the promoted product emblazoned prominently on it, that logo or brand name addition makes the gift unusual, but it is still not unique. What counts in practice is whether a Trading Standards Officer would consider that such a technical misdescription will in fact be misleading to redeemers.

Added value

2.33.4 If that personalised gift has never been before, and will never again be, provided as a gift for a promotion by the manufacturer, and if it is not available, and never will be available, from any other source, then one would be more justified in claiming that the gift is unique as a category of "added value" product. If the added value is the personalised brand name of the product, that will not be the first or the last promotion for which that added value will be used. The quantity of such a gift which is needed to satisfy the whole of a potential redemption demand ensures that the gift itself cannot be unique in its traditional and narrow definition.

"LIMITED EDITION" GIFTS

No legal definition

2.34.1 The same reasoning applies to other descriptions of the gift, such as "limited edition". Apart from the same implication of the gift being only available through the promotion, the words "limited edition" are associated with something of special value, of which only a few copies have been produced. There is no exact legal definition of what constitutes a limited edition, so the validity of that description must be judged in the context in which it is used. There is a general consumer assumption that a limited edition refers to specially produced items, being of high value compared to normal redemption gifts, or which will have a scarcity value as a collector's item in the future.

Media advertisements

2.34.2 The British Code of Advertising Practice (Part C.IX) states that for the purposes of the Code an edition may be advertised as being limited by either:

    (a) a pre-announced specified number of items; or

    (b) a time limit within which an application or subscription for the item must be made.

Part C.IX of the Code deals with the different possibilities under both (a) and (b) above. The Sales Promotion Code makes no reference to what would be a fair reference to a limited edition promotional gift, but in practice applications for promotional gifts are always limited under (b) above simply because all promotions have a closing date. In promotion terms that does not automatically make the gift a limited edition, and being described as an open-ended "limited edition" in that style would be misleading. Therefore the Code definition in (a) above would be the correct one in sales promotion terms. This is not necessarily the same as being "subject to availability". Nevertheless the following comments should be considered.

Forms of limited edition

2.34.3 A popular painting by a famous artist may be reproduced as special prints with his authority on a strictly one-off basis with a maximum print run of, say, 500 copies. The prints are numbered serially and are signed and dated by the artist. It is of some significance to own one of the prints, because there will never be any more, as the signed print edition is genuinely limited. If 500 prints are reproduced as a numbered limited edition, and only the first 100 of them are signed by the artist, that creates another form of limited edition. The numbered and signed prints will have a higher value than the ordinary unsigned but numbered prints.

What is a limited edition?

2.34.4 Subject to the possible application of Part C.IX of the ASA Code of Advertising Practice, points to watch when running a promotion which describes gifts as being a limited edition are set out below. The Code is not legally binding, only an industry guide. Part C.IX will not prevent a promotion from being found to be misleading in law if consumers are genuinely misled by the description of the gift.

(a) While an ordinary gift item, such as a sweatshirt, may only be available bearing the product logo and brand name through the promotion, it has a certain attraction, but it does not have any recognised intrinsic value greater than that of the plain, unmarked item which is generally available and cannot therefore be described as a limited edition.

(b) The description "limited edition" is normally only used for special quality or crafted creative products, such as specially illustrated and bound copies of a book, or a limited number of reproductions of a painting or sculpture, the value of which is enhanced by the master item being an original work, and by the scarcity of copies of the limited edition. Ordinary promotional gifts, such as personalised T-shirts, do not come within this definition.

(c) The words "limited edition" in the accepted sense described in (b) above imply a low limit on the numbers of the quality gift reproductions which are being used for the promotion, such as 250 or 500. A highly successful promotion may have tens of thousands of redemption applications, so the description of "only 25,000 items" of a gift required in that quantity as being a limited edition could not be correct.

(d) The essence of the definition of a limited edition is that the limit is set at the time when the launch of the edition is announced. If the edition limit is 500, then the first 500 applicants for copies of that edition are successful, and all others will have to have their money returned. The print or manufacturing run of the limited edition article should never be extended under any circumstances, even to replace an edition copy which can be shown beyond doubt to have been damaged or destroyed.

(e) The printing plates, statue mould or other means of reproducing the limited edition item should be destroyed after the complete edition has been successfully produced from them, to prevent any fraudulent extension of the numbers of the edition from being produced. It is that certain limit which gives the edition copies their rarity value.

(f) If a promotion with a purported "limited edition" gift, such as a personalised sweatshirt, is so successful that the initial production run of the gift is inadequate to fulfil the redemption demand, the manufacturer may authorise a further production run of the gift to enable the handling house to satisfy the outstanding demand from redemption applications. That act alone would destroy the claim that the gift is a limited edition. It would also cause the promotion to become misleading, because the "limited" element, which will have prompted quick redemption applications in order to be in time before stocks of the gift run out, will have been removed. In this sense a limited edition promotion is like a "subject to availability" promotion.

"EXCLUSIVE" GIFTS

Definition

2.35.1 The word "exclusive" is used frequently to describe a promotion gift which has been personalised by the addition of the brand name and logo of the product. The most appropriate of the dictionary definitions of exclusive is "not obtainable elsewhere", so when examining the promotion the question is whether the use of "exclusive" is justified. If it is not justified, then the gift description would be a misleading advertisement. The use of "exclusive" here is similar to that of unique, as it implies a class of goods which, when personalised as a gift, will not be available elsewhere. The goods on which the gift is based, whether they are sweatshirts or alarm clocks, are not exclusive to the promotion in their standard form. Does personalising them create an exclusivity? If the combination of gift and availability is exclusive to the promotion at the time, that description is considered in sales promotion terms to be valid. As the brand name of the product will be a protected trade mark, the commercial use of it is exclusive to that manufacturer.

Source and availability

2.35.2   Some manufacturers licence the use of their brand names and brand logos to merchandising companies to be placed on clothing and other articles which are offered for sale to the public. If the brand-personalised "exclusive sweatshirt gift" for the promotion is also available to the public from other sources because an authorised merchandising company is producing and selling them, then the claim of exclusivity for the promotion gift, even under the most relaxed of interpretations, would not be correct. If the merchandiser agrees not to produce competing products to the promotion gift during the period between the start of three months before the promotion launch date and the end of three months after its closing date, there would be a limited form of exclusivity for the personalised gift, but only during the promotion period. The promotion text would have to be worded carefully to avoid being misleading.

STOCKS OF GIFTS

"WHILE STOCKS LAST"

Limited availability

2.36.1   If the promotion gift is a common item which is always readily available, the manufacturer or the handling house will simply order as many gifts as it needs initially, and re-order them on a batch basis during the promotion period to fulfil all valid redemption applications. Where gift availability is limited, it is possible for the anticipated total number of redemption applications to exceed the available quantities of the gift. The promotion material and the rules should specify clearly that the entitlement of the redeemer to receive one of the advertised gifts continues only "while stocks last". If the list of rules is tucked away in the promotion text, the "while stocks last" condition should be repeated in a prominent position on the promotion package where it will be immediately visible to a buyer who is looking at the major features of the promotion. It should also be prominent on any advertising material for the promotion.

Realistic redemption estimate

2.36.2   To avoid the "while stocks last" limitation from being a misleading means of running a promotion, before placing the order for a once-only special gift the product manufacturer must make a genuine and reasonable estimate of the likely number of redemption applications which may be received by the handling house during the promotion period. Where it is able to control the

55

size of the special order, the manufacturer must provide the handling house with a quantity of gifts which should be sufficient to fulfil that estimated likely redemption demand. If the gift availability limit is beyond its control, it must assess whether what is available is genuinely likely to prove sufficient for the promotion before deciding to use that gift.

A genuine estimate is not misleading

2.36.3 If the manufacturer has taken the advice of his sales promotion agency, and has made a genuinely reasonable estimate of the likely redemption level for a one-off special gift promotion, what happens if the number of redemption applications exceeds expectations by a substantial margin? There are two possibilities:

(a) If the rules state that the availability of the gift is limited, and if there is no misrepresentation as to that availability in the promotion text, the promotion will not have been misleading just because of the shortfall in availability.
(b) If the promotion rules state or imply that all redemption applicants will receive their gift, or if there is no warning that stocks of the gift are limited, the promotion would be misleading for those redeemers who fail to get a gift because the limited stock of gifts ran out. If there is a possibility of there being a shortfall in gift availability for any reason, the "while stocks last" rule should be included in the promotion text as a safety measure.

Defining the limit of availability

2.36.4 If despite all reasonable efforts the manufacturer has only been able to obtain 10,000 of the special gift items for a reasonably anticipated redemption application level of 20,000, the promotion material and the rules should state that only the first 10,000 applicants will receive a gift. In the absence of specifying the application limit, that margin of discrepancy is not acceptable unless there will be a suitable substitute gift for all unsatisfied redeemers, because the stock of gifts may be exhausted too early in the promotion period. Shortly before the stock runs out, the promoter would have to put out extensive advertising to let the public know that the promotion has been terminated. Where the gift availability should just about match the reasonably estimated redemption numbers, the "while stocks last" limited availability can be emphasised without specifying a numerical limit.

Nominal availability is misleading

2.36.5 A "while stocks last" statement for an attractive gift can have the effect of making a large number of consumers purchase the product during the period immediately after the promotion launch, in order to be one of the lucky limited number of redeemers. The gift advertisement and the promotion will be misleading if the manufacturer supplies only a nominal quantity of gifts to the handling house to satisfy redemption applications, even if a limited availability statement is contained in the promotion text and rules. Where "mistaken judgment" of a realistic redemption rate ends and "misleading statement" begins is a matter of degree. There is no specific percentage error which determines whether there is a misleading statement.

Misleading availability statements

2.36.6 Would it be misleading for the manufacturer to claim in the promotion text that the gift has a limited availability when that is not the case? Would this cause a higher product purchase and therefore a faster redemption rate because it appears to consumers from the promotion text that there is a scarcity value to the gift? It will be a misleading statement if the stated reason for the limitation of availability is not true. Availability of a gift is thought of by the public as a matter of source, so that "limited availability" implies that only so many gifts can be obtained for the promotion. There is nothing to stop the manufacturer from claiming that the availability of the gift for the promotion will be limited because it only intends to buy in a limited quantity of a gift which has an otherwise unlimited source of supply; there is no obligation on the manufacturer to make an open-ended gift offer of an ordinary, readily available item. In those circumstances the promotion text would have to be worded carefully to avoid any implication that the gift is something more than its description. People may believe that it is different or better simply because it appears to have a limited availability, as that normally implies that the gift is something special.

DISPOSING OF STOCK OF GIFTS

Alternative uses

2.37 If the gift is a one-off special, and therefore the redemption availability is stated in the rules to be limited to "while stocks last", what happens if the redemption rate is surprisingly low, and there is a residual stock of the gift left unredeemed at the closing date of the promotion? The possibilities are as follows.

(a) The gift is a one-off personalised or otherwise special-order production of an ordinary gift item which is taken and paid for by the manufacturer of the promoted product, so that it cannot be returned to the supplier. In this case, excess stocks may be distributed through an internal promotion for the manufacturer's sales force or something similar, or they can be given out as individual promotional gifts. It could also be used in another promotion for the brand of personalised product with a "limited availability" rule provided that:

57

(i) it has not been advertised in the previous promotion as "unique" or as a "limited edition" gift for that specific promotion, and provided that it has not been represented in any other way which would make the promotional re-use of it misleading; and

(ii) there is a sufficient quantity of the gift left over to fulfil most of a likely redemption level.

(b) Where the gift is a third-party brand product, the supplier (being the proprietor of the brand name and logo) may have imposed restrictions on what can be done with any excess stocks at the end of the promotion. This is to prevent them from being dumped on the market at give-away prices, or from being disposed of through an unsuitable outlet, which would be detrimental to the image and reputation of that brand of product. Such restrictions would also be imposed to protect the reasonable interests of authorised retailers of that product, who would be harmed if a significant excess quantity of unused promotional gifts were to be sold publicly by the promoter for substantially less than their recognised retail price. This is not a form of illegal resale price maintenance (for which see Chapter 3, paragraph 3.29 onwards).

ALTERNATIVE GIFTS

Contractual substitution

2.38.1 The promotion rules may state that if the "limited availability" gifts have been exhausted by the time the redemption application has been received, the manufacturer has the right to substitute a suitable alternative gift to satisfy the redemption application. For a proof-of-purchase-only promotion where the gift is not of significant value, this offer of substitution of an alternative gift is a fair and reasonable means of ensuring that the redeemer receives a benefit from participating in the promotion. If no alternative gift is offered in the promotion rules, there is no obligation on the manufacturer to supply one when the stock of a properly advertised limited availability gift has been exhausted, subject to paragraph 5.9.4 of the Code of Sales Promotion Practice.

Misleading advertisements

2.38.2 If there is no reference in the rules to the gift availability being limited, but the stock of that gift nevertheless runs out and cannot be renewed, leaving a number of unfulfilled redemption applications, what is the manufacturer's position? If the manufacturer has advertised in the promotion that a gift will be delivered upon receipt of a valid application, one must be provided as advertised. Whatever substituted gift is supplied to the redeemer to fulfil that promotion obligation, it will not be the one which was advertised in the promotion. This could lead to a valid complaint that the promotion offer at that time has become misleading in its description of the gift, although this would not have been the case originally. This offence is not affected by the reason for the gift which is delivered not being the gift which was advertised. Failure to provide the advertised gift is also a breach of the promotion contract by the manufacturer. If the gift description is so vague that it covers equally well two or more available gift articles, it is immaterial which of them is sent to redeemers, provided that they each comply with the description in all respects. This can happen where one brand name covers a range of the same product from the primitive to the deluxe. These may be identified by numbers or letters added to the brand name, and it is the number or letter identifying the promotion gift which is omitted from the promotion text.

AUTOMATIC SUBSTITUTION

Inapplicable to cash redemption

2.39 An automatic gift substitution rule should not be included where the advertised limited availability gift is so different or valuable that a cash balance requirement is part of the redemption cost. In that case, if the gift which is applied for cannot be provided, but some suitable alternative gift is proposed, the handling house should contact the disappointed redeemer to see whether he will be prepared to accept the alternative gift, or whether he wants the return of his money. The redeemer's choice should be complied with promptly.

VALUE AND NATURE OF SUBSTITUTED GIFT

Comparable substitution

2.40 The alternative gifts offered should be of an equivalent value and quality to the advertised gift, and they should also be of a similar nature if possible. For a voucher-only promotion where stocks of the original limited availability gift have been exhausted, the manufacturer would not be recommended to offer a more valuable substitute gift for which an additional cash balance payment is required, unless there is also an adequate alternative straight voucher-only substitute gift. Such an offer would change the original nature of the promotion, which could make it misleading, and the rules may not cover the possibility. The proposal would also add an unnecessary complication to an otherwise straightforward promotion.

EXCESS REDEMPTION INSURANCE

INFORMATION REQUIRED BY INSURER

Nature of the risk

2.41.1   There is a financial risk to the manufacturer in having a very successful gift redemption promotion. This is caused by a redemption rate which is far in excess of that which was anticipated and budgeted for. The loss which will be incurred by the manufacturer as a result of an excessive number of redemption applications is that the notional discount on the promoted product price which is attributable by the manufacturer to the cost of the redemption gifts plus their handling charges becomes uneconomically high. There will not be such a risk for a promotion where a limited quantity of the gift is "subject to availability", as there cannot be a redemption overrun.

Fixed prize promotions

2.41.2   The promotion may have a fixed cost prize, such as £50,000, which can only be won by chance. The most popular kind of chance promotion is the use of a random choice scratchcard mechanic which has no skill element (see Chapter 4, paragraph 4.39), but which has a "saving grace" provision in the rules (see Chapter 4, paragraph 4.21.2). The more difficult the scratchcard is, *i.e.*, the greater the number of random scratches which have to be made in order to get the correct answer, the higher the prize is likely to be. Depending on the mathematical odds of a randomly scratched scratchcard being successful and winning the prize, and also depending on the value of the prize, the risk of there being a winner should be insured against.

Insurance available

2.41.3   The manufacturer can get special insurance against the additional costs it incurred as a result of an excessive rate of redemption, or as the result of a scratchcard promotion prize being won. The information which is needed by the insurers so that they can assess their risk and calculate the level of premium which they will charge to the manufacturer will include those listed below.

(a) The nature of the promotion, the number of promotion packages of the product to be distributed, the promotion launch and closing dates, whether the promotion launch is national or regional, and the previous redemption level experience of the manufacturer in respect of similar promotions for its products.

(b) The anticipated redemption rate of promotion gifts and how it has been calculated, and the actual redemption rate at which the excess insurance cover is to come into effect. If the anticipated average redemption rate for the promotion is 5 per cent., then the insurance cover will take effect at a slightly higher percentage, which will be stated in the policy. The higher the redemption level is at which the insurance becomes effective in comparison with the likely redemption rate, the lower the risk is to the insurance company, and the lower will be the premium charged to the manufacturer.

(c) The nature, cost and redemption value of the gift, and how that information relates to the anticipated redemption level. The cost of redemption for the insurance cover will not include postage or delivery charges, and the charges of the handling house for managing the whole process of redemption unless they are specifically referred to in the policy.

(d) The formula for calculating the amount which can be claimed by the manufacturer under the insurance policy if there is an excessive redemption rate which is covered by it.

(e) A copy of the final version of the mechanic and the rules of the promotion, and a copy of any other relevant promotion documents.

INSURANCE PROPOSAL FORM

Completion in good faith

2.42.1 The manufacturer will have to complete the insurer's proposal form, and the questions have to be answered "in good faith", *i.e.* fully and absolutely correctly. Good faith is the foundation of any contract of insurance, and it means that all answers to questions, and all information which is provided to the insurer must be true, complete, and in its right context, and it must not be misleading in any way.

Third party information

2.42.2 If any of the relevant information is being provided to the insurer by a third party on behalf of the manufacturer, checks should be made that the third party has complied with the insurance company's requirements of enquiry and good faith as carefully as the manufacturer would have done. All information which is provided to the insurer as being fact should have documentary back-up confirmation, and all statements of opinion should be reasonably based and "to the best of the knowledge" of the party giving it. To have the "knowledge", the manufacturer (or whoever is providing the information to the insurer) must carry out reasonably detailed research on the subject of the opinion, if that is necessary to satisfy the condition.

Consequences of bad faith

2.42.3 If the manufacturer does not act in good faith towards the insurer, and if this failure is discovered by the insurer, the latter will be able to cancel the insurance contract if no claim has yet been made under it, or it can refuse to pay out on any claim which has been made by the manufacturer. A payment which has already been made to the manufacturer under a policy claim could be recovered by the insurer, by legal action if necessary. In each case the insurance company keeps the premium which has been paid to it. There may be a question of how material the breach of good faith by the manufacturer is, and whether the failure to provide the relevant information or to answer the proposal form correctly was deliberate. Dispute may also arise in the extent of a claim over whether the manufacturer ought to have been aware of information which has suddenly become relevant and which was not disclosed originally to the insurer.

DISCLOSURE OF RELEVANT INFORMATION

Voluntary disclosure

2.43.1 Because of the fundamental nature of the good faith requirement in all insurance contracts the manufacturer will have to disclose to the insurer any relevant information which the manufacturer has in its possession or of which it is aware relating to the promotion and to the insurer's risk, or what could reasonably be expected to be the insurer's perception of risk, even though that information was not specifically asked for by the insurer in the proposal form or elsewhere. The insurer cannot be expected to have all the knowledge which will enable him to ask specifically about everything which is pertinent to the promotion. There will normally be a sweeping-up question in the proposal form asking for voluntary disclosure by the manufacturer of any other relevant information of which it is aware. Awareness may be deemed where the relevant information is known to the agent or representative of the manufacturer. This is information which could affect the judgment of the insurer:

    (a) whether or not to accept the risk in the first place and to insure the manufacturer against it; and

    (b) on the level of premium to be charged; and

    (c) as to the imposition of any conditions on the policy.

Post-contract disclosure

2.43.2 If pertinent information which is required by the insurer is not known to the manufacturer when the insurance is taken out, but it becomes aware of such information later, the manufacturer must provide it promptly to the insurer. Subsequent disclosure in those circumstances should not affect the insurance contract which has already been signed. If the manufacturer could reasonably be expected to have known about that information before the insurance contract was issued, the question of whether it acted in good faith or whether it made sufficient and diligent enquiry might arise.

THE CONTRACT OF INSURANCE

Terms and conditions

2.44.1 An over redemption insurance contract has to define very clearly the terms and conditions which are legally binding on the insurer, *i.e.* when it has to pay out under the policy. The contract is constituted by the completed proposal form, any documents attached to it or referred to in it, and the terms and conditions of the policy issued by the insurers. Before the policy is issued and the premium becomes due:

(a) the manufacturer must be absolutely clear on what it has to do to comply with the policy terms; and what action or inaction could cause the insurance policy to be breached, and therefore nullified; and

(b) the insurers must be absolutely clear on what statements they consider constitute contractual representations and conditions on the part of the insured manufacturer for the purposes of the policy. The manufacturer may disagree with the legal significance being put on those statements by the insurer, and they will have to reach a mutually acceptable compromise.

Problem areas

2.44.2 For most over-redemption insurance contracts the promotion is a standard format where there should be no nasty surprises, such as a simple gift redemption, a large free prize draw first prize or a money-off voucher redemption. Where the promotion is more complicated, or where the amount insured is substantial, the potential problem areas will include the following:

(a) the insurer taking for granted that vague verbal proposals discussed during the promotion development period will actually be finalised and undertaken, without making them a specific warranty or condition of the insurance contract;

(b) significant documents such as agency briefings, and contact reports of meetings between the various parties involved in the promotion, being circulated, seen, but (again) not being legally incorporated into the contract of insurance where they are relevant to the risk;

(c) critical policy terms and conditions being ambiguous in their language. There is a rule in insurance contracts, known as the *contra proferentem* rule, under which any ambiguous insurance contract term is construed in favour of the insured party, and against the insurer;

(d) a distinction between what is fair and reasonable but unenforceable, and what applies contractually and legally. The only time an insurance contract is scrutinised carefully tends to be when a claim is made by the manufacturer, and which the insurer would like to avoid paying.

3 Promotion Gifts and Loss-Leaders

LEGAL ASPECTS

RECOGNITION OF RESPONSIBILITIES

Where legal problems may arise

3.1.1 Commonly available goods, which are used frequently as redemption gifts for promotions, will not normally be involved in any intellectual property or consumer safety problems. However, care should be taken in choosing more expensive or unusual redemption gifts for special promotions, or prizes of a significant value to be won in a competition. Two likely sources of legal problems are set out below.

(a) Where the gift or prize is an independent, well known branded product the availability of which is heavily advertised for the promotion, and where the consent of the proprietor of the brand name trademark of that product has not been sought for its use as a promotional gift, or has been refused. The main legal risk here arises from the unauthorised use and consequent infringement of the brand name trademark or logo associated with that product. For example, if a well known branded goods manufacturer refuses to provide its products as competition prizes, the agency may just buy some of those products and use them as prizes in any case. The physical products now belong to the agency, but using their brand names in the description of the competition prizes to publicise the promoted product will be an infringement of the use of the trademark brand name (Trademarks Act 1938, s.4). In this case, the branded product (together with its trademark, image and reputation) is being used only for the benefit of the promoted product; it is not being advertised for its own benefit in the normal course of trade.

(b) Where the gift or prize is defective, in that:
  (i)   it does not function according to its advertised specifications;
  (ii) it is not fit for its intended purpose;
  (iii) it is defective in its materials or workmanship (not necessarily the same as (i) above);
  (iv) it is dangerous to use; or

65

    (v) it does not conform to a material degree with its description in the promotional material.

Manufacturer and agency

3.1.2   It may not always be clear from the contract between the manufacturer and the agency who is responsible for any consequences arising from the choice and purchase of the promotional gift. There is not likely to be a specific contract between them for each promotion. Their respective responsibilities will normally be set out in a promotion brief after agreement on the style and presentation of the promotion has been reached in discussions. The agency will be acting at all times under the terms of its general agency contract with the manufacturer, and the promotion brief is subject to that contract, so the principle should be dealt with in the main agreement between them. The promotion brief which is agreed between the agency and the manufacturer should deal with all points which are pertinent to the promotion mechanic and rules, and respecting the obtaining, checking and delivery of the promotion gift. Whatever the contract for the supply of the promotion gift to the manufacturer says, the manufacturer will still be liable for any damage suffered by participants in the promotion, because it will be deemed to be the supplier of the gift under the promotion. (See paragraphs 13 to 16 for legal liabilities.)

ANONYMOUS GIFTS

PROPRIETARY RIGHTS

Use of brand name

3.2.1   The manufacturer may use ordinary unbranded goods as a gift in a promotion, although in a sense all available goods are proprietary as they are manufactured by a third party. Anonymous goods such as drinking glasses, T-shirts and beach towels come within the category of unbranded goods. In this context "branded" means that the goods have an identifiable and publicly recognised and advertised named manufacturer, and that the goods are sold under an established trade mark which consists of a brand name or logo. The basic distinction between branded and anonymous goods is that the producer of branded goods can control the unauthorised use of the brand name; whereas the marketing, distribution and sale of anonymous goods does not concern their producers or suppliers after they have been paid for those goods.

PERSONALISED BRANDING

Additional advertising potential

3.3.1 The manufacturer may personalise the anonymous goods by having them marked with the name and/or logo which is the trade mark or brand name of the promoted product. This will easily identify the goods as the promotional gift and it is another means of publicising the promoted product. Personalised branding does not infringe any rights of the original producer of the anonymous goods by representing an "added value" to the promotion gift. Personalised branding of anonymous goods for sales promotion gifts does not represent to the redeemers that the goods are produced by the manufacturer of the promoted product.

Added value gift

3.3.2 Personalised branding will give an ordinary item an added attraction, and will give a greater "hook" to the thrust of the advertising and publicity for the promoted product. There are two benefits from personalised branding: the first is that the gift is made more attractive and is no longer perceived by consumers as being anonymous, and the second is that the gift becomes a permanent advertising vehicle for the promoted product for as long as the gift is worn or used, at no further cost to the manufacturer.

Purchasing procedures

3.3.3 For convenience and economy the supplier of the gift may be asked to mark the whole of the ordered quantity with the brand name and logo of the promoted product at the same time. This will cover the bulk of the anticipated redemption demand in the early part of the promotion period. If the redemption rate for the promotion gift exceeds expectations, then more gifts will have to be personalised in sufficient time to enable the 28 day gift delivery period in the rules to be maintained. If the redemption level by the promotion closing date does not use up the quantity of gifts which have already been personalised for the promotion, the question arises of what should be done with them.

Use of excess gifts

3.3.4 As the manufacturer would be committed to take and pay for all of the gifts which have been ordered and personalised there may be internal or other promotional uses to which the manufacturer can put the excess stock of gifts. If the personalising is only done by the supplier when a specific number of the gifts is ordered by the handling house in response to redemption applications which have already been received, the likelihood of an end-of-promotion excess of gifts is minimised. The 28-day standard period in the promotion rules for delivery of the redeemed gift enables the handling house to match the redemption demand, and to order and supply in time, the gifts which are needed to satisfy those applications.

LIMITED AVAILABILITY

Personalised during production run

3.4.1   For some anonymous goods which are used as special promotion gifts, such as beach towels, or ceramic mugs or plates, the manufacturer of the promoted product can commission the production of a limited quantity of personalised gifts with the brand name and logo of the promoted product woven into the towel as part of its design, or inserted as a design upon the surface of the ceramic gift when it is made. This kind of gift may be subject to a once-only manufacturing run for the promotion, because the lead-time and cost of a new production run in relatively small quantities would not be practical or economic for the manufacturer. The quantity to be ordered of such a special gift will depend on a realistic assessment of the potential redemption level for the promotion. The promotion rules would require a "while stocks last" statement so as not to be misleading should stocks of the special gift be exhausted before all redemption demand has been satisfied.

Fulfilling excess applications

3.4.2   If the number of unfulfilled redemption applications is great enough to make a second production run of the personalised gift economically viable, the handling house could send out a standard letter to unlucky redeemers telling them about the second run, as they will have to wait for the gifts to be ordered and delivered to the handling house. The only effect on the redeemers is that the gifts will be delivered outside the 28-day period stated in the promotion rules. The production of an additional quantity of "limited availability" gifts does not make that original statement misleading, as it was only a warning of a potential shortage.

PROPRIETARY BRAND GOODS

USE OF PROPRIETARY GOODS

Recognition value

3.5.1   Proprietary branded goods can be used as a more prestigious form of promotion gift because the brand name and the reputation of the goods are the main attractions of the gift and thus the promotion. These goods also tend to be more expensive than personalised anonymous goods. For convenience the owner and producer of proprietary branded goods is called "the proprietor" in this section. This distinguishes it from the manufacturer of the promoted product and the supplier of anonymous third-party goods. If the promotion package of the product refers prominently to the brand identity or trademark of popular goods which are being used as the promotion gift, buyers will be encouraged to purchase the product.

Relative cost of product and gift

3.5.2 Because of their cost and reputation, major branded goods which are used for promotion gifts are usually limited to being prizes in competitions. Alternatively a promotion which has quality proprietary brand goods as the gift may have to be one in which there is a cash balance to be paid as well as providing a number of proofs of purchase of the promoted product with the redemption application for the gift.

CONSENT OF BRAND TRADEMARK PROPRIETOR

Use of the brand trademark

3.6.1 The manufacturer will not be entitled to use branded goods, and therefore the protected trademark of those goods, as the gift to promote sales of the promoted product without the prior agreement of the proprietor of the relevant branded goods. This is because the promotion package and any advertising, publicity or other printed material for the promotion will refer prominently to the brand name of the goods (by name, illustration or otherwise) which are being used for the gift. Every reference in the promotion text to the brand name of the goods being used as the gift will constitute use of the trade mark and a potential infringement unless authorised. Therefore there must be consent to such use from the proprietor, otherwise the whole purpose of using high profile branded goods will be lost.

Unauthorised trademark use

3.6.2 The gift of branded goods is not being promoted and sold separately for its own sake in the ordinary course of a retail trade, where its availability is being advertised. In a promotion the branded goods are being advertised and offered by the manufacturer of the promoted product as an incentive reward to a consumer for having bought a quantity of the promoted product. The promotion is making commercial use of the branded goods' reputation and trademark goodwill, not for the benefit of the branded goods, but for the benefit of the unconnected product which is being promoted. Therefore the use of the branded goods' trademark in that context is *not* a permitted use without the consent of the proprietor. Unauthorised use of a brand name trademark to promote a third party product can be damaging to the public image, reputation and status of the branded goods.

Rights of trade mark owner

3.6.3 The proprietor, as the owner of the branded goods trademark, has a right of legal action against the manufacturer and whoever else prints and distributes the promotion material containing any trademark infringement of that brand name. The proprietor may use a court injunction to stop the unauthorised advertising use of the branded goods as a gift in the promotion, and it may also be entitled to a claim for damages.

FAILURE TO USE THE BRAND TRADEMARK

Trademark infringement

3.7 Even if there is no reference in the promotion material to the brand name of the goods which are being used as the promotion gift, or if there is no reference to the identity of the brand trademark proprietor, it will become evident that use is being made of the trademark proprietor's goods in the promotion. The proprietor of branded trademark goods is entitled to have the goods publicly associated with the trademark. Such "non-association" is a trademark infringement. The proprietor of the branded and trademarked goods could claim an injunction and damages against the manufacturer of the promoted product for failing to identify and state the brand name trade mark in connection with the goods. It could be damaging for the reputation of the branded goods and the proprietor for the manufacturer of the promoted product not to identify the goods with their recognised brand name. The business and reputation of the proprietor of the branded goods will also have been deprived of the benefit of the goodwill which can be generated as a result of the proprietor being publicly associated and advertised as the proprietor of the goods which it produces.

CONTROL OF BRAND NAME USE

Proprietor of branded goods can refuse consent

3.8 A proprietor who does not want its branded goods to be advertised and used as the prize for a competition to promote another manufacturer's product has no implied obligation to agree to that use; it can refuse consent without giving any reason. A proprietor prepared to give consent will not normally authorise the use of its branded goods as a prize unless it is satisfied that it will receive an acceptable benefit over and above the sale of the goods themselves, and that the use will not damage its corporate reputation, or that of the branded goods. The proprietor will also want to check that the product which is being promoted is suitable for association with the branded goods, and that the presentation of the promotion is legal.

DAMAGE TO NORMAL RETAIL SALES

Quality branded goods

3.9 Where the branded goods are a recognised quality product the consumer sector for them is usually serviced through selected authorised retail outlets. The retail prices for the branded goods are recommended by their proprietor, but set competitively by each outlet to reflect a reasonable profit on sales, and to be consistent with the image of the retailer and of the reputation of the branded goods. If a substantial quantity of the branded goods is supplied to buyers as the "free gift" in a national and highly publicised, but short-lived promotion for another (even though non-competitive) product, it may be considered by the affected retail trade to be unfair competition. The reason is that each redeemer of a promotion gift might otherwise have bought the branded item at the normal retail price from a regular shop. If the branded goods are the first twenty prizes in a competition, the number involved is insignificant to the retail trade. The retail trade can even benefit from a successfully promoted competition because of the additional advertising for the branded goods prize which is generated through the competition.

LOSS-LEADING AND USE OF BRANDED GOODS

Not loss-leading

3.10.1 The use of branded goods as gifts to promote a totally different product is not loss-leading as defined in section 13 of the Resale Prices Act 1976 (see paragraph 3.32 below). The branded goods are not being offered for sale by an outlet at an uneconomical price for the purpose of enticing customers to go to that outlet to encourage them to buy other goods while they are there.

Similar effect

3.10.2 As the use of branded goods as gifts or prizes in a promotion is a commercial enticement to a buyer to purchase the promoted product, it could be argued that the same "loss- leading" principles should apply. The price which is being charged by the manufacturer of the promoted product for the third-party branded goods is certainly uneconomical in retail terms, because it is either nothing (a "free" gift or a competition prize), or there is a modest cash balance payment (with proofs of purchase of the promoted product) under the promotion rules. The "loss" is picked up by the manufacturer of the promoted product as part of its marketing cost for that product. The disposal of the third party branded goods as a promotion gift is not a sale of those goods in the course of a bona fide retail trade disposal.

CONTRACT FOR USE OF BRANDED GOODS

WRITTEN AGREEMENT

Commercial protection

3.11.1   The proprietor of branded goods should have a written agreement with the manufacturer of the promoted product setting out the terms on which the branded goods will be supplied for use as the promotion gift. An agreement is necessary for the protection of both parties, because:

(a) the proprietor must protect its trade mark rights by a contract which he can sue on if the manufacturer defaults in a material manner;

(b) any restrictions on the use and advertising of the brand name, trademark and logo must be set out clearly;

(c) a written and properly negotiated contract makes each party consider the relevant commercial points carefully. Nothing of significance should be left out of the contract;

(d) without the correct written authority of the proprietor, the manufacturer may be accused of trademark infringement if the parties fall out.

Manufacturer's minimum commitment

3.11.2   Where branded goods are used as a redemption gift, the proprietor might commit the manufacturer to placing a minimum order, whatever the redemption rate may be, subject to paragraph 3.11.5 below. Without such a minimum commitment, the proprietor will be the loser if the availability of the branded gifts is highly publicised, but the redemption rate of the promotion is so low that the proprietor gets an inadequate benefit from sales of the branded goods to the manufacturer in return for having agreed to their use as the promotion gift. An alternative safety feature can be the payment to the proprietor by the manufacturer of a minimum sum of money representing the value in sales to the proprietor of the manufacturer's minimum purchase obligation. The unit cost risk to the manufacturer for redemptions is increased if the quantity of branded goods actually ordered from the proprietor is less than the quantity upon which the minimum payment was calculated. If such a proposal is agreed to by the manufacturer, it should consider having an "under redemption" insurance policy to cover any redemption shortfall loss. (See Chapter 2, paragraph 2.41 onwards.)

Maintaining supplies

3.11.3 The proprietor must consider how the schedule of supplying the branded goods as promotion gifts to the handling house will affect its manufacturing and distribution capacity to satisfy its retail orders in the ordinary course of business. The proprietor must be able to fulfil orders for the gift as well as being able to supply normal trade requirements. Any difficulty must be resolved by producing the promotion gifts over a period of time, and setting the promotion dates accordingly.

Conditions of use

3.11.4 In its agreement with the promoted product manufacturer, the proprietor should lay down strict conditions to ensure that all stocks of the branded goods which are provided to the handling house are only used as gifts for that specific promotion. The proprietor should make its agreement to supply the branded goods conditional on being able to approve the promotion terms and rules as being suitable for that gift. The reasons are that:

(a) the proprietor has the opportunity to check independently that the promotion is legal and that it complies with the Code of Sales Promotion Practice;
(b) the proprietor can ensure that all references to the brand name trade mark in artwork, promotional text and advertisements is approved as being in conformity with the agreement with the manufacturer (see paragraph 3.12.2);
(c) if there are any useful comments which it can make, or if it requires changes to the promotion material to comply with the agreement, the agency which is dealing with the promotion has time to do so without incurring unnecessary expense or inconvenience;
(d) there should be a promotion rule to limit the number of redemption applications, as there must be no opportunity for the branded goods to be redeemed by any one applicant in any significant quantity, indicating that they may not be intended for personal use only.

Disposal of residual stocks

3.11.5 The branded goods which are unredeemed at the end of the promotion period must not be dumped on any sector of the consumer market. On the other hand the manufacturer does not want to have a significant residual stock of the gift, for which it has paid, and for which it cannot find any suitable use within the restrictions of the supply agreement with the proprietor. It should be entitled to make internal corporate or dealer promotional use of them, provided this does not entail any form of commercial disposal.

TRADEMARK PROTECTION

Control by proprietor

3.12.1 The use of the brand name, trademark and logo of the proprietor's branded goods in any printed material, promoted product packaging and advertising relating to the promotion must be closely controlled by the proprietor for trademark protection purposes. The manufacturer must comply with the directions of the proprietor in respect of how the logo and any distinctive style in which the brand name is set out can be used in the promotion material. The trademark must be used accurately, in the same way as it appears on its registration. For this purpose the agreement between the proprietor and the manufacturer should contain a representation of the trademark as it is to be used on the gifts. As logos and brand names may be stylistic, those styles also should be represented accurately. Personalised use of either of them, such as by making modifications which are designed to fit in with the promotion concept or packaging, should not be allowed by the proprietor. An example of this would be the conjunction of the brand name or logo with those of the promoted product into one new artistic device to denote the connection between them for the promotion.

Proprietary notices

3.12.2 The correct trademark and copyright notices have to be stated wherever the brand name or logo of the gift appears on any material for the promotion, and in a manner required by the proprietor (so long as this is reasonable). This should warn imitators that the brand identity words and/or logo have protection as trademarks, and should publicise the proprietor as being their registered owner. The logo, being an artistic device, will also be protected by copyright if it is sufficiently substantial, distinctive and original to be a protectable artistic work under section 4 of the Copyright Designs and Patents Act 1988. Samples of all printed material containing the trademark should be submitted to the proprietor before that material is finalised and printed, so that the proprietor can be satisfied that the protective obligations for the trademarks set out in the agreement are being complied with accurately by the agency which is designing the artwork for the promotion.

Modification of goods

3.12.3 The manufacturer should be prohibited by the agreement from modifying the branded goods without the consent of the proprietor, for example by adding to them in a prominent manner the brand name and logo of the promoted product. In this case there would be two infringements by the manufacturer:

(a) There would be a trademark infringement for which, if the claim is not resolved amicably, the proprietor could sue the manufacturer, obtain an injunction to stop such infringement and claim damages. The infringed goods still in the hands of the manufacturer would have to be returned to their original condition or handed over to the proprietor.

(b) The manufacturer would be open to an action for passing off, or for defaming the branded goods, depending on the nature of the modifications.

DEFECTIVE PROMOTION GIFTS

SUPPLY OF GOODS

A gift is a trade supply

3.13   The fact that the goods which represent the promotion gift are being provided on a commercial basis to a buyer indirectly, *i.e.* not through a normal retailer, does not change some of the legal requirements relating to such supply. The supply of the gift to redeemers is made in the course of the manufacturer's business, which is that of selling the promoted product. Although the promotion gift is supplied "free" or for a nominal payment as the result of a redemption application being made, or upon the competition being won, this form of disposal can be a trade supply of the gift. The manufacturer or the handling house (whichever is legally considered to be the supplier of the gift to redeemers), is in the same position as any other trade supplier of goods to the public.

CONSUMER PROTECTION LEGISLATION

Meaning of defective

3.14.1   For the purposes of this section, "deficient" means that the promotion gift is incomplete or does not work properly when it is delivered to the redeemer, whereas it is "defective" when it comes within the Consumer Protection Act 1987 , s.3. "Product" or "goods" refer to the promotion gift, as those are the words used in the relevant legislation. This section states that there is a defect in the product "if the safety of the product is not such as persons generally are entitled to expect". This reference does not refer to what a consumer might reasonably do with the product, but what the *manufacturer* might reasonably expect a consumer to do with it. Therefore the more idiot proof the product is, the safer it will be to use. The Act requires that the following matters must be taken into account when considering the safety aspects of the product:

(a) the manner in which and the purpose for which the product has been marketed, as well as its get up, the use of any trademark in relation to the product, and any instructions or warnings given with the product;
(b) what might reasonably be expected to be done by any person with, or in relation to, the product; and
(c) the date when the product was supplied by its producer.

Legal position of supplier

3.14.2   The liability of a supplier for defective products is largely a matter of contract. Sales promotion contracts as between manufacturers and consumers (see Chapter 1, paragraph 1) never contain references to defective promotion gifts or prizes. In the absence of a specific reference in the relevant contracts, the law implies certain minimum contractual requirements under the Sale of Goods Act 1979 and the Supply of Goods and Services Act 1983. Under section 14(6) of the 1979 Act there is an implied term that goods which are supplied in the course of business should be of merchantable quality, which is defined as being "as fit for the purpose for which goods of that kind are commonly bought as is reasonable to expect having regard to any description applied to them, the price (if relevant) and all other relevant circumstances". The parties who are liable for defective products under the Consumer Protection Act 1987 are:

(a) the manufacturer of the defective product;
(b) if the product is produced outside the E.C., the importer to the E.C. carries the same liabilities as the manufacturer;
(c) an O.E.M. "own brand" supplier has the same liability as the manufacturer, as it is putting itself out to the public as being the manufacturer of its own brand product;
(d) any person who supplied the product can be as liable as the manufacturer, if he does not identify who is the manufacturer, importer or own brander of the defective goods within a reasonable time of being asked to do so by a person who has been injured by them. Distributors and retailers of defective products can therefore have the same liability as the manufacturer of the defective products, whether or not they are aware of that risk.

Under section 46 of the 1987 Act, supplying goods, whether as principal or agent, includes providing the goods in exchange for any consideration other than money, and giving the goods as a prize or otherwise making a gift of the goods. Therefore, supplying gifts to promotion gift redeemers and prizes to competition winners, is supplying goods for the purposes of the relevant legislation. This is a point which fundamentally affects promoters and handling houses, who seldom think of themselves as having such a potentially serious liability for defective goods which are supplied to the public under the terms of a sales promotion, either as gifts or as prizes.

Legal position of promoter

3.14.3 If the manufacturer of the promoted product acts as its own handling house and manages the promotion internally, it would buy the gift from its appropriate supplier, and it would deliver a gift to each valid redemption applicant. It would then be the legal supplier of the gifts to members of the public for the purposes of the consumer protection legislation, and paragraph 3.14.2(d) above will apply to it.

Legal position of agency

3.14.4 If the sales promotion agency buys the promotion gifts on behalf of the manufacturer, it does so as a principal. It would invoice the manufacturer for them, and it would arrange for them to be delivered to the handling house on behalf of the manufacturer. In that event, the agency is the supplier of those goods in legal terms as it has bought the gifts for onward transfer to redeemers, although it does not actually undertake that transfer. The agency in those circumstances could have a responsibility to a redeemer, unless (possibly) it cannot provide the information referred to in paragraph 3.15.3.

E.C. Directive

3.14.5 The E.C. Directive 92/59 of June 29, 1992 relates to general product safety, and its application to sales promotions follows the same lines as the U.K. Consumer Protection Act 1987. The relevant definitions under Article 2 of the Directive are:

(a) "product" shall mean any product intended for consumers or likely to be used by consumers, supplied whether for consideration or not in the course of a commercial activity, and whether new, used or reconditioned;

(b) "safe product" shall mean any product which, under normal or reasonably foreseeable conditions of use, including duration, does not present a risk or only the minimum risks compatible with the product's use, considered as acceptable and consistent with a high level of protection for the safety and health of persons, taking into account the following points in particular;

    (i) the characteristics of the product, including its composition, packaging, instructions for assembly and maintenance,

    (ii) the effect on other products, where it is reasonably foreseeable that it will be used with other products,

    (iii) the presentation of the products, the labelling, any instructions for its use and disposal and any other indication or information provided by the producer,

    (iv) the categories of consumers at serious risk when using the product, in particular children,

(c) "distributor" shall mean any professional in the supply chain whose authority does not affect the safety aspects of a product.

Article 3.3 states that "distributors shall be required to act with due care in order to help to ensure compliance with the general safety requirement, in particular by not supplying products which they know or should have presumed, on the basis of the information in their possession and as professionals, do not comply with this requirement".

HANDLING HOUSE

3.15.1 If the handling house, and not the manufacturer of the promoted product, is to be treated legally as the supplier of defective goods under the Consumer Protection Act 1987 to redeemers of the promotion gifts, it will have to operate as an independent contractor under an appropriate contract with the promoted product manufacturer, and with the gift supplier. Under these contracts the handling house would purchase the redemption gifts from their source, supply them to redeemers under the promotion rules, and would charge the manufacturer for buying and distributing those gifts.

Handling house as agent

3.15.2 Normally the manufacturer of the promoted product should be treated as the supplier, because the defective gift is delivered by the handling house only as its agent in connection with the manufacturer's trade, *i.e.* the promotion of its products. The handling house will be treated as an agent of the manufacturer where:

(a) the manufacturer or its agency has a contract with the gift supplier to sell and supply the gifts to the manufacturer; and
(b) the manufacturer has a separate contract with the handling house appointing it to receive stocks of the gift from the supplier, and to deliver them to valid redemption applicants on behalf of the manufacturer according to the promotion rules.

Manufacturer's indemnity

3.15.3 If the handling house has had no part in choosing or evaluating the gift for the promotion, because of the risk of it being treated as the supplier of a defective gift, it should require an adequate indemnity from the manufacturer in its agreement relating to the gift redemption management for the promotion. In order to pass on to the ultimately responsible party the risk and consequences of a prosecution or a claim for damages under the Act for supplying defective goods, the manufacturer of the promoted product must keep full details of where the gift came from, so the identity of the gift manufacturer, supplier or importer can be given promptly to any person who is injured, or who suffers actionable loss, resulting from a defective gift.

Public assumptions

3.15.4 Members of the public may assume that the manufacturer of the promoted product is responsible for defective gifts, because of the connection between the product and the gift through the promotion. The role of the handling house in dealing with redemption applications appears to redeemers to be only administrative.

LEGAL POSITION OF GIFT SUPPLIER

Cause of defect

3.16.1 The redeemer has a good cause of action against the original supplier or the manufacturer of the promotion gift if the gift is defective and if it injures the redeemer. The promoted product manufacturer must provide the injured redeemer with the particulars of the manufacturer or the importer of the defective gift to avoid being held responsible themselves. If any such claim is made by the redeemer, and if he cannot get the necessary information about the gift manufacturer or its importer from the promoted product manufacturer, he may be advised to take legal action against the manufacturer, since in the absence of such information the manufacturer is legally responsible for the consequences of supplying him with the defective gift.

Deficiency not a defect

3.16.2 The supplier of the gift would not be responsible for a characteristic deficiency (as opposed to a physical defect) which the promotion rules legitimately compel the applicant to accept as a condition of participating in the promotion. For example, if the promotion advertises Gift A, and Gift B is delivered to a redeemer, as the original supplier of Gift B is not connected with the promotion it is not liable to the redeemer for the wrong gift being delivered to him. Neither will the supplier be liable for any misleading description of the gift which is contained in any of the promotion material originating from the manufacturer of the promoted product, and which has not been provided or approved by the supplier. The manufacturer might have a right of indemnity against the supplier if the supplier provided the misleading description in the first place.

Inadequate description

3.16.3 The gift may be described in the promotion material as being within a range of products, such as "a steam iron made by X Co. Ltd.", without specifying the exact model to be supplied to the redemption applicant. If the redeemer gets an X Co. Ltd iron which is not of the steam variety, the advertisement for the gift is misleading. If the redeemer gets a steam iron, but not the one which is illustrated in the promotion text, that will also be misleading. If there is no indication in the promotion material of which steam iron it is, the redeemer cannot complain if he gets the most basic model in the steam iron range, although he had hoped for the de luxe model. This is not a defect in consumer protection legislation terms.

CONTRACT WITH GIFT SUPPLIER

MANUFACTURER'S REQUIREMENTS

Choice of agencies

3.17.1 A manufacturer who has several major-brand products which are constantly being subject to promotions may be dealing with several agencies, different handling houses and different gift suppliers. Each of these parties will have their own terms and conditions of business, and none of them will be precisely the same. Each of them is providing services or goods to the same customer, *i.e.* the manufacturer of the promoted product, and they will each do their best to accommodate the manufacturer's reasonable requirements. It would save the agency a lot of time and effort if the manufacturer "standardised" his usual needs in a checklist for each of the above organisations. As the promotion is proposed and developed, that checklist will be a starting-point for negotiation of an agreement with the relevant organisation. The checklist can be updated and modified according to experience and, in each individual case, to satisfy the specific needs of the promotion.

Terms of supply

3.17.2 There are many companies which specialise in supplying clever or interesting relatively low-cost goods which are designed for use as promotion gifts. Doing a deal with such a supplier should not need a special contract for any of its standard range of gifts outside its standard terms and conditions of supply. These should be reviewed by the agency on behalf of the manufacturer for acceptability, and any desired changes should be negotiated if necessary. Where unusual goods may be used for the promotion gift, such as a special design of plate or personalised branded goods, the manufacturer should have a properly negotiated agreement in writing with the supplier of the goods. Some of the main features of such an agreement are explained in the following paragraphs.

GIFT-ORDERING COMMITMENT

Approve samples

3.18.1 Where the promotion gift is modified or personalised for the promotion by the supplier, or where the gift is a "one-off" limited-availability production run for something special, it should be examined at the sample (pre-production) stage by the agency and the manufacturer. This enables them to check whether:

(a) the basic gift is what the manufacturer understood it to be;
(b) the quality of the finished gift is acceptable; the gift's production-run quality must match the sample quality;
(c) the personalising of the brand name and logo of the promoted product is correctly expressed, correctly positioned, of the agreed size and in accordance with any agreement affecting it;
(d) the correct trademark or copyright symbols or notices are there, and that they are reasonably prominent; and
(e) in the case of a regular item, such as a sports bag, that there are no other product brand names, logos or insignia on it apart from those of the manufacturer of the promoted product.

Where the type of gift makes it desirable, the agreement with the supplier of the gift must contain relevant warranties covering each of the above representations or requirements. A material breach of any of the warranties should also have a stated responsibility of the supplier for the consequences, as a remedy and as protection for the manufacturer of the promoted product.

Size of order

3.18.2 The quantity of promotion gifts which will be ordered over the promotion period from the supplier will ideally be just enough to enable the handling house to fulfil all of the redemption applications which will be received by it during the period of the promotion. The 28 day rule for the delivery of promotion gifts enables the handling house (or the agency) to order batches of the promotion gift from the supplier as redemption applications are received. This should enable the ordering and the delivery of gifts to be kept in line. The quantity cannot be forecast precisely when the promotion is being scheduled, so for unusual goods the handling house should establish first whether for economic or other reasons it will be necessary to have a once-only run of the personalised gift production. The estimate of the overall likely rate of redemption may have to be on the generous side to avoid the risk of not having sufficient stocks of the gift if the promotion is more successful than anticipated. The handling house should also establish if there is likely to be an excessive time-delay or an uneconomical cost in the supplier producing a small additional run of the personalised gift to cover the tail-end of redemption applications.

Lead-time for gift supply

3.18.3 The starting and closing dates of the promotion are known well in advance of the final arrangements for the launch of the promotion. The supplier of a personalised gift for the promotion should be committed to supplying the agreed gift quantity by specified dates. Working backwards from a final delivery date for personalised gifts, the supplier will have a minimum lead-time which it requires for their production or personalising. The timetable for providing the supplier with artwork for the stylised product brand name and logo, for samples of the personalised gift to be submitted to the manufacturer for quality approval, and for delivery of stocks to the handling house can then be calculated. There should always be a contingency period built into the timetable to deal with any unexpected problems or delays so that the launch of the promotion is not prejudiced.

QUALITY OF GIFTS

Product guarantee

3.19.1 Where the gift is a proprietary branded product the manufacturer's supplier may provide it with a guarantee if that is appropriate. This will put a redeemer in the same position as a retail purchaser of that branded product. If the supplier is making a one-off run of unusual personalised gifts which are not to a standard product design, and for which it does not have any printed specifications or warranty, the supplier should give a warranty of the quality of their workmanship and materials in the gift supply agreement. That quality control will be applied to the production run to ensure that the bulk order which is delivered to the handling house conforms to the approved sample. The agreement should also set out the rights and remedies of the manufacturer if the supplier of the promotion gift fails to maintain the gift quality or the agreed delivery schedule. The supplier should indemnify the manufacturer in the agreement from any real damage or expense it incurs as a result of such breaches.

Accurate promotion description

3.19.2 If the promotion material contains any description of the gift in performance or qualitative terms, the agency should check with the supplier that the description given to it in the promotion terms and in any related advertising is accurate. Any material inconsistency or inaccuracy in the gift description will make the promotion misleading in that respect. Some major retail outlets are particularly sensitive about the legality of promotions which are advertised on products which they sell. In a blatant case the outlet may refuse to sell the promoted product because of the risk of prosecution.

Supplier's indemnity

3.19.3 If the supplier is the producer or the importer of the gifts it should indemnify the manufacturer from the adverse consequences of any complaint or claim which may be made by any third party (including a Trading Standards Authority) in respect of the gifts which it supplies for the promotion being defective. If a deficiency in the gift is the cause of the manufacturer of the promoted product being prosecuted for running a misleading promotion or for publishing a misleading advertisement (such as where the supplier's own description of the gift in the promotional material is inaccurate) no indemnity can prevent a conviction, but it can cover the costs and fine incurred by the manufacturer.

THE PROMOTION GIFT MUST BE LEGAL

Safe to use

3.20.1 The promotion gift as provided by the supplier must be legal, so it must comply with any applicable U.K. and E.C. regulations governing its design and construction, and it must be safe to use. Examples of causes of liability are where a cuddly teddy bear has a dangerous method of fixing glass eyes into its head, or where a novel device for cutting vegetables cannot be operated without harm to the user's hand. Where it is reasonable to do so, the manufacturer should obtain confirmation in the supplier's agreement that the supplier or the gift manufacturer has adequate product liability insurance and that it would cover the supplier's goods being used by the manufacturer as promotion gifts. The insurance cover should be insisted on for gifts which could be hazardous if they are not made or used correctly whether or not the supplier is the manufacturer. If the supplier is not the manufacturer or the importer of the gifts, it should be required to notify the promoted product manufacturer in writing of the identity of the manufacturer or importer of the gift, in case there are any personal injury claims from redeemers in respect of defective gifts.

No infringement of proprietary rights

3.20.2 The promotion gift must not be an infringement of any third-party proprietary design right or copyright, such as where the manufacturer had commissioned a one-off design gift to be produced by the supplier especially for the promotion. Examples are an "original" furry toy which infringes the copyright in a well-known animal character, or a special artwork poster which turns out not to be original, or a new cassette tape compilation of Country and Western artists' performances, where the reproduction rights have not been cleared with the relevant copyright owners of the music and the recordings. An indemnity against third-party claims for infringement of intellectual property rights should always be required by the manufacturer in these circumstances, as such infringements can be expensive to rectify or to compensate for.

DELIVERY OF GIFT BY HANDLING HOUSE

SHIPMENT AND PACKAGING

Responsibility for breakages

3.21.1 If the gifts are fragile, such as glass or ceramics, the agreement with the supplier should deal with the responsibility for packing and delivering them safely to the premises of the handling house. If a fragile gift is to be delivered to the redemption applicants in special packaging, the supplier may be required to deliver them to the handling house in an already packaged state ready for delivery.

No applicable rule

3.21.2 Promotions do not normally have rules which deal with the procedures for delivery errors, breakages and deficiencies in gifts delivered to a redeemer. The following paragraphs deal with the normal situations, and section 5.10.3 of the Sales Promotion Code sets out the procedures which should be adopted in these cases.

INSPECTION ON SHIPMENT TO REDEEMER

Practicability of examination

3.22.1 It is not possible for the handling house to examine all of the promotion gifts for deficiency or breakage prior to shipment to each redeemer. Inspection should not even be considered for standard mass produced gifts, or those which do not need inspection. Examination may be considered on a random sample basis where the gift is a more expensive item which is breakable. The gifts may have been supplied to the handling house in secured safety packaging, and it is impractical to open each package and to examine each item before despatch to redeemers.

Risk of damage to fragile gifts

3.22.2 Fragile items, such as a set of drinking glasses, have a risk of damage in the delivery process both from the supplier and from the handling house.

Examination by the handling house of broken glasses which have been returned by a redeemer will not be able to show one way or the other whether they were broken before or after delivery to the redeemer. The incidence of dishonesty among redeemers is not great, and for a low value promotion gift that risk is worth taking. As a consequence some fraudulent claims for replacement of broken gifts will get through the system.

NOTIFICATION OF DAMAGED GIFT

Return damaged gift

3.23.1   Damage to a promotion gift may be visible immediately on inspection by the redeemer, or it may become apparent only when the redeemer attempts to use it. The redeemer should contact the handling house immediately to report the damage, and if requested to do so he should ship the damaged gift back to the handling house for inspection. The cost of returning the gift will be paid by the redeemer initially, but that expense should be reimbursed by the handling house if the redeemer's complaint is found to be justified.

Automatic replacement

3.23.2   If the promotion gift has a modest value and is an ordinary item, as a matter of customer goodwill and economic convenience the handling house may send a replacement without asking for the return of the defective or broken gift. For a more valuable gift the handling house may want a short written report on how the damage was discovered, and what it was, in case a warranty claim can be made against the supplier. The supplier's contract for higher value fragile gifts should contain a right in reasonable circumstances for the manufacturer of the promoted product to claim for broken gifts without giving the supplier the opportunity to examine them. In most cases a handling house report should be sufficient, except where the manufacturer of the gift permits its return.

REPLACEMENT POLICY

Genuine or fraudulent claim?

3.24.1   If the handling house is reasonably satisfied that the damage to the gift was not caused by the careless handling or use of the gift by the redeemer, a replacement should be provided promptly. If the handling house reasonably believes that any damage to the gift has been caused by the redeemer or that he is fraudulently trying to get a second gift, the claim should be rejected, or at least queried closely. The response of the handling house should depend on the value of the gift. For some gifts it may be more expensive to query a claim than to satisfy it, even knowing it may be fraudulent. There is also the usual commercial goodwill question of balancing the aggravation and cost of having an argument with the redeemer, against maintaining good customer relations, just in case the suspicion that the claim was fraudulent proves to be unfounded.

Limited availability gift

3.24.2 If the promotion is one in which the promotion gift is subject to a "while stocks last" limitation, there may be no more items of the gift available to effect a replacement for the damaged item returned by the redeemer. The handling house should provide the redeemer with some other gift of a comparable value, and if possible of a similar nature. If the promotion required a proof-of-purchase plus a cash balance for a special higher value gift, the redeemer should be given the opportunity to have his money back or to accept a suitable substitute gift in the case of a genuine claim.

GIFT MANUFACTURER'S GUARANTEE

Not affected by promotion

3.25.1 Promotion gifts which are branded mechanical or electrical goods, such as digital alarm clocks, should carry a guarantee from the gift manufacturer for a period of time after its retail disposal against failure by reason of defective materials or workmanship. The conditions of the manufacturer's guarantee must be observed by the redeemer if he is to make a valid claim under it for the replacement or repair of the damaged or defective item. If the manufacturer of the promoted product has any doubt about the application of the promotion gift manufacturer's guarantee, it should be resolved with the supplier *before* a commitment is made to buy stocks of that gift for the promotion.

Guarantee terms

3.25.2 The manufacturer's guarantee of the promotion gift may only be valid for the original purchaser of the gift, and it may only last for a specified period of time from the date of the retail sale of the item to a consumer. The manufacturer of the promoted product should check when the guarantee for the gift will commence if the gift is used in the promotion. In this case there is no retail sale of the gift, but for all practical purposes the redeemer is in the same position as a retail purchaser. The guarantee period should run from the date of delivery of the promotion gift to the redeemer, not from the date of supply to the handling house, if there is a substantial time-lag between these two dates.

CONDITIONS OF DELIVERY

Report on inspection discoveries

3.26   Terms and conditions of delivery of the handling house or the transport company, as stated on the back of the delivery note or the receipt acknowledgment form signed by the redeemer, may state that if no complaint is received in writing within, say, seven days after delivery, the promotion gift will be deemed to have been examined by him and found to be in good order. In this context "good order" relates to there being no visible signs of damage to the gift in transit, and to ensuring that all relevant attachments and documentation have been included in the gift package. A specified time limit for the notification of any damage or defect is a contractual matter and can be enforced if it is reasonable. For example, a requirement to give notification of damage within 24 hours after receiving the gift would be unreasonable. Contractual time limits do not affect the rights of the redeemer under any consumer protection legislation should the gift be found at a later date to be damaged or defective. Neither does a time limit for notification affect his right to complain to the gift supplier under the guarantee terms if the promotion gift has a valid warranty failure within the guarantee period. In the absence of a contractual time limit for making a damage or defect notification, the redeemer will have a "reasonable" time in which to do so. What is considered to be reasonable will depend on the circumstances of each claim.

WARRANTY CLAIMS FOR FAULTY GIFTS

Checking cause of fault

3.27.1   The promotion gift may be electronic or mechanical, and may work perfectly for two weeks and then expire. The redeemer may open up the gift or fiddle with it to see whether the cessation of function is due to some obvious and simple cause which is not visible from the outside. For example, batteries can run down and wires can become detached.

Interference prohibited

3.27.2   If the redeemer does more than just check the batteries, which are accessible without having to dismantle any sealed part of the gift, he may lose his right to complain about a defect. This is not the case if the gift comes with a set of instructions upon how to find and resolve operational problems and if he follows them correctly. The gift manufacturer's guarantee prohibits any unauthorised interference with the gift, the happening of which automatically causes the guarantee to become void in respect of that defect, and in respect of any other fault which is caused, or which is materially contributed to by the unauthorised interference. Any necessary repairs to the gift then become chargeable to the redeemer.

Reason for prohibition

3.27.3 If the redeemer interferes with the gift and returns it to the supplier because it still will not work, it may be impossible for the supplier to be reasonably satisfied that the fault complained of existed in the first place, and that it was not caused or aggravated by such interference. The gift manufacturer will only accept responsibility under its guarantee for a defect which is clearly not the redeemer's fault, provided that it comes within the guarantee terms.

Warranty invalidity by certain use

3.27.4 Any right of the redeemer to return the defective gift to its manufacturer under the guarantee in expectation of a replacement, or of it being repaired free of charge, will usually become void under the guarantee terms if the gift is used or stored in a manner which is:

(a) not in compliance with the manufacturer's instructions and recommendations;
(b) likely to cause it damage or deteriorate; or
(c) inconsistent with the use for which the gift would normally and reasonably be intended.

NON-DELIVERY OF PROMOTION GIFT

Lost in transit

3.28.1 If the promotion gift is shipped by the handling house to the redeemer by ordinary post, *i.e.* not by using a door-to-door carrier system, it is possible for it to become delayed in the post, and it is possible but unlikely for it never to be delivered at all. It is also possible that the gift may be delivered to the wrong premises, such as where the redeemer's address is incorrectly stated on the application form, or where it is not stated clearly and had to be guessed at by the handling house. An illegible or incomplete application form is invalidated under the promotion rules, but the handling house may have made an attempt to interpret whatever was not clear or what was missing. The handling house may decide not to recover a misdirected gift from the person who had a pleasant surprise in receiving it, although legally it may be entitled to do so.

No liability

3.28.2 After the expiry of the 28 day period for delivery of the gift specified in the promotion rules, the redeemer should notify the handling house that the long awaited gift has not yet arrived. A check in the handling house records ought to show the date upon which the gift was despatched, and where it was sent to. If the handling house had the wrong address for the redeemer because the application form was incorrectly or illegibly completed, the handling house should have no further obligation to despatch a replacement gift to the right address. If the handling house is satisfied that the gift was delivered correctly, the complaint may be a fraudulent one, and the handling house will have to take a view on how to deal with it.

Delivery failure

3.28.3 If the handling house is satisfied that it did not despatch the gift, or that the post office is at fault in not delivering it to the complainant, the handling house should apologise immediately and arrange for the gift to be delivered. If the gift was subject to availability, and if there are none left to despatch, a suitable alternative gift should be supplied.

IN-STORE PROMOTIONS AND LOSS-LEADERS

DEFINITION OF IN-STORE PROMOTIONS

Promotions for outlet benefit

3.29.1 "Promotions" generally refer to promotions run by product manu-facturers which are contained on the product package. This section deals with in-store or live promotions, which are limited to the retail outlet, or to a chain of retail outlets. In-store promotions are run and controlled by the outlet, and they are intended to generate increased sales of all of the products which are stocked by the outlet. The proprietors of retail outlets do not make any of the products which they sell, although many major chain store chains have their "own brand" versions of some popular products which are made for them.

Bargain prices

3.29.2 A common in-store promotion is the offer for sale of a popular and high selling product at a bargain price. This is done to entice shoppers (who might not otherwise have entered the store) into the outlet, where they may buy that product at that price and where they will be encouraged to do the rest of their shopping while they are in the store. If the product is sold in this way, at a very low price, which is close to or below the wholesale cost of the product to the outlet, the outlet may be accused by the manufacturer of the bargain price product of using that product as a loss-leader, as to which see paragraphs 3.31 onwards. Bargain prices are usually associated with "was £X, is now £Y" price reduction claims. Whenever an outlet wants to have a "reduced price" sale promotion for any goods, the DTI Code of Practice for Traders on Price Indications (see Appendix 2) will govern the legality of how that outlet can represent those price reductions. The Code is clear and concise, and failure by an outlet to comply with its requirements will be a breach of the Consumer Protection Act 1987, s. 20, on which the Code is based. The outlet risks prosecution by its local Trading Standards Officer if he becomes aware of any illegal price promotions.

PRINCIPLE OF FREE COMPETITION

Protection of competition

3.30 Fair competitive price retail trading on a commercially sound basis has to be protected from undue pressure brought by manufacturers. This is why resale price maintenance was abolished by the Resale Prices Act 1976. Once a retailer has obtained and paid for a manufacturer's products they belong to that outlet. How that retailer wishes to promote its business through the advertising and sale of that product is outside the control of the product manufacturer, with the exceptions listed below:

- (a) the physical product and its packaging must not be interfered with or modified by the retailer so as to:
  - (i)   infringe the copyright and other proprietary rights of the manufacturer in the get-up and the trade mark branding of its product;
  - (ii) infringe any patent or design right the manufacturer has in the product;
  - (iii) adversely affect the constituent elements of any perishable products;
  - (iv) invalidate any warranty given by the manufacturer in its product guarantee;
  - (v)   make unsafe any mechanical or electrical product; or
  - (vi) invalidate any European type approval (CE) or British Standard with which the product has to comply to be legally sold to the public;
- (b) there must be no misrepresentation by the retailer of the quality, function or origin of the product to the detriment of the manufacturer. Both (a)(i) and this provision would be breached if, for example, the store re-packaged branded frozen food products which had been produced in a politically sensitive country so as to remove any references to that country;
- (c) the public must not be misled by the retailer in connection with the advertising or sale of the product; and

(d) there must be no contravention by the retailer of any legislative or other legally enforceable protection which is given to the product manufacturer to ensure that its business as well as its image and reputation and that of the product are not denigrated or damaged.

LOSS-LEADING

THE RESALE PRICES ACT 1976

Purpose of the Act

3.31.1   The Resale Prices Act 1976 ("the Act") deals with the prohibition of anti-competitive practices which may otherwise be applied by product manufacturers to retailers who do not charge what the manufacturer considers to be reasonable and commercially competitive prices for its product. There has to be a balance between the freedom of retailers to be competitive, and the right of a manufacturer to protect its legitimate business interests, and the Act provides a balance with a sensible set of enforceable rules.

What is loss-leading?

3.31.2   Loss-leading occurs when an outlet purchases from the manufacturer a substantial quantity of a popular range of quality branded products and sells them at a price which is irresistible because it is close to or below the wholesale price at which the outlet bought the product from the manufacturer. In those circumstances the outlet is not stocking, advertising and selling the branded product for the purpose of making a commercial profit on the sale of each item. On the contrary, the outlet is deliberately making only a nominal profit, or it may even make a trading loss on each item of the branded product disposed of at that price. The outlet is prepared to take a loss on sales of the product by using it as bait to attract customers into the shop. Other unrelated retail outlets which stock and sell the product at a normal profitable price may put pressure on the manufacturer to stop supplying the product to the "offending" outlet because it is seen as unfair trading.

Loss-leading as an incentive gift

3.31.3   Another form of loss-leading is for the retail outlet to offer that branded product as a free gift to any customer whose invoiced purchases of other products at any visit to the outlet exceeds a stated amount. This is disposing of the branded product otherwise than for its own benefit in the ordinary course of business, and has the same effect as cut price loss-leading.

Ensure that supply refusal is lawful

3.31.4 No supplier or manufacturer of branded products should arbitrarily refuse to supply a retail outlet on the grounds of suspected loss-leading of its products unless it has thoroughly researched the circumstances of the low price sales. It must be able to prove that the product is being loss-leadered in accordance with the definition in the Act, and it should seek legal advice before it takes any action against the offending outlet which could be an offence under the Act. Sections 11, 12 and 13 of the Act are set out below to explain the statutory provisions. Their interpretation and operation depend entirely upon the context and the merits of each given case. The kind of evidence which would be necessary to back up a claim by a manufacturer that an outlet is guilty of loss-leading its products would include the answers to the following questions:

(a) What is the wholesale price of the branded product which is charged by the manufacturer to all retailers?
(b) What is the manufacturer's standard price discount structure for bulk purchases of the branded product?
(c) What has been the average (monthly) quantity of the branded product ordered by the offending retailer during the last 12 months?
(d) How does that compare with its ordering rate leading up to, and during, the period of loss-leader selling of the branded product?
(e) What has been the offending retailer's average selling price for that product prior to it charging the loss-leading price?
(f) What was the estimated profit of the retailer per item of branded product sold during its normal-priced trading period?
(g) How does that compare with the estimated profit at a price at which it is being sold as a loss-leader?
(h) What is an average sale price and profit margin on the branded product when it is sold in reputable retail outlets of a comparable size?
(i) What is the offending retailer's estimated profit or loss per item of the branded product in relation to the loss-leading price being charged?
(j) How is the price reduction being advertised by the retailer?
(k) How do (e), (f), (h) and (i) for the loss-led product compare with similar products of other manufacturers being sold by the retailer?
(l) Is the cut-price sale of the branded product by the outlet only for a limited period, such as at Christmas, or is it a regular feature of its trading?

This is to find out whether there is a pattern of discount pricing by that outlet. Using loss-leading only seasonally does not validate it, subject to section 13(3) of the Act.

Relevant sections of the Act

3.32   The sections of the Act which deal with loss-leading are sections 11, 12 and 13, which are well drafted and can be understood easily if followed carefully. They are set out in full below because there is no better or more concise way of describing the details which have to be considered when assessing the existence of loss-leading, or when dealing with it on a safe legal basis.

11.– (1) It is unlawful for a supplier to withhold supplies for any goods from a dealer seeking to obtain them for resale in the United Kingdom on the ground that the dealer—

> (a) has sold in the United Kingdom at a price below the resale price goods obtained, either directly or indirectly, from that supplier, or has supplied such goods, either directly or indirectly, to a third party who had done so; or
>
> (b) is likely, if the goods are supplied to him, to sell them in the United Kingdom at a price below that price, or supply them, either directly or indirectly, to a third party who would be likely to do so.

(2) In this section "the resale price" in relation to a sale of any description means—

> (a) any price notified to the dealer or otherwise published by or on behalf of a supplier of the goods in question (whether lawfully or not) as the price or minimum price which is to be charged on or is recommended as appropriate for a sale of that description; or
>
> (b) any price prescribed or purporting to be prescribed for that purpose by a contract or agreement between the dealer any such supplier.

(3) Where under this section it would be unlawful for a supplier to withhold supplies of goods it is also unlawful for him to cause or procure any other supplier to do so.

12.– (1) For the purposes of this Part of this Act a supplier of goods shall be treated as withholding supplies of goods from a dealer—

> (a) if he refuses or fails to supply those goods to the order of the dealer;
>
> (b) if he refuses to supply those goods to the dealer except at prices, or on terms or conditions as to credit, discount or other matters, which are significantly less favourable than those at or on which he normally supplies those goods to other dealers carrying on business in similar circumstances; or
>
> (c) if, although he contracts to supply the goods to the dealer, he treats him in a manner significantly less favourable than that in which he normally treats other such dealers in respect of times or methods of delivery or other matters arising in the execution of the contract.

(2) For the purposes of this Part a supplier shall not be treated as withholding supplies of goods on any such ground as is mentioned in section 11(1) above if, in addition to that ground, he has other grounds which, standing alone, would have led him to withhold those supplies.

(3) If in proceedings brought against a supplier of goods in respect of a contravention of section 11 it is proved that supplies of goods were withheld by the supplier from a dealer, and it is further proved:

(a) that down to the time when supplies were so withheld the supplier was doing business with the dealer or was supplying goods of the same description to other dealers carrying on business in similar circumstances, and

(b) that the dealer, to the knowledge of the supplier, had within the previous six months acted as described in section 11(1)(a), or had indicated his intention to act as described in paragraph (b) of that subsection in relation to the goods in question,

it shall be presumed, unless the contrary is proved, that the supplies were withheld on the ground that the dealer had so acted or was likely so to act.

This subsection does not apply where the proof that supplies were withheld consists only of evidence of requirements imposed by the supplier in respect of the time at which or the form in which payment was to be made to goods supplied or to be supplied.

13.– (1) It is not unlawful by virtue of section 11 above for a supplier to withhold supplies of any goods from a dealer, or to cause or procure another supplier to do so, if he has reasonable cause to believe that within the previous twelve months the dealer or any other dealer to whom the dealer supplies goods has been using as loss-leaders any goods of the same or a similar description, whether obtained from that supplier or not.

(2) The reference in this section to the use of goods as loss-leaders is a reference to a resale of the goods effected by the dealer, not for the purposes of making a profit on the sale of those goods, but for the purpose of attracting to the establishment at which the goods are sold customers likely to purchase other goods or otherwise for the purpose of advertising the business of the dealer.

(3) A sale of goods shall not be treated for the purposes of this section as the use of those goods as loss-leaders—

(a) where the goods are sold by the dealer at a genuine seasonal or clearance sale, not having been acquired by the dealer for the purpose of being resold as mentioned in this section; or

(b) where the goods are resold as mentioned in this section with the consent of the manufacturer of the goods or, in the case of goods made to the design of a supplier or to the order and bearing the trade mark of a supplier, of that supplier.

ECONOMIC VIABILITY OF SALE PRICE

3.33.1   Any outlet which offers uneconomic cut price bargains of a reputable branded product will be either:

(a) a major outlet or chain of outlets which relies on a huge and rapid turnover of stock to be economically viable from the marginal profit made on each "bargain" item of branded product sold; or

(b) an established but aggressively marketed small outlet which uses the cut price device selectively in order to attract more customers, although it makes a loss (or no profit) on the sale of each item of the cut price branded product. The outlet anticipates that the extra profit which it gets from the increased sales of all other stocked products which is generated through the attraction of the loss-leader more than compensates it for the marginal loss it incurs in selling just that one branded product at a loss-leading price.

Hence the expression "loss-leading", *i.e.* deliberately making a marginal profit or even a loss on the sale of a chosen brand of product at a highly publicised knock down price for the sole purpose of generating greater interest in the outlet and improving its business overall.

Uncommercial sale price

3.33.2   The essence of loss-leading is that there is no intention of making a commercially sensible profit on the sale of the branded product which is being offered at that unrealistically low price. In the case of a reputable branded product which has a "class" image, with a recognised and generally observed average retail price within which is built a hefty profit-margin for the outlet, there can be room for spectacular price reductions before a loss-leading position exists.

Beneficial effect

3.33.3   If a major retail outlet decides to loss-lead a major branded product for the Christmas market, there are both beneficial and prejudicial effects on the manufacturer of that product. The beneficial effect is that the retailer will be ordering greater than normal quantities of the branded product because it expects "loss-led" sales of the product at that unrealistic price to be far higher than they would have been at its normal competitive price. The manufacturer of the branded product does not itself lose any money on what it sells to the outlet, because it is paid its regular wholesale price subject to its usual trade discounts.

Detrimental effects

3.33.4   Unless the loss-led product is obsolete stock and has been deleted from the manufacturer's current product catalogue, a detrimental effect is that a highly publicised loss-leadered availability of currently popular product can damage the reputation of that product, as well as damaging the trading relationship between the product manufacturer and its normal wholesale or retail outlets which are within the catchment area of the loss-leading outlet. Regular outlets do not mind competing on a fair basis against other retailers who sell the product at a competitive but economic and profitable price in the ordinary course of business, but they do not object to what they consider to be uneconomic, cut-price and unfair competition.

RIGHTS OF RETAILER IN PURCHASED STOCK

Product ownership and control

3.34.1 If the manufacturer objects to the use (or abuse) of its branded product by the retail outlet as a low price of free premium incentive, what can he do about it? Once the outlet has bought a stock of the manufacturer's products, nothing can be done by the manufacturer if the retail price charged for that stock by the outlet is very low; it cannot demand to repurchase the product to prevent that happening, and neither can it enforce a minimum retail price. The retailer can give those branded products away if it chooses to do so, such as to a charity or to some other needy cause, and achieve publicity for having done so. The key point is that such a disposal is not in the course of trade so far as that branded product is concerned. The loss-leading provisions of the Resale Prices Act 1976 only refer to *trading* transactions, because they are set in the context of what can be defined as fair or unfair competition.

Consumer perception of loss-leading

3.34.2 A loss-leading use of the branded product by the outlet, which is going to be heavily advertised, may lead consumers to believe that either:

(a) the manufacturer of the branded product has authorised it to be "sacrificed" as a promotional bargain offer incentive for the benefit of the outlet; or

(b) there must be something wrong with those branded products, such as being "seconds" or otherwise not being up to the expected standard of quality for those products which would justify a proper retail price being charged for them.

Each of these inferences is incorrect, misleading, and potentially damaging to the reputation of the branded product and to that of its manufacturer.

Outlet justification

3.34.3 It can be argued by the loss-leading outlet that it will still have bought its stock of the loss-led branded product from the manufacturer or its wholesaler at the normal wholesale prices, with the appropriate bulk purchase trade discounts which are available to any retailer, so financially the manufacturer loses nothing. The argument goes on to state that if the outlet decides that it does not mind losing money on each item of the branded product which is purchased by its customers at that price, or which is given away to them free (even if that is a "reward" incentive for buying something else), should that be any concern of the manufacturer of that branded product.

Remedies of Manufacturer

Refusal to supply outlet

3.35.1 If the manufacturer wants to stop the outlet from using its branded product as a loss-leadered customer inducement, particularly if it is on a large scale and is done persistently, how can this be achieved legally? If all requests to the outlet to stop the misuse of the product should fail, to protect its legitimate business interests, the only recourse of the manufacturer is to refuse to supply the outlet with any further product. The manufacturer may decide to resume supply when it gets a written assurance that the outlet will immediately cease the loss-leading sales of the product, and that it will return to a proper commercial competitive pricing for it. This condition must not represent any form of price-fixing by the manufacturer, and so must be worded very carefully.

Be sure of the facts

3.35.2 In the absence of any legal right of the manufacturer under the Act to stop the supply of its product to a legitimate retailer who pays its invoices in time, that action will be deemed to be an illegal means of trying to enforce on the retailer a price structure which is dictated by the manufacturer. If a manufacturer believes that an outlet is selling its products at what amounts to a loss-leading price, it must on no account threaten in any way to stop supplying product to the retailer unless the manufacturer is absolutely certain that it will be legally entitled to do so.

Illegal discrimination

3.35.3 Refusal by the manufacturer to sell branded products to the outlet purely on the ground that the outlet's retail price is too low or too competitive when compared with the range of "reasonable profit" prices which are charged for that product by other reputable retailers, is an illegal trade discrimination under section 11 of the Act, because it is an indirect means of enforcing against the outlet a minimum resale price policy for the branded product.

Genuinely competitive pricing

3.35.4 The product should be sold by outlets at a reasonable, commercially competitive price which is consistent with good business practice, and which produces for them a sensible profit on sales. The fact that some retailers can still be commercially profitable while charging lower prices than other retailers does not of itself make them loss-leaders, since there will always be variation in the retail prices of different outlets. Economical shopping by consumers makes the retail trade very conscious of price competitiveness, so the normal variations in prices charged by different outlets on an economical basis for the same product will not normally be significant.

Lawful refusal to supply

3.35.5   The law recognises that product manufacturers must be able to protect their legitimate business interests. As a result, under section 13 of the Act a manufacturer will be entitled to refuse to supply its product to an outlet if it has reasonable cause to believe that the outlet has been using those products as loss-leaders. If the outlet also stocks other products of the manufacturer, even though they are being sold at reasonable competitive prices, the manufacturer will also be able to refuse to supply those regular priced products until the loss-leading sale of the disputed product has stopped. A dilemma for the manufacturer is where only one outlet in a chain of outlets is making the loss-leading sales. The chain will have a centralised system for the bulk purchase of products, which are distributed to each outlet as required. For this purpose the manufacturer may refuse to supply the central purchasing office of the chain, unless there is a guarantee that supplies will not be delivered to the loss-leading outlet.

WITHDRAWAL OF DISCOUNT BY MANUFACTURER

Increase of base cost

3.36.1   Where the outlet pricing of the product is too low to be genuinely competitive, but where it may not amount to loss-leading, the manufacturer may be tempted to try other forms of persuasion to get the outlet to price the products reasonably. For example, he may decide to continue to supply the outlet with the product, but to refuse to give it any bulk purchase discounts, which are ordinarily available to any bona fide trade purchaser of the product from the manufacturer. These discounts may be on a sliding scale depending on the quantities for which a firm order is given by the outlet. The purpose of withdrawing the discount would be to ensure that it is costing the offending outlet even more to maintain the bargain basement price for the product, because without the bulk purchase discounts it will pay more for the branded product. The loss-leading bargain price for that branded product would have to be increased by the outlet if it does not want to make any greater loss on each item of the product which it sells at the unrealistic price.

Illegal to withhold discount

3.36.2   An ability to withhold the discount on an arbitrary basis would make the usual trading terms of the branded product manufacturer a discretionary benefit to selected customers, which the manufacturer could exercise as a discriminatory weapon to favour some customers and to punish others.

However attractive this form of retribution on the outlet may sound, in the absence of a proven case of loss-leading it will be illegal under section 12 of the Act as representing another form of withholding supplies from a customer. Under that section any bona fide trade customer is entitled to get the benefit of bulk purchase discounts which are given by the manufacturer as part of its normal trading terms. Refusing to give that benefit to a trader without legal justification represents a refusal to supply. If the manufacturer is legally justified in withholding supplies of the product under the protective provisions of section 13 of the Act, then a reasonable interpretation would be that any withdrawal of discount could equally well be justified in the same circumstances, and so would not be an offence under section 12.

RATIONING SUPPLIES TO OUTLET

Commercial justification

3.37.1 Where low prices charged by an outlet for the branded product are not commercial, but technically they do not amount to loss-leading, another possibility the branded product manufacturer may be tempted to consider is to accept only some of the orders for the branded product which are placed by the outlet, or to delay deliveries so as to minimise the rate of delivery. The objective would be to minimise the adverse effects on the status of the products being sold by that outlet at an uncompetitive price. The manufacturer will try to justify its actions commercially on the basis it also has to provide adequate supplies of the branded product to other retailers, and it also has to maintain a proper level of stock to cover unexpected fluctuations in supply and demand.

Is this legal?

3.37.2 The rationale put forward by the manufacturer is that fulfilment of the unusually massive orders which are received from the offending outlet in anticipation of a high level of sales of the cut-price branded product may make it difficult for the manufacturer to satisfy all other wholesale and retail orders which are placed with it for the product in the ordinary course of business during the same sales period. Any artificial limitation of supplies by the manufacturer would also be illegal under section 12 of the Act, in the absence of a provable claim of loss-leading sales of that product by the outlet. Such a loss-leading claim would have to be fully justified with genuine and reasonable back-up evidence under the provisions of section 13 of the Act. If the manufacturer can genuinely show that the fulfilment of unusually massive orders by the offending chain of retailers cannot be met without adversely affecting its ability to supply all of the orders of its other customers, it would be entitled to ration the offending outlet to its normal rate of product delivery. The manufacturer would have to be very careful in maintaining a complete record of justification, to answer any claim by the outlet of illegal withholding of supplies. For example, if that outlet was the only one to be rationed, as opposed to all major customers having a *pro rata* cut in supplies while stocks of the product are insufficient to fulfil all orders, it would be considered to be a discriminatory selective and unlawful withholding of supply.

Anticipating withholding of supplies

3.37.3 If an outlet has not previously had a loss-leading history, can the manufacturer withhold or restrict supplies of its branded products to that outlet where it has reason to believe that they will be used in the future as a loss-leading sales promotion to boost the popularity of that outlet? For example, a major chain of outlets may advertise nationally that, with effect from a future date, it will be selling that brand of product "at only £X", where clearly that is a loss-leading price. Some interesting points come out of this example:

    (a) in such a clear case the manufacturer will be entitled not to supply the outlet prior to the declared loss-leading period to prevent it from having stocks of the branded product to sell at that price during that time. The date from which the manufacturer can stop delivering the product to the outlet will depend on its good faith reasonable estimate of ensuring that the outlet's stock of normal priced branded products will be exhausted just before the promotion start date;

    (b) if the declared loss-leading promotion period is six months ahead, the manufacturer will not be entitled to withhold supplies now, as these will be sold by that outlet at normal prices until the promotion start date;

    (c) if the outlet's advance advertising of the attraction of the loss-leading price promotion for that product is very successful, and its rate of customer attendance increases dramatically in the promotion period as a result of it, that advertising could turn out to be misleading if the outlet does not stock at that time any of the branded product to be sold at the advertised loss-leading price, due to the withholding of supplies by the manufacturer;

    (d) if the outlet subsequently obtains a court order for the product supply to be renewed by the manufacturer because the court decided that, although it is a border line case, the extremely low advertised price for sales of that product in fact did not amount to loss-leading, or that the anticipatory withholding was illegal, then:

        (i) could the outlet sue the manufacturer of the withheld product for the loss of anticipated increased overall outlet profits because it was not able to sell the product at the low price in accordance with its advance publicity and advertising? Such a claim would be indirect, and would not be quantifiable, and so would be unlikely to succeed. Neither would there be a claim for loss of profits on the missed sales of the withheld product, as it was not going to be sold at a profitable price;

(ii) could the outlet reclaim from the manufacturer its costs and damages incurred through being prosecuted successfully for running misleading advertising for sales of the product as described in (c) above? This claim would have been reasonably foreseeable by the manufacturer if it had reviewed in advance of its decision the potential consequences of withholding supplies of the product. Therefore the outlet might succeed in claiming that compensation if a court decides that the withholding was illegal. As a balance the outlet should have mitigated its embarrassment and loss by ceasing the advertising as soon as it knew it would not be getting any stocks of the product which it could offer for sale at the low advertised price.

In these circumstances, because of the lead time for ordering and delivering products, the outlet would know well in advance of the promotion start date that the manufacturer was not going to supply the product so as to be available for sale during the promotion period. If the outlet believes it has pitched the "invitation" price of the product to the public outside the definition of loss-leadng, it could make an immediate application to the Court to resolve the legal position of the refusing manufacturer well before the promotion starts.

One-off differential discounts

3.37.4 To what extent can a product manufacturer give some outlets a more favourable discount structure than set out in its standard terms of supply without having to offer it also to all other outlets? Could such a one-off differential be deemed to be a form of "reverse" refusal to supply other outlets under section 12(1)(*b*) of the Act? As a general rule the following points should be considered by the product manufacturer before it becomes involved in any form of pricing discount ddifferentials which are not to be offered to all of its bulk trade purchasers.

(a) national established standard trade price discounts should never be modified for the benefit of selected customers on a permanent basis which could reasonably be considered discriminatory or unfair to other comparable customers.
(b) local area managers can agree different forms of trade incentives for selected local customers, provided that there are beneficial considerations to the product manufacturer which are not within its standard discount terms. These local trade incentives must be short term and "one-off", and must not amount to a material distortion of local trade and retail price competitiveness.

Any proposed deviation from the manufacturer's normal trading terms and price discounting structure for the supply of products to selected outlets which could have an adverse impact on other outlets which stock those products should be examined carefully before any such offer is made to ensure that section 12 of the Act is not infringed.

4 Lotteries, Competitions and Free Prize Draws

INTRODUCTION

PURPOSE OF THIS CHAPTER

Practical approach

4.1.1 This chapter provides a practical explanation of the law on lotteries, competitions and free prize draws, as it relates to the business of creating and running promotions. It is essential for any person who takes part in the promotions and advertising industry to understand the parameters of what is (or may be) considered to be an unlawful promotion, and why it is illegal.

Explained by means of examples

4.1.2 The statute law relating to lotteries, competitions and free prize draws can be stated relatively simply; in every case the problem is how to apply the legal principles to the particular promotion which is being examined for legality. The decided cases give some guidance, but most of them happened a long time ago and promotions today are far more sophisticated; nevertheless they are still subject to the same basic legal principles. The best way to see how these principles work in today's terms is to set up examples and analyse them, and so this has been done below. The opinions expressed as to the application of the law to the examples are only those of the author—the reader must make his own judgment in each case.

LOTTERIES

WHAT IS A LOTTERY?

Readers Digest case

4.2 The best definition of a lottery was set out in *Reader's Digest Association Ltd.* v. *Williams* [1976] 3 All E.R. 737, [1976] 1 W.L.R. 1109, when Lord Widgery said that:

"A lottery is the distribution of prizes by chance when the persons taking part in the operation, or a substantial number of them, make a payment or consideration in return for obtaining their chance of a prize. There are really three points one must look for in deciding whether a lottery has been established:

(a) the distribution of prizes;
(b) the fact that this was to be done by means of a chance; and
(c) there must be some actual contribution made by the participants in return for their obtaining a chance to take part in the lottery."

LOTTERIES AND FREE PRIZE DRAWS

Elements of a lottery

4.3.1 The definition of a lottery requires the existence of each of the elements set out in (a), (b) and (c) in paragraph 4.2. The Lotteries and Amusements Act 1976 (the Act), which is the legislation dealing with lotteries, does not contain a legal definition of what exactly constitutes a lottery. Nor is there any specific definition of a free prize draw. It has been left to the courts to provide an interpretation of what kind of activities will be deemed under the Act to constitute an illegal lottery.

Contribution distinction

4.3.2 It can be seen from the *Reader's Digest* case definition when read in conjunction with section 14 of the Act (see paragraph 4.5) that the only difference between an illegal lottery and a lawful free prize draw is that in the case of a free prize draw there must be no payment or contribution by the participant for entering the draw. Their similarity is that neither of them has any element of skill.

PAYMENT FOR "LOTTERY" STAKE

Public perception

4.4.1 A lottery is normally understood to be the risking of something (the payment or contribution) by the participant in return for a chance either to gain more (the prize) or to lose the whole payment. If a lottery could be run legally as part of a product purchase promotion, then having to purchase a quantity of the product as a condition of being entitled to enter the "lottery" promotion would not be seen by the public as taking a financial risk. The participant would purchase the product to use it, and an added bonus for doing so would be the possibility of winning a prize through participating in the lottery promotion.

Initial value of contribution

4.4.2 The payment or contribution by the participant for entry to a legitimised product purchase lottery would be limited to the purchase price of the product. This concept is analagous to the question of what is "free" in sales promotion terms. (See Chapter 2, paras. 2.28 onwards). It would not be considered a wasted payment if the prize is not won, because the participant would have already received full value for money for that payment, *i.e.* the purchased product. In contrast, a legal registered, ticket-purchase lottery, such as a raffle, requires a payment of some risk contribution to be made by the participant for the lottery ticket. In that case no other independent value is obtained by the purchaser of the lottery ticket at the time of making the payment, so that the ticket purchaser is gambling with his money. The law on lotteries needs to be changed to take into account this distinction.

STATUTORY PROVISIONS

Lotteries and Amusements Act 1976

4.5.1 The legality of promotions which employ the mechanic of skill or of chance to enable a participant to win a prize is dealt with in the Act. Section 14(1) of the Act states:

"It shall be unlawful to conduct in or through any newspaper, or in connection with any trade or business, or the sale of any article to the public:
(a) any competition in which prizes are offered for the forecast of the result either:
  (i) of a future event, or
  (ii) of a past event the result of which is not yet ascertained or is not yet generally known;
(b) any other competition in which success does not depend to a substantial degree on the exercise of skill."

Reference to competitions

4.5.2 Section 14(1) of the Act refers in both (a) and (b) to "competitions", and states that they will be unlawful if they depend upon the element of forecast, or where there is no skill which can be applied to get the correct result. The "unlawful" aspect is derived from the first part of the section, where there is a presumption that a participant is making a payment, such as in the purchase price of a product or in connection with any trade or business. As stated in the *Reader's Digest* case, a payment or contribution for the right of participation is what distinguishes an (unlawful) lottery from a (lawful) free prize draw in circumstances where the exercise of skill is not relevant to the promotion.

Application of the Act

4.5.3 However the mechanic and rules of a promotion are dressed up to present it as a free prize draw, if it is in reality a lottery in its operation within the terms of section 14 of the Act, and of the *Reader's Digest* case judgment, it will be illegal. Which side of the line it is can be a very fine judgment of interpretation. This is where the distinction between "the form and the substance" must be considered, *i.e.* between what the promotion looks like and what it really is in legal terms. (See paras. 4.17 and 4.21.3).

Legal lotteries

Non-commercial use

4.6 Under the Act there are restricted forms of lottery which are legal provided that the conditions set out in the Act relating to them are complied with. They are not dealt with in this book because they are not appropriate for promoting the sale of consumer products on a public commercial basis.

Illegalities of lotteries are absolute

Belief is not relevant

4.7 Ignorance of the fact that the promotion is illegal because it constitutes a lottery is not a defence to a prosecution, and neither is a firm belief that it is legal. Manufacturers and agencies may take the view, or they may be legally advised, that the promotion which is being examined for clearance is not an illegal lottery, because of the apparent saving grace of some mechanism of its operation (see para. 4.21.2) or because of the existence of some promotion rule. If the promotion is clearly legal, there will be no cause for concern. However, if the "saving grace" mechanic or rule has no other purpose than to be a cosmetic device which in reality does not validate or remove the illegal element of the promotion, that device will not prevent a prosecution of the promoter for running an illegal lottery from being successful.

Illegal activities relating to lotteries

Third party risks

4.8.1 Where an illegal lottery exists, section 2(1) of the Act sets out those activities connected with the lottery which are offences. If the promoter of an illegal lottery, or any party which is directly involved in running an illegal lottery, does any of these activities, he will have committed a criminal offence for which he could be prosecuted. Section 2(1) of the Act states that:

"Every person who in connection with any lottery promoted or proposed to be promoted either in Great Britain or elsewhere—

(a) prints any tickets for use in the lottery;
(b) sells or distributes or offers or advertises for sale or distribution, or has in his possession for the purpose of publication or distribution any tickets or chances in the lottery; or
(c) prints publishes or distributes, or has in his possession for the purpose of publication or distribution:
   (i) any advertisement of the lottery
   (ii) any list, whether complete or not, of prize winners or winning tickets in the lottery
   (iii) any such matter descriptive of the drawing or intended drawing of the lottery, or otherwise relating to the lottery, as is calculated to act as an inducement to persons to participate in that lottery or in other lotteries;
(d) brings, or invites any person to send into Great Britain for the purpose of sale or distribution, any ticket in, or advertisement of, the lottery;
(e) sends or attempts to send out of Great Britain any money or valuable things received in respect of the sale or distribution, or any document recording the sale or distribution, or the identity of the holder, of any ticket or chance in the lottery;
(f) uses any premises, or causes or knowingly permits any premises to be used, for purposes connected with the promotion or conduct of the lottery; or
(g) causes, procures or attempts to procure any person to do any of the above-mentioned acts,
   shall be guilty of an offence."

Extent of illegal participation

4.8.2 The potential offences which are set out in section 2(1) of the Act indicate how serious the running of an illegal lottery can be, and how extensive can be the illegal activities which are connected with it. It is unlikely that a prosecution would be brought unless the criteria referred to in paragraph 4.21.3 are complied with. The wording of section 2(1) assumes that it is dealing with a traditional lottery, which will have advertising, a distribution of tickets, and a draw for the prize, so the application of the section to promotions has to be a matter of interpretation.

European Community application

4.8.3 The illegal activities in the U.K. under the Act apply to a lottery which is being run in "Great Britain or elsewhere". If any party in the U.K. becomes involved in the promotion in the U.K. of any European or other foreign

107

lottery which may be legal in its own country, until the Act is amended they will be committing an offence.

WHO CAN BE CRIMINALLY LIABLE?

Statutory provisions

4.9.1 In the absence of any specific statutory guidance in the Act in respect of who could come within the section 2(1) categories, the following points should be considered by the manufacturer and by the agency when they are putting together a promotion which has any features in its mechanic or its rules which could result in it being treated as a lottery.

Personal liability for offences

4.9.2. Section 2(1) of the Act states that an offence will be committed by "every person who in connection with any lottery" does any of those things referred to in paragraph 4.8.1(a)–(g). The only "persons" who are likely to be involved in the creation and running of an illegal lottery as a promotion are the relevant executives and employees of the organisations which are set out in the following paragraphs.

Persons as principals

4.9.3 There is no statutory definition of "person" and there is no exclusion from any liability which is referred to in the Act on the basis that the "person" is an employee who was only following directions and doing his job. All of the reported prosecutions under the Act appear to have been against the company which ran the lottery in connection with the promotion of its products, see *Reader's Digest* case (para. 4.2) and *Imperial Tobacco Ltd* v. *A–G* (1981) A.C. 718. From this it may be concluded that "persons" mean people who are operating as principals, and who are therefore personally responsible for their own actions.

Officers of a company

4.9.4 Section 21 of the Act recognises that corporations are incapable of independent thought and action, and that they can only act in accordance with the directions of their officers. While ordinary employees do not appear to have the risk of personal liability under the Act, officers of a company can be personally liable for the criminal offences of the company under the Act, as according to section 21:

"Where an offence under this Act committed by a body corporate is proved to have been committed with the consent or connivance of, or to have been attributable to any neglect on the part of, any director, manager, secretary or other similar officer of the body corporate or any person who was purporting to act in any such capacity, he as well as the body corporate shall be guilty of that offence, and shall be liable to be proceeded against and punished accordingly."

Management executives

4.9.5 Section 21 of the Act includes "manager" as being an "other similar officer", although a manager is not normally considered to be a corporate officer in company law terms. Within the legal *'ejusdem generis'* rule a manager in this context means a person who is involved in managing the company's business to the same extent as a director, although he may not be officially a director of that company (see section 741(1) of the Companies Act 1985). This would fit in with the definition of a "shadow" director under section 742(2) of the Companies Act 1985. The definition might include a manager who is the head of a marketing department because:

(a) apparently he does not have to be a director to come within the definition of person who can be made liable for lottery offences committed by his company; and

(b) at that level he may be exercising the powers and authority of direction and decision-making, at least in connection with promotions, as if he were a director of his company.

Consent or connivance

4.9.6 According to section 21 of the Act a manager or other officer of the company would have to *consent to* or *connive at* the production of the illegal lottery promotion to be liable as a potential prosecution defendant. The meaning and extent of these words have not yet been tested in Court under the Act, so their common sense meaning should be given. To consent to something denotes a positive action of consent being sought and the officer agreeing to it being done. This would be the case whether or not that officer has been active in the production of the illegal promotion. Connivance denotes a positive involvement in creating the illegal promotion and in its commercial publication.

Knowledge of illegality

4.9.7 Significantly section 21 of the Act does not include a fairly common statutory caveat in similar circumstances, such as in dealing with infringing material under the Copyright, Designs and Patents Act 1988. The caveat is that for such persons to have committed a criminal offence they "must have known, or had reasonable cause to believe" that the activity is illegal. Without such a caveat in section 21, the persons and other officers of a company which is found guilty of running an illegal lottery, and who consent to or connive at it, could also be committing a criminal offence even if they did not know one was being committed.

Effect on partnership

4.9.8 If a small agency is being run as a partnership, and not as a limited liability company, then the partners who are responsible for the illegal sales promotion lottery will have a potential personal criminal liability under section 2(1) of the Act. This liability would apparently not extend to a partner who can satisfy the court that he had no connection at all with the lottery by way of consent or connivance. This may be difficult to prove where the partners work as a co-ordinated creative team when designing promotions for their clients. Section 21 refers to corporations, not to partnerships, and officers of the corporation can be equally liable if they had some participation in the offence. Using that distinction as an analogy, it is reasonable to assume that a partner who has no knowledge of the illegal lottery will not be committing an offence.

LIABILITY OF PARTIES CONNECTED WITH THE PROMOTION

The manufacturer

4.10.1 Promotions are published, that is made available to the public, by the manufacturer of the promoted product, and therefore the manufacturer is primarily responsible for an illegal lottery promotion. Criminal liability is not like civil liability (such as under a contract). The agency in its contract with the manufacturer may have indemnified the manufacturer from the adverse consequences of a breach of contract by the agency (such as of the agency's obligation to design legal promotions for the manufacturer), but that would not affect the manufacturer's criminal liability for running an illegal promotion. Under a properly worded indemnity the agency would have to reimburse the manufacturer all financial penalties and all legal costs incurred as result of the prosecution. Whether the indemnity would extend to reimbursement of any commercial expense or loss (such as wasted product or packaging) if the illegally promoted product has to be withdrawn from sale, will depend on the wording of the indemnity.

The agency

4.10.2 The agency is not directly connected with the distribution or publication of the offending lottery material, and it is questionable whether it has such material "in its possession for the purpose of publication or distribution" in the sense referred to in section 2(1)(c) of the Act. The agency will certainly have samples of the material in its possession, as it originated it. It will only be distributing those samples to certain parties, such as to the client for approval, and the agency is not involved in the storage and distribution of commercial quantities of any material which contains the illegal promotion.

The handling house

4.10.3   If the handling house is involved in the management of the lottery, it will publish or distribute the list of winners, and its premises will be used for purposes which are connected with the promotion or the conduct of the lottery, as referred to in section 2(1)(*f*) of the Act. The handling house will be receiving and processing the illegal lottery entry forms, so it will be active in the administration of the illegal promotion. However slight the risk of prosecution may be, a handling house should have in its standard form of contract, or in its standard terms and conditions, a warranty and an indemnity from the manufacturer or agency (as the case may be) relating to illegal promotions.

INDIRECT INVOLVEMENT OF PARTIES

Awareness and responsibility

4.11.1   The less obvious candidates for prosecution in connection with the running of an illegal lottery could be the printer of promotional material, newspaper and magazine proprietors and retailers of the promoted goods. Although they may have a technical liability under the Act, a decision not to prosecute them would be based on the fact that they are not likely to be aware of the illegality of the material which they are producing for a third party, or which they are selling through their outlets or publishing through their magazines. They have no connection at all with the design of the illegal promotion or with the distribution of the product which contains the illegal promotion on its packaging. If the point of sale material advertising an illegal promotion also constitutes misleading advertising, the outlet could be prosecuted for that separate offence. Their contractual position would be covered by having in their standard terms and conditions an indemnity from their customers against the consequences of being involved in printing any material which is illegal, or which infringes any third party proprietary rights.

The printer of the promotion package

4.11.2   The printer's business is not the promotion of products or lotteries. The printer's responsibility is to ensure that the printed material is in accordance with the order's specifications, and that the quality and finish of the printed material are acceptable to the agency which orders it. In regard to the illegality of a promotion, the printer cannot reasonably be expected to examine or to understand the contents of the material which it is printing, and it cannot be expected to take legal advice on every promotion-related job

111

which it takes on, to ensure that it is not committing a criminal offence under section 2(1)(*a*) of the Act.

Sales outlets

4.11.3 As a high proportion of consumer products have a promotion attached to them at some time, most retailers would not bother to check whether any of those promotions is illegal. If one is illegal, they have a potential liability under section 2(1)(*b*) and (*f*) of the Act. Therefore all retailers should review on-pack promotions as a routine precaution. However, this is not a practical proposition because of the sheer volume of promoted products which are stocked. Some retailers may decide not to burden themselves with that administrative expense on the basis that if a reputable manufacturer has a high profile promotion running on its prime branded product, it can reasonably be assumed by the retailer that the promotion has gone through sensible vetting procedures, and therefore that the promotion must be legal. In any event the risk of a retailer being prosecuted for selling a branded product which carries an illegal promotion is remote.

Risk on sales

4.11.4 If a retailer reads the text of a promotion which is on the package of goods it is about to stock, and concludes on a reasonable basis that it is not legal as being a lottery, or as being misleading, in theory it should not offer the product for sale to the public. If the suspicions are correct and the promotion is illegal, then to do so would be committing a criminal offence. Even with that knowledge, the retailer may decide that the chances of being prosecuted are not great, so it may take a commercial risk judgment and sell the illegally promoted product. If the product which carries the illegal promotion is popular, and is being sold through all other usual outlets without any query or complaint from consumers or Trading Standards Departments, then the commercial judgment of the retailer would take that into account, but that would not affect any decision which is taken by the authorities to prosecute the retailer.

Promotion in publications

4.11.5 It is not an offence for a marketing publication to comment on or to review the attraction of a promotion which happens to be an illegal lottery. However, if the publication is carrying the lottery "competition" as a means of promoting the major first-prize product through the magazine, and as a means of boosting the sales of that month's issue, the publisher of that magazine will be either the sole or a joint promoter of the illegal lottery. The competition entry form will be cut out of the magazine, which is effectively a proof of purchase of the magazine. The publisher of the magazine will then be in the same position as the promoted product manufacturer under paragraph 4.10.1 above.

INTERPRETATION OF LOTTERY TICKET

Promotion entry form

4.12 By section 23(1) of the Act, the word "ticket" includes any document which evidences the claim of a person to participate in the lottery. Where that competition or prize draw is found to be an illegal lottery, the entry form for the purported "free prize draw" or the "competition" which is contained in the product package, and which is completed by the participant in the promotion, constitutes the lottery "ticket" for the purposes of the Act.

RISK OF PROSECUTION

New point of law

4.13.1 Where the promotion is of major national interest and has a novel mechanic and rules which have the effect of apparently legitimising an otherwise obvious lottery, there may be pressure for a prosecution to be brought against the manufacturer. This would be to establish a new point of law, or to confirm or to test the effect of current legislation in the light of an apparently doubtful interpretation of it which is being applied to that promotion. Parliamentary or judicial review of the outdated stringent law on illegal lotteries is long overdue, but see paragraph 4.21.3 below. Amongst the mass of short-life consumer product promotions, the likelihood of an illegal lottery on one of them being discovered, and the manufacturer or the retailers of that product being prosecuted, is not great. But that does not reduce the necessity for the manufacturer and its agency to make every reasonable effort to ensure that there is not even a remote possibility of the promotion being an illegal lottery.

Modification and removal of novelty

4.13.2 The removal of all illegality risks can have the result of sanitising what looks like an exciting "new idea" promotion, possibly to the point where it is not worth running in its legal form. If the manufacturer decides to run the promotion notwithstanding the risk of its illegality, it should at least be well aware of the potential problem areas, and what consequences or costs may flow from the risk of prosecution becoming a reality.

DISTINGUISHING LOTTERIES FROM FREE PRIZE DRAWS

Similar characteristics

4.14.1   Under section 14 of the Act, a skill-related promotion or competition is excluded from the definition of a lottery. The difficulty in some promotions is to distinguish between what constitutes a legal free prize draw, and what can be an illegal lottery. They have two similar characteristics, as in each case:

> (a) a participant obtains a ticket or other means of entitling him to enter the promotion, the basis of which is the possibility of winning a prize; and
>
> (b) the prize is won purely by chance.

Legal differences

4.14.2   The differences which determine on which side of the legality borderline the promotion falls are as follows:

> (a) in the case of a legal free prize draw, the participants or a "substantial number of them" (see para. 4.21.1), must not make any payment or other contribution, whether directly or indirectly, for obtaining an entry to the draw. Entry to a free prize draw must be totally unconditional; and
>
> (b) in the case of an illegal lottery the participants have to make some payment or contribution to obtain the chance to enter, either directly or indirectly. Therefore entry to an illegal lottery is conditional upon something being done by the entrant, and it is not free. Whether the income which is derived from the sale of lottery tickets goes to a deserving cause such as a charity, or whether it is used for paying for prizes, has no bearing on the legality of the promotion.

These differences must be read in conjunction with paragraph 4.21.2 in respect of a possible "saving grace" mechanism in promotion rules which is intended to avoid illegality in what would otherwise be an illegal lottery.

DISTINGUISHING BETWEEN LOTTERIES AND COMPETITIONS

The element of chance

4.15.1   The essential distinguishing feature between a lawful competition and an illegal lottery is that the former contains an element of skill which is needed for successful participation, while the latter relies entirely upon chance for any participant to be successful. "Chance" means that the answer or the result can only be achieved by luck or random guesswork, and success is beyond the influence of any application of skill. Each ticket-holder in a lottery has the same chance of success and a participant may enter the lottery as many times as he likes, subject to the promotion rules. His chances of success on a traditional draw of tickets are in the ratio of the number of tickets which are purchased by him to the total number of tickets which are sold. In most sales promotion lotteries his chance of success is indeterminate, especially where there is a very high value prize, such as a motor car or a "pool prize" of (say) £50,000 in cash.

Guessing the answer is not relevant

4.15.2   Where the competition is legal because it contains an adequate element of skill in its mechanic, the fact that the entrant may just disregard the effort required to exercise the skill and rely purely on chance to guess the right answer is not material, provided that the structure of the promotion follows the legal requirements.

HIDDEN CONTRIBUTION

Difficult to identify

4.16.1   The element of chance may be disguised in a much more sophisticated promotion mechanic, and therefore the element which makes the promotion into an illegal lottery may not be identified so easily. For example:

(a) To promote ticket sales to a certain destination, an airline may run a promotion to the effect that either:
(i)   all purchases of that airline's tickets to that destination during the stated promotion period will be eligible to be entered for a "free prize draw" with an attractive prize; or
(ii) every 50th passenger who books in for a particular flight, or any passenger who books a first class ticket to that promoted destination, will receive a gift to be chosen at random by an electronic device from a stated selection of gifts, a few of which are valuable, and most of which are just "interesting".
(b) A motor car distributor wants to sell his lingering excess stocks of last year's model before the new models are made available in the showroom. To do this he advertises a promotion whereby all purchasers of any new vehicle "this month" will get a free car radio, and, as an added bonus, their names will go into a "free draw" for an expensive mobile car phone which will be supplied to the lucky winner and fitted free of charge.

Acceptable to buyers

4.16.2   The above examples are promotions which would not alarm any buyer, and they appear to be reasonable sales incentive offers. Any buyer who takes up the offer and who is entered into the relevant "free draw" would consider that the incentive has been provided "free", as entering involves no extra cost to him.

A hidden contribution is a condition of entry

4.16.3 Each of those promotion examples set out in paragraph 4.16.1 is an illegal lottery because winning the "prize" is purely by chance. Although the participants in the draws have not paid any more than the cost of the airline ticket or the car, each of them has thereby made a contribution, which cancels the purported legal "free prize draw" status of the promotion. The reason for the illegality is that to be entered for what is described as a "free draw" there was a hidden condition that the participant had to spend money on buying the airline tickets or the car, as the case may be. There is no means in either case whereby any person can enter the draw unconditionally, or at no direct or indirect cost.

Indirect contribution

4.16.4 Would it make any difference if an employer company bought the airline tickets or the car, in each case for the benefit and use of the employee? The person who is participating in the promotion has not made any contribution to the "entry" for the promotion, so can it be considered to be free? The answer is no. It is immaterial who pays for the entry or who takes the benefit of it. In each case the company is entitled to the promotion benefit as it paid for the right to participate in it; all it has done in this example is to assign the right to enjoy the benefit to the employee. The legality of the promotion depends on its mechanic and its rules, not upon the identity of the participant.

OPERATION DETERMINES LEGALITY

Disregard the form and look at the substance

4.17.1 When examining a promotion to see whether it is an illegal lottery, the examiner must look at the operative substance of the promotion, not just at its form. He should disregard how the promotion is expressed in its presentation and description, if an analysis of its structure and operation shows it to be a potential lottery. The examiner's investigation should be directed towards looking into the elements of skill and chance and whether there is any direct or indirect payment. This research should indicate what kind of promotion it is. The examiner would have to be careful not to be fooled by an elaborate mechanic which, when carefully analysed, is not what is appears to be.

Disregard promotion description

4.17.2 In the examples given in paragraph 4.16.1 there are various components, all of which point to a lottery. These include a purchase price contribution for entry, no skill being needed by the entrant, and reliance by the participant for success purely upon the element of chance. Describing the promotion as a "free prize draw" does not remove the reality that it is an illegal lottery, and that the allocation of the main prize to only one of all of those who are entitled to enter the promotion is only achieved by chance.

FREE PRIZE DRAWS

CHARACTERISTICS OF A FREE PRIZE DRAW

What is a free prize draw?

4.18.1 A free prize draw is a promotion in which a participant:

(a) can enter only by obtaining a free ticket or any other free means of entry, subject to paragraphs 4.18.2, 4.21.2 and 4.21.3(c). "Free" in this context means that there is no payment or other indirect contribution which has to be made directly or indirectly by the participant as a condition of being entitled to the entry;

(b) relies entirely upon chance to win a prize, as the winning ticket, or its promoted product equivalent, is chosen entirely at random; and

(c) cannot do anything to give himself a greater chance of success than any other participant except by making several entries to the draw if the rules allow him to do so.

New legal interpretation

4.18.2 By reason of paragraph 4.21.3(c) and (d) it appears that sub-paragraph (a) above may not be correct, although it has been the traditional view of the strict law. If by reason of the Crown Prosecution Service indications (see paragraph 4.21.3) it is assumed that the law will evolve to give statutory substance to the principles laid down by its sub-paragraphs (c) and (d), they must also be equally applicable in the reverse *i.e.*; to free prize draws. If that is the case, a free prize draw will be legal even though a substantial number of participants *have* to purchase a promoted product to participate in it. The reason is that the basis of the promotion is the availability of a totally free and uninhibited entry as described in paragraph 4.21.2, so (d) of the C.P.S. Statement is complied with. Therefore, if half the participants have bought the promoted product to participate in the promotion, and half take the unconditional free entry option, the promotion would be considered to be legal whether it started off as a lottery or as a free prize draw—in fact they would not be distinguishable.

Draws distinguished from lotteries and competitions

4.18.3   By definition a free prize draw does not contain any element of skill; the winner is chosen (drawn) purely by chance. Therefore a prize draw can be distinguished:

    (a) from a competition, by the lack of any skill in its simple mechanic; and

    (b) from an unlawful lottery, because it has no form of contribution as a condition of entry.

PAYMENT OR CONTRIBUTION

Relevance of contribution

4.19.1   In the absence of the element of skill which is required for a lawful competition, the promotion will be either a lawful free prize draw or an illegal lottery. In deciding which of these alternatives will apply to the promotion, the question is whether at any stage in the promotion the participant has to make a contribution as a condition of participation. Subject to paragraph 4.21.3 any form of contribution which is reasonably connected with the promotion will prevent it from being a legal free prize draw and consequently it would be an illegal lottery.

Entry condition

4.19.2   "Contribution" covers any form of direct or indirect consideration, which is not necessarily money or money's worth, and which is made or paid by the entrant or by any other party for the benefit of the entrant as a condition of entry to the promotion. If the contribution is indirect, there has to be some reasonably close connection between it and the obtaining of an entry to the draw to change it into an illegal lottery.

Connection between contribution and entry

4.19.3   A superstore may advertise a free prize draw where entry forms are freely available without question from a central dispenser. The rules of the draw include a "no purchase necessary" rule. If an entrant to the draw has bought something in the store prior to discovering the existence of the draw, or even afterwards but before making the draw entry, the price of that purchase will not constitute a contribution which has been paid for the chance to enter the draw. If the dispenser of the "free prize draw" tickets is situated at the store checkout, and if it can only be reached by a person who has paid for the purchases and checked out, it is arguable that even though the entry forms are advertised as being available free that is not the case in practice. If the only way for a hopeful participant to get a draw entry is to have purchased something in the store, that becomes an apparent condition, and the promotion runs the risk of being a lottery. The store could argue that it is equally possible for a person to enter the store and walk through the checkout without purchasing anything in the store, and to take the draw entry form without making any contribution. It is not obligatory for a customer to buy anything when he visits the store, but there may be a strong psychological pressure upon him to do so. This is an example of where the interpretation of the promotion will be in accordance with the points made in paragraph 4.17.

"NO PURCHASE NECESSARY" RULE

Not a legal requirement

4.20.1 The rules of a free prize draw promotion should specify clearly and prominently that no payment or purchase is required to be made by the entrant as a condition of entry. This is normally done by putting the promotion rules on the entry forms for the free prize draw and the ticket dispenser and any other material advertising the promotion. A promotion rule to the effect that "no purchase necessary" is not a statutory requirement for a free prize draw, so if it is inadvertently omitted from the rules of a genuine free prize draw that by itself will not automatically invalidate the promotion. The statement is a reminder to entrants that the prize draw is "free" to enter, and that they do not have to purchase any products or make any other payment to enter the free prize draw. The same rule is used, but in a different context, where an "on pack" promotion would be an illegal lottery but for the "saving grace" rule referred to in paragraph 4.21.2, as supported by paragraph 4.21.3.

Independent purchase

4.20.2 Even though entry forms for a free prize draw are freely available, what happens where the participant also receives an entry form for the draw as a matter of courtesy after buying goods in the outlet which is holding the draw? All customers in the outlet have the choice of buying goods, and acceptance of an entry form by some of the customers after making a non-compulsory purchase will not of itself make the promotion an illegal lottery. The rule need not state that it is a condition of entry to the promotion that no purchase is made by the customer. A purchaser of goods in the store who is given a free prize draw entry form is not compelled to fill it in and enter the draw, and he may choose not to do so. If he does so, will the purchase of the goods be considered to have a close connection with the entry? For a properly drafted and run in-store promotion for a free prize draw, unrelated product purchases should be considered as incidental, and not as a condition of entry.

Associated purchase

4.20.3 If entry to the prize draw in an in-store promotion is automatic on the customer buying the goods, then for those entries the purchase price would be a clear contribution. This would also be the case where no cash is paid for the goods, but they are charged to the customer by credit card or through an in-store credit account. If there is no other means of entering the draw, then the promotion would be a lottery. If the circumstances set out in paragraph 4.20.2 apply predominently, the promotion can still be legal.

WHERE MOST ENTRANTS ARE PURCHASERS

Degree of product purchase necessary

4.21.1 If most of the participants in what is advertised as a free prize draw purchase products in order to enter, will the promotion be legal? For example, a producer of a canned product may run a promotion whereby the purchaser of a can automatically has an entry to the promotion, which is printed on the inside of the can top, and which states whether or not he is the winner of a prize. As it stands that promotion would clearly be an illegal lottery because:

(a) The entry "ticket" is the can top.
(b) Whether the "ticket" entitles its holder to a prize depends entirely on chance.
(c) The "ticket" can only be acquired through buying the can to which it is attached.
(d) There is no skill element in the promotion.

"Saving grace" rule

4.21.2 A crucial rule in the promotion is that "no purchase is necessary" to enter it. This rule is supported by the statement that any person, whether or not they have bought any of the promotion cans of the product, may apply to the handling house for a "free can top". Any person may apply for any number of the free can tops during the promotion period, but they will only get one can top per application. This rule is considered to be the "saving grace" rule which transforms an illegal lottery into a legal free prize draw, because participation is not *necessarily* dependent on purchasing the can, and therefore making a contribution is not an absolute condition of entry. Is that argument valid? According to the *Reader's Digest* case (see paragraph 4.2) a lottery can exist where a "substantial number" of participants make a payment for the chance to enter. Therefore, if the case is still good law, the legal assessment of the character of the promotion will depend on the ratio of the product purchasers to those people who make the free applications for can tops. If the "saving grace" rule is challenged by a prosecution of the promoter of a similar promotion, and if only a minimal number of people take the free entry option, the promotion may well be adjudicated by the court to be an illegal lottery.

Crown Prosecution Service Statement

4.21.3 Because the "free entry" alternative participation has caused considerable confusion as to whether it is a legal means of running what would otherwise be an illegal lottery, in December 1991 the Crown Prosecution Service wrote to the Institute of Sales Promotion to confirm that (as at that time) its official view was that:

(a) any prosecution of a manufacturer would have to be supported by "admissible, substantial and reliable" evidence which would provide a realistic prospect of a conviction;

(b) even if such evidence were to be available, a prosecution would only be brought if the public interest required it.

(c) it is not in itself sufficient to make a scheme lawful that some participants do not purchase a chance in the draw.

(d) the position is likely to be different where there is a genuine, realistic and unlimited alternative method of entry which is free.

This timely and useful indication does not represent a change in the law, and would not hinder any prosecution which may subsequently be brought by the C.P.S. It is a policy statement which is in line with the reality of current promotion trends (see paragraph 4.4.2.). While the C.P.S. statement is of broad principle (d) above does not wholly resolve (c) above. The grey area is where the free entry conditions comply wholly with (d), but in fact very few consumers avail themselves of that freedom of entry in comparison with those who participate through purchasing the promoted product. Does (d) override (c) whatever happens, or will the *Reader's Digest* case be followed, favouring (c) as the prime criterion of legality.

Operation overrides description

4.21.4 If the "no purchase necessary" rule is not observed by any of the entrants to the prize draw, so that no free applications are made, the rule becomes meaningless. The rule does not by itself protect the legality of the promotion if its operation wholly disregards the rule. This view is supported by subparagraph (c) in paragraph 4.21.3 above. In those circumstances it appears that the promotion can have its legality determined by the actions of the people who participate in it; it is not necessarily bound to be interpreted by the way in which the rules are drafted or by the way the promotion is presented.

Change in the law

4.21.5 The law needs to be changed to qualify the present illegality of this kind of lottery promotion because it is used so widely on consumer products, and because it is not harmful to consumers. One practical answer would be to set a percentage of promotion entries which are made by the "free application" route over which the promotion is deemed to be legal. One weakness of this proposal is that such a promotion would start out by being illegal, and would only become legal if the free entries exceed that percentage of all participants by the promotion's closing date. A promoter could "fix" the number of free entries towards the end of the promotion period in order to attain legality. Another weakness is that any illegality would only be decided a long time after the promotion took place. An alternative is to legalise all such promotions provided that their rules contain a "saving grace" rule which complies with paragraph 4.21.3(d).

If the minimum percentage of free entries alternative were to be adopted judicially, it would work for voucher and proof of purchase promotions, as these are positive action promotions, where the number of product purchase participants are known as well those who apply for free entries. In contrast, the promotion which is described in paragraph 4.21.1 is a passive promotion, as every person who buys and opens a tin of the product is effectively participating in the promotion. In that case the number of people who write in for a free can lid will never be significant in comparison with the number of cans which are opened.

A LOCAL CLUB PROMOTION

Special incentives

4.22.1 A club may put on a promotion whereby each purchaser of a nominated "Today's Special" drink on a Saturday evening at the bar gets a ticket, and all those tickets are entered for a draw to be held at the end of the evening for a stated prize. The reasoning which is put forward by the club for the legality of the promotion is that although each purchaser of that promoted brand of drink is given a ticket, it is "free" because he did not have to pay anything extra for it. Is this promotion legal?

Is there a contribution?

4.22.2 It is the effect of the promotion that counts, and not how it is described in the advertising material relating to it. The wording of the notice at the bar may be that purchasers of a stated drink will be "given free" a ticket to the draw. This wording indicates that each purchaser of the drink is entitled to get a ticket, and that tickets will not be given to people who do not buy that drink. On that basis the promotion would not be a free prize draw, as the entry is conditional on the product purchase "contribution".

Timing of contribution is not material

4.22.3 It would make no difference to the legality of the promotion if, as an added precaution, the names of the purchasers of those drinks, and the number of the drinks which they bought, are marked down and the tickets are issued "free" to those people if they are still at the bar at the end of the evening, just before the draw is made. The association between the ticket entitlement and the purchase of those drinks is what still governs participation in the promotion.

Combined purchase

4.22.4 *Imperial Tobacco Ltd.* v. *A–G* [1981] A.C. 718; [1980] 1 All E.R. 866 (see Chapter 2, paragraph 2.29.1) decided that a payment for a product which ensures that the purchaser receives a "free" ticket with the purchased product has the legal effect that the payment is deemed to be in respect of a "combined purchase" of the product and of the ticket. Therefore in the example described in paragraph 4.22.1 the ticket is not "free" in terms of a legal free prize draw.

One-off spontaneous draw

4.22.5 If the club decides at the end of one Saturday evening, without any prior notification or advertising, to hand out tickets to all who are present and to have a draw immediately for some suitable prize, would that be legal? Each of the participants will have already spent some money on drinks at the bar, so can those payments be deemed to be contributions for an entry into the draw? The relevant points are:

(a) People did not buy drinks earlier in the evening in the expectation of being entered into a draw as they did not know that the draw would be held, so any such payments are not connected with it.
(b) It is unlikely that all of the people will have been at the bar for the same length of time, or that they will have spent the same amount on drinks, and there may be some people who have spent nothing at all during the evening.
(c) Even if the barman tried to find out which of them drank a promoted product, and how many drinks of it they had, so that the draw would be limited to those people, the same principle as in (a) above would apply.

In these circumstances the spontaneous promotion will be a legal free prize draw. But if it became a regular feature of the club's Saturday night activities, it would lose its original spontaneity and would become a lottery. People would stay at the bar and buy drinks until closing time just to be there when the draw tickets are handed out, which encouragement would be the purpose of running the promotion. Buying drinks is not a condition of entry to the draw, and that is not an inevitable consequence of waiting in a bar until the end of the evening. But enough of those people who are waiting for the draw are likely to buy drinks for those purchases to be deemed to be an indirect contribution by a substantial number of the participants to the draw at the end of the evening.

Effect of prize destination

4.22.6   Does it have any effect on whether the promotion is a lottery or a free prize draw if the prize is not collected by the winner but:

(a) is voluntarily given by him to charity although he is entitled to keep it, or
(b) a rule of the promotion is that the prize will go to a charity to be nominated by the winner?

Section 14 of the Act does not refer to any prize entitlement or to any prize destination. So even if the winner does not receive the prize personally, nevertheless if it is won on his ticket by chance alone, and if a contribution is made by him as a condition for the entry, the promotion will be an illegal lottery.

RESTAURANT PROMOTION

Moral pressure for contribution

4.23   If in a self-service restaurant the only dispenser of the "free" prize draw entry forms and the box in which completed entries are deposited are both immediately beside the cashier, many people might be embarrassed to enter the restaurant, walk up to the cashier, take an entry form and fill it in and then deposit it in the completed entry box and walk away. They might feel so uncomfortable that they would prefer to buy something, and in the course of paying take an entry form, and complete it while eating what they had bought. The question will be whether a potential participant believes that there is a genuinely free availability of the entry forms, if in practice all or most of them are only collected in connection with a purchase in the restaurant. There does not seem to be a distinction between what is legally and what is morally considered to be free availability, so moral pressure does not count. A "no purchase necessary" statement on the entry form and the dispenser make the position clear, but see paragraph 4.17.

EXHIBITION PROGRAMME DRAW

Automatic entry

4.24.1   What is the position if an art exhibition's printed souvenir programme contains a serial number which is automatically entered into a much-publicised free prize draw after the close of the exhibition? The alternatives are as follows:

(a) There is no entry charge to the exhibition, and no charge for the programme. The advertised free draw would be legal, as there is no contribution made by the holders of the programmes in consideration for entry to the draw.

(b) There is an entry charge for the exhibition, but the programmes are given out free of charge inside the exhibition and nowhere else. Whether each visitor who pays to get into the exhibition gets one programme only, or if they can be picked up freely from a table inside the exhibition, is not material. There is no immediate charge for the programmes which have the draw numbers on them, so apparently they are free. But it is not possible to obtain a "free" programme without having to pay first to get into the exhibition. There is no difference between being given the programme at the time when payment is made to enter the exhibition, and getting the programme after entry. That entry payment is an indirect and reasonably connected contribution which is a condition (although unspecified) of obtaining a programme, as there is no other way of getting it, and there is no other way of entering the "free draw". In those circumstances the promotion will be a lottery.

(c) There is a charge for each programme, irrespective of whether there is any entry fee to the exhibition. That would be a direct payment for the entry to the draw, which would then clearly be a lottery.

Alternative entry method

4.24.2   The exhibition organisers may decide to have a more interesting way of running the free prize draw:

(a) The exhibition is by invitation only, and the printed invitation states that if the invitation is returned before the opening date confirming that the invitee will be attending the exhibition, the name of the invitee will be put into the free prize draw. There is no actual attendance qualification or condition for eligibility, other than the invitation acceptance. Even if there is an exhibition entry fee payable at the door, as the participation in the draw is independent of the visitor's attendance, and the entry to the draw has been completed before the visitor reaches the exhibition, the entry fee will not be a contribution which turns the draw into a lottery.

(b) The programme contains a tear-out section which, when completed and put in the box, is the draw entry. If paragraph 4.24.1(b) or (c) applies, there will be a lottery. If the tear-out portion contains a skilled competition question relating to the subject of the exhibition then:
(i) if there is a tie breaker or some other means of finding a winner based on skill it will be a lawful competition;

125

(ii) if the winner is found by putting all the correct entries into a hat and making a draw of the winning ticket, it will be an illegal lottery, unless paragraph 4.24.1(a) applies, in which case the draw will be legal.

LIMITATION ON PRIZE DRAW ENTRIES

Effect of limitation

4.25.1 Will a limitation on the number of entries which can be made by a participant in an otherwise legitimate free prize draw affect the legal status of the promotion? In a widely publicised free prize draw, because of the quantity of tickets which are made available to the public, it does not matter to the promoter of the draw that an individual makes it a personal challenge to obtain as many entry tickets to the draw as he can. As there is no payment or other consideration for the entry, the number of entries does not affect the cost or the benefit of the promotion to its promoter. There will only be a problem if the limit on entries is in some reasonably direct way a means of ensuring that the entrant has to make a contribution for the entry.

Small venue draw

4.25.2 Where the promotion is a small free prize draw which complies with the relevant legal requirements, and which is being held in a pub or a club over a short period, it would be legal to have the following kind of limit. Tickets for the draw will be freely available at the bar to any person without any product purchase being required, so that anyone can walk in and take a ticket without any obligation. A rule of the draw is that there is a limitation whereby only one ticket can be asked for at a time, or even that there is a limit of one ticket per person per evening. This limitation does not affect the availability of the tickets or their being free of charge, and the limitation is not associated with any form of contribution. The limitation rule is only intended to make the promotion fair and manageable, and to prevent a deliberate abuse of it by people who might ask for a ticket once every minute.

Discriminatory limit

4.25.3 Will the position be different if there is a limit of one ticket per person per night for those who take them off the bar, but two "courtesy tickets" are given each time to anybody who buys a particular brand of beer? This promotion appears to fulfil the "no purchase necessary" rule because a free ticket is available to any person on application at the bar. The limit is relaxed to encourage the product purchase, but there is no obligation to make the purchase. Does that form of discrimination make the promotion illegal? The principle is the same as for the promotion described in paragraph 4.20.2, and the promotion should be legal.

PRIVATE MEMBERS' CLUB DRAW

Is the membership fee a contribution?

4.26.1 In a private members' club the prize draw tickets contain a rule that they are made freely available on request and one each to members of the club only. Tickets are not available to their guests or to other visitors to the club, as a natural form of limiting entry only to those people who should be able to benefit from it. Although no payment is made by a club member when he gets his ticket, as he had to pay an annual membership fee to belong to the club, and as only club members can get the draw tickets, could the club membership fee be deemed to be a rather remote and indirect contribution for the entry? The logic is that without the payment of the membership fee the person could not be a club member, in which case he would not be eligible to take a ticket for the draw. Membership of the club is a condition of getting a ticket, and the payment of membership fees is a condition of club membership.

Privity of contribution

4.26.2 If that argument were to be successful, the free prize draw would become an illegal lottery. There has to be some sensible privity between the right to obtain the ticket, and what can reasonably be considered to be a contribution which is paid for the ticket. The membership fee payment is wholly unconnected with the promotion, and therefore it will not be deemed to be a related contribution causing its illegality.

Legality depends on circumstances

4.26.3 The annual club subscription is not in the same class as the exhibition entry fee, because the exhibition programme draw is an integral part of persuading paying visitors to come to the exhibition. If the club needs more new members, and advertises that all new members (and only new members) who join the club "before March 31" will have their names entered into a "free prize draw", it would be a lottery. The reason is that the new membership and the promotion are directly connected, and the payment of the new membership fee is a condition of becoming eligible for the entry to the draw, as only the new members will be entered. Therefore the subscription fee in that case is a clear contribution for the chance to win the draw prize.

TOUR OPERATOR DRAW

Limited entry

4.27.1 A tour operator, having been successful in persuading a number of people to choose and pay for an expensive and unusual holiday which was included in its brochure last year for the first time, subsequently, and without any premeditation, decides to celebrate the event by promoting a limited entry free prize draw. The tour operator makes eligible for the draw only the names of all those people who took and paid for that specific holiday. They are automatically entered for the draw without their being aware of it until they are notified about it by the tour operator. Is that promotion legal? What about the previous holiday payments being deemed to have been indirect contributions for eligibility to the draw because only those people were entered for it? If the prize draw promotion was not proposed by the tour operator until after all the holidays had been taken, so that the holiday-makers were not aware of it at the time they booked their holidays, they could not have been influenced to buy that holiday in anticipation of being eligible for the draw. There can be no connection, as a condition of participation, between the holiday payments and any intention of the holiday makers to enter the draw, so the promotion would be legal. The position would be the same for the previous holiday makers even if the tour operator heavily advertises that it is going to repeat the special holiday offer. The purpose of holding the prize draw (and at that particular time) is clearly calculated to encourage repeat bookings by those previous holiday makers, although such a booking is not a condition of entry. That encouragement by itself would not make the draw illegal, because the original basis of eligibility for entry to the draw has not changed.

Circumstances affect legal status

4.27.2   If the class of entrant to the above free prize draw is the same, but according to its rules eligibility for the draw is conditional on the holiday-maker booking the repeat holiday, that cost would clearly be a contribution, and would make the promotion into a lottery. The reason is that the unconditional eligibility basis set out in paragraph 4.27.1 no longer applies; entry to the promotion is now conditional on a new booking being made. Even if eligibility for the draw is limited to the original holidaymakers who re-book the holiday, so that other people booking the second holiday are not included in the draw, it will still be an illegal lottery.

UNUSUAL PROMOTIONS

Interpretation of the law

4.28.1   Unusual promotions which are designed to get the benefit of a "ticket with purchase" illegal lottery incentive, but which are trying at the same time to bypass that potential illegality through sheer ingenuity and convolution of mechanic and rules, cause the most concern when trying to decide upon their legality. While the Act is the statutory basis on which a promotion is judged to be a draw or a lottery, the cases over the years have shown a wide variety of attempts to bypass the law.

Product-promoted free draw

4.28.2   A pub may for one evening promote a new brand of beer by stating that the first order which is placed by each individual customer for one pint of that beer will be free of charge, and that with each such first free pint there will be handed over a "free" prize draw ticket, and the draw will be made at closing time. Is that legal? No contribution is made by the customer for that free first pint, so the promotion should be legal. The draw promotes and encourages the consumption of the new brand of beer, but that of itself is not illegal. The fact that the class of participant is limited accordingly does not matter, as a free prize draw does not have to be open to the world at large.

Modified promotions

4.28.3   Would the answer be different if the promotion rules stated that the *third* pint of that beer ordered by a customer who has already bought two pints that evening would be given away free, and with that free pint the customer would be given a ticket in the free prize draw? Leaving aside the point that the third pint would have to be carefully defined (to take care of half pint consumption), what now is the legal position of the promotion? It can be argued both ways:

(a) The first possibility is that the third pint has no purchase price and therefore there is no contribution made at that point for the draw ticket, in which case it should be a legal free prize draw.
(b) The second possibility is that there is a necessary (but unstated) condition of the promotion that the customer will have had to pay for the first two pints before the third, free pint and its associated free draw ticket are given to that customer.

Total promotion context

4.28.4   The third-pint promotion would be an illegal lottery, because it could be argued more strongly that there is a compulsory two-pint purchase cost to achieve eligibility for the prize draw, as there is no other means of a customer drinking a third pint. The claim that the third "free" pint is not related to any contribution is a red herring in legal terms. As those first two pints have to be bought, any "no purchase is necessary" rule for the promotion would be inappropriate, and could not be complied with, although it would be intended to apply only to the third (and free) pint.

FREE PRIZE DRAW RULES

What the rules should cover

4.29 Chapter 8 deals in detail with certain promotion rules. For a free prize draw the rules should cover the following matters, and anything else which is relevant for the circumstances in which the free prize draw is being run:

(a) How the free prize draw can be entered, and specifying that no purchase of any product is necessary for an entry to be made. There should be no pre-condition or requirement which would be tantamount to the participant in the promotion making any form of direct or indirect contribution for the opportunity to enter the draw where there is no "no purchase necessary" rule. Any limitation which is placed upon when tickets can be obtained, who can obtain them, and any limit on the number of tickets which can be taken at one time should be stated prominently.

(b) What the free draw prize is, or what the prizes are. The description of the prizes must be correct and not misleading.

(c) Lesser prizes for runners up will normally be won in the order in which the tickets are drawn, as for large scale "commercial" draws the entrants are not present at that time. For a small-scale draw, such as at a charity gala evening, where anybody who has a ticket will be present when the draw is made, the tickets may be drawn with the major prize winner first, or they may be drawn in reverse order.

(d) To draw the tickets in reverse order could cause a problem if the promotion has a rule that, irrespective of the number of entries which he had, no entrant can win more than one prize. If he won a lesser prize half way through the draw process, and coincidentally also had a ticket drawn for the major first prize, he would not be entitled to claim the second (and greater) prize through the operation of that rule, as that would be the second prize he had won in the draw. The major prize ticket would have to be redrawn, but it would still be a controversial decision. To solve this controversy the rule could state that the winner of more than one prize can choose which to keep, providing the choice is made immediately upon his winning the subsequent prize, so that the discarded prize can go back to be drawn for again. The rule would also have to deal with the possibility of that winner of two prizes not being present at the time of the draw. To solve the dilemma the rule should state that the lucky person will be awarded the more valuable prize.

(e) When the draw will be made, and by what date the winner will be notified of his success.

SCRATCHCARD PROMOTIONS

BASIS OF SCRATCHCARD APPEAL

Instant gambling

4.30.1 A scratchcard promotion is another means of running a free prize draw, or a skill-related promotion which is not a competition. Where there is no skill question, the "ticket" for the draw (or the lottery) is the scratchcard itself. Instead of there being many tickets in one draw, each scratchcard acts as an individual "one ticket" draw when the choice of scratchpatch is made, and it is scratched. Scratch card promotions are popular because they have an appeal to the gambling instinct—the choice of which little patch to scratch makes the difference between losing or gaining. Where there is no cost incurred in acquiring the scratchcard, if it is not a winner it is not so much a case of the participant "losing", but more of his "not gaining". Scratchcards are easy to produce and distribute in large quantities, they are addictive to use, and the prize claim risk factor can be controlled easily.

Differences between draws and scratchcards

4.30.2 The differences between a conventional free prize draw and a legal draw scratchcard are:

(a) The chances of getting something may be more favourable for a scratchcard than for a large public draw.

(b) However many entries a person makes to a draw, the result is entirely beyond his control. For each non-skill scratchcard the person has some control because he decides which patch to scratch and he can make a different decision for each scratchcard he tries. Success is still based on chance.

(c) The results of a draw are not known until the promotion date when tickets are drawn, and only the winners are notified. A scratchcard result is known instantly.

(d) Where the scratchcard contains skill questions as a legal precaution it is fun and can be educational. Draws do not have a skill element.

(e) A scratchcard promotion is easier to run than a draw. It is also more flexible for use in different locations and at different times, so it is ideal for a chain of petrol stations or fast food outlets.

Different questions

4.30.3 There is no requirement in law that each skill-based scratchcard must have the same questions. Each scratchcard can be different providing they all have skill questions and they comply with the rules of a lawful competition. There is no legal requirement that the potential prizes which can be won for the successful answering of any scratchcard in the same promotion must all be the same, either as to their value or as to what they consist of, providing the prize for each card is fixed. If there is a choice of prizes, the choice can only be determined by skill in a lawful competition scratchcard.

SCRATCHCARD PROMOTIONS

Where there is no skill involved

4.31.1 The scratchcard has a number of boxes which are covered with the scratch material, and under one of them may be a prize. Alternatively a selection of boxes may have to be scratched correctly in a random sequence to see whether a prize has been won. If the prize box is uncovered, then the participant is entitled to redeem the prize from whoever is running the scratchcard promotion. Alternatively the scratchcard may only have one scratch box, which may or may not have a prize entitlement under it. It is not legally necessary for a scratchcard to have any prize in any of the scratch boxes, so there may be scratchcards which have no prize at all. Where in such a case a prize is obtained only by chance, the scratchcard has to comply with the rules governing free prize draws. Shortage of space on the scratchcard is the only limitation on how complex the scratch box combinations can be made to win a prize by chance.

Where there is an element of skill

4.31.2 One or more skillful questions may be set out on the scratchcard, with several alternative answers to each question, only one of which will be the correct answer. If the correct answer is "scratched", that stage is successfully completed. The scratchcard rules will determine whether the correctly scratched card entitles its holder to an immediate prize, or whether something else has to be done by him to obtain it. If there is an immediate prize, the scratchcard comes under the rule governing skilful competitions. A legal, skill-based scratchcard must have a prize for a correct answer, or for a combination of correct answers through different stages. If there is a second stage where the winning of a prize, or the value of the prize which has been won, is decided purely by chance, the scratchcard has to comply with the free prize draw rules to avoid being an illegal lottery.

Added value gamble

4.31.3 A variation on a skilful scratchcard theme may be that the correct answer will always provide a prize of modest value, but there will also be an additional selection of boxes which are hiding the possibility of a more valuable prize. There may also be a "lose" box. Where this form of refinement exists, the rules on the scratchcard must set out in simple language exactly what attempting any alternative added value "scratch" means. The added value variation can be that:

(a) The original correct answer prize is retained with a successful scratch, even if the additional prize selection is attempted; and if it is attempted, the original prize is retained whether or not the second attempt is successful.

(b) Attempting the second selection prize puts the first successful answer prize at risk, *i.e.* if the second scratch attempt is a loser, then the original prize is also lost.

(c) If the second-stage attempt is successful, that greater prize is in addition to, or is in substitution for, the lesser first successful answer prize.

Basic rules still apply

4.31.4 Whenever an added value element is included on the scratchcard, how it operates and the way in which anything is won or lost still has to comply with the rules which determine whether it is a legal draw, a once-only legal form of competition, or an illegal lottery. Whichever category the first phase of the scratchcard fits into, the added value section must also comply with the same rules. For example:

(a) If the first phase is a pure chance one, and if it is a legal free prize draw at that stage, the second stage can be a chance one or a skill one without affecting its legality.

(b) If the first phase has to be skilful to make the scratchcard legal, the second phase also has to be skilful to retain its legal status, and the winning of a prize, and the determining of the prize value, must not be a matter of chance.

ASSESSMENT OF SCRATCHCARD FOR LEGALITY

Established form of promotion

4.32.1 From a legal point of view a scratchcard is no different from any other promotion, which could be a competition, a lottery or a free prize draw, so it has to comply with the appropriate rules relating to chance, contribution and skill. How it does so will determine its legal identity. If the attainment of the correct answer and the winning of the prize for the scratchcard promotion is wholly based on a skill element, the scratchcard can be given out free or it can be distributed as part of a product sales transaction. That is because each scratchcard is treated as an individual lawful competition. If the scratchcard only provides a random choice as to which patch to scratch, with an equally random chance of being successful, it will only be legal if it is distributed without being conditional upon the purchase of products. It is the scratchcard equivalent of a free prize draw, and must comply with the relevant rules.

Restrictions of chance element scratchcard

4.32.2 If the "correct" scratchbox of a skill scratchcard entitles the holder of the card to a prize and if that is all there is to do, the card is legal. If, having scratched the correct answer box, the card holder then has to scratch a special patch to see whether or not he gets a prize at all, then no skill is applicable to that second stage. The scratchcard will not be legal in that case if it is only given out as a product purchase reward, as the obtaining of the scratchcard prize is decided purely by chance. The fact that the possibility of winning the initial prize depended on the exercise of skill is irrelevant, as it has been overridden by the later pure chance condition.

Multi-stage assessment

4.32.3   Where there is a multi-stage scratchcard promotion, each stage must be examined to see whether it is skill-related in its own right, or whether any stage is dependent wholly on chance for success. Here also it is not material that a cardholder may guess the correct answer to a skilful question; the essence of the legality is whether the correct exercise of skill in all the stages will inevitably produce the right result and the prize.

SCRATCHCARD TO SUIT PROMOTION

Distribution determines design

4.33   Whether the scratchcard is only to be acquired by the participant upon a product purchase, or whether it is to be made freely available will determine whether a skill version is necessary, or whether a lottery version of the scratchcard can be used safely by the promoter. There are two main factors to be considered:

(a) The legality requirements for the kind of promotion which is to be run must be ascertained, and the mechanic and the rules of the scratchcard which is used must be designed accordingly.

(b) From a commercial point of view, the potential redemption cost in prizes to the manufacturer in relation to the number of scratchcards to be issued for the promotion, may determine whether it can afford a prize for every scratchcard. If not, a free prize draw style should be used, so that legally only a proportion of the scratchcards may have prizes for success, and there may be a selection of potential prizes.

CREATING A SKILL SCRATCHCARD

Used with product purchase

4.34.1   If the scratchcard is to be distributed only to people who purchase the product, it must comply with the rules for competitions to ensure that it is a form of promotion involving some element of skill. The simplest form of scratchcard would be one which has a question with only one correct answer out of a number of scratch boxes which give alternative answers.

Chance element introduced through indeterminate question

4.34.2   There may be a legal risk where the skill question is so badly worded that it has more than one answer, so that it is a matter of chance as to which of the two answer boxes contains the prize. The risk is that the ambiguity, leading to two possible correct answers, makes the successful "scratch" a matter of chance as to which of them is considered to be the correct answer under the rules. A question such as "Who was the first man to land on the moon's surface?" is capable of having two answers, as two astronauts were in the lunar module which was the first to *land* on the moon. The question may have been intended to ask who actually *stepped on to* the moon's surface first, to which there is only one answer. Because of the question, if only that astronaut or only one of the two astronauts is on the list of possible answers it will be the right answer. Owing to the wording of the question, if both of those astronauts are on the list of possible answers, the scratchcard promoter would have to accept that either of them would be the correct answer. In that case it would be impossible to answer the question incorrectly, and the prize redemption cost to the promoter would be unexpectedly substantial. The careless wording of the question would also probably invalidate any excess redemption insurance policy.

All correct or nothing

4.34.3   A two-stage legal card may be produced by adding another question to the example in paragraph 4.34.2, for instance, "In which year did the first moon landing take place?" If the participant has found the right answer to the first question, he is likely to have at the same time the right answer to the second question, but this is not necessarily the case. So what is to happen if the participant gets only one of the questions right? The scratchcard promotion rules should ensure that the prize will only be won if he gets them both right, unless there is a separate prize for the correct answer to each stage.

Speculative questions

4.34.4   If the second question in the two-stage scratchcard is purely speculative, the scratchcard will become an illegal lottery despite the first question being a skill-based one. If the second question is "In which year will the first man land on Mars?", it can only be answered by a guess. In the scratchcard promotion rules the answer may be subject to the judgment of a panel of experts who are appointed to decide the most likely year, but in the absence of enough information on which to base a reasoned answer, it could come within the wording of section 14(1)(*a*)(i) of the Act, and so would make the promotion illegal (see paragraph 4.5.1). There is nothing upon which the participants could rely for the exercise of any skill in estimating the likely year. This is not the same as the panel of judges as described in paragraph 4.46, as they are assessing the relative merits of applied skill.

FREE PRIZE DRAW SCRATCHCARD

Must be freely available

4.35 Where the scratchcard is intended to be a public fun promotion for a product, but with no skill element, it must be made freely available to the world at large and not exclusively to purchasers of the product, since it must have all the genuine characteristics of a free prize draw to be legal. A free prize draw scratchcard promotion gives greater scope for the design of a gambling mechanic. Prominent point-of-sale material promoting the product, and polite enquiries by counter staff are fine, but any heavy pressure on the buyer which clearly demonstrates a reluctance of the outlet to hand over free scratchcards without a purchase being made must be avoided.

SCRATCHCARD RULES

Clear and legible

4.36 The scratchcard should contain legibly all of the conditions and rules which are being applied to the promotion. These will depend upon what kind of promotion it is, and upon any unusual element in its structure. The most important rules applicable to all scratchcard promotions are:

(a) Instructions as to how the card is to be activated, *i.e.* what can be "scratched" and (where applicable) in what order.
(b) Instructions as to what cannot be scratched under any circumstances, such as a security check box, and an explanation of what else will invalidate the scratchcard.
(c) How to check whether a prize has been won, and how to claim the prize, and by what date.

POOL PRIZE SCRATCHCARDS

Form of promotion

4.37.1 A popular form of scratchcard promotion is one with a large cash prize, such as £50,000, which can be won by scratching successfully a random sequence of patches. The prize is made difficult to win by there being many choices of patches, within which is a long sequence of "correct" patches which have to be scratched for the card to be a winner. There is also a very high number of different variations of the scratchcard, so that the chances of a consumer getting duplicated cards are remote, even with bulk purchase of the product to which they are attached.

Prize structure

4.37.2   The attraction of the promotion is the high cash prize, despite the odds against scratching one card successfully on a random basis being possibly several millions to one. To avoid financial disaster for the promoter the £50,000 prize must be a pool prize, so it is crucial to have a promotion rule which states that if there are several winners they will share in the prize equally. (See paragraph 4.37.3(g)) If no winning scratchcards are submitted to the handling house by the promotion closing date, then the promoter does not award the prize. It is not the kind of competition where there has to be a winner, as it is possible that no successfully scratched card which is valid according to the promotion rules will be submitted to claim the prize. The calculation of the risk of there being a winner is part of the assessment by the promoter of how high the odds should be set against a successful card being submitted when designing the scratchcard for the promotion. Notwithstanding the high odds against there being a winner, for a big prize fund it would be prudent for the promoter to take out excess redemption insurance against that possibility. (See Chapter 2, paragraphs 2.41 onwards).

Security features

4.37.3   The following security features are common to all scratchcard promotions. Depending on the level of the risk and the size of the prize, the insurance company may require stringent checks in the management of the promotion to ensure that its rules and the policy condition security features have been complied with. The details of the checks to be carried out by the promoter, the agency and the handling house should be included clearly in the written instructions to be given by the promoter or the agency to all of the parties which are involved in the administration of the promotion. They should also be included as obligations in the contracts between the promoter and each of those parties. The insurers are taking the ultimate risk of having to pay a winner, and any failure by the promoting manufacturer to comply with any of the insurer's conditions of providing the cover will invalidate it. For that reason the manufacturer must ensure that the insurance terms are clear, and that they are notified to and understood by those who have to comply with them.

(*a*) *quality of the scratchcard* The scratchcard must be of sufficiently thick paper, and the latex overprinting of the scratch boxes must be sufficiently solid, that it is not possible to see the contents of the scratch box through either of them, even by using sophisticated technology. As a precaution, a sample scratchcard should be submitted to the insurers for approval of its quality and visible security.

(*b*) *number of patches* The ratio of the number of patches to be scratched to the total number of patches on the card, and what has to be scratched to achieve a winning card, determines the mathematical odds against the participant scratching successfully an all correct card at random. The size of the cash prize, and the number of cards which will be printed, and the number of patch content variations will influence the premium which will be charged by the insurers for covering the prize value against a valid winning claim.

(c) *sequence variation* For a large national promotion, where possibly millions of cards may be produced, there must be a great number of different combinations of hidden symbols within the patch layout on each of the scratchcards. This reduces the possibility of a professional "scratcher" obtaining enough scratchcards to find a pattern from which he will finally deduce the correct sequence for a winning card.

(d) *printing quality control* The precautions taken under (a) above will be meaningless if the latex is not printed accurately on the cards, so that the numbers, letters or symbols which should be hidden can be seen. Where that happens, short of the participant spoiling the card in the excitement, it must be a winner, subject to (f) below. Printing security should also extend to ensuring that there is no opportunity for fraud or theft in the printer's works.

(e) *random distribution* To reduce the "professional winner" risk even further, the distribution of the scratchcards should be planned so that duplication of similar winning sequence cards at any source of collection by consumers is minimised.

(f) *the promotion rules* When submitting a winning card, they will ensure that they comply with the eligibility rules of the promotion. The defacing and similar invalidation rules used for other forms of promotion must be included. There should also be a rule to exclude as entries any scratchcard which has been misprinted, or which is otherwise incorrectly produced, whereby the guesswork is taken out of getting the winning combination of scratches.

(g) *definition of cash prize* It may seem obvious, but the promoter must ensure that the wording of the promotion text, and in particular the definition of the cash prize, makes it one prize which is shared amongst all valid winners. If the definition of the prize is so badly worded that each of the winners could claim the prize in full, that could be an extremely expensive error to the extent that the payout commitment exceeds the redemption insurance cover.

Relevant contracts

4.37.4 The promoter or its agency will be dealing with the scratchcard printer, the insurance broker the handling house and any other party which is directly involved in managing the promotion. If the scratchcards are supplied "on pack" to consumers, then the printer or a handling house should attach the scratchcards to the product packages in accordance with the terms of their contractual instructions. The insurer will have its own form of contract with the manufacturer, and the manufacturer (or its agency) must have effective contracts with all other parties setting out clearly all of the material obligations of those parties within the promotion administration.

Indemnities

4.37.5 All third party contracts must contain an indemnity to protect the promoter against any loss or damage (including legal fees) it incurs as a result of something going wrong with the promotion due to the default of the relevant party. The indemnity must also cover the reimbursement of the manufacturer where that party does something which invalidates the insurance cover of the promoter in respect of the prize which has to be paid out to a winner or winners.

Risk areas and winners

4.37.6 If payment of the promotion prize by the manufacturer is insured against, the premium is a normal promotion expense, and the only risk the promoter faces in the event of there being a winner is if the insurance policy is invalidated. In that case the manufacturer's monetary loss will be the prize paid out, and the wasted insurance premium. The risk of there being a winner against all of the statistical odds are increased by there being:

(a) incorrectly printed cards which show the hidden symbols, and
(b) such bad randomising of distribution of the cards that "professional scratchers" win against all the odds.

A winner will be any person who submits a scratchcard duly "scratched" in compliance with what the promotion rules define as a valid card and as a winner. In the absence of any rule to the contrary, this will include all correctly scratched cards which are defectively printed, or which are known to come from professional scratchers. (See paragraph 4.37.3.(f))

Exclusions from the insurance policy

4.37.7 Unless the rules of the promotion and the conditions of the insurance policy are matched with care when drafting the promotion text, the definition of a winner for the purpose of the insurance policy may not be the same as the definition of a winner in the promotion rules. If the circumstances set out in (a) and (b) of paragraph 4.37.6 above are stated in the insurance policy terms as invalidating any claim by the promoter under the policy for reimbursement of the paid out prize, the promotion rules should include 4.37.6 (a) above as an entry invalidation cause. However, 4.37.6 (b) is a promotion management matter, and has nothing to do with the consumers who collect the scratchcards, and so cannot be in the promotion rules. For example, in the case of 4.37.6 (a) above the possibilities are that:

    (a) there are no winning cards submitted to claim the prize.

    (b) there are winning cards, but they are all defective in their latex overprinting so that the random symbols are visible.

    (c) there are winning cards, which are all properly printed valid claims to the prize,

    (d) there is a mixture of valid winners and misprinted winners.

Printing errors

4.37.8 Assuming that all "printing error" cards which are submitted as winners are excluded for reimbursement purposes by the terms of the insurance policy, but they are not excluded as winners under the promotion rules, then all the winners under paragraph 3.37.7(b) and (d) above would have to be paid by the promoter, and the insurer will not have to reimburse the prize payout to the promoter. The promoter would have to try to recover its loss, (*i.e.* the prize payout), from the printer which caused the invalidation of the policy by reason of the faulty scratchcard printing. The promoter's contract with the printer must contain an effective indemnity clause in favour of the promoter to cover the claim, and the printer must also have adequate negligence insurance.

Grey area resolution

4.37.9 A dispute between the promoter and the insurer may arise where the policy excludes misprinted cards from the cover, and the promotion rules do not contain such an exclusion, and there is a mix of winning cards as in paragraph 4.37.7(d) above. As just one valid winner under the policy terms will trigger the insurer's liability to pay the whole of the "pool prize" money, the possibilities are that the wording of the exclusion clause in the insurance policy means either:

    (a) that the existence of any misprint winners will invalidate any claim under the policy, irrespective of the number of valid winners, or

    (b) that the existence of one or more valid winners makes the insurer liable to pay out the pool prize money, even though there is at least one misprint winner.

Analysis of exclusion Clause

4.37.10 Assuming that the insurer is relying on its policy exclusion clause to cover the position described in paragraph 4.37.9 (a) above, what is the legal position? Any exclusion clause is strictly interpreted in favour of the insured party (in this case the promoter), and will only exclude payment under the policy in circumstances which are clearly defined. The promoter and its agency must consider any exclusion clause in the policy very carefully before accepting the policy, and before finalising the rules of the promotion. If the clause simply "excludes" from the policy any misprint winners, a reasonable interpretation is that it still "includes" valid winning scratch cards, in which case the insurer must pay the promoter. The loss to the insurer of paying the promoter a pool prize where there is at least one valid winner is not increased by the existence of any number of misprint winners or of any more valid winners.

Therefore the existence of misprint winners in this example has no adverse effect on the insurer and should be disregarded. For the same reason it would not be logical for the insurer to pay the promoter pro rata according to the number of valid winners within all of winners who have to be paid by the promoter, except where the promotion gives a prize payment to each valid winner, irrespective of their number. This is not likely except for small sums of money, with a limit on the number of winners to be paid. If the insurance policy offered to the promoter is specifically invalidated by the existence of any misprint winners even where there are also valid winners, this should not be acceptable to the promoter. Its risk on paying out the prize, and its insurance against that happening, must be "back to back" in those circumstances.

COMPETITIONS

ELEMENTS OF A COMPETITION

Basic mechanic

4.38   The elements of a normal competition which is used as a promotion for the marketing of a product are that:

- (a) There are major prizes to be won, and there may also be a number of consolation prizes.
- (b) The participant has to complete an entry form, which is either a separate leaflet or part of the promoted products promotion label or package. The entry form will include the entrant's name and address, space for the competition answer, and a tie breaker which has to be completed where that is applicable.
- (c) The competition mechanic consists of some questions, which have to be answered, or a list of qualities which have to be put into an order of priority, or something else which has to be done for which the exercise of skill is necessary.
- (d) Because there may be many correct entries to the competition, there must be some legal means of elimination to find the winners of the prizes. This is usually done by a tie-breaker, so that the exercise of skill is applicable throughout the promotion activity.
- (e) The entry form has to be accompanied by some proof that the promoted product has been purchased by the entrant. This is normally the entry

form itself which has to be cut out of the product package, or it may be a detachable label or wrapper or sometimes a till receipt.

(f) There will be a set of competition rules which govern its operation, and a set of instructions explaining the mechanic of the competition. These are part of the competition material, and completion and submission of the entry form must be in compliance with the rules. They must still be complete after removal of the entry form.

Minimum skill level

Reasonable for promotion

4.39.1 Section 14 of the Act does not explain what is considered in law to be a minimum level of skill which has to be applied by the entrant in order to qualify the promotion as a lawful competition. The skill level should be consistent with the competition mechanic without making it either very simplistic or absurdly difficult. The absence of any appreciable skill would make any product-purchase competition an illegal lottery. Conversely, any promotion which requires an unreasonably high intellect to compete the competition entry correctly would not be considered to be consumer-friendly.

Skill must apply throughout

4.39.2 If the winner is chosen by chance from a number of finalists after the conclusion of a skilful means of eliminating unsuccessful entrants, then notwithstanding the original qualifying application of skill, the second stage will make the whole promotion into an illegal lottery. The skilful eliminating round is advertised as the main promotion, but all it achieves is the reduction of the number of original entrants to a few finalists who participate in a separate lottery among themselves to find the winner.

A substantial degree of skill

4.39.3 Section 14(1)(*b*) of the Act refers to "any other competition in which success does not depend to a substantial degree on the exercise of skill." What does "substantial degree" refer to or mean? It is not clear whether the words "substantial degree" qualify the word "success", or whether they qualify the word "skill". Section 14(1) differentiates between pure chance and pure skill, and section 14(1)(*b*) is a "sweeping up" reference to all other competitions which do not contain any skill. The subclause might have been clearer if it had stated that "success does not depend on the exercise of a substantial degree of skill". If the "substantial degree" does not refer to the exercise of skill, then it could mean that a competition would still be legal if the exercise of skill applied only to a "substantial degree" of the competition, *i.e.* only to some of it. The decided cases do not favour this interpretation, so for a competition to be lawful success must depend throughout the promotion on the exercise of a substantial degree of skill.

Skill is applicable to each stage

4.39.4 Each stage of a multi-stage competition which determines by a test whether a participant goes through to the next stage must comply with the skill rule. If there are five stages of which four are skilful and the last one relies purely upon chance to find the winner, the "substantial degree" test cannot reasonably be said to have been fulfilled just because four out of five stages were skilful if all five have to be completed successfully to win. If each stage of a competition is a separate question, then each question is (in legal terms) an independent mini-competition which is subject to section 14 of the Act. What is the position if the competition consists of one question consisting of several related sections, all of which have to be answered correctly to be a prize winner? An imaginary example relating to the football World Cup might be:

> "In the most recent World Cup Finals England only reached the second round. Please answer the following:
>
> (a) Which team beat England to knock it out?
> (b) What was the final score?
> (c) Who was England's goalkeeper?
> (d) What was the exact spectator attendance figure for that match?"

In this example there is only one stage, but it is a multi-section question, of which 25 per cent. (the answer to question (d)) is reliant on chance, because no competitor could be expected to know the answer, although in theory it might be ascertainable. How does the "substantial degree" of skill requirement apply? Is it to the overall skill to be applied to the whole question, or is it to the skill which is applied only to a substantial part of the question? If it is the first, the above example will be an illegal lottery because skill cannot realistically be applied to question (d); if it is the second, the promotion would be legitimate. However, to interpret section 14 of the Act in the second way would open a whole new vista for "semi- skill" promotions which would make a mockery of the current legislation.

Skill overrides chance

4.39.5 What would be the legal position where a product-purchased-based three-stage promotion is devised, whereby:

(a) initial entry is unconditional;
(b) fifty finalists are picked at random from all of the successful entrants; and
(c) those finalists are subjected to a quiz-game-show style of skill or knowledge test on a knock-out basis until only the winner is left?

In this case the chance choice of finalists, although it is an initial random elimination process, only reduces to a manageable number the participants in the skilful last stage knockout competition. As the winner of the competition succeeds through the application of skill, and not by chance, it will be a lawful competition. It would be too remote to argue that any of the randomly rejected original applicants might equally well have had the knowledge to win if they had been among the finalists. The conclusion appears to contradict the statement that the "substantial degree" of skill has to apply to the whole competition, but this is not so. The reason is that the competition only starts at (c) above, the random choice at (b) is not related directly to any success or prize.

Superficial skill

4.39.6 If the competition only requires the entrant to put a random jumble of the letters of the alphabet into their correct order, that may not be considered to be a sufficient test of skill to justify it as being a legal competition. It may be argued that a significant section of the public, such as the dyslexic or the near-illiterate would in fact find it a test of skill, but for others, the skill requirement would be insufficient. If the classical Greek or the Russian alphabet were to be used in such a competition, they are both so different from the English alphabet that there would be a sufficient element of research and skill which would have to be undertaken by an average English person in putting that alphabet into the correct sequence.

Priority order listing

4.39.7 The compilation style of promotion, such as "place the following eight characteristics (or products) in descending order of importance to a man on a desert island", is not so much an exercise of skill as it is a matter of personal judgment, and to that extent it could be argued that the winning order of priority can only be achieved by reasoned guesswork. However, section 14(1) of the Act makes no reference to judgment having an equivalent to the exercise of skill. There is no absolute answer which can only be given correctly through the exercise of skill, and different people will have different priorities. The only benchmark could be the order of priority which is agreed by a panel of judges who are appointed for that purpose in accordance with the promotion rules. Each competition entry should be checked to see whether it accords with the listed order which is determined by the judges to be the correct answer. On balance there is some element of skill in working out why one item would be more important than another if the list is of a sensible range of items which enables a rational judgment to be made.

Section 14(1)(a)(i) and (ii)

4.39.8 If judgment and skill are not the same within the context of section 14(1)(A)(i) and (ii) (see paragraph 4.5.1) of the Act, then the exercise of judgment is only the exercise of chance, *e.g.*, the chance of guessing what sequence the panel of judges will have chosen as being the correct one for the competition. In this kind of competition the judges will have made their definitive listing before the competition takes place, so as to avoid any possible manipulation of the result subsequent to the receipt of all the competition entries. In that event clearly the judge's decision is a "past event" for the purposes of section 14(1)1(a)(ii), and therefore any listing sequence competition based on the panel of judges method of finding the winner will not be legal. Similarly, if the judge's decision on the correct sequence of listing is not to be ascertained until after the closing date of the competition, section 14(1)(a)(i) would apply to make the competition illegal.

As there has not been any judicial decision on this specific question, the assumption must be that, until a judicial decision states otherwise, a sensible sequence listing competition complies with the skill qualifications for a lawful competition. (See also paragraphs 4.42.2 and 4.45.2.) All tie-breaker competitions depend on the panel of judges deciding the winner being a lawful mechanism.

SKILL IS DEPENDENT ON ADEQUATE INFORMATION

Complete and pertinent information

4.40.1   The construction and instructions of the competition mechanic must give enough information to the entrant to enable a sufficient element of skill to be genuinely exercised by him in solving the competition test. An example of this need of skill is a form of competition such as "Assuming that all the normally available tube trains ran on time, how long would it take a person to visit all of the stations on the London Underground system?"

Finite resolution required

4.40.2   In those instructions there is a lack of necessary information, such as train speeds or distances between stations, etc., and as the routing of the journey is left to each entrant to choose, there is no absolute answer. In the above competition wording there is nothing which an entrant can use in order to apply any skill to resolving the problem and getting an even reasonably accurate answer, and so each answer can only be obtained by guesswork. Therefore it could not be a lawful competition. Even if the functions of distance and speed were known and constant, different start and finish points and different routes taken would produce different overall times.

CHOICE OF SKILL OR GUESSWORK

Does not affect validity

4.41.1   Every answer to a competition which is capable of being arrived at by the exercise of skill is equally capable of being solved by guesswork. Whether the entrant chooses to use skill or guesswork in arriving at the correct answer to the skilful competition is not relevant to the legality of the competition. The material question is whether the solution to the competition mechanic can be achieved, and is intended to be achieved, through the exercise of skill.

Checklist

4.41.2   As each competition is developed by the agency, it has to be examined to see whether there is anything else which needs to be added in order to comply with the following list of points which must be dealt with.

(a) The result of the competition mechanic must be capable of being resolved on a skilful basis.

(b) Enough pertinent information must be provided in the mechanic instructions to enable the necessary skill to be applied to the competition by the entrant. The best way to check this is for an agency executive to try to solve the competition using the information which has been provided. If it becomes evident that further information is needed, it should be added.

(c) It is permissible for the competition instructions to include references to the source of any necessary information which is not contained already in the on-pack competition material. Despite the intention of the manufacturer to produce a skill-based competition, if the necessary information is not made available to enable the skill to be exercised, the end result will have to be a matter of guesswork.

DIFFERENT APPLICATIONS OF SKILL

Skill and creativity

4.42.1   The competition does not have to be a logic test which requires a skilful solution. It may be a creative competition, such as:

(a) to design a new logo or brand name for a new product yet to be marketed by the manufacturer which is promoting the competition; or

(b) to compose a new advertising slogan or concept for the product; or

(c) to undertake some other original creative task, such as paint a picture, which will be compared with all other entries to the competition by a panel of judges to decide upon the winner.

Judgmental answers

4.42.2   The possibilities of this kind of competition are endless, and while they each need the exercise of skill to produce the entry, each entrant is not attempting to provide precisely the same answer. As all the answers will be different, the competition must contain a legal mechanism to decide the winner. Could it be argued that any winner who has been chosen by a panel of judges has won more by chance than by the exercise of skill? The competition entry will be a skilful original work, but out of many thousands of entries is it not a matter of chance as to which one the judges pick as a winner? If the same entries were independently reviewed by 10 judges who did not confer with each other on the merits of the entries, it is most likely that each of them would choose a different winner, based upon their personal preference. That could be seen as a sophisticated form of random choice. It could also be argued that, in devising their entry to such a competition, the entrants are trying to forecast the result of a future event, *i.e.* the decision of the judges. Alternatively, it may be argued that success by an entrant (being chosen by a judge as the winner) does not necessarily "depend to a substantial degree on the exercise of skill" as required by section 14(1)(*b*) of the Act. In fact the entry may be skilful, and all the judge is doing is deciding which of all of the entrants' skills is most appealing to him. (See also paragraph 4.45.2.)

CHOOSING THE WINNER

Elimination required

4.43.1　A reasonably simple competition which is based on the skill of the entrant may have a large number of correct entries, and there may be only one major prize (such as a foreign holiday for two people), and ten consolation prizes of a relatively minor nature. Some form of elimination is therefore required.

Creative competitions

4.43.2　As there is no specific answer in a creative competition, the winner or winners can only be chosen by a panel of judges. The instructions for this kind of competition can only define the parameters of the competition, such as the logo or slogan to be designed to depict or project a certain kind of image for the product. The panel of judges will assess each of the entries accordingly.

Logic-based competitions

4.43.3　Where there are many correct entries to a logic-based competition, that only reduces the number of entrants who still have to go through some process of selection or elimination to ascertain the final winner. The usual mechanism for legally determining the winner in the case of a logic competition is for it to contain what is known as a tie-breaker.

Tie-breaker

4.43.4　A tie-breaker is an eliminating secondary competition, which is normally along the lines of "In not more than 12 words say what appeals to you

147

about the Gizmo Gadget", where that is the product which is being promoted by the competition. This is exactly the same as running a mini-original creative competition which does not have a finite answer. It must have a panel of judges which reviews all of the tie-breakers, and decides which of them is the most appropriate to the promoted product.

FINDING WINNER OF DEFECTIVE COMPETITION

Tie-breaker missing

4.44.1 What happens if several people get the correct answer to a logic-based skilful competition, and its instructions and rules do not have any mechanism to ascertain who is the ultimate winner? Through an error or oversight when designing the competition a tie-breaker may not have been included in the competition rules. To maintain the legality of the competition, the names of the successful entrants cannot be put into a hat for a random draw, nor can the identity of the winner be established by any other random means.

Costly defect

4.44.2 If there are one thousand correct entries, the promoter of the competition has to "find" a winner by some means despite the elimination procedure deficiency in the rules, or it will be faced with providing one thousand first prizes. It would be a form of fraud on all of the successful entrants if the promoter simply ignored the deficiency in the rules and arbitrarily announced the "winner" and the "runners up" as if nothing was wrong. As the promotion represents a contract between the promoter and each of the participants, if each of them is entitled to a main prize because that is the only and the correct interpretation of the promotion rules, then they can all enforce a claim to it.

Danger of imprecision

4.44.3 If the only definition of the winner in the rules is, for example, "The entrant with an all correct entry will win a holiday for two", that may be construed as meaning "Any entrant with an all correct entry . . . .", *i.e.* each of the correct entrants. It could not be construed as meaning "the first all correct entry received by the handling house" on the basis that the word "first" had obviously been omitted in error, because nothing is to be judged until the promotion's closing date. If it is found to mean "the first all correct entry examined" then the final decision of a winner is made at random, which makes it a lottery. What is missing from that definition of the winner is something like "and if there are two or more all correct entrants, then their tie-breakers will be examined by a panel of judges . . . ."

Rules are absolute

4.44.4 There is no equitable principle which the promoter could rely on so as to have "deemed" in hindsight the inclusion as a rule of the promotion that the promoter should be entitled to limit its prizewinner payout exposure to just one by the subsequent unilateral and compulsory inclusion of a suitable elimination mechanism. It would be possible to have a rule which states "The [promoter] reserves the right to amend or add to these rules at any time without notifying participants except for rules [ ]." The exceptions would be the proof of purchase requirement, the closing date and other rules which would affect entries which have already been received by the handling house. Such a rule is seldom included because it should not be necessary in most promotions, and space for text is scarce for on-pack promotions.

Panel of judges

Appointment of judges

4.45.1 In the absence of any other means of finding the winner, judgmental competitions which have a creative mechanic should also have a rule providing for a panel of judges to be appointed as the final means of deciding upon the winner. The rules do not have to state who are to be appointed to the panel of judges, nor how they are chosen for that purpose. In making the choice of who should be judges, consideration should be given to what qualifications or experience (if any) they need to make them suitable as judges for that specific competition. They ought to be independent of any party which is involved in running the promotion.

Judgment or lottery?

4.45.2 Few people believe that thousands of entries to a creative competition, or tie-breakers in a logic competition, are really examined individually by each member of a panel of judges, as the time which would be involved in doing so would make that process wholly impractical. If it could be proved that the judges did not, or could not, review each of the entries to judge its merits, but did (or must have) picked a winner arbitrarily and at random from all of the correct entries, that act will transform what would have been a lawful competition into an illegal lottery. The reason is that the ultimate means of winning was purely by chance, and the skill which was exercised in creating each entry or in completing each tie-breaker had no influence at all on the outcome of who was chosen as the winner. This is not the same point which was discussed in paragraph 4.42.2.

Panel guidelines

4.45.3 The judges should be given guidance as to the approach they should adopt in examining the competition entries in the case of literary or artistic competitions. This will go some way to eliminating any personal bias which is bound to be inherent in each judge. One judge may favour a classical style of art, whereas another may be attracted to impressionist works. Their guidance when examining the tie-breakers of the all-correct entries to a logic competition will be contained in the tie-breaker instruction. The tie-breaker sentence may have to be "the most apt" or "the most amusing" statement in the opinion of the judges.

COPYRIGHT IN COMPETITION ENTRIES

Preliminary precautions

4.46.1 Where the competition is to suggest an original brand name or to design an artistic logo for a new line of product, or where the manufacturer wants the right to make commercial use of any other form of artistic or literary competition entries, the relevant legal issues should be dealt with in the competition rules. Because of the reason for the competition, the manufacturer must be able to make unconditional use of the winning (or any other) brand name or logo which is submitted by an entrant. To do this the manufacturer must own all of the copyright and the other proprietary rights in the entries. The four essential conditions of the promotion which must be set out in the rules, are that the brand name or logo which is the competition entry must be:

(a) The original work of the entrant, who must be the sole "author" of it so as to be the first copyright owner under section 11 of the Copyright, Designs and Patents Act 1988.

(b) Original in the sense of not being a copy of, or derived from, or an infringement of, any copyright work or of any trade mark or any other third party proprietary right.

(c) Assigned to the competition promoter together with all of its copyright and other proprietary rights.

(d) Free from any encumbrance, so that the copyright in it can be assigned unconditionally by the entrant to the manufacturer under the competition rules. There should be a rule whereby the entrant confirms that he is free to enter the competition, and that he is not prevented by any circumstances from complying with its rules, or from assigning to the promoter the proprietary rights in the competition entry. Nevertheless the legal position on the copyright may not be clear where, for example, the entrant is a full-time employee designer in an artwork house and is dealing exclusively with brand identity development for his employer's clients. His service contract and section 11(2) of the 1988 Copyright Act would give his employers the copyright in whatever he produces during the course of his employment within the scope of his job specification, which would include the design of logos and brand names. The employee would also be prohibited from producing any similar work for any other party under the terms of his service contract.

Unauthorised assignment

4.46.2 What would be the competition promoter's legal position if the winning entrant was found to be legally incapable of complying with the requirements of paragraph 4.46.1(c) and (d)? The entrant would also be in breach of the "assurance" rule referred to in paragraph 4.46.1(d) above. The sequence of events could well be that:

(a) The winning entrant did not tell his employer that he was entering the competition.
(b) The new product is launched, using the brand name and logo of the winning competition entry.
(c) Because of the publicity which is given to the competition the employer of the winning entrant becomes aware that the new, high-profile product brand identity was created by one of its employees.
(d) The employer contacts the product manufacturer to claim:
    (i) the copyright in the logo, and the right to own the brand name, although the name is not protected by copyright; and
    (ii) that the manufacturer must cease immediately to use them, or it must negotiate a purchase or a licence of the rights in them from the employer for a large sum of money.

Employer's rights in the logo

4.46.3 If the copyright in the original artistic logo submitted by the winning entrant belongs to his employer by reason of his exclusive service contract, and through the operation of section 11(2) of the Copyright Designs and Patents Act 1988, the proprietary rights in the artistic logo of the winning entry will automatically belong to the employer. In that case the employee entrant never had any legal rights over his entry to assign to the promoter of the competition. As the promoter could not receive any rights in the entry despite the purported assignment by the winner, which had no legal effect, the promoter has no claim for any rights in the entry as against the employer. The promoter may well have a claim against the employee for misrepresentation and breach of contract, and for any loss which it may have sustained in relying upon its assumption that it had the proprietary rights in the logo due to the operation of the rules.

In any specific case the employer's rights in the entry will depend upon whether, for the purposes of section 11(2) of the Act, it can prove that the competition entry was done by the employee in the course of his employment, and/or whether his service contract wording would cover it. Entering a competition would not be "in the course of" the employee's employment, but if designing new brand names and logos for the employer is his prime responsibility and job specification with the right wording giving the employer exclusive rights over the relevant results of the employee's creativity then both of section 11(2) and the service contract would apply. The employer's rights to what is created for it under an employee's exclusive service contract are not necessarily restricted to work which is done by that employee only during office hours and within the office premises.

Employer's rights in the brand name

4.46.4 The brand name entry, being one or two words, is not protected by copyright (as it is not sufficient to be a literary work), so section 11(2) of the Copyright Designs and Patents Act 1988 would not apply to it unless it is in the form of an original artistic logo. The employer's rights in the brand name as against the employee will depend on whether the wording of the employee's service contract is sufficiently extensive to cover the creation of brand names. But, although the employer has a claim against the employee, on what legal basis would the employer sue the manufacturer of the promoted product for using the brand name? At the time of the competition the brand name will not have been used commercially, and so it would have no goodwill value. An application for the registration of the winning entry as a trade mark will have been made by the competition promoter at the earliest opportunity, and before the employer becomes aware of its existence. There is no proprietary right in an unregistered non-copyright brand name until either:

(a) it is used commercially as an unregistered trademark for a product to such an extent that it generates widespread public recognition and a substantial goodwill value. But those values only exist through the association of the brand name and the product. If they are sufficiently extensive the goodwill and the public recognition of the brand name make it protectable under the common law rules relating to "passing-off" (See Chapter 7, paragraph 7.30 onwards), or

(b) it becomes a registered trademark. In this case it has statutory protection for the benefit of the registered proprietor.

If, in the above example, the employer has no proprietary right in the brand name at the time when it is created, it has no legal grounds either for reclaiming it from the promoter of the competition, or for claiming damages for using it commercially. The employer may have a right of action against its employee for breach of his obligations of exclusivity and good faith within his service contract.

Competition promoter's safeguards

4.46.5 The four conditions set out in paragraph 4.46.1 should be supported for the safeguard of the competition promoter by at least:

(a) An indemnity from the entrant to compensate the promoter for any loss, damage or expense it incurs as a result of the warranties which are set out in the promotion rules of originality, non-infringement and assignability being breached by the entrant.

(b) The entry form asking the occupation of the entrant. If it is "designer" or "commercial artist", then the promoter can make precautionary enquiries if that entrant is the winner, to satisfy itself that the kind of problem referred to in paragraph 4.46.2 does not exist.

(c) Independent insurance by the promoter in case its enquiries do not show up a warranty breach by the winner, which is claimed by a third party at a later stage. An indemnity from an individual entrant will not be worth collecting by the manufacturer where there is a massive liability to a third party.

However, in practice these precautionary rules are never included in the competition text, as they would look too formal and legal. They could be included in "user friendly" language in a complete set of rules which can be applied for by an entrant. Section 5.8 of the Code of Sales Promotion Practice requires all essential rules to be displayed prominently on the promotion packaging and material.

Consideration for assignment

4.46.6 As the competition entrant is assigning potentially valuable proprietary rights to the promoter, and as the promoter must be able to rely on the assignment if it wants to use the winning entry commercially, the assignment has to be legally enforceable by the promoter. The copyright and any other proprietary rights in the winning brand name or logo can be assigned by the winner to the manufacturer either:

(a) Free of charge and unconditionally at the time of entering the competition, the implied consideration for doing so being either the entry opportunity or the first prize he receives for winning the competition, or

(b) In consideration of a reasonable financial deal which would have to be set out in the competition rules.

The first is the standard approach, because the purpose of the competition is to find a logo or slogan which the manufacturer can use commercially. The second approach would make the competition text look too much like a business contract, and would be far too complicated to set up and operate. The amount of a cash prize may reflect to some extent the potential value of the winning entry to the promoter, and would be adequate legal consideration. The assignment must be worded carefully.

Copyright assignment rule

4.46.7   A copyright assignment of the competition entry should be included in the rules, as (where appropriate) the future copyright in something which has yet to be created or produced can be assigned before its creation. (Section 91 of the Copyright Designs and Patents Act 1988). However:

(a) Copyright can only be assigned by a written document which is signed by the assignor of the copyright. The rule will represent an unconditional assignment of the copyright from the entrant to the manufacturer provided that it is worded correctly, and it should be repeated on the competition entry form. To make that assignment effective in accordance with an appropriately worded rule, the entry form should have a space for the signature of the entrant where he prints his name and address to represent the assignment execution. Non-signature should invalidate the entry as being "incomplete", so the agency should make sure that the promotion entry validity rule covers the point. Bold print should stress that condition prominently.

(b) If there is no copyright assignment rule in the competition, and subsequently the winner is sent a form of assignment of the copyright in his winning entry to the manufacturer, if he does not sign it and return it the document would be ineffective. The manufacturer could not claim that the assignment is deemed to be completed by the winner just by sending him one to sign.

(c) If the winner refuses to assign the copyright in his entry as in (b) above, or if there is no mention of copyright, either in the competition rules or afterwards, what rights does the manufacturer have in the winning entry? If it does not own the copyright in the logo, or the trademark rights in the brand name, and if it does not negotiate a licence as in paragraph 4.46.8(b) below, the position of the manufacturer will be either that:

(i) it cannot legally use the winning entry for the purpose for which it was intended in the competition; or

(ii) as the purpose of the competition is clear to each entrant, the entrant will be deemed to accept that his entry (if successful) will be used by the manufacturer, and by entering the competition he is deemed to grant to the manufacturer an implied licence to make such use of it free of charge, and on a non-terminable basis.

If the copyright aspect has not occurred to either the manufacturer or the winner, the manufacturer will assume that it owns the proprietary rights in the winning entry. It will make a trade mark registration application to protect the new brand name and logo before the launch of the new product. If after all that has happened the winner claims that the manufacturer has no rights in the band name and logo, as a balance of convenience the position set out in (ii) above is likely to apply.

Refusal of assignment

4.46.8 What would be the position if the entrant who designed the winning logo had refused to accept the assignment of copyright rule *when making his entry*? He could do so by returning with his entry a copy of the promotion rules with that rule deleted and countersigned by him, or he could do so in a covering letter which enclosed his entry. The possible answers are that:

(a) The entry is declared invalid as the complete rules are not being accepted by the entrant; in which case it should be rejected when it is scrutinised on receipt by the handling house.

(b) If the modified entry is not rejected, the promoter will be deemed to have accepted it as a valid competition entry in its modified form, even though it wins the competition because that is exactly the logo or brand name the manufacturer wants to use. As the copyright assignment rule does not apply, the promoter would have no alternative but to negotiate with the winner for a commercial licence for the use of the logo or brand name if it wants to use them for the new product. The disadvantages of not owning the copyright in the entry are:

(i)   A licence may not be adequate for, or appropriate to, the use for which the manufacturer wants the winning entry. The brand name chosen through the competition must be registered as a trade mark to protect it, and the manufacturer should be the registered proprietor and the beneficial owner of it. Registrations may have to be made in many countries, and the entrant licensor will not want to go to this trouble and expense.

(ii) Through extensive publicity and advertising and promotion expenditure a valuable goodwill is built up for products bearing the brand name, and the manufacturer must retain the benefit of that goodwill as part of its business assets.

(iii) There is always a risk of a licence being terminated, which is not an acceptable risk in the above circumstances.

(iv) The manufacturer must have unconditional control over the worldwide marketing of the product, including all brand name uses and derivations of that brand name to suit foreign territory needs. It must have legal ownership of intellectual property rights in the brand name and logo to protect them and to give it the legal right to sue infringers.

(c) The manufacturer could negotiate an outright purchase of the logo or brand name. The fact that the entrant specifically deleted the copyright assignment rule suggests that either he is not prepared to sell them, or he wants a price which is greater than the value of the first prize.

(d) The manufacturer would not be entitled to make any changes to the design of the logo, or to the brand name, without first getting the consent of the winner (as the owner of the proprietary rights in them).

Exception to copyright assignment

4.46.9   In the case of a competition which consists of the painting of a picture, or the creation of any other work of art, where the promotion is of a non-commercial nature, the winning entrant would not be expected to assign to the manufacturer any rights in his entry. The manufacturer may require a licence to exhibit or to make some uses of the artistic work entry, but not necessarily on a commercial basis.

Copyright in winning entry only

4.46.10   While the rules of a brand name and logo competition should assign the copyright in each entry to the manufacturer, in a perfect world there should be some qualification for the protection of entrants to the effect that the copyright assignment will only apply to the winning entry. The point is seldom, if ever, taken in the rules, but the reasons for such a proposition are:

    (a) The winning entrant will receive the competition prize as the consideration value for the copyright assignment.

    (b) All other entrants will receive no valuable consideration for their assignments, except for the rather tenuous one of having the opportunity to enter the competition.

    (c) Without that qualification the manufacturer would be entitled to make commercial use of any brand name or logo entered into the competition, even though the entrant won nothing for it, and for no additional payment. The rules will not say that only the winning entry will be used by the manufacturer.

    (d) If the entrant is a professional designer, and his entry is not in the prize list, it is a reasonable assumption that the manufacturer does not intend to use it. In that case the designer should be entitled to make alternative commercial use of his original design if he can.

Moral rights

4.46.11   By reason of the moral rights provisions under Chapter IV of the Copyright, Designs and Patents Act 1988, if commercial use of an artistic entry will be made by the manufacturer, the competition rules should contain a waiver by each entrant of his moral rights to his entry. Moral rights are dealt with in Chapter 5, paragraph 5.46 onwards.

Description of competition prize

Must be accurate

4.47   The description of the prize in the competition literature must be accurate, and must not be misleading. There can be an impulse for the manufacturer to enhance the general impression given by the competition by making more of the prize in its description than is warranted in real life. The description of the prize must also be complete, so that no material reference to it is omitted. For example, if the prize is a portable telephone, but the prizewinner will have to pay for the initial cost of delivery, such as a substantial security deposit, the prize description must say so, particularly if the prize is advertised in the promotion as being "free".

EXCHANGE OF PRIZES

No right of exchange

4.48.1   Competition rules never cover this point because it is so unlikely, but if the winner wants to decline the first prize and would prefer instead to accept the second prize, would he be entitled to do so? In the absence of a specific rule covering that remote possibility, what should happen? Any entrant is only entitled to claim the prize which he has won, and he has no right to demand an exchange with another and lesser competition prize. It is difficult to imagine the runner-up not being willing to trade places with a reluctant winner, so an agreed substitution should be possible, but not as an official part of the competition procedure.

Nominate prize-taker

4.48.2   The first prize may be a one-day return flight to an exotic place in Concorde, and the runner up prize may be dinner for two at the Savoy. If the winner of the first prize has an overpowering fear of flying, but has never been able to afford a splendid dinner at the Savoy, he might prefer to exchange the greater prize for the lesser prize. The runner-up may be willing to make the substitution, in which case all is well. If he does not want to do an exchange, the winner of the first prize can always nominate a substitute to enjoy the first prize. If there are several runners up, which of them should be given the opportunity to make the exchange of prizes? If all their names went into a draw to decide who will benefit from the exchange, does that lottery affect the validity of the competition? The answer is that as the prize exchange takes place after the competition has been completed, and as it is not an official part of the competition, the draw has no effect on its legality.

ANALYSIS OF ACTIVITY PRIZES

HOLIDAY PRIZES

Problem areas

4.49.1 A popular choice of main prize in a competition is a holiday for two in some exotic place. Holiday prizes have points of their own which can become controversial unless they are understood and are dealt with in the competition rules, and also in the follow-up material which is given to the holiday prizewinner. The holiday prize is examined in some detail to demonstrate that whenever a major prize consists of something of a personal use nature, or where the competition promoter relies on third parties for the prize to be fulfilled, anything which could be reasonably foreseen as a potential cause of a material problem should be covered in the rules.

CLARIFICATION OF HOLIDAY PRIZE

Specific prize

4.50.1 The competition material should define the prize clearly. For example, it may be a specific holiday, such as a two-week stay in a named hotel in Barbados, in accordance with the regular holiday arrangements which are provided by a nominated tour operator and which are advertised in its current brochure. Alternatively, the prize may be any holiday of the winner's choice provided by a nominated tour operator to a total brochure cost of, say, £1,000. The prize will normally be the former, as the promoter of the competition will have negotiated a discount with that tour operator for that specific package holiday to be the competition's first prize. The only choice left open to the winner will be the date upon which the holiday will be taken.

Winner's choice holiday

4.50.2 In the case of a "winner's choice" holiday, the rules must clarify what is meant by the value of the holiday prize being "up to £1,000". If a holiday is chosen by the winner which costs £750 according to the tour operator's brochure, is the balance of £250 going to be paid to the winner by the competition promoter to make the value of the prize "up to £1,000?" The competition promoter would only pay £750 to the tour operator, being the brochure cost of the holiday which has been chosen by the prizewinner. The "up to £1,000 holiday value" should be described as being the tour operator's brochure cost of whichever holiday is chosen by the winner. The fact that it might have cost the promoter of the competition less because of an agreed discount the promoter has negotiated with the tour operator is not relevant. If extra payments, such as spending money, are to be made to the winner as part of the prize, these should be stated separately. Whether that holiday cost limit is to include or exclude all additional prudent holiday insurances and other related costs should be stated.

No cash alternative

4.50.3   There should be a competition rule which states that there will be no cash alternative to the prize which has been won. Depending on the wording of the prize description, this rule would normally prohibit a claim for the difference between the prize value and the cost of the chosen prize. So if in the above example the winner chooses a holiday with a brochure cost of less than £1,000, he would not be entitled to claim the balance of the holiday value in cash. If that were not the case, the prize winner could choose a holiday for £199 and ask for £800 as the cash balance. The prize is a holiday, not a payment of £1,000 in cash.

BOOKING OF HOLIDAY

Winner's instructions

4.51   The holiday prizewinner will receive a letter from the handling house explaining that he has won the prize, and enclosing the nominated tour operator's brochure, plus all instructions and guidelines on how to book his holiday. The prizewinner will book his holiday in the normal way by personally completing the tour operator's booking form and dealing with any other matters, such as holiday insurance, directly with the tour operator. The holiday booking will be a contract directly between the prizewinner and the tour operator, with the result that the promoter of the competition is not involved in the holiday booking contract, and has no responsibility for the tour operator, the hotel, or anything else connected with the holiday. The competition promoter will simply pay the tour operator for the holiday which is booked, within the limits set out in the competition rules. (See paragraph 4.57.)

WHEN A HOLIDAY IS TO BE TAKEN

Advance notice

4.52.1   Most people who book foreign holidays do so reasonably well in advance, and so holiday prize promotions which are run in the summer or autumn of one year will have flexibility to enable the prize holiday to be taken in the following year. The competition closing date may be close to or just after the end of the normal high season for holidays during the year in which the competition is held. If the competition prize is specifically a summer holiday or a winter holiday, the competition would have to be run at a time of the year to suit the next relevant prize holiday season.

Latest starting date

4.52.2   The dates within which the holiday can be taken should be stated in the full competition rules, and if it is in a high season it may have to be booked by the winner many months ahead to ensure that the desired dates are available. High season bookings may be excluded under the promotion rules. There may also be an advisory date by which the holiday booking should be made, so that the tour operator still has available a reasonable selection of dates before the season or the hotel is booked up. If the prizewinner fails to book his free holiday prize at all, or if he fails to book sufficiently far ahead with the result that there are no dates available in the holiday prize period, the holiday will be lost. (See paragraph 4.56.)

Transferability of holiday

Should be permitted

4.53   If the prize winner does not want to use the first prize by taking a holiday, he should be entitled to transfer the holiday benefit to members of his family, or to anyone else. The manufacturer gets the publicity from running a successful competition, and the tour operator will be paid for the holiday which is taken, so it does not concern either of them as to who actually goes on holiday. That will even be the case where the winner of the prize "sells" it to someone else.

Spending money

How much?

4.54.1   Part of the first prize holiday may be a supplementary prize of spending money, such as £500. As the usual prize is a holiday for two people, and if the prize includes an amount of spending money, the rules of the competition must explain clearly whether the £500 spending money is to cover both people, *i.e.* is it £250 each, or is it £500 each? The effect depends on the wording of the rule. If the prize is advertised as "A holiday for two people with spending money of £500", what is the payment to be made? It does not say "£500 each" but can that be implied? The £500 relates to the holiday in that example, and would be interpreted as being a total of £500. What if the prize is described as "A holiday plus £500 spending money for two?" That is an ambiguous statement, because does "for two" mean "between two" or "each"? On balance it is likely to be held to mean "between them". Wording such as "A holiday for two people who will be given £500 to spend" could be interpreted as awarding each of them £500 to spend. To be safe, the wording should be precise.

Further considerations

4.54.2 If spending money is provided to the winner, further considerations which should be dealt with in the competition rules, and which should be repeated in the material dealing with the holiday details given to the prizewinner are:

(a) Is the £500 severable from the holiday? Could the prizewinner take the cash, and allow another couple to take the holiday, providing their own spending money? This would not infringe the "no cash alternative" rule, as there is no substitution of cash for something else; there is simply a splitting of the value of the prize.

(b) At what point is the £500 paid, and to whom? If the cash and the holiday elements of the prize are not severable, then the cash may be provided together with the tickets when they are issued by the tour operator. Alternatively the prizewinner may be sent a cheque for £500 together with the letter confirming that he has won the first prize. What he then does with the money and the tickets is no concern of the promoter of the competition.

(c) Is the spending money payable at all if the holiday is not taken by the prize winner or by any couple in his place? Failure to take the holiday may be for a good reason, such as sickness or some other intervening event, even though it may have been booked. There is no obligation on the prizewinner to take the holiday, so the payment of the £500 should not be conditional upon him doing so. The wording of the rule does not oblige the winner to spend that £500 while he is on holiday. Therefore the spending money should be paid in any event.

ADDITIONAL HOLIDAY COSTS

Define expenses

4.55.1 Care must be taken when describing the holiday in the competition material. If it is advertised as being "An all expenses paid holiday for two . . .", what does the reference to "all expenses" mean? That is a dangerous open-ended commitment unless the expression is clearly defined or limited. The same applies to an "all inclusive" holiday. If the prize description is badly worded, expenses which might be claimed by the prizewinner could include the cost of meals, transport to and from the airport, tours and excursions, fuel cost surcharges and any extra facilities made available at the hotel.

Strict interpretation of description

4.55.2 When interpreting the description of the extent or the value of the prize, only what is stated in the promotion text is relevant, as that is the contract. If the material which is subsequently provided to the prizewinner attempts to modify the prize, that is too late. The promotion terms are not subject to the promoter trying to explain later that "What we meant was . . ." or that "Nobody expects an open-ended commitment . . .". This shows again that every meaningful statement in promotional text, and especially in the rules has to be vetted carefully for interpretation and effect.

Misleading advertisement

4.55.3   If there is a disagreement between the prizewinner and the competition promoter as to what "all expenses" covers, and if that expression within the context of all of the competition material strongly implies that the prizewinner is entitled to get much more than the competition promoter is prepared to provide him with, that promotion material could constitute a misleading advertisement.

Expenses or unallocated payment

4.55.4   For an "expenses paid" holiday prize which does not come within clause 4.54 the competition rules should stipulate exactly what expenses will be reimbursed to the winner or will be paid for by the promoter directly. How will the expenses be paid to the winner? What evidence will be required to validate the expenses claim, and will there have to be an accounting from the winner at the end of the holiday? If the small print explains that "all expenses paid" means a cheque for £500 and no more, the expression "all expenses paid" could be considered misleading, as "all expenses" is an indeterminate value which (depending on the holiday) is unlikely to be wholly covered by £500.

Beware the "free" holiday

4.55.5   There would be a materially misleading description of the prize if the competition details referred to it as a "free holiday" without dealing specifically with who pays for the inevitable extra costs, and without explaining precisely which parts of the holiday are indeed "free", and which parts will be at the cost of the winner. In the absence of any qualifications, a "free holiday" is in the same category as the "all expenses paid" holiday, with an unknown liability for the total cost of the prize being incurred by the competition promoter as a result.

MODIFICATION OF HOLIDAY

Prizewinner's preference

4.56.1   The prizewinner may be interested in seeing whether, at his additional cost where necessary, the holiday prize can be modified or extended to fit in with what he would really like to do. If the holiday is for only one week in Jamaica, he may want to extend it to two weeks if that can be done. Alternatively he may prefer to take one week in Hawaii, so both the location and the cost will be different.

Promoter not affected

4.56.2   This will be no concern of the promoter of the competition, provided it only pays to the tour operator the cost of the original holiday which was advertised as the prize in the competition. Any modified holiday arrangements would have to be made directly between the prizewinner and the tour operator, which has no obligation to change a fixed deal which it made with the promoter for providing the prize. If the holiday is "one week in Jamaica at the X hotel between the following dates . . . ", under the terms of a special deal which the competition promoter has with that hotel, a change of time may be possible, but not a change of location. The additional cost of any alteration in the specific prize will be the responsibility of the prizewinner.

LIABILITY FOR SPOILT HOLIDAY

Exclude promoter

4.57.1   For the protection of the competition promoter the rules should state that the rights of the winner arising from a spoilt holiday will only be against the tour operator, the holiday hotel or some other party which is directly connected with the provision or the administration of the holiday. This warning should be repeated in the holiday material which is sent to the winner. Under the rules the competition promoter specifically should have no liability to the prizewinner for any aspect of the holiday. The promoter will have provided the holiday only in the sense of paying for it. One of the reasons for a prizewinner dealing directly with the tour operator is to give him all of the contractual rights against the tour operator as the person who books and takes the holiday.

Prize performance is not guaranteed

4.57.2   By arranging for the holiday to be a competition prize, the promoter is not recommending or guaranteeing the performance of any contractual or other obligations of any third parties such as the tour operator, or the airline carrier, or the holiday resort hotel. Ideally there should be some reference to this in the competition rules, but it is frequently omitted. This exclusion of liability of the competition promoter should also extend to any consequences arising from the cancellation of the holiday, or from the prizewiner being unable to get back from the holiday resort for any reason.

Effect of prize

4.57.3 By awarding the prize the competition promoter gives the winner the opportunity to travel; it does not guarantee that he will actually travel, or that he will travel happily and safely. The promoter will not be obliged to provide a substitute holiday if the first one is a disaster. The promoter of a major competition should take reasonable steps to check that the chosen tour operator is reputable, and that the advertised holiday is consistent with its description in the brochure.

EFFECT OF CANCELLED HOLIDAY

Refund entitlement

4.58.1 In the case of a cancellation by the prizewinner or the tour operator of a firm booking of the holiday for any reason in circumstances where, under the tour operator's terms and conditions, a refund is due of the whole or any part of the booking payment, and if no substituted holiday is booked by the prize winner, who would be entitled to get the refund? Although the competition promoter would have paid for the holiday, the winner will have been the contracting party with the tour operator, so the terms and conditions of the booking will be effective only as between them. Those terms will contain the refund provisions, without reference to who actually paid for the holiday; therefore the prizewinner who booked the holiday will receive any refund which is due.

Right to retain refund

4.58.2 If the tour operator has been paid in full by the competition promoter by the date when the refund is claimed, the winner would get the refund. As a means of getting cash, if the prizewinner prefers to accept the refund rather than take a substitute holiday, that would not be in breach of the "no cash alternative" rule, even if the prizewinner deliberately cancels the holiday to get the refund. However, any refund is subject to the appropriate cancellation charges contained in the booking contract, which may itself be declared to be non-cancellable.

No claim for refund equivalent

4.58.3 When the holiday booking is made by the prizewinner well in advance of the proposed travel date, the tour operator may not invoice the competition promoter for some time. If the prizewinner then cancels the holiday booking quickly before there are significant refund retentions by the tour operator, but before the competition promoter receives the invoice for the booked holiday from the tour operator, no invoice will be issued by it except for the amount of any cancellation charges which have been incurred. When the refund is claimed nothing would have been paid by the promoter to the tour operator, so there would be nothing for the tour operator to refund to the prizewinner. Would the prizewinner be entitled to claim from the promoter the outstanding cash value of what the refund from the tour operator would have been if it had been paid by the date of the cancellation? Within the interpretation of the "no cash alternative" rule, if it is worded appropriately, the promoter will not be obliged to pay the refund value of the holiday to the prizewinner. The possibilities are:

(a) As the prizewinner has paid nothing to the tour operator, and as the prize winner cancelled the holiday, he has lost nothing for which he can claim against either the tour operator or the competition promoter. The competition promoter's obligation under the rules is to provide a holiday, but the prizewinner voluntarily cancelled that obligation.

(b) Even if the prizewinner does have a claim for a refund under the holiday booking contract, there can only be a refund by the tour operator of something which has been paid to it. In this example the tour operator has not been paid whatever is due under the booking contract, either by the prizewinner or by the competition promoter. The booking contract will probably refer to the prizewinner as "the Customer". The refund clause would refer to "money paid by the Customer", which will not have been the case.

(c) Can the prizewinner force the competition promoter to pay the balance of the cost of the prize to the tour operator so that it can make the appropriate refund to the prizewinner? The prize offered was a holiday, with a "no cash alternative" rule applying to the competition. If the prizewinner does not want to take the holiday, he cannot ask for a cash alternative. To force the refund procedure in this artificial way would only be an extreme means of the winner getting the cash alternative. Such a claim against the promoter would not succeed under the competition rules.

No cash alternative to prize

Must accept prize

4.59.1 One of the competition rules should be that there is no cash alternative to any of the prizes. The prize is awarded in accordance with the competition rules, and what the prizewinner does with it after he receives it is his concern. If the prize is something which is not a permanent physical acquisition, such as a holiday, it is taken by the prizewinner, or by someone nominated by him, or it is wasted. If the nominee pays the winner something for the holiday transfer, that is not an infringement of the "no cash value" rule.

165

Prize cash value

4.59.2   If the prize is something physical and permanent, such as a car, then once it has been delivered to the prizewinner he is free to keep it or to do a deal on it with the original supplier, or he can simply sell the car to a third party for cash.

TEMPORARY USE PRIZES

No residual cash value

4.60.1   There are competitions which have as the first prize the temporary use of something. Where the competition has been run by a local motor car distributor, the prize may be "free use" of a fully taxed, insured and maintained motor car for twelve months. In those circumstances it will not be possible for the prizewinner to "sell" the benefit of the use of the car, and there will be restrictions on who he can allow to use the car for that period. The prize has no cash value to the winner other than the cash saved by not having to pay for what is provided as the prize.

Special rules

4.60.2   There should also be a comprehensive set of special rules for this kind of competition to protect the promoter, and to specify any limitations upon what is meant by "free use", such as:

(a) Any "free insurance" which is provided with the use of the car may be conditional upon the prizewinner:
  (i)   being over 21 or 25 years of age;
  (ii) having had a clean full driving licence for not less than 5 years,
  (iii) completing the competition promoter's nominated insurance company proposal form and being an acceptable insurance risk at normal rates, and
  (iv) living at a permanent residential address.
(b) In what circumstances the competition promoter can cancel the prize and take back the car, such as where the prizewinner:
  (i)   crashes the car badly, or has more than (say) three minor accidents,
  (ii) is convicted of any serious driving offence or has any other material criminal conviction during the twelve month prize period,
  (iii) becomes uninsurable, or becomes insurable only with a high excess loading, or
  (iv) fails to comply with any material obligation contained in the agreement referred to in paragraph 4.60.3 below.

Written agreement

4.60.3 A condition of the prize being awarded should be a rule that the prizewinner will sign an agreement with the competition promoter which sets out the terms and conditions on which the prizewinner may retain and use the car during the twelve-month period. These conditions must be set out clearly within the rules, and would include stipulations that the prizewinner:

(a) be the only driver of the car, or have only his wife as a nominated driver. She would also have to comply with the insurance requirements;

(b) maintain the car in a clean and roadworthy condition, and have it serviced regularly and properly by the promoter;

(c) do nothing with the car which is illegal or dangerous or which may affect the validity of the insurance policy, or the rate of insurance premium which has been accepted for him;

(d) must not take the car abroad or part with it for any purpose;

(e) must not be convicted of any serious motoring offence during the period of hire; and

(f) must hold a valid full driving licence throughout the prize use period.

EXAMPLES OF OTHER PRIZES

A DAY AT THE RACES

What is a "free day"?

4.61.1 If the competition prize is a "free day for two at the races", what does the "free" cover? The same considerations have to be given to this style of promotion as apply to an "all expenses paid" holiday promotion. (See para. 4.55.1). Apart from the entry fee to the event, the possible costs which can be incurred by the lucky winner of the competition include travel to and from the racecourse, costs of meals, bets and any special enclosure costs.

What prizewinner pays for

4.61.2 The rules should state the costs which will be paid for by the competition promoter as part of the prize, so it is clear that the winner will have to pay for any other costs himself. As well as not misleading the prizewinner, and not misdescribing the true extent of the prize, it would be most embarrassing if the winner did not take enough money to enjoy the event properly, because he assumed reasonably from the terms of the promotion that he had little or nothing to pay for personally.

167

Special conditions of prize

4.61.3 If the first prize event, such as a VIP day out at the Henley Regatta, is one where the mode of dress is stipulated by the organisers as a condition of entry to the event or to special guest areas, the prizewinner should be notified of these conditions when he receives the event tickets. To be excluded from a special guest enclosure for not knowing that he had to comply with the conditions of dress would be embarrassing and would prevent him from carrying out his prize.

Transferability of prize

4.61.4 Any impersonal competition prize such as a holiday or a car (subject to paragraph 4.60) is transferable from the winner to any other person. Where the subject of the competition is the creation of an artistic work, and where the first prize is (say) a certificate of merit and a free art course at a local college, by their nature these prizes are personal and cannot be transferable. If there is no self-evident reason why transferability of the prize should be allowed, or if there are to be restrictions on the transfer, the rules should say so. If the prize is transferred by the winner so that someone who is not the declared winner of the competition comes forward to claim it, the promoter should satisfy itself that a transfer is acceptable under the promotion rules, and that the person who is claiming the prize has been authorised to do so by the winner.

FREE WEEKEND BREAK PRIZE

Emphasise prizewinner's costs

4.62.1 If there are any costs or responsibilities which may apply to a prizewinner, and of which he may not be aware at the time he won the prize because they were not stated in the competition details, they should be explained to him in the material which will be sent with the written confirmation of winning the prize. Even so, if the competition advertisement states or implies that these costs will not be for the prizewinner to pay, it will still be a misleading promotion. The promoter should ensure that Section 5.8 of the Code of Sales Promotion Practice is complied with.

Compulsory meal

4.62.2 This caveat will apply to "free weekend break" prizes which emphasise that the accommodation is free. This can be of a substantial value in a good hotel. The catch is that the offer of free accommodation will be based on the condition that one main meal each day has to be taken at the "free weekend" hotel by each of the people who are taking the break, and they will normally be subject to a minimum charge. These meals have to be paid for by the prizewinner in the absence of any "free weekend" promotion rule making the promoter responsible for paying for them. If the prizewinner has to pay for the meals, the weekend is not entirely free and so should be advertised as a "free accommodation" weekend break prize, with a prominent reference to the extra meal costs. There may be a commitment on the prizewinner plus guest to stay at the hotel for at least two nights as a condition of the accommodation being free, in which case two main meals have to be paid for by the winner and his guest during their stay. What must be made clear to the prizewinner is that the compulsory meal charge for each person has to be paid for whether or not the meal is taken.

TIME SHARE WEEK PRIZES

Prizewinner signs contract, not promoter

4.63.1 The first prize may be a free time share week in a block of apartments on the Spanish coast. As for a package holiday prize, the winner is treated contractually and for all other purposes as the purchaser of the time share week, although the competition promoter pays the bill. The winner signs all the relevant documentation with the time share company direct; this will include contracts for the purchase of the timeshare week in a specific apartment, and for payment of the appropriate proportion of its annual maintenance and management charge.

Winner's rights and obligations

4.63.2 Except where a time share company is running a competition to promote its own time share accommodation, there is no connection between the promoter of the competition and the time share premises' owner. The initial "purchase price" which is set out in the time share purchase and maintenance contracts is paid directly to the time share company by the competition promoter on behalf of the prizewinner. The following points must be set out in the competition prize description which is sent to the winner, so that he is under no illusions as to his future rights and obligations in relation to the time share company and the time share premises. Once all the agreements have been signed by the prizewinner, they will be legally binding on him subject to any legislation which allows cancellation during a compulsory cooling off period.

No representations as to prize by promoter

4.63.3 The competition promoter should state clearly in the follow-up material (if such is the case) that it does not represent to the winner that it:

(a) recommends or has investigated the time share company;

(b) has examined or surveyed the time share property to verify its existence and to check its stage of construction and repair; or

(c) has taken any English or Spanish legal advice in respect of the legality or commercial fairness or security of the contractual arrangements to be entered into by the prizewinner with the time share company. However, before putting the time share week up for the main prize, the competition promoter should take reasonable precautions to satisfy itself the prize and the timeshare company are not likely to give the prizewinner or the promoter an immediate good cause for complaint.

Prizewinner is ordinary purchaser

4.63.5 The prizewinner will be taking the same risks, and will be accepting the same liabilities in respect of the time share deal, as any other purchaser in normal circumstances of a time share week at those premises from that company. The only difference is that the prizewinner will not have paid the initial purchase price for the time share week, and so that is one less risk of loss he has should the exercise turn out to be a disaster.

Take legal advice

4.63.6 The prizewinner should be strongly recommended within the competition follow-up documentation to take independent expert legal and financial advice on the arrangement, and the timeshare documentation, although he is getting it free as the competition prize. This advice should be sought before he signs any commitment to the timeshare company, and should concentrate on the law and property practices of the country where the time share property is. If the property is in Spain and the contracts are made with an English or tax haven country company, then the advice should cover both jurisdictions. Unless the competition rules state otherwise, this would be at his own expense. If the prizewinner is advised that the potential liabilities which he may have in the future as the owner of a time share week in that block of apartments are likely to incur risks, or if he does not want to risk having uncertain future financial obligations to the time share company it may be safer for him not to accept the prize. The time share company may have instigated the competition in the first place, as a means of promoting a time share scheme which is new, or which the company is having difficulty in selling; in which case, the prizewinner should be even more cautious about accepting it.

Time share "come-on" prizes

4.63.7 A common cause for complaint by the public is that some timeshare promoters or owners direct mail consumers with advertisements for time share properties which are invitations to attend a demonstration, and which give the impression that the recipient has "won" a valuable prize, which can be collected merely by attending the sales pitch. To some consumers this sounds too good to be true and usually that impression is correct. All too often the advertisement/invitation is wholly misleading, as any "prize" is likely to be of minimal value unless the consumer signs a purchase order for a time share property.

5 Consumer Product Advertising

ADVERTISING AND THE LAW

LEGAL REQUIREMENTS

All advertising is affected

5.1.1 Advertising, whether it is printed or broadcast, is affected by some legal right or constraint. All advertising is subject to the law from its inception to its ultimate conclusion, and those who produce and disseminate any advertising material are equally subject to the law. Advertising covers a wide range of prime and support activities, and it is used universally to promote consumer products. Sometimes the finer points of the applicable law can easily be forgotten, or they can be adapted as far as possible within the current interpretation of the law to get provocative or exciting advertising before the public. But this does not mean that the strict legal requirements can be overlooked safely.

Origin of advertising material

5.1.2 Everything which is used in advertisements is either created specifically for that purpose as original copyright material, or the advertisement uses existing material the rights in which will either be owned by somebody, or in the public domain. The application of the law to an advertisement depends upon its contents, and in this connection four questions need to be asked:

(a) Does the advertisement fail to comply with a specific legal requirement?
(b) Is the advertisement misleading?
(c) Is it in accordance with the ASA Code of Advertising Practice and any other applicable Code?
(d) What intellectual property rights does it contain, and has their use been authorised?

Approach to advertising

5.1.3 This chapter does not explain how to create advertising or how to use it effectively as a marketing tool. In non-technical language and based upon working examples, it explains the main principles of what can and cannot be done within the legal framework in the creation and use of material for advertisements. Finding out what the law says is not difficult; recognising when there may be a legal problem in the structure or content of a proposed advertisement, and dealing with it accordingly, is much more difficult.

Understanding advertising

5.1.4   To explain how the law applies to advertising, there must first be a brief explanation of what advertising is, and how it relates to intellectual property, promotions and to brand names. It sets the background to an understanding of which legal principles apply, what they mean and what effect they have on the freedom of expression which is allowed in advertising material.

WHAT IS ADVERTISING?

DEFINITION OF ADVERTISING

Passive promotion

5.2.1   Advertising is a passive form of promoting products, whether it is through printed material, TV, radio, posters, leaflets or by any other audio or visual means. The practical difference between media advertising and promotions is that a promotion is an on-pack, point of sale or other form of advertisement which is also an active product purchase incentive; whereas media advertising only appeals to the senses and thus develops product awareness. It does not provide an immediate opportunity for any purchase of the product, or for participation in any promotion which is attached to or associated with that product.

Promotions are advertising

5.2.2   Technically an on-pack promotion is also an advertisement for the product, and for the competition or the redemption gift which is the promotion benefit. Therefore it is subject to the legal restraints on misleading advertisements, and the use of intellectual property. As the on-pack advertising is taking place at the point of sale, the consumer can immediately purchase the product in response to that advertisement, so that he can participate in the promotion which is being advertised.

Advertising a corporate identity

5.2.3   Advertising is also widely applied to the publicising of a manufacturer's or a distributor's corporate identity. When a major food chainstore pays for a full-page-spread national newspaper advertisement which shows what prices it charges for baked beans or other ordinary commodities, it is not just advertising the fact that baked beans can be bought there economically; it is suggesting that the advertised chainstore is the best place to buy them.

Advertising brand names

5.2.4   Brand names, logos and packaging for products are specialised forms of advertising, as they are all intended to identify and promote visually and commercially the products with which they are associated. In this chapter all references to advertising, the rules applicable to advertisements, and what may or may not be legally permissible for advertisements, relate only to advertising for consumer goods and services, and for a manufacturer's corporate image. For convenience all references are only to goods, unless something special relates to services, as they will be broadly similar.

Slogans are advertisements

5.2.5   A successful advertisement is one which sticks in the consumer's memory, so that the sight or sound of a feature of the advertisement immediately brings the whole of it, and the brand name of the advertised product, to the consumer's mind. One of the most elementary human learning processes is the repetition of a catchy phrase or keyword in association with what is to be remembered. This process is used with great success in relation to slogans which are created to advertise products.

Musical link

5.2.6   A clever or funny slogan, particularly if it is supported in TV advertisements by a catchy musical jingle, can outlast in recollection terms the publication of the advertisement which made that slogan famous. The catchy tune of "A million housewives every day pick up a tin of beans and say . . .", or even just the first five words, immediately brings the complete jingle to the mind of anyone who has seen that advertisement. Slogans are useful as a foundation to enable different advertising campaigns for the same product to be complementary, as the development of a successful slogan has an already inbuilt sense of recognition and familiarity with the product.

DISTINCTIONS BETWEEN ADVERTISING AND PROMOTIONS

Different functions

5.3.1   While media advertising and promotions are complementary as instruments for the publicity and promotion of products, their functions are entirely different. Experience shows that a product for which there is no promotion or advertising to the public at all will not sell as well as it might do if it is heavily promoted and advertised. However, it can be difficult to establish a precise relationship between the different kinds of marketing of a product and any influence over its sales figures which is produced by a specific promotion or advertisement.

Long-term effect of advertising

5.3.2 Media advertising is a reminder and an unconscious trigger to buyers that the product exists, that it has excellent qualities, and that it is widely available. To respond to an advertisement, a buyer has to find an outlet which sells the product and then he has consciously to pick it off the shelf and pay for it.

Marketable advertising

5.3.3 If the advertising agency can create advertising for a product which becomes a cult of humour or sophistication so that it can be transformed into a marketable feature in its own right, then the additional promotional possibilities for the associated product are extensive. These will include the production and sale of posters and other suitable forms of merchandise using the marketable advertising, so that the "hallmark" of the central theme of the advertising becomes the source of a mini-industry. This supplementary advertising format benefits the advertised product, because it is getting free additional advertising through a new and cost effective medium which is developed by other parties. Promotions do not generate such possibilities, because the useful commercial life of a promotion is limited to the short term availability of the special promotion package of the product.

STRUCTURE OF ADVERTISEMENTS

Creative assembly

5.4.1 Advertising does not have a formal structure in the same way that a promotion may be structured as a coupon promotion or a competition, with the recognised ways of designing them. Neither does advertising have any other recognisable means of highlighting a product at the point of sale except for limited in-store advertising and the design of the product pack itself. The different media for which advertisements are created need different skills for their conception, design and production. They also use different proprietary rights, or similar proprietary rights are used in a different manner. The specific advertisement determines what rights are used in it, and those rights determine what consents are needed from their proprietors. The impression and presentation of advertisements for the product will be different for printed or televised media. Advertising can be categorised by styles rather than by structures, but the legal regulations and Code of Practice refer only to the specific contents of the advertisement and to the visual and mental impression it gives to the public.

Association with the product

5.4.2   The presentation of an advertisement can be analogous to the specially designed promotional package of the product, for instance where it becomes inseparable from the brand of product which is associated with it. All advertising obviously relates to the product which is advertised, but some advertisements are transient while others can achieve a hallmark status. When a memorable style of advertising is developed for the product on a long-term basis its recognition factor can be so strong and permanent that it can become a form of brand identity.

ADVERTISING AGENCY AND CLIENT RELATIONSHIP

AGENCY OBLIGATIONS TO CLIENT

Media exposure for products

5.5.1   The client of an advertising agency will be a company or a business which is the manufacturer or importer of products, or which is the provider of services. Agencies use their specialist skills, experience and contacts to advise the client upon its media advertising and related marketing strategy. They will also design advertising material, plan advertising campaigns and book media space for those advertisements, as well as providing many other support activities.

Agency responsibilities to client

5.5.2   There should always be a written contract between the agency and the client, which must deal with the following matters:

(a) the brands of the client's product which will be within the brief of the agency;
(b) the areas of advertising which will be covered by the agency, such as TV, press, billboards, or whatever else the client uses for advertising;
(c) the agency contract period, and the notice periods each should give to the other to terminate the contract;
(d) the rights of the client to use after the agency contract termination any advertising which was produced by the agency during the contract period, and what payments the agency should get from such use;

(e) the assignment to the client of the copyright in any original material which is commissioned for advertisements, whether that is produced by the agency or by an independent contractor;

(f) the physical ownership of original artwork created by or for the agency;

(g) the procedures for concept origination, development, approval and signing-off final artwork as ready to use,

(h) the agency fee basis, such as for:
   (i) project work which may not proceed beyond an early stage,
   (ii) production costs which are incurred internally by the agency,
   (iii) third-party contracted services.
   (iv) media booking, with specific references to the discounts available from rate card charges,
   (v) ordinary agency support service expenses,
   (vi) extraordinary expenses.
   (vii) accounting and payment procedures.

(i) who will be responsible for finding out what third-party consents are required for the use of proprietary material, and for obtaining them;

(j) the agency's responsibility for providing legal and non-infringing advertisements, including obtaining legal clearance of all advertising material, and ensuring compliance with the ASA Code of Advertising Practice. The client may want the concepts and copy of new advertisements to be checked by its own legal advisers, but that should only be a backstop precaution.

Agency's terms of business

5.5.3 All agencies have their own standard terms of doing business, but they will not all be the same, and they may not all be wholly acceptable to a major client. Standard contracts are not sacrosanct, and they are all subject to negotiation where the client requires different terms. For example the client may want a "key man" clause to identify who will be responsible for the account, and a responsive agency will not be unreasonable over the individual requirements of a significant client in a very competitive industry.

Agency acts as a principal

5.5.4 The agency is not an agency in the accepted legal sense; it is not the appointed representative of the client in the manner of a "go between". The agency in an independent contractor, which operates as a principal in its own right in its dealings with the client and with all third parties which provide facilities or services to the client through the agency. The client is not directly contracted to any such third party, and the client is not responsible for any of the obligations of the agency to third parties. The agency does not contract with third parties on behalf of the client. The agency is wholly responsible to each of them independently for the performance of obligations and for the payment of money which becomes due under their respective contracts.

Who owns agency-originated material?

5.5.5 Where the ownership of copyright is an issue for artwork, TV film or any other original material which is created "in-house" by the agency for the client's advertising, it will be owned initially by the agency and not by the client. Section 11(2) of the Copyright, Designs and Patents Act 1988 (employers owning the copyright in their employees' original work) does not apply as between the agency and the client. The agency contract normally commits it to assigning the copyright in any advertising material to the client when the work for that advertisement has been completed and all payments due to the agency for the production of that advertisement have been made. In the case of jingles or music for TV advertisements, the composer (or the jingle company) will insist on retaining the copyright in the music, and will only grant a licence to the client through the agency for the limited use of the music in the soundtrack of that advertisement. With that one exception, the agency should always ensure that the copyright in material produced for the client by sub-contractors of the agency will be assignable to the client without any further charge when all the appropriate fees have been paid to the subcontractor.

Agency's responsibility

5.5.6 The agency designs and puts the advertisement together, and under the terms of its contract with the client the agency should be responsible for ensuring that nothing in the advertisement will infringe the proprietary rights of any third party. The only exception to that responsibility will be in respect of any material which is provided to the agency by the client advertiser, in which case the client takes on the responsibility for any infringement if it has not obtained the necessary intellectual property clearance for the use of that material in the advertisement. Any legal actions will be brought by the proprietors of infringed material against the advertiser (the client), and not the agency even if the infringing material was provided by the agency. That is because it is the advertiser who has published or used commercially the infringing material.

Advertising agency indemnity

5.5.7 The primary legal liability of the client advertiser for copyright or other intellectual property infringement which is caused by the publication of its advertisement cannot be removed or assigned by the advertiser to the agency through the agency's contractual responsibilities to provide the client with non-infringing material. Any such infringement is an absolute legal responsibility of the advertiser, the adverse consequences of which should be covered by an indemnity from the agency to the advertiser in the agency agreement. Under the indemnity the agency should agree to reimburse the advertiser for the whole of the monetary loss or damage (including legal costs) which it may suffer as a direct result of any intellectual property infringement or defamation in an advertisement for which the agency is responsible. (See paragraphs 5.38.5 and 5.38.6). Agencies will never extend the scope of their indemnity to indirect consequential loss, or loss of profits by the advertiser. For example, the consequences to the advertiser of a successful intellectual property infringement action against it could include:

(a) the payment of damages to the plaintiff;
(b) the payment of the plaintiff's legal costs;
(c) the wasted cost element of any advertising which has been withdrawn, either voluntarily or under an injunction;
(d) any media cancellation costs caused by withdrawing that advertisement; and
(e) the cost of re-creating similar advertising which is not infringing.

Even if the agency agreement contains no indemnity of the advertiser for the consequences of intellectual property infringements in advertising produced wholly by the agency, the advertiser will still have a right to claim against the agency for damages and compensation. As the agency is acting as a principal, and is therefore responsible for its own actions, in the absence of any contractual release or waiver from the advertiser in the agency agreement there will be an implied responsibility upon the agency for the consequences of it being negligent or in breach of contract in providing infringing advertising to its advertiser client.

Legal clearance

5.5.8   Agency agreements always contain a condition that the client has the ultimate responsibility for "approving" the advertising copy. The condition may not define what that approval represents, such as whether it merely refers to the concept and final artwork or whether it is deemed to include the responsibility for legal and Code of Practice clearance. Both the agency and the client should ensure that their respective contractual responsibilities are made absolutely clear. From the client's point of view, the agency should be responsible for legal clearance, as through experience it is in a better position than the client to know the legal requirements for the kind of material used in the advertising campaign. In any event the agency must accept legal responsibility for material it provides to the advertiser. The client may still withhold approval on legal grounds if it is advised accordingly.

CREATIVE ASPECTS OF ADVERTISING

CONCEPT AND FORM

Expression of creativity

5.6.1 The contents of advertisements are creative and original, including a substantive and original arrangement or display of material which may itself be in the public domain. That arrangement is an original work, and will have a copyright of its own if it has been achieved through the use of skill in creating a sufficiently original and distinctive layout. The same will apply to an original arrangement of a number of copyright works, such as a photographic montage. In the creation of an advertisement there are two basic elements:

(a) The first element is the concept or the idea upon which the advertisement is based, being the design of its layout, and the idea which the advertisement is intended to convey.
(b) The second element is the permanent form in which that idea is expressed.

COPYRIGHT IN ADVERTISING CONCEPTS

Ownership of concepts

5.7.1 There is no copyright in a new advertising concept otherwise than in the permanent form in which it is presented, such as an artistic work. If any form of "ownership" of an original concept as between an agency and its client is going to be recognised, that is a matter of contract. A concept is a moving target, as it is the idea at any time which is represented by the then current version of the artwork. When trying to identify "who owns what" in relation to the concept, such as at the termination of the agency contract, it is important to establish whether the concept originates from the agency or from the client. The concept may be a one-off original idea, or it may be yet another variation or extension of a series of linked advertisements which are based loosely on the same concept.

Competing use of concept

5.7.2 On termination of the agency contract, an acceptance by the agency that the client "owns" the advertising concept which is original or which is distinctive to the client, should be supported by an undertaking from the agency not to use a confusingly similar concept unless it becomes "flavour of the month" style by being used by other agencies as the basis of their own clients' advertising. The undertaking could be linked to a confidentiality commitment by the agency, to prevent a novel advertising concept from becoming public knowledge, and so losing its impact before the publication of the client's advertising based upon it.

Agency transfer of concept

5.7.3   Where it is practical to do so upon its termination, the agreement between the client and the agency should deal with the transfer to the client of new or developed concepts for the client's advertising, including the copyright in any early stage artwork. It is possible that at the termination date of the agency agreement there will be at least one advertising project which is being formulated by the agency for the client, and which is still at the concept stage. There may be nothing special about the concept, but the client does not want any interruption in its advertising production schedule, and the agency wants some recompense for its time, effort and creativity. The client should have the option, upon agreed terms of payment for work done, and possibly for a split of future agency commission, to take an unusual concept at its then design stage with it to another agency, so that the project can be completed. Whether a split of agency commission is justified will depend on the extent of the original agency's creative input to the final version of the advertisement.

Rights in storyboard

5.7.4   The storyboard, which illustrates the use of the concept within the proposed advertisement design, will have copyright protection for the illustrations as artistic works. However that would not protect the concept from being illustrated in a wholly different and original manner by a third party. Therefore the transfer of any current advertising project to the new agency, or to the client, must include an assignment in writing of the copyright in the storyboard and in any other text or material which has already been produced by the agency in connection with that project. If any artwork for the storyboard has been commissioned by the agency from an independent contractor, the agency will have to obtain an assignment in writing to the advertiser of any copyright owned by the contractor in the storyboard.

IMAGINATION VERSUS TECHNOLOGY

Protecting the creative element

5.8   Creating artwork or taking a photograph or making a film is a process which can be undertaken by most people who have the technical ability and who are trained to do so. However, thinking of *what* to paint or *what* to photograph, and *how* to present it as a promotional concept, is inspirational rather than mechanical. If it could be said that the creativity of an ingenious and attractive advertisement can be apportioned as to eighty per cent. for the inspiration which was behind the original concept and twenty per cent. for transforming that concept into a memorable visual form, it is no wonder that a frequent question is whether the inspirational value and effort behind an original concept can be protected from copycat third-party use.

ADVERTISING AGENCY CHECKLIST

Reduces risk

5.9 Agencies should have an efficient standard checklist or other system to be followed when an advertising campaign is being originated for submission to the client. Once the advertising concept has been approved, and the artwork for it is going through the creative development stages, it is even more important to ensure that any possible risk elements in the style of advertising (such as passing-off) or the advertisement contents (such as a breach of copyright or trade mark infringement) are identified by using the checklist, so that they can be dealt with promptly. In all advertising design and preparation there has to be a balance between the need for caution, the creation of interesting advertising and completing the project within the time and cost constraints which normally apply.

ASSESSING PROPRIETARY RIGHTS

Basic checklist headings

5.10 (1) Is it a press advertisement and if so is it to be used to support a TV campaign, or is it to be a TV or a radio advertisement?
   (2) Is the advertising to be related to a current on-pack promotion, or will it be limited to other forms of advertising, such as billboards and posters?
   (3) Who will do the voice-over? What are his contractual terms?
   (4) Will the advertisement contain featured performers, not being endorsing personalities? If so, the rights and obligations of the advertiser in respect of those performers must be properly documented.
   (5) Endorsing personalities must negotiate an agreement with the advertiser.
   (6) If the advertisement contains third-party trademarks or copyright material, written consents to use them must be obtained. The third-party rights must be identified, the rights' owners must be found, and correctly worded consents for use must be obtained in writing. The consent must specifically cover all intended uses of the rights and the period of use.
   (7) Background music should be properly licensed (for existing music) or contracted from a jingle company (if original music is to be commissioned).
   (8) "Copycat", comparative advertising or spoof (similarity advertising) should be legally checked for passing off or for any form of trade defamation. (See paragraph 5.68 onwards.) If any such advertising may be used outside the U.K. it should be cleared separately for such use.

(9) Are there any potential breaches of the ASA Code of Advertising Practice?
(10) Can any part of the advertisement be interpreted as being misleading?
(11) If the advertisement is to be based upon an adaptation or modification of a copyright work, check the position of moral rights of the original author or artist.
(12) Check the source and veracity of all facts which are stated in the advertisement, as well as the context in which they are placed, to ensure that they are not misleading. Also check that all opinions which are stated are reasonably based, and that they can be substantiated. In each case the agency should keep a file of the authoritative source material from which any statement of fact or of opinion has been taken. Check that the overall impression given by the complete final version of the advertisement is accurate, and that there is nothing which prompts a query even at that stage.

COPYRIGHT AND ADVERTISING

INTRODUCTION

Underlying proprietary right

5.11.1 The main proprietary right which is relevant to the creation and protection of advertisements in all media is copyright. If the artwork or the photography for an advertisement is an original modern work, then its permanent visual form is protected by copyright. If an advertisement contains any infringing material, it will normally relate to the copyright, the brand name or to trade marks which belong to a third party. Trade marks are dealt with in Chapter 7, paragraph 7.18 onwards.

Passing-off

5.11.2 The common law action of "passing-off" can also apply to advertisements which make misleading statements or implications relating to the identity or origin of the advertised product, and which cause a wrongful misappropriation of the goodwill and reputation of another product, and which cause damage to its manufacturer. It is possible for an advertisement to contain an infringement of copyright and for it to be at the same time a "passing-off" off a third party product. Passing-off is dealt with in Chapter 7, paragraph 7.30 onwards.

Relevance of copyright

5.11.3 To understand why copyright is such an important element of advertisements, and how it affects and protects the original material which is created by artists, scriptwriters, photographers, film producers, and any others who are actively involved in producing advertising material, it is necessary to analyse what can go into the production of an advertisement. When considering an advertisement to see whether there are any legal, proprietary or Advertising Code of Practice points to deal with, all the components of the advertisement have to be identified. The main concern is to establish whether any third-party consents are necessary for the use of intellectual property, and from whom such consents have to be obtained.

Print media references

5.11.4 Except where it is otherwise stated, for convenience the references to advertisements in this section refer to those in the printed media. The making of TV advertisements, and the rights relating to their contents, have a similar basic foundation, but where they have other features which are pertinent to film and music rather than to print, these will be referred to as they arise.

U.K. COPYRIGHT LEGISLATION

References limited to advertising

5.12.1 The Copyright, Designs and Patents Act 1988 (the Act) contains the current U.K. copyright legislation. This chapter deals only with the copyright aspects of advertising material, which will cover printed, filmed or recorded material as well as musical works which are contained in a TV advertisement sound track. Appendix 4 contains those sections of the Act which are pertinent to this chapter.

Simplified Act reference

5.12.2 For convenience, explanations in this chapter of the relevant sections of the Act have been simplified, paraphrased or abridged so as to exclude references to matters which are unrelated to the advertising industry.

WHAT IS PROTECTED BY COPYRIGHT

Original works

5.13.1 Under section 1(1) of the Act copyright will subsist in original literary, musical or artistic works, sound recordings and films. By section 3(1) of the Act a literary work will include any work which is written, spoken or sung. Section 3(2) states that copyright does not subsist in a literary or musical work unless and until it is recorded in writing or otherwise, and that such a work is "made" when it is so recorded. The relevance of section 3(2) is that:

(a) A concept is not protected by copyright insofar as it is an idea which is not expressed in a permanent form.
(b) When a concept is expressed in a permanent form, it is only protected by copyright in that specific form.
(c) Therefore it is possible for a concept to be expressed in a permanent form in any number of different ways, each of which is capable of having its own copyright if it originated independently of any other, so there is no question of copying. In copyright terms an agency or a client cannot make a concept or an idea exclusive to itself in copyright terms simply by producing it, or an explanation of it, in a permanent form.
(d) It is important to produce the advertisement artwork of a concept at an early stage to settle its copyright.
(e) Each developed but significantly different stage of artwork will have its own copyright, although it is based on the previous version. Therefore an assignment to the agency of the copyright in the work of an independent contractor which is done for the agency must be worded to include specifically *all* original artwork, irrespective of its relevance to the final version which is published as the advertisement.

Slogans and titles

5.13.2   The Act does not define precisely what is deemed to constitute a literary work, for instance, it does not say it must have a minimum number of words. It has been judicially decided that just one or a very few words, such as a song title, book title or an advertising slogan, although they convey a message, are not sufficiently substantial to be deemed to be a literary work, so they are not protected by copyright (See the case of *Exxon Corporation* v. *Exxon Insurance Consultants International* [1982] Ch. 119, C.A.). Where it is applicable, a title or a slogan can be protected by an action for passing off, or as a trademark where it is associated with the product in a trademark sense.

Artistic works

5.13.3   By section 4(1) of the Act an artistic work includes an original graphic work, photograph, sculpture or collage, irrespective of its artistic quality. "Artistic quality" means the aesthetic sense of the work. Whether or not it is appreciated by its viewers as being good, bad or indifferent from a visual or artistic point of view, if it is an original work of sufficient substance, it will be protected by copyright. It does not have to be a particular size, or have a minimum amount of "work" done on it to be an artistic work. An artistic work will include a design logo, even though the artistic element may incorporate the brand name of a product in a stylised manner. A logo may be protected both by copyright and as a trade mark if it complies with their relevant criteria.

No "substance" test

5.13.4 Section 4(1) of the Act does not refer to an artistic work as having to be of "sufficient substance". Therefore even a simple original work which has some degree of skill and labour will be protected by copyright. The question may arise where an agency produces for a printed advertisement graphics of a very simple nature which may resemble a portion of some modern "art" where merit (and copyright) is claimed by the artist, such as for a basic and unexciting compilation of geometrical shapes or patterns. A resemblance and a copy are not the same thing. The artist does not get any exclusivity over the artistic reproduction of geometrical shapes just by painting a picture based upon them.

What is artistic?

5.13.5 The definition in section 4(1) of the Act explains what can be an artistic work, and in this respect:

(a) a graphic work includes any painting, drawing, diagram, map, chart or plan. If the graphic work, such as an advertisement, also includes a substantial amount of text, the words and the graphics will each have separate copyrights, and the whole combined picture will also be a single artistic copyright work. If the text consists of words which are not all associated with each other to form a complete work, each phrase on its own will not individually have copyright protection;

(b) a photograph means a recording of light or other radiation on any medium on which an image is produced, or from which an image may be produced by any means, and which is not part of a film. A photograph of a photograph with nothing else in sight will not have a separate copyright, as that would have no more effect than taking another print from the negative or the original photograph, or making a facsimile copy of it. This prevents the possibility of a perpetual copyright being created in the original photograph;

(c) there is no copyright in a "style" of painting or of photography, no matter how original and distinctive that style may be. The use of a copy-cat style could amount to a passing off of the original style if the criteria for a passing off legal action are met. (See Chapter 7, paragraph 7.30 onwards);

APPLICATION OF COPYRIGHT

Automatic copyright protection

5.14.1 Copyright in the U.K. attaches to each literary, musical and artistic work as it is created; it is an automatic process which does not need any formal registration or notification—in fact there is no mechanism for doing so in the U.K. There are Copyright Conventions (such as the Universal Copyright Convention and the Berne Convention) which give reciprocal copyright protection between member states for their citizens' copyright works. Therefore the fact that the work or photograph was not produced in the U.K. does not make it a candidate for unauthorised reproduction.

First copyright date

5.14.2   The common question is "How can I prove the priority date when my recording or painting came into existence if I cannot register it with some authority?" Where there is a potential breach of copyright claim it will be essential to be able to prove whose version existed first, as whoever created their version first could not have copied the other one. Evidence will have to be provided to show when it was created, but as any artistic project evolves over a period of time, the precise start date can be difficult to prove if none of the originating material has been retained.

COPYRIGHT IN "COMPILATION" ADVERTISEMENTS

Composite advertisements

5.15.1   Any substantive element or a composite part of an advertisement which makes artistic sense in its own right will have copyright protection provided that it is original. An advertisement may include something which is in the public domain without adversely affecting its overall copyright protection. For example, a printed advertisement which is based upon nostalgia may contain as only an incidental part of it an old, out of copyright photograph. The advertisement as a whole, being a combination of all of its original and public domain features is still copyright, despite the inclusion of the public domain photograph. This does not operate to recreate copyright in the old photograph itself. If the public domain photograph is the sole or main feature of the advertisement, that does not entitle any other party to reproduce that advertisement, but they could reproduce the original public domain photograph if they had access to it.

Different sources of material

5.15.2   A printed advertisement may be a compilation of a variety of copyright items, and each of those items may have a different copyright owner. For example, an existing original painting, the copyright of which is owned by the artist, may be used as the main feature of an advertisement. With the consent of the artist the painting may be photographed for use in the advertisement by an independent photographer who will own the copyright in his photograph. The first few words of a popular song may be reproduced in the advertisement as the "message" and a "glowing praise" extract from a published independent review of the advertised product may also be included.

Compilation is an independent work

5.15.3   Provided that the inclusion of all the copyright items is authorised, the whole graphic display of the advertisement itself is an independent copyright work, as it is an original and skilful arrangement of all of the contents. This separate copyright for the whole advertisement exists despite the fact that several existing copyrights are contained within it, as the artistic arrangement of all of them in the advertisement creates a new work in its own right. The overall copyright in the advertisement does not give the agency or the advertiser any individual copyright claim over the separate elements which are already copyright. Nor does the inclusion of that copyright work in the compilation advertisement give the advertiser any right to use the included work in any other way.

Another example of an independent work occurs where the representation of a country scene is the whole of an ecologically based advertisement. The painting or the photograph depicting the scene which constitutes the advertisement is itself copyright. Therefore the advertisement cannot be reproduced without the copyright owner's consent, even though precisely the same presentation could be created by any other person taking a photograph of that scene, or painting it, while standing at the same spot at the same time of day and in the same weather conditions. If he did so, his original work would have its own copyright which would not infringe that of the first work, although it could be virtually identical with it.

WHAT IS AN ORIGINAL WORK?

Preliminary stages

5.16.1   In accordance with the Act, the work must be original to obtain copyright protection, the "work" being the end result of the efforts of the creator, such as a photograph or artwork. The advertisement is all that is seen by the public, but copyright will also subsist in all of the preliminary sketches for the graphic artwork of the advertisement. For copyright purposes each sketch is an original work in its own right, independently of any previous version or the final version of the artwork.

Effort and skill

5.16.2   The word "original" is not defined in the Act and so will have its ordinary meaning, which is not being a copy of something which already exists. That is only one of the meanings of "original", because a photograph of something which already exists has copyright protection although in a sense it is a copy of what has been photographed. Originality is derived from the exercise of skill and effort in producing the copyright work. "Original" can also be used as a description of the distinctive layout, design or concept of an advertisement, in the sense of being new and different.

Originality of related works

5.16.3   Another example is a page of strip cartoons which tell a complete story in pictures. Each individual frame will have been drawn from scratch as an original work, although it has considerable similarities to the previous frame and to the subsequent frame in the series. Each frame will have a copyright protection of its own, as well as being part of the overall copyright of the complete page of the cartoon strip.

USE OF PUBLIC DOMAIN MATERIAL

Copyright version

5.17.1   The use in an advertisement of a new photograph of a public domain work, such as an old master painting, will not recreate copyright protection for that old master, although the photograph itself will enjoy copyright. An original creation in oils or watercolours of a public domain familiar painting "in the style of" the old master will have copyright protection. It is an original work of the artist which required skill and effort, although the painting is based on a public domain subject. Taking a photograph of that new painting without the consent of the copyright owner will be a copyright infringement, even though photographing the old master will not. An authorised photograph of the new painting will also have a copyright of its own as a photograph, although it reproduces the copyright painting.

Protectable compilation

5.17.2   Any form of original compilation of public domain information which is contained in an advertisement will be protected by copyright, where there has been some skill and effort in selecting it and putting it together. Therefore an advertisement for a railway or cross-channel ferry company which consists substantially of its timetable will have copyright protection, as the assembly of that information has required some original effort, although it is not what is generally recognised as creative skill.

Nostalgic artwork

5.17.3   If classic advertising of the past is to be used it is essential for the agency to confirm that any copyright in it has expired. If that is the case it will be safe to use. What is the position if the new advertisement, being a poster which reproduces wholly and only the public domain work, is itself reproduced by a third party for commercial sale? Is there a copyright infringement? Infringement will only happen if the copied advertisement itself had an independent copyright. An advertisement which is a copy of a public domain work reproduced by a fax machine with no added new material will not have a copyright just because the reproduction advertisement has been created through the use of new technology, as no skill or effort has been applied to make it an original work. Therefore the advertisement which is produced in that way is not protected by copyright, and the poster company is not infringing any rights in the advertisement with the posters. This is not the same as having copyright in a new and original edition of a public domain work, such as where a public domain book has been re-set as a different edition. But if it can be shown that the advertisement reproduction of the public domain work incurred recognisable skill or effort, such as by using photography with colour enhancement, the photographic advertisement would be protected as an original work, and the poster produced from it would infringe its copyright. Again, a similar but independent production of the original work would not infringe that photographer's copyright.

MULTI-COPYRIGHT ADVERTISEMENTS

Print media

5.18   Advertisers want to take advantage of any legal means of using third party material in their advertisements. Identifying the relevant rights and their owners may be difficult. Examples of areas of concern are:

(a) The advertisement may contain the facsimile reproduction of part of a newspaper page, such as to illustrate a published comment on the advertised product, or as part of a comparative advertisement. The published comment is reproduced in the advertisement with jagged edges surrounding the included material, to indicate that it is an exact replication of the original page of the newspaper. The reproduced portion of the newspaper page may itself contain part of an original article, or a supplier's advertisement, which is clearly identifiable and readable. Each of these has a different copyright, and the supplier's advertisement may also contain its product's trademark. Depending on the substantiality of the reproduced third party items, and if no consents are obtained for such use, three proprietary rights may be infringed by the advertisement which contains the extract from the newspaper page: the copyright in the article, the copyright in the advertisement and the trademark.

(b) The advertisement may consist entirely of a collection of photographs which are used to compile a montage. If they are modern each of these photographs will have their own copyrights, even if they all come from a photo library. It is easier to get copyright clearance if they can all be approved by the same person or organisation. If there is any doubt as to their still being in copyright, an agency should always check the source of photographs for copyright clearance before using them.

BLUEPRINTS AND PLANS

5.19 The architect owns the copyright in his design of a new building through the copyright in his original drawings of that building. It is assumed that he has not assigned the copyright in the plans to the builder. Without the consent of that architect copyright owner, a substantial and instantly recognisable reproduction of that building design must not be used by a property developer in the construction of its houses. If the property developer issues an advertisement for its new estate project, depicting that architect's building design, then:

(a) under section 62(2) of the Act there will be no copyright infringement; but

(b) to build houses to that design would be a copyright infringement; and

(c) if that design will not be used for the buildings on the new estate, the advertisement will be misleading.

INDIVIDUAL COPYRIGHT OWNERS

Limited to their copyright

5.20.1 The advertisement as a whole, whether it consists of a single photograph, or whether it contains many third party copyrights all of which have been cleared for use, will have a copyright of its own. The advertisement cannot be reproduced without the consent of the overall copyright owner, and also without the consent of the copyright owner of each of the individual copyright contributions to the contents of the advertisement.

Individual promotional use

5.20.2 Where the advertisement is a montage of photographs, one of the individual copyright owners may be proud of his photograph being part of the advertisement, and he may want to reproduce the whole of the advertisement in his company's corporate brochure to demonstrate its commerciality. Any unauthorised reproduction of the whole advertisement by the owner of one of the copyright contributions would breach the advertiser's overall copyright in the advertisement, as well as the other copyrights which are also contained within the advertisement. There is nothing to prevent one of the copyright owners from using his own contributed photograph commercially in any other way, subject to any temporary restrictions or exclusivity he may have agreed with the advertiser to give the advertisement exclusive publication rights in the photograph for a period of time.

TELEVISION ADVERTISEMENTS

5.21 TV advertising provides as much scope for a multi-copyright production as printed media advertising does. In a TV advertisement the potential copyright or other proprietary rights clearances will be of:

(a) *The music* on the advertisement sound track. The copyright clearance from the music publisher should be an automatic part of the commissioning of new music directly from a composer. Where an original recording is to be used in the soundtrack the advertiser will need the written consent of the music publisher which owns the copyright in the music and of the record company which owns the copyright in the recording. The separate consent of the recording artist is not required.

(b) *The "voice-over"* which is used to extol the virtues of the product which is being advertised. There is no copyright in a voice as such, but the voice-over actor is providing a performance, the recording and commercial use of which needs his written consent. There is a different problem altogether where the voice-over is instantly recognisable as being that of a well known personality, but in fact it is an imitator's voice. (See Chapter 6, paragraph 6.33 onwards).

(c) *The personalities who are visually featured in the advertisement*, even though they may not have any speaking parts. Because they are contracted to be filmed in the advertisement they must sign a consent giving the agency and the advertiser the right to exploit that filming as an advertisement. If the advertisement film is to be used for any other purpose, such as featuring in an "out-takes" humorous programme for TV entertainment, the consent of its copyright owner will be needed. Whether the consent of the personalities in it will be required depends on the extent of, or the restriction placed upon their original consent to appear.

(d) *Any other trademark or copyright owner* whose products also feature in the advertisement.

THIRD-PARTY PROPRIETARY RIGHTS

REFLECTED USE OF OTHER PRODUCTS' REPUTATIONS

Pertinent attributes

5.22.1 There is an appeal in associating a product in its advertising material with the attributes of another product, to give the advertised product some reflected affinity with the image and reputation of the second product, such as its quality, speed or reliability. This is not the same as comparative advertising, and is not a form of endorsement of the advertised product by the associated product. It is a trademark infringement to use a "trademark feature" of a third-party product in a trademark sense in connection with advertising unrelated goods without its owner's authority. (Trademarks Act 1938, s.4).

Favourable comparison

5.22.2   In the "affinity" style of advertising the third party trademark is not being connected directly with the advertised product in the sense of leading viewers or readers of the advertisement to believe that the trademark relates to that product. The third-party trademark is being deliberately used to promote and advertise an unconnected product, and not the product with which it is associated and to which it belongs. It is not an acceptable response in law for the manufacturer of the advertised product to state that, as an incidental consequence of the unauthorised use of that trademark, the third party is getting valuable free advertising of its own products, and so should not complain about the featuring of its products in the advertisement.

TRADEMARK USE IN ADVERTISING

Example of use

5.23.1   So that the relevant points can be examined in detail, it is useful to follow a theoretical example. The example is that the agency wants to make prominent use of a full frontal shot of the radiator grille and the mascot of a Rolls Royce motor car which is parked outside Harrods of Knightsbridge as the main setting for the national printed media advertising for a new model of a trendy, but cheap cellular portable telephone. In the advertisement the telephone will be held by a voluptuous woman who is leaning against the radiator of the Rolls Royce car. The advertising will be repeated as a hoarding poster in choice locations.

Establish proprietary rights

5.23.2   The advertiser has no intention of making any direct comparisons between the advertised product and the car or Harrods because there is nothing comparable between them. Neither does the advertiser intend to give any impression that its products are in any way associated with either the Rolls Royce (such as being a standard in-car installation), or Harrods (such as being sold there). Use of those third party "products" is not intended to represent an endorsement or recommendation of the cellular telephone by either organisation. The agency which is creating the advertising must research thoroughly what proprietary rights are involved in the advertisement, and whose consents (if any) have to be obtained. This is in addition to establishing what legal requirements and what Code of Practice guidelines have to be complied with for that style of advertisement. The agency does not want the advertiser client to be sued or injuncted for infringing any third-party rights in the advertisement it is about to publish, particularly if the client has negotiated a suitable indemnity clause into its contract with the agency. The risks in this example are that:

(a) There will be an infringement of the Rolls Royce and Harrods trade marks.
(b) Either of them may claim an infringement of copyright in the artistic logo or representation which constitutes its trademark.
(c) They may each claim the equivalent of trade defamation of their respective businesses or products as a result of the titillating advertisement damaging their reputation and bringing them into disrepute, and implying a form of endorsement of the advertised product. Because of the prominence of the car and of the emporium in the advertisement, viewers might reasonably conclude that their proprietors had consented to participate in it.

Infringement is a matter of degree

5.23.3 Whether any proprietary rights may actually be infringed in this example will depend upon the extent to which the Rolls Royce car and Harrods are made deliberately prominent, and are obviously posed central features in the advertisement. There would have to be a significant image projection within the advertisement for there to be an infringement of their trademarks. This does not necessarily mean that they must have the same space allocation in the advertisement as the advertised product; it is more a question of the visual impression which is given to the viewer of the advertisement.

Incidental inclusion

5.23.4 The legal position will be different where the siting of the car and the shop front in relation to the display of the advertised product is incidental to the advertisement. The risk of infringement reduces as the inclusion becomes only an inconsequential background glimpse which has no impact on the visual message given out by the advertisement. In this case the lady and the phone will be nowhere near the Rolls Royce car or Harrods, and the model and telephone will be the only prominent features of the advertisement. In a clear case of an accidental inclusion, where the presence of the car and Harrods in the advertisement is so insignificant that they are only noticed if they are pointed out, there should be no infringement of their trademarks.

Trademark owner's consent

.5.23.5   Where the Rolls Royce radiator grille and the Harrods logo are prominent features of the advertisement, and where they are deliberately and artistically placed in the advertisement "frame" to maximise their reputation factor for the advertised product, the agency must obtain the consent of the trademark proprietors for such use to be made of their trademarks. The whole purpose of having the prominent Rolls Royce and the Harrods shop front in the advertisement is to associate their style, class and quality with the advertised product.

Risk of commercial association

5.23.6   If the advertisement which features the Rolls Royce car is for a motor vehicle component product, there is another risk of infringement of a proprietary right if the advertisement implies that the advertised product is actually associated with, or is being recommended by, the makers of Rolls Royce cars.

True advertising

5.23.7   Even if the advertisement is true, such as where the Rolls Royce car does indeed contain that specific component, the unauthorised commercial use of its trademark will still be an actionable infringement. To establish a trademark infringement in this context is not always easy, as there must be the freedom to refer to Rolls Royce motor cars in connection with motoring matters, *i.e.* not in a trademark sense, without the fear or threat of legal proceedings. If it is true, it would be legitimate for the manufacturer of the hypothetical Widget fuel injection systems to advertise ". . . Widget fuel injection systems are installed in . . ." followed by a list of makes of motor cars, using just their names, and not their logos. The simple-statement style of advertising, if properly drafted, will not be a trademark infringement. There *would* be an infringement if the logos of the car manufacturers are used, or if the names of the cars are set out in any trademark style of script or presentation. An example is the Ford name contained in its oval logo.

Consequence of infringement

5.23.8   If an infringement is proved, the plaintiff trademark proprietor can get an injunction against the infringer to prevent any further publication of its trademark or logo in the infringing advertising, and it may also get an award of damages. A successful plaintiff will also get repaid the costs of the legal action against the advertiser. Withdrawing an infringing advertisement and settling an unsuccessfully contested trademark infringement claim can be expensive.

196

USE OF THIRD-PARTY COPYRIGHT

Favourable editorials

5.24.1 Third-party copyright material which is useful for advertising a product includes a favourable independent review of the product in a trade magazine, or it could be an "advertorial" review. The latter is a commercial mix of blatant advertising and an apparently independent review of the product which is set out with a disguised editorial front. If it is an advertisement, however cleverly disguised, under Part B.11 of the ASA Code of Advertising Practice it must be identified as such so as not to be misleading. The difference between the two approaches is that a totally independent review should be on a "warts and all" basis without any influence from the product manufacturer. An advertorial will be "advertiser friendly", and will not criticise the product in a potentially harmful way. In a specialist publication it is also possible for an expert on the advertised product to write an article about some specific feature of it. This may be a subjective personal view, or it may be a scientific or technical performance analysis.

Value of independent comment

5.24.2 The public may be more impressed by paid advertising if it publicises the praises which are heaped upon the product by independent third parties. This is why it is popular to quote from independent articles, reviews and comments which are favourable to the product, and which are originally published in authoritative magazines or as independent consumer test reports. Credibility is given to the quotation in the advertisement if such reviews are written by people whose opinions and reputations are respected, and who are honestly expressing their own opinion on the product, irrespective of the reaction of the manufacturer to that opinion.

Value of comparative analysis

5.24.3 If a consumer product testing and reporting publication closely examined and tested a revolutionary widget, and gave it a glowing write up with the conclusion that it was the best kind of widget available on the market for technology, performance and price, that report would be a valuable source of publicity and promotion for the widget, and for the reputation of its manufacturer. Can such a report legitimately be used by the manufacturer to advertise the product without obtaining copyright consent?

Identifying copyright owner

5.24.4 The magazine article, review or editorial, and the consumer test report, are each protected by copyright. This may belong to the magazine publisher, or it may belong to the author of the article. Which of them is the owner of the copyright depends on the relationship between the magazine and the author, and the terms upon which the review or article was undertaken and written (Copyright Designs and Patents Act 1988 s.11). If the review or editorial was written by any member of staff of the publication in the ordinary course of his job, the copyright in it will belong to the proprietor of the publication. If the article or review was written by an independent journalist and was submitted to the magazine for publication, the copyright in it will belong to the journalist. If the journalist is not an employee of the publication, but is retained by it as a regular contributor of articles and reviews on his special interest subjects, the question of who owns the copyright will depend on the agreement between them. If there is nothing under contract, the copyright will belong to the journalist.

Effect of consent refusal

5.24.5 If consent for the proposed use of the review in an advertisement for the reviewed product is refused by the copyright owner, because, say, it would detract from the reputation of impartiality of the magazine in which the review was published, then the review, or any substantial part of it, cannot be reproduced in the advertisement. If any substantial part of the review is reproduced within the advertisement without the copyright owner's consent, an injunction can be obtained by him against the advertiser to prevent any further publication, and damages can also be claimed against him for having done so. Very short quotations from a favourable article about a product can be published in an advertisement for that product, with a sufficient acknowledgment of its origin and of its copyright owner, without infringing the copyright in it. Reproduction of significant sections of the review in the advertisement does not come within the "fair dealing" exemption in the Act (see paragraph 5.24.7 below).

What is reproduction?

5.24.6 "Reproduction" of a printed text review means either a facsimile copy of the review or of a substantial part of it; or a verbatim version of the review which has been re-set and displayed differently. An edited version of the review, which is included in the advertisement as originally written and being the substance of the review, will still be a breach of copyright. A "restated" review, which is only a transparent paraphrasing of it, explaining or analysing its favourable conclusions about the reviewed product, could still be a breach of the copyright in the review if it is sufficiently similar to it.

Fair dealing

5.24.7 A wholly different and original work which analyses and comments upon the review, and which emphasises its favourable comments upon the product, will not be a copyright infringement. In this case it could be legitimate to use pertinent and not extensive quotations from the original review, taking advantage of the "fair dealing" exemption in the Act, if is not a disguised advertisement for the product. Section 30 of the Act states that fair dealing for the purpose of criticism or review will not be a copyright infringement provided that it is accompanied by a sufficient acknowledgment of the author and of the copyright owner. The question will be whether the inclusion of an excerpt from a favourable article about a product can be published in an advertisement for that product, with a sufficient acknowledgment of its origin and its copyright owner, without infringing its copyright. Can the advertisement really be considered to be a "criticism or review" under section 30 of the Act? The advertisement will not contain a review of the article in the normal sense. "Review" is defined in the *Oxford Dictionary* as including "a general survey of a subject" and a "report assessing the merits of [a work]". The advertisement will be using extracts from the review solely to advertise the reviewed product. An advertisement is not the appropriate medium for "fair dealing" as envisaged by section 30, so it would not be a good defence to a claim of breach of copyright in these circumstances.

Extension of infringement

5.24.8   If an advertisement which contained an edited version of the review deliberately highlighted all the praise of the advertised product, and omitted all of the adverse criticism directed at it by the reviewer, that would not only be a breach of copyright, it would also be a wholly distorted and incorrect interpretation of the review. This would make the advertisement which contains the edited version of the review misleading. The deliberately selective misrepresentation of the review could also constitute a defamation of the author, as it could well put his reputation as an impartial and truthful expert in question. This could happen where on balance he concluded in his review that the product had more to criticise than to praise, but only the praise is set out in the edited version in the advertisement. The editing process would breach the author's moral rights in his review, where they have been asserted, which would be yet another infringement. (See paragraph 46 onwards.)

What is a substantial part?

5.24.9   In copyright infringement terms it is necessary to establish what is a "substantial" part of the review, and where the point is reached at which so little has been reproduced in the advertisement that it could not be confidently claimed by the author to be a breach of copyright. "Substantial" refers not only to the quantity of the words of the review which are reproduced, but also to how much of the essence of the review has been reproduced in the advertisement. An edited version of the review which incorporates all of its essence will be a substantial part of it, irrespective of the word count ratio.

Qualitative test

5.24.10   If a half-page review of a product which is comprised only of a comparative table of the results of various independent expert tests which have been undertaken upon the advertised product, and which are dull and factual statements, ends up by saying "In view of the above results in my opinion this widget is the best on the market", those quoted words could reasonably be considered to be the substance or the essence of the review. It is also possible that apart from a few introductory words at the beginning of the review, those are the only original words which were actually written by the reviewer, as the comparative table consists entirely of existing third-party data. If the test results were included in the review with the consent of their copyright owners, the above quoted words are effectively the whole review in the author's own copyright terms, as they are his only original contribution to the review. For the purposes of this example, ignore the possibility that those words may not be sufficient to represent a literary work.

What constitutes the review?

5.24.11   The assessment by the reviewer of the independent test data is the basis of the opinion expressed by him in his review. The fact that the word count of the quoted sentence may be modest in relation to the extent of the whole published review does not affect its essential contribution to the review, as without those quoted words the review has no meaning. Should the author of the review be entitled to stop the manufacturer of that product from using the opinion he states in the review to advertise the reviewed product? A technical examination of the review shows that a basic question has to be resolved first.

(a) The review as a whole has a copyright, as it is an original work, being an analysis of the various copyright tests in a new combination or configuration of text, plus the author's short original contribution to the review. The quoted sentence is then the essence of the whole review.

(b) Could it be claimed that the original contribution of the reviewer is so short that it cannot have a copyright in its own right, on the basis that it does not by itself constitute a literary work? (See again the case of *Exxon Corporation* v. *Exxon Insurance Consultants International* [1982] Ch. 119 C.A.) If that is the only part of the review that the author could attempt to protect by a copyright infringement action, he would have to prove that it is protected by copyright, and that such copyright has been infringed by reproducing the quotation in the advertisement.

The use of the simple quotation in an advertisement, even though an acknowledgement is made of its source and that it is copyright material, will still infringe the copyright in the review if it can be shown that the quotation is the substance of the whole of the author's copyright work. This example may seem far-fetched, but it illustrates a point which any product advertiser in similar circumstances should consider very carefully.

Non-infringing references: paraphrasing the review

5.24.12   In the advertisement the agency could make a brief paraphrased reference to the review, such as, "According to the latest XYZ report, the widget is the best on the market." The object is to present a comment on the review, not a quotation from it, although the last eight words are a substantial part of the review. However, without using exactly those words which are taken directly from the review, it is not possible for the advertisement to express the opinion of the reviewer accurately. If there is no practical alternative to using those words in any fair and representative comment on the review, it is unlikely that the courts would consider such a use to be a copyright infringement. Where the advertisement refers directly to the review, and to the conclusion of the reviewer on the merits of the widget, any other form of expression would not represent correctly what the reviewer actually said. To misrepresent his opinion would be worse than running the risk of a copyright infringement complaint. The use of different words to express the same intended meaning could create good grounds for the reviewer and the magazine publisher to complain that the advertiser did not provide an accurate statement of the review.

Reference without quotation

5.24.13   As an alternative to the agency trying to paraphrase the wording of the review, it could simply refer in the advertisement to the existence of the review in the magazine, and invite people to read what the review says about the advertised widget. This is not an effective form of advertising, and is meaningless in promotional terms. The product only gets a value from the favourable review if its conclusion is publicised and quoted in the advertisement.

USE OF PUBLIC DOMAIN WORKS

Consent of owner not required

5.25   The agency may want to use a famous old master painting as the basis of the advertisement. The idea is to re-draw and modify the old master painting slightly for the advertisement so that it contains a representation of the product as if the old master had included it in the original painting. Reproduction of the *Mona Lisa* or the *Laughing Cavalier* holding a can of the world's favourite lager might make appealing advertising. So would a similarly modified reproduction of *"When did you last see your father"*, but with the inquisitor asking, "When did you last drink this product?". Does the agency have to get the consent of the gallery in which it hangs to reproduce the old master in a modified form, and what could the agency suffer if the gallery complains because its consent was not sought? This modified old master concept could be the basis of an amusing advertisement, or one of a series of "spoof" advertisements created to set the scene for a campaign with a central theme of various updated old masters. The relevant points for advertising purposes are:

(a) The fact that the gallery is the owner of the old master, or is just exhibiting it, does not give it any proprietary right over any form of reproduction of it. Therefore the gallery has no ground for complaining to the agency.

(b) There is no copyright in an old master painting, so it may be reproduced freely in its original form or in any modified form because there is no proprietary right of the long-dead artist to infringe.

(c) If some person has in recent times taken a photograph of the old master painting, or if he has painted a copy of it as a new original work of art, each of these will have a copyright of its own. The fact that the subject-matter of the new work is in the public domain does not invalidate the copyright protection which is given to the new original work. Therefore any use of that photograph or painting requires the consent of its copyright owner. That does not prevent any other person from going to the source of the work and creating a different copyright in his own photograph or painting.

CONTRAST WITH COPYRIGHT WORK

Distinguish ownership and copyright

5.26   If the copyright work is being exhibited in the gallery, and an unauthorised reproduction of it is used within an advertisement without obtaining the copyright owner's permission to do so, does that infringement give the gallery any legal right to make a claim against the advertiser or the agency? Ownership or possession of the physical painting will not give the gallery the right to take any legal action against the infringer unless it has also acquired the copyright in it, as otherwise it does not have any proprietary right in it to be infringed. The only party who has that right is the artist, or whoever else is the owner of the copyright in the painting where it has been assigned by the artist. If the copyright owner is the gallery, it has a right of action against the advertiser for the infringement, but because of its copyright ownership, not because it is the owner of the physical painting.

USE OF PHOTOGRAPH OF AN OLD MASTER

Rights of gallery

5.27.1   The agency may want to use in an advertisement an unmodified version of an old master painting which is hanging in the gallery, but the agency is refused permission by the gallery to photograph it for the proposed advertisement use. The gallery is entitled to do so; it may consider that the proposed use of the painting is not in keeping with its status and dignity, and that the use of it in the advertisement would reflect adversely on the gallery if it was known to have given its consent, and to have been paid for authorising the use.

Photograph of painting

5.27.2   The agency would then have to find a suitable photograph of that painting. The most likely sources will be a photographic library or the publishers of a "coffee-table publication" on old masters. Before any such photograph can be used, the agency must get copyright clearance in writing from the owner of the copyright in the photograph for the use of it in the advertisement. Although there is no copyright in the original old master painting, there is a copyright in that coffee-table book photograph. There is also a separate copyright in the print of the photograph in the coffee table book. If the advertising material is produced by photographing the book's printed picture, that will infringe the publisher's copyright in the book, as well as the photographer's copyright in the photograph which is reproduced in the book.

No control over photographs

5.27.3   The gallery in which the old master hangs has no control over the use of any photograph which has been taken of it, unless it owns the copyright in the photograph. The possibilities are:

(a) The gallery commissions photographs for its own use in brochures or as postcards for sale in the gallery shop. If these are taken by a gallery employee as part of his work, the copyright in them will belong to the gallery. If an independent photographer takes them he will own the copyright in the absence of a specific assignment of it to the gallery in writing.

(b) If a visitor to the gallery gets permission to take a photograph of the painting, he is in the same position as an independent photographer under (a) above. The gallery gets no proprietary right in the photograph merely by consenting to it being taken.

(c) If the taking of photographs of the old master painting is forbidden by the gallery, but nevertheless a photographer succeeds in taking one surreptitiously, the copyright position is the same as under (b) above. The photographer is not infringing any proprietary right, and the ownership of the copyright in the photograph in this case is not affected by whether or not permission to take it was obtained. If access to the painting is given under the terms of a contract forbidding photography, the gallery may be able to prevent the publication or use of any photograph as a contractual right.

Different copyrights

5.27.4   Although the photograph is solely of the old master painting, that does not reincarnate any copyright protection for the old master itself. The photograph of it has copyright protection by reason of its being a separate original work. If access to the old master could be obtained by someone else for the purpose of taking another photograph of it, which would be identical to the coffee-table book photograph, it too would be an original copyright work. The two photographs would have an independent origin, although they may appear to be identical. They would have separate copyrights and neither of them would be an infringement of the copyright in the other.

USE OF A COPYRIGHT PAINTING

Find all proprietary rights

5.28.1   The agency may want to use a modern copyright painting for the advertisement. It may have been refused permission by the gallery to photograph the painting, which is owned by the gallery. The agency may also have found from an independent source a photograph of that painting which it would like to use for the advertisement. There are two copyrights to consider, that of the painting and that of the photograph, and therefore there are two copyright owners from whom consent is required to use the photograph for the advertisement.

CONSENT OF THE ARTIST

5.28.2   The original copyright owner is the artist who painted the picture. Even though he has sold the painting to the gallery, unless he also assigned to it the copyright in the painting, he is still the owner of the copyright, so the agency must get his consent first to use the painting in the advertisement. If the artist has sold the copyright, the agency must find out who now owns it, and it must get his or her consent. If the owner of the copyright in the painting refuses to give his consent to its use in the advertisement, there is no point in the agency approaching the owner of the copyright in the photograph, although that is a separate proprietary right. If the artist agrees, the agency still has to get the consent of the photographer. They may each charge a separate fee for the use of their work in the advertisement.

Consent of the photographer

5.28.3   The second copyright is in the photograph itself, so the owner of that copyright will normally be the photographer. If he gives his consent to the use of the photograph for the advertisement, and copyright clearance has also been obtained from the artist in respect of the painting, then the use of the photograph of that painting within the advertisement is legitimate. If the taking of the photograph of the painting was unauthorised and so it is a copyright infringement, then its use in the advertisement would be an infringement of the copyright in the painting.

Moral rights

5.28.4 If the copyright painting is to be reproduced in a modified form for the advertisement, such as for a satirical or amusing purpose, the agency must also consider the moral rights of the artist. (See paragraph 5.46 onwards.) Where the moral rights apply, and they have been asserted or they have not been waived, the artist's consent will be required for the production of an adapted version of the copyright work which could be considered a derogatory treatment, even though he no longer owns either the physical work or the copyright in it. Although it is based upon the original copyright painting, a substantially modified version will be an original work in its own right, and it will have a copyright of its own. The agreement between the advertiser and the artist of the modified work should deal with this aspect to ensure that there are no "grey areas" at a later date in the ownership of the intellectual property rights in the modified version. The relevant points are:

(a) if the modified version is produced by the artist as a commission from the agency, in the absence of a copyright assignment to the agency, the artist will own the copyright in it. The client advertiser will be licensed to make use of it only for the advertisement.

(b) if an independent contractor produces the modified version for the agency with the artist's consent, the copyright in the modified version (as an original work) must be assigned by the contractor to the artist, or to the agency if the artist agrees.

(c) if the artwork for the modified version is done "in house" by the agency, the normal copyright rules will apply, subject to its agreement with the artist of the original version.

USE OF PHOTOGRAPHS

Authorised photograph

5.29.1 The agency should check that the copyright owner of the painting gave permission for the photograph of the painting to be taken otherwise the photograph will be a copyright infringement (section 16 of the Act). Before agreeing to use the photograph for the advertisement the agency should require from the photographer a written assurance satisfactory to the agency that:

(a) The taking of the photograph was authorised in writing by the artist and that it is not an infringement of the copyright in the painting.

(b) Written clearance has been obtained by the photographer from the owner of the copyright in the painting for the commercial use of the photograph. The terms of the clearance will have to be wide enough to cover use of the photograph in an advertisement. The agency should ask for a copy of that written clearance to check its validity and extent.

(c) The photographer will indemnify the agency and the advertiser from all financial and other consequences which may be caused by the use of the photograph in the advertisement, such as by being an infringement of the copyright in the original painting.

Choice from selection

5.29.2   If the agency has commissioned a photographer to "shoot" a series of photographs around the theme for the advertisement, it is likely that no decision will be made immediately upon which of the photographs will be used. Once the decision to proceed has been made, one or more of the photographs will be chosen for use in the advertisement. One question is what happens to the rejected photographs.

Photographic commission terms

5.29.3   The terms of the commission agreement between the agency and the photographer could be any of the following:

(a) The photographer takes the complete "shoot" for a fee which includes payment for the assignment of copyright in all of the photographs to the agency. The fee would take into account that the agency, as the copyright owner, can make whatever commercial use of them the advertiser wants. Whether or not they are used in the advertisement is no concern of the photographer.

(b) A lesser fee than under (a) above may be agreed on the basis that the photographs will only be used for media advertising, although their copyright will belong to the agency. Agreed additional payments will be made to the photographer if other commercial use is made of any of the photographs outside media advertising (such as for posters), but with the photographer not having any control over such extended use.

(c) The photographer could be paid a fee for taking the photographs, on the basis that he retains the copyright in them and licences specific uses of them to the agency for agreed fees set out in the commission agreement, with an obligation not to refuse any use. The agreed fees fixed in advance are to prevent the agency from being held to ransom by the photographer for any additional requested use of the photographs. He would also undertake not to make any other commercial use of any of the photographs, or to authorise their publication, without the agency's written consent.

IN-HOUSE OR COMMISSIONED ARTWORK

WHO IS THE COPYRIGHT OWNER?

Artist as full-time employee

5.30.1   By section 11(1) of the Act, the author of a work is the first owner of the copyright in the work. The statutory exception to that basic rule is under section 11(2) of the Act, where a literary, musical or artistic work is made by an employee in the course of his employment. In that case his employer is the first owner of any copyright in the work, subject to any written agreement with the author to the contrary.

Contract of service

5.30.2   The main conditions which create a contract of service for an employee are as follows:

(a) The author works for the agency on a full-time basis under either a personal service contract or subject to the standard terms of service for all of the agency's employees. The employee will be prohibited by his service contract from having any other employment. Moonlighting as a graphics artist for another agency would be a fundamental breach of his service contract, even if that work is done outside his normal working hours.

(b) The author is paid a regular salary for doing his job, with tax deducted at source under PAYE, irrespective of what his job entails or how much work he actually does on a daily basis.

(c) The author will be provided by the agency with a remuneration package which is compatible with his employee status, such as paid holidays, and (depending on his status), a company car and BUPA. The author will also be entitled to become a member of the agency's employee pension scheme, to which he contributes a percentage of his salary.

(d) The carrying out of his job by the author is subject to the absolute control and direction of the agency in what he does, when he does it, and how he does it.

(e) The author who is an employee is required to work at the agency's premises or wherever else the agency directs, and the agency provides him with all the facilities to enable him to do so.

Private work excluded

5.30.3   If the agency employee's job is creating artwork for clients of the agency, but independently he is a gifted artist in his leisure time, the agency

207

will have no claim on paintings which are produced by him outside the scope of his employment. Sometimes there may be a grey area between what he does for his job and what he does for his pleasure. His hobby could not include the creation of any commercial artwork for other parties in circumstances where he would be in breach of his full-time employment contract.

ARTWORK PRODUCED BY INDEPENDENT CONTRACTOR

Contract governs copyright

5.31.1 The copyright position is different where the artwork has been commissioned by the agency from an independent contractor. Because the independent contractor is not an employee of the agency, section 11(2) of the Act will not apply to the original work he produces, and in the absence of a written agreement to the contrary, the copyright in the artwork will remain with the contractor as the author. If there is an assignment of copyright by the contractor to the agency, it must refer to all of the originating artwork, not just to the final version which becomes the advertisement. If the contractor party to the commission agreement is not a person but an artwork house, it must ensure that it owns the copyright in the artwork which it assigns to the agency. Therefore it must use its own employee, or an independent artist who assigns the copyright in his work to the contractor, or direct to the agency. Where the ownership of the copyright in the artwork is critical to the agency, it should satisfy itself that the assignment will be legally effective.

Contract for services

5.31.2 The main conditions which demonstrate an independent contractor status are as follows:

(a) The contractor is not a regular employee of the agency, but is commissioned by the agency only to do a specific job. He will usually do that job at his own premises in his own time, and he will provide his own working facilities.

(b) The contractor does not get a regular remuneration package. The fee for the job is negotiated freely, and will be different from job to job. The fee will be paid by the agency in response to an invoice submitted by the contractor.

(c) The contractor is (or can be) VAT registered, and if so, he charges VAT on his invoices.

(d) The contractor will have his own terms and conditions of doing business, and each commission for work from the agency represents a new and separate contract. The contractor and the agency must agree on whose terms and conditions will apply to each commission agreement. The terms and conditions of each of them will normally claim the ownership of the copyright in the commissioned work. This contradiction has to be resolved in the commission agreement between them.

(e) The contractor does not work exclusively for the commissioning agency.

(f) Apart from the commission agreement conditions for the project, the contractor is not subject to the control of the commissioning agency in how he undertakes the work.

Clarify contractual status

5.31.3 The wording of the agreement between the agency and the contractor must reflect accurately in legal terms what the parties have agreed to in commercial terms. Any assignment of copyright to the agency must be clear, specific and in writing; woolly words of intent may not be effective in law. The commission agreement for the artwork sometimes refers to the contractor as being an employee of the agency, such as "We hereby employ you to produce the artwork specified . . . ". The use of the word "employ" does *not* make the contractor the employee of the agency; in law he retains his independent contractor status. The danger is that using the word "employ" may confuse the agency into believing that the contractor somehow becomes its employee in legal terms just for the limited purpose of the artwork preparation, and therefore that copyright in the artwork he creates will be assigned automatically to the agency in accordance with the provision of section 11(2) of the Act. This is not the case. The advertiser client, which is expecting the agency to produce the artwork, is also expecting to get an assignment of the copyright in it in accordance with its contract with the agency. The ownership of the copyright in the artwork will enable the client, without reference to the originating contractor, to make unlimited use of the artwork in promotional and publicity projects to support the media advertising for the product. If the contractor is an individual, he must also waive his moral rights.

Alternative is a licence

5.31.4 If the contractor does not assign the copyright in the artwork to the agency, and if there is no other agreement between the agency and the contractor referring to the proprietary rights in the artwork, the client will only have an implied licence to use the artwork for the specific advertising in the U.K. for which it is being designed. The same will apply where a purported assignment in fact turns out not to be effective legally. If the agency has to negotiate a licence with the contractor for the use of the artwork in the advertisement, it must set out in detail what licenced rights the client will be getting and what the total cost to the client will be.

Additional licensed rights

5.31.5 If the client wants to make any use of the artwork beyond the limited licensed rights, such as for promotional posters or corporate brochures, it

209

cannot do so without getting a further licence from the artwork contractor and paying him an additional fee. This "additional use" process (and fee paying) is potentially an endless and expensive one for the client, and it is a profitable one for the contractor. Unless the original agreement between the agency and the contractor ensures that its consent would not be withheld, and that the additional fees would not be excessive, the client will have no control over those items.

Subsequent copyright purchase

5.31.6 If the original artwork contract is on the basis of a licence, and if the client subsequently wants the unconditional and absolute use of the artwork which only comes through owning the copyright in it, the client will have to negotiate through the agency for an assignment of the copyright from the contractor. There is always the possibility that, unless he is obliged to do so under the terms of his commission agreement with the agency, the contractor may refuse to sell the copyright to the client at any price. There is no means of legally enforcing a sale of the copyright from the contractor in those circumstances.

OWNERSHIP OF ORIGINAL PHYSICAL ARTWORK

Creative graphics

5.32.1 The other potential source of contention and misunderstanding by the agency in connection with artwork contractors is the ownership of the original physical artwork. Most originating artwork is typeset or is photo-graphed material, in which case it has no attraction or value as a physical object. Where the artwork is an original painting or graphics, or any other original form of personal creativity, the one and only original work does have an attraction and a value to the client.

Contractual rights

5.32.2 In the absence of any specific reference in the artwork commission agreement, the agency will receive a copy of the finished graphic or original artwork, but the agency does not necessarily get permanent possession or ownership of the original graphic artwork after the advertisement production processes have been completed. Ownership of original artwork is unrelated to ownership of the copyright in it so even if the agency has the copyright in the artwork assigned to it, it may still not get the original artwork unless that is stipulated in the contract. If the contractor is a well- known artist, the final version of the original artwork could have a substantial value in its own right. Therefore if the original artwork is intended to be owned by the client, the transfer of the ownership has to be specifically dealt with by the agency in the artwork commission agreement with the contractor.

210

Separation of artwork and copyright

5.32.3 It is a common misconception that if the agency pays for and becomes the owner of the original artwork which is produced for it by an independent contractor, the copyright in it is also automatically transferred to the agency as a result of the sale. This is not the case unless the commission agreement contains a specific assignment of copyright. If the agency or the client believes in that erroneous assumption, and does not ensure that there is a specific assignment of the artwork copyright in the commission agreement, any use of the artwork commercially will constitute an infringement of the contractor's retained copyright.

SECONDED EMPLOYEE

Copyright and employment

5.33.1 With greater integration through the European Community, what would be the legal position in the case of the temporary secondment of a graphic artist from one agency to another? If an artist who is a full-time employee of Company A in France is seconded to Company B in England for six months' work experience, that artist is then working full time for Company B in creating original material for the advertisements of clients of Company B. There is a distinction between working full-time and being employed full-time for the purposes of section 11(2) of the Act. The alternatives are that:

(a) Company A remains the contractual employer of the artist, and seconds the artist to Company B. Company A then invoices Company B on a monthly basis for an agreed overall fee to cover the remuneration and other payments which Company A pays to its artist employee. The secondment means that Company A has no connection with or control over the work which is done by the artist for Company B.

(b) Although Company A is still the contractual employer of the artist, Company B agrees for convenience to be fully responsible for the direct payment to the artist of his remuneration while he works for Company B, and provides him with all facilities which are available to all employees. To all intents and purposes the artist has become a Company B employee for the period of his secondment.

Which agency is the copyright owner

5.33.2 In both of the above cases the intention is that the artist is under the direction and control of Company B during his period of work experience. The question then is which company owns the copyright in the original artwork which is created by the artist while working for Company B during his period of secondment. In his original contract of service with Company A there will be an implied or specific assignment to Company A of the copyright in whatever is produced by the artist in the course of his employment. If that is not the case, the copyright position as between them will be subject to the relevant French law.

Specific assignment

5.33.3 In the above example the artist would be considered by the two companies to be a full-time employee of Company B for the period during which he works for Company B, but section 11(2) of the Act is only likely to apply in favour of Company B in the case of paragraph 5.33.1(b). To be safe, the agreement covering the secondment of the artist should deal specifically with the copyright position of all of the work which is created by him for Company B. This should be an assignment of all such future copyright to Company B, in consideration of payment of the agreed fee made by Company B to Company A, or in consideration of Company B paying the artist his remuneration direct. The assignment document should be signed by Company B, Company A and the artist to remove any doubt.

RETAINED INDEPENDENT CONTRACTOR

Potentially grey area

5.34.1 If a self-employed artist is renowned for his work, and the advertising agency pays him a retainer to get priority of access to him for work to be done for its clients, and all or most of the agency's outside artwork is commissioned from this artist, how close is he to becoming an employee for copyright purposes? Would it make any difference if he never did graphic design work for any other party, although all of the other criteria for identifying him as being an independent contractor are present? If his position is genuinely as set out in paragraph 5.31.2, he will still be an independent contractor in law.

Is employment transition effective?

5.34.2 This exclusivity of availability on an independent basis may happen where, with the consent of his agency employer, an artist terminates his contract of full-time employment and becomes legitimately self-employed for tax and other reasons. For all practical purposes the artist may otherwise retain the same day to day working relationship with the agency. If he ceases technically and legally to be an employee of the agency, and is accepted by the Inland Revenue as having a self-employed status, the copyright position in respect of his work for the agency would have to be covered by a contract and an assignment of copyright. This is because from that date the agency will not automatically become the copyright owner of his work under section 11(2) of the Act. The contract would also have to cover what happens to projects which were not finished by the employee by the transition date when he becomes an independent contractor. The artist may do the preliminary artwork for the agency while he is an employee, and he will complete the final artwork some time after becoming a self-employed independent contractor. Therefore the copyright assignment should extend to these works in progress.

Practical reality

5.34.3   There might come a time in the above example when the practical and legal distinctions between the artist now being an independent contractor and him previously having been an employee of the agency are blurred. In the event of a dispute over copyright ownership, or even the true tax status of the artist, the Court would look at both the form and the substance of the arrangements between the parties in deciding which status is the real one.

Identifying risk factors

5.34.4   If a valued employee of the agency wants to become an independent contractor, but by agreement the following factors are retained in his future relationship with the agency, then notwithstanding the apparent change of status, it could be deemed by the Inland Revenue to be a sham. The points to be aware of are:

(a) Any regular retainer which the agency pays to the contractor should only be an amount which could genuinely be fair value for the agency having priority call over the contractor's services. The retainer should be separate from the fees which are negotiated on a proper arms length basis with the contractor for each job which is commissioned by the agency. If the retainer is excessive, and is regular and close in amount to the contractors' previous salary, and if commission fees are adjusted against the retainer, it might be considered by the Inland Revenue to be just a reduced continued salary.

(b) The break between the agency and the contractor would have to be complete, as he will cease to be employed by the agency. For example, he could not continue to have the uninterrupted use of in-house facilities to undertake his work for the agency, unless he genuinely paid a market rate for them. Even then that continued close association would be risky to his self-employed status.

Grossed up tax liability

5.34.5   The agency faces a risk if the Inland Revenue does not accept the validity of the purported change of status for the employee, and if he is deemed by them to have been in law a continuing employee of the agency despite having apparently complied with the formalities of becoming a self-employed independent contractor. In that situation the risk is that:

213

(a) the agency would have retained the employer's obligation to deduct tax and to make all the other usual deductions from the "employees" salary throughout the "self-employed" period; and

(b) all "fees" which have been paid to the employee by the agency for work done without deducting income tax will be deemed to have been net salary payments in the employee's hands.

If that claim by the Inland Revenue succeeds, the consequence is that either the employee will have to pay the tax element of what he has already received as gross payments, or the agency will have to gross up that total "net" amount which the employee has been paid, treating it as net salary, and pay to the Inland Revenue the appropriate amount of unpaid tax. If the Inland Revenue takes the view that the whole procedure is a deliberate attempt to defraud them, the consequences could be even more serious.

(c) If the self-employed status claim fails, another (beneficial) consequence is that the copyright in all the material which has been produced for the agency by the contractor/employee during that period will belong automatically to the agency, because section 11(2) of the Act must also have been operative during that period.

FULL-TIME EMPLOYMENT

Specific terms of service

5.35.1 In-house designers, photographers, draughtsmen and artists will be full-time employees, who should always have properly drafted and signed employment contracts with the employer. The agency's standard terms and conditions of employment should have clauses which cover the following points.

Full-time employment

5.35.2 The employee must be a full-time exclusive employee, and his job specification must cover the whole of the likely activities for which he is employed. In an agency these activities may be far-ranging because of all of the various aspects which are connected with creative work. Apart from his primary occupations, there should be a clause stating that the agency can ask the employee to do anything which is lawful and within the broad scope of his intended job specification.

Copyright

5.35.3 The copyright in everything which he creates, designs, draws or produces for the agency as part of his job, and whether or not the creative work is done during office hours or at home, will belong to the agency under the operation of section 11(2) of the Act. Therefore it is important to define his scope of employment and job specification. The rights of the agency in the copyright of the material which is produced by an employee are not affected by whether the client or the agency ever uses it. Despite the automatic operation of the Act, for employee awareness there should still be a copyright assignment in employees' service contracts. Under section 91(1) of the Act a copyright assignment contained in the employee's service contract when he signs it which refers to all future work to be done by him will be effective for the work which he creates throughout his period of employment. Under that section of the Act it is possible for an author to assign the future copyright of something which does not exist at the assignment date.

Non-infringing material

5.35.4 The employee must warrant that all of the material which is produced by him for the agency will be original to him. It must not be a copy of, nor must it otherwise infringe, any third-party copyright, design right, trademark or any other proprietary right. His original material must also not be defamatory, illegal or otherwise actionable by an offended third party. An independent contractor should be required in any commission agreement to indemnify the agency and the advertiser client from any breach by the contractor or (if it is a company) by any of its employees of any warranty of originality and of non-infringement. A full-time employee is not usually required to give an indemnity to his employer, but the point should be considered by the employer in unusual circumstances.

Good taste

3.35.5 Material contained in an advertisement which is politically, racially or otherwise offensive to good taste, but which is not defamatory, may not be actionable in a court of law, but should be avoided. It is the responsibility of the agency to ensure that all material which is produced by its employees and its sub-contractors, and which is cleared for presentation to the client, does not cause any liability or embarrassment to the client. This can happen inadvertently in humorous advertisements which rely on puns for their punchline.

No moral rights

5.35.6 In accordance with section 79(3)(*a*) of the Act, the artist employee will not have any moral rights in the artwork which he produces, so the question of exercising those rights does not arise. (See paragraph 5.46 onwards.) A famous artist may be credited as the author of a painting which is used for the advertisement, because of the kudos of having him produce it. Otherwise the identity of who did it is of no interest to the advertiser, or to the public. The publication of the advertisement is not intended to be a vehicle for promoting the name and reputation of the employee artist or the photographer who created it. In any event, the final version of an advertisement will have been produced by a team of contributors, so giving credits is not practical.

COMMISSIONED ARTWORK CONTRACTS

Signing contractor's agreements

5.36.1 The development of the artwork of an advertisement from concept to publication is often a rapid process, particularly if the advertisement is topical. Consequently there may be no time in which to organise such administrative matters as agreeing the artwork terms with the contractor and getting an order form or an agreement delivered and accepted before the work is begun. A telephone call may get the job on its way, followed in due course by a pro-forma order which contains the minimum of details of a contractual nature.

Whose contract prevails?

5.36.2 The agency may be commissioning an artwork contractor for the first time, and there may have been no discussion on the copyright terms prior to the delivery of the artwork commission order from the agency. The phone call may have been limited to a description of what is needed by the agency, the date by when it is required, and what the fee will be. The questions of copyright and any other relevant items are left to the follow up document-ation, if any. What is the position if, when the time comes to document the telephone call deal, the parties dispute the ownership of the copyright in what the contractor produces? The agency confirms the commission by sending the contractor an order form, which states clearly and prominently that it is "subject to our terms and conditions of business". They may be printed on the order form, or may be obtainable from the agency on request, and they state that the copyright in the contractor's work will be assigned to the agency. The independent contractor then sends the agency an invoice with his terms and conditions printed on the back, and which gives the contractor copyright retention on all of his original artwork. Each party's terms and conditions also state that theirs will override the other party's, which will be deemed to be inapplicable. At the time neither party reads the fine print of the other's order or invoice, and neither of them queries the contradiction on the copyright ownership until after the artwork has been delivered. Who wins?

Contract analysis

5.36.3 An oral agreement is valid, and the question is whether one was made in respect of the copyright at the time of the original telephone conversation. Even if it was, copyright can only be assigned in writing, so the oral agreement would only be concluded when such an assignment is made. Each party believed that its terms and conditions relating to the ownership of the copyright applied to the artwork commission agreement. In the event of an exchange of quotations, orders or confirmations in the circumstances set out in paragraph 5.36.2 above, the general rule is that the terms and conditions which are attached to the last document to be submitted by one party to the other in the transaction, and *before* the work has been done, will govern the transaction. This fact is seldom considered by the parties, such as an agency and an artwork contractor, but it has a fundamental affect on their contractual rights. Therefore in the above example the terms and conditions of the contractor will apply.

Familiarity with contractor's terms

5.36.4   The agency may have frequent dealings with the same independent artwork contractor without any formal exchange of documents containing contractual terms and conditions. Whether or not the agency is aware that the contractor states in his terms and conditions that he retains copyright, if the agency has never challenged that condition will be deemed to accept that position unless the contractor agrees otherwise in writing for a specific commission.

Action by agency

5.36.5   Whenever an agency deals for the first time with an artwork contractor it should ask for a copy of its terms and conditions before commissioning it to do any work, even of a preliminary nature. The copyright position, and any other unsatisfactory stipulation contained in the contractor's standard terms and conditions, must be challenged and revised to the satisfaction of the agency before it uses that contractor. The better alternative is for the agency to supply a copy of its terms and conditions to the contractor before any work is commissioned and to require the contractor to agree in writing that they will apply to all artwork which will be produced by the contractor for the agency in the future.

FEES FOR COMMISSIONED WORK

5.37   Before the artwork order is placed by the agency with the contractor, or before the commission agreement for the artwork is signed by the agency, the agency should agree the fee which is to be paid for the work which will be done by the contractor. This may be a fixed fee, or it may be a formula establishing the basis upon which the fee will be calculated after the job has been completed. If it is a fixed fee, the agency must make clear precisely what it covers. Any extension of the work specification will attract an additional fee. Fee disputes for a "rolling" project are not unusual. If the contractor is assigning the copyright in the artwork to the agency, it should check whether the quoted fee is "all-in", or whether it will be increased to take account of the copyright assignment. If it is agreed that different presentations for the same project will be submitted to the agency by the contractor, the agency will choose which representation of the concept it and the client likes best, and that will become the basis of the second stage of the commissioned work. If the contractor has submitted two or three presentations to the agency for consideration, does it get paid for the work it did on the presentations which were not chosen? Is this cost factor wrapped up in an initial project fee? The agency does not want an unexpected invoice for the rejected work, so the position must be made clear in the arrangements for the presentations.

COPYRIGHT USE CONSENT

CONSENT MUST BE SPECIFIC

Consent cannot be assumed

25.38.1 Consent for the reproduction and use of copyright material must always be obtained, and should be given in writing by or on behalf of the copyright owner. Written consent is not a legal requirement, but is an essential precaution. Consent must never be assumed by the agency to have been granted where there is nothing in writing from the copyright owner; if necessary the existence of the written consent should be checked, and a copy of it obtained. Neither should an agency assume that copyright use clearance will be forthcoming if it is sought after the event. There is no legal obligation on a copyright owner to give his consent to the use of a copyright work in an advertisement, even though a refusal will mean that the advertiser is caused to be infringing the copyright, with all the consequences that flow accordingly. A copyright use consent will not be created merely by the agency writing to the copyright owner asking for his consent, and stating that if he does not respond to the contrary within a given time his consent will be deemed by the agency to have been given. If any conditions are to be attached to the consent by the copyright owner, the agency should ensure that they are reasonable, and that the agency can fulfil them, and that they are not so inhibiting as to make the consent unsuitable for the required use of the copyright material.

Course of conduct

5.38.2 Consent will not be deemed to have been given by the copyright owner simply because he does not take immediate legal action to challenge or to prevent the unauthorised use of his copyright material in the advertisement. For example:

(1) The copyright owner may not be aware of the advertisement, or if he does see it he may not recognise immediately that any of his copyright material has been used in it.

(2) The agency knows that the material it wants to use in the advertisement is protected by copyright, but it cannot find the copyright owner to get his consent after making reasonable efforts to do so. Can it use the material despite not getting consent, and what can the copyright owner do if he subsequently decides to take action against the advertiser for copyright infringement? The unauthorised use of the material will still be an infringement of the copyright in it, and the advertiser can be injuncted and sued for damages by the copyright owner. The law does not permit an infringing use in the hope that it will be subject to subsequent validation, although a licence which is subsequently given by the copyright owner for that unauthorised use will validate the infringement retrospectively.

(3) What is the position where the agency uses the copyright material as in (2) above, and the copyright owner becomes aware of the infringement, but does nothing about it at that time? Let us suppose that, to the knowledge of the copyright owner, the advertising campaign finishes after a successful three month run, and six months later the copyright owner claims infringement damages from the advertiser. They cannot reach an agreement on the amount to be paid by the advertiser, so the copyright owner issues a writ for infringement damages and seeks an injunction to prevent further publication of the infringing advertisement. Leaving aside the formalities of litigation procedure, can he do so? Has he not waived his rights to complain about that advertisement by not taking action promptly when he became aware of the infringement? Some of the factors to consider are:

(a) The copyright owner's right to prevent further publication is not necessarily prejudiced by his delay in taking legal action over the first infringement. An injunction might not be granted where he can be shown to have tacitly agreed to the publication, or where the "balance of convenience" between an injunction and compensatory damages is in favour of the advertiser paying compensation to the copyright owner. This will also depend on the seriousness and flagrancy of the infringement.

(b) Neither is his entitlement to damages for the first infringement prejudiced, although the amount of damages awarded by the court may be influenced by how long afterwards the claim is made, and by how serious the infringement is. However, if the circumstances are such that the copyright owner is legally deemed to have tacitly approved of that use, or to have waived his claim for infringement, all he could claim would be a fair fee for that use.

(c) The advertiser cannot claim that as the copyright owner had allowed the first running of the advertisement without complaining about it, he can be compelled by law to agree to its being run again, upon payment of a reasonable fee to legitimise the otherwise infringing use of the copyright material. That would amount to creating a form of compulsory licensing, which does not exist currently in these circumstances. The advertiser would be in a vulnerable position if the advertisement is highly successful, and the copyright material is an essential part of it.

Balance of convenience

5.38.3 The plaintiff has to issue a High Court writ if it wants to claim an injunction to prevent further unauthorised publication by the defendant of the advertisement which is infringing the plaintiff's copyright. The Court has a discretion in deciding whether or not to grant an injunction where the culpability of the defendant is in question, and relevant factors include the following:

(i) whether there has been any unreasonable delay in the plaintiff making the application for an injunction after first becoming aware of the breach;

(ii) whether irreparable damage will be done to the plaintiff if the injunction is not granted. Nominal damage will put the balance in favour of the defendant; and

(iii) whether substantial damage would be done to the defendant if the injunction is granted, and whether in all the circumstances the payment of damages by the defendant would be an adequate remedy to the plaintiff if the infringement is proved.

Consequences of infringement

5.38.5 Where a copyright owner takes legal action successfully against an infringer the possible consequences will include:

(a) an injunction being granted to the copyright owner to prevent the infringer from continuing with the infringement. The court order would require the immediate cessation of the publication and distribution or broadcasting of the infringing advertisement, and the withdrawal from circulation of any printed material, videos and sound tapes or any other medium which contains the infringement which has been issued by the infringer. That can be a very expensive process;

(b) the payment of damages to the copyright owner, for which there are three categories:

(i) compensatory damages where the infringement has caused calculable and reasonably direct loss to the copyright owner;

(ii) profits related damages, where any profit received by the infringer arising from the infringing use of the copyright is made payable to the copyright owner; or

(iii) punitive damages.

These categories of compensation to the copyright owner are not mutually exclusive, if the circumstances apply all three of them can be ordered by the court; and

(b) the reimbursement of all, or a substantial portion of, the legal costs incurred by the successful copyright owner in the pursuit of his claim against the infringer.

Advertiser's indemnity

5.38.6   The copyright infringer will be the advertiser which published the advertisement containing the infringement, not the agency. That is why the advertiser should have the protection in their agreement of an indemnity from the agency which prepared and presented the infringing material to the advertiser.

GET COMPREHENSIVE CONSENT

Client protection

5.39.1   A comprehensive agreement between the copyright owner and the agency for the consent to use copyright material ensures that everything which is relevant to the advertisement, and to all spin-off uses for it, have been discussed and agreed. A comprehensive agreement should also ensure that the client advertiser is protected from the copyright owner demanding unreasonable and unacceptable conditions for an extended licence if rights for easily foreseeable additional uses of the copyright material are sought by the agency for the client at a later date. It can be dangerous for the agency to assume that the copyright owner will always be reasonable when he is approached for an extended licence.

Fee for consent

5.39.2   If the copyright consents are sought by the agency at a late stage in the production of the advertisement, and if consent is available subject to the payment of a fee, the agency is not in a strong position when it negotiates the amount of the use fees with the copyright owners. The use of copyright material in the advertisement will not be subject to an industry-wide standard rate of fee, and the fee to be charged depends on the copyright owner's perception of the value of the copyright material to himself and to the advertisement. If the agency is late in requesting the copyright clearance, and has to pay what is demonstrably a substantially excessive fee, which would not have been the case had it acted in time, the client advertiser might be entitled to refuse to pay if the excess amount over the expected fee.

COPYRIGHT CONSENT CONSIDERATIONS

Essential priority

5.40.1 Because of the expense of creating and publishing and broadcasting advertisements, and the expense, inconvenience and embarrassment of being forced to withdraw them for copyright or trademark infringement, getting written clearance and consents from the owners of those rights *must* have priority in the project timetable. Obtaining oral consent in principle is one thing, but drafting a comprehensive individually structured agreement with each copyright owner is another. Set out below are some of the main points which should be considered by the agency when obtaining copyright consents.

Authority for consent

5.40.2 Where necessary the agency should satisfy itself that the person who is giving the consent is entitled to do so, particularly if it is a company or if he claims to be a representative of the copyright owner. If the "consent" is not given with the authority of the copyright owner it will not be valid, even if the agency has relied upon it, and use of the copyright material in the advertisement will be an infringement. Acceptance by the agency of an invalid third party assurance of authority does not entitle the agency to use the material in the advertisement, even if it believed in good faith that the consent was valid. The invalidly authorised use is an infringement, but the agency would have some right of action against the bogus "representative" of the copyright owner for breach of any express or implied warranty of authority, and for obtaining a use fee payment by deception. If the copyright owner had given his authority to the representative to grant a licence for such use, and the agency knew of that fact and relied upon it in good faith to include the material in the advertisement, that authority cannot subsequently be withdrawn retrospectively by the copyright owner.

Clear and unconditional

5.40.3 The written copyright consent must be in clear, unambiguous language. It must also be unconditional except for any specifically agreed terms of the consent, such as where further approval of the artwork is required by the copyright owner of a merchandisable cartoon character or a trade mark logo. It is important for the proprietor's legal protection that the final advertisement artwork is a correct representation of what is being licensed. This is not intended to be an artistic approval of the advertisement as such; it is only required to check whether the agreed terms of the proprietary right use have been observed.

Define authorised uses

5.40.4   The consent should be set out exactly what use can be made of the copyright material, for how long and where it can be used, and any conditions which will apply to that use. The agency and the client must be able to check without doubt at any time whether what they have in mind as a use of the copyright material is covered by the licence. For example, artwork which is intended for print media advertisements may have its use extended to hoarding advertising, or to being produced and sold as posters or put on shopping carrier bags. The copyright material, or variations of it, may also be intended for use in a variety of different advertisements on the same theme.

Rights are not implied

5.40.5   Any use of the copyright material which is not referred to specifically in the consent licence, or which is not contractually implied by the wording of the consent, will not have been granted to the advertiser. There cannot be an assumption by the agency that an extension of the use of copyright material which has not been granted contractually will be deemed to be granted "because it is logical".

Media use

5.40.6   The authorised media use of the copyright material should be stated in the licence such as for print advertising or TV advertising, and whether that is to be regionally, nationally or even internationally.

Use fees

5.40.7   The agreement should state what the fee will be and what that fee will cover. The licence for the use may be limited to one year or to one or several different advertising campaigns, and the amount of the fee may be calculated accordingly. Alternatively there may be a "shopping list" of agreed uses, to be taken up during the licence period as the advertiser wants at the time, with a tariff of fees set out in the consent licence to match the exercise of each of the available use options. In this case there may be a minimum fee payable irrespective of how little use is made of the copyright material by the advertiser under the "shopping list".

Advertiser's indemnity

5.40.8 The copyright owner may want an assurance from the advertiser that the use of the copyright material in the advertisement will not incur the copyright owner in any form of liability, and that the advertisement will be legal and in compliance with the ASA Code of Advertising Practice, and any other applicable English or European advertising regulations. The fact that consent is given for a specifically requested use of the copyright material does not imply any representation from the copyright owner that the ultimate use of it by the advertiser will be legal, or that (apart from copyright infringements) such use will not infringe third party rights. The use consent licence should make all of these representations clear.

English bank notes

5.40.9 The Bank of England has issued guidelines for the reproduction of its bank notes in advertisements, to ensure that reproductions cannot be used to defraud the public. The Bank of England is the owner of the copyright in the original designs of its bank notes and therefore section 16 of the Copyright Designs and Patents Act 1988 protects the Bank from unauthorised uses of its copyright material. Further statutory protection is given to the Bank by section 18(1) of the Forgery and Counterfeiting Act 1981:

> "It is an offence for any person, unless the relevant authority has previously consented in writing, to reproduce on any substance whatsoever, and whether or not on the correct scale, any British currency note or any part of a British currency note."

Section 18(2) explains that for the purposes of section 18(1) a British currency note is any note which has been lawfully issued and is or has been customarily used as money in the country in which it was issued. Therefore notes which have ceased to be legal tender will still come within this prohibition.

Bank of England criteria

5.40.10 The Bank of England has set out the following criteria for the reproduction of its bank notes:

(a) no reproduction is allowed on articles for sale;
(b) for advertising and sales promotion (and all other) printed material, the consent of the Bank must be obtained, and the criteria for consent are:

(i) reproduction of notes, whether in black and white or colour, must not be the same size as actual notes. If they are smaller, they can be up to half as long and half as wide. If they are to be larger, they must be at least twice as long and twice as wide. Reproductions of parts of notes must be in the same proportions;

(ii) notes should be shown on the slant and not flat, and should also form part of a larger pictorial design;

(c) the reproduction of notes issued before 1960 must meet the size criteria but need not be slanted or over printed "specimen". If the reproduction meets the criteria, the consent of the Bank of England will not be required.

5.40.11 The making of imitation British coins is covered by section 19(1) of the Forgery and Counterfeiting Act 1981 which says:

It is an offence for a person—

(a) to make an imitation British coin in connection with a scheme intended to promote the sale of any product or the making of contracts for the supply of any service; or

(b) to sell or distribute imitation British coins in connection with any such scheme, or to have imitation British coins in his custody or under his control with a view to such sale or distribution

Unless the Treasury have previously consented in writing to the sale or distribution of such imitation British coins in connection with that scheme. Section 19(2) states that a British coin means any coin which is legal tender in any part of the U.K. From this definition it would appear that it would not be an infringement of the Act to reproduce for sales promotion or advertising purposes a coin which is British but which has ceased to be legal tender.

ASSIGNMENT OF COPYRIGHT

VALIDITY CONDITIONS

Assignment must be in writing

5.41.1 Except where the author of an original work is not deemed to be the first owner of the copyright in it under section 11(2) of the Act because he is an employee, copyright in the work can only be assigned by a written document which is signed by the copyright owner, or by a person who has the legal authority to do so on his behalf. The meaning and effect of the assignment must be clear. The words "copyright" and "assign" should appear in the assignment document, to avoid any possible claim that the copyright owner has only granted a licence to the client advertiser through the agency to use the material for limited purposes. If there is any doubt whether a signed copyright assignment is effective, it is advisable to have another assignment signed and specifically having effect from the original assignment date.

Assignment must be signed

5.41.2   If a commission agreement for artwork, whether it is a formal document or a letter, submitted by the advertising agency to an independent contractor artist states that "You hereby assign to the Agency the copyright in the artwork you produce under this agreement", and if no written acknowledgment of the commission agreement is signed by the artist, then the copyright will not have been assigned to the agency by that document.

Part performance

5.41.3   In the above example, if the artist receives but does not respond to the agreement, but he does the artwork which was commissioned, he will be deemed to have accepted all of the contractual terms of the agreement. Therefore he will be deemed to have agreed to assign the copyright in the artwork to the agency. However, until the artist executes a copyright assignment pursuant to the commission agreement, the copyright will not have passed to the agency, and it cannot legally deal with the artwork as if it were the copyright owner.

Beware the English language

5.41.4   The use of the English language is seldom precise in casually drafted documents, and the same risk exists when trying too hard to make the document "user-friendly". For example, it is possible for the words "I hereby agree to assign" to mean either that an assignment will be made in due course, or that the document being signed is an actual assignment. The wording of the rest of the document should confirm whether the assignment is to be interpreted as absolute now, or as a future commitment. On the other hand the words "I hereby assign", or just "I assign" would be an effective immediate assignment, provided the rest of the document is worded correctly.

PRESENT ASSIGNMENT OF FUTURE COPYRIGHT

Immediate effect

5.42.1   It is possible under section 91 of the Act for an independent contractor artist to assign immediately the copyright in an original work which has not
yet been created by him. Where the copyright is to be assigned to the agency,
the agreement relating to a present commission of future artwork should
contain an immediate assignment by the artist to the agency of the copyright in
that future work. The assignment will automatically become effective when
the work has been done. There is nothing further which needs to be assigned
or formalised on the copyright front when the artist has completed the
commissioned work; the agency will already own the copyright in it.

Confirmatory assignment

5.42.2   Where the artist has made a general assignment of the future
copyright of work which is to be done by him under the commission
agreement, the agency or the client may want to have a separate form of
copyright assignment for a completed piece of artwork where different works
under the agreement need to be identified separately, or where the rest of the
commission agreement is to remain confidential. The signing by the artist of a
confirmatory copyright assignment in respect of completed artwork produced
under the original agreement does not grant the agency a new right; it simply
confirms the existing copyright ownership position. If the artist refuses to sign
a confirmatory assignment, he does not thereby retain the copyright—he has
already assigned it in general terms under the original agreement. Therefore it
is not a bargaining counter for the artist if there is a dispute on fees. There is no
obligation on the artist to sign such a document unless the commission
agreement contains a "further assurance" clause which obliges the artist to do
anything which is reasonably necessary to confirm his assignment of proprietary rights at the request and at the cost of the agency.

CONDITIONAL COPYRIGHT ASSIGNMENT

Artist's safeguard

5.43.1   For his protection the copyright in the artwork should only be
assigned to the agency by the artist when all of the agreed fees for that artwork
have been paid in full to the artist. The artist who assigns the future copyright
in his work to the agency at the time the commission agreement is signed will
only be able to sue the agency for unpaid fees: he has not retained any
proprietary interest in the artwork. Under a conditional obligation to make an
assignment, as a form of pressure, he can refuse to assign the copyright to the

227

agency until the fees are paid. The commission agreement must make it clear whether the assignment of copyright for a piece of artwork is conditional on just the fees for that artwork being paid, or whether the condition extends to the payment of all outstanding fees due to the artist for any other work he has done for the agency.

Effective wording

5.43.2 From the agency's point of view it is safer to have a conditional copyright assignment which should become effective immediately upon payment for that artwork in full, and without any further formalities having to be completed by the artist. This prevents the agency from being inconvenienced or delayed in receiving a copyright assignment by an awkward or unreasonable artist, or if he is not personally available to sign the document for a long time. A conditional copyright assignment would have to be worded carefully to make sense.

Conditions must be absolute

5.43.3 The transfer of the copyright under a conditional copyright assignment may be delayed where payment is withheld because there is a dispute about the fees between the artist and the agency, because the artist will claim that the copyright assignment will not be effective until "the fees are paid in *full*". A dispute might arise where some of the fee is dependent on the quality or quantity of the work to be done by the artist, or on the timing for its delivery to the agency. Any unresolved fee assessment under the commission agreement which is based upon the quality of the artwork must have a foolproof benchmark against which the quality can be judged. (Acceptability of artwork is discussed below.) This is for the safety of both parties. The agency cannot unreasonably reject artwork and refuse to pay for it; and the artist cannot enforce payment for substandard artwork. If the time of delivery of the artwork to the agency is expressed in the commission agreement as being "of the essence", and if the artist is late in delivering the artwork, but blames the delay on the agency because it did not give approvals of preliminary artwork in time, there will be a dispute.

ACCEPTABILITY OF ARTWORK

Quality approval

5.44.1 There is no problem if the artwork is completed and delivered by the artist in accordance with the commission agreement, and it is approved by the agency. In this context "artwork" is not standard typesetting, but original creative artwork. But what is the situation where some or all of the artwork is found on delivery not to be acceptable to the agency in accordance with its quality standards? In theory this should never happen because of the artist's established reputation and because of constant liaison between artist and agency, but the question does arise occasionally. To meet its quality standards, the agency may require the artist to do the work again, or to modify what has already been done. Three potential dispute areas are:

(a) whether or not the artwork has been produced to a reasonable standard acceptable to the agency;
(b) the delivery date for the artwork modification; and
(c) whether the work to be done for the modification will increase the fee for the artwork.

Standard of artwork quality

5.44.2   The commission agreement for the artwork may not contain any reference to quality control, or (if it does), it may not specify what kind of quality standard is applied by the agency. The artwork quality standard which is applied by the agency may be no more than a matter of approval to its reasonable satisfaction. If the work of the artist is not known to the agency because he is being used for the first time, samples should be requested or a more explicit quality standard should be set out in the commission agreement. If the quality of the artwork is disputed, what is to be the benchmark? Either party may simply express a personal opinion on the merits of what has been delivered to the agency and it can be difficult for the agency to prove that the artist has not fulfilled his side of the agreement. Cognisance must be taken of the distinction between unsatisfactory artwork, and good artwork which just does not depict what the agency wanted to project to the viewer.

LATE DELIVERY OF ARTWORK

Subject to applicable contract

5.45   The delivery of the artwork may have been seriously delayed, and by the time it is delivered it may be too late for the client's requirements. Assuming that the agency did not contribute to or cause the delay, the dispute between the agency and the artist will be upon whether the full fee should be paid despite the late delivery, or whether a reduced fee or even no fee at all is due to the artist. The terms of the commission agreement have to be examined to see what the rights of the parties are in those circumstances. Timely artwork delivery is obviously important to the agency, and where it does not issue commission agreements its standard terms and conditions should deal with the question specifically.

MORAL RIGHTS

AUTHOR'S MORAL RIGHTS

Statutory right

5.46 Under the Act, for the first time in English law, in certain circumstances the author of a copyright literary, musical or artistic work, and the director of a copyright film, have personal rights in respect of their original work. These are the right to be identified as the author or the director of the work, and the right to prevent it from being adapted in a derogatory manner, provided that the author:

(a) has "asserted" his moral right; and
(b) is not a full-time employee of the party for which the work is done.

Throughout these paragraphs all references to the author exercising his moral rights is on the assumption that he is entitled to do so, and that he has asserted his right to do so. (See sections 77 to 83 of the Copyright Designs and Patents Act 1988.)

RELEVANCE TO ADVERTISING

Advertisements have authors

5.47.1 How do the moral rights provisions of the Act affect the advertising industry? Advertising consists of original creative works which are produced for the purpose of being published by television or radio broadcasting or press media coverage, or through any other means of bringing the advertised product to the attention of the public. Not all advertisements will be affected by the application of moral rights, such as where they are purely printed text advertising, unless they are sufficiently substantial to be a literary or artistic work under the Act attributable to an author as his personal creativity. The author will be the photographer or the artist who produced the artistic or literary material which constitutes, or which is included in the advertisement. Where the agency has any doubt as to the potential relevance of the moral rights provisions to the use of existing material in a specific advertisement, it must find out what the position is before the material is used or modified. The advertisement is the end result of the creative and artistic input of several different people, so that in many cases no substantial individual contribution can be separately identified. In that case there would be no single person who could claim any moral rights in the advertising material.

Television advertising

5.47.2 The relevance of the moral rights provision to the broadcasting of TV filmed advertisements will depend upon the circumstances in which they are produced:

(a) In respect of the visual film the director will be an individual who may be entitled to exercise his moral rights. The author of the film will be the film production company, as being the party which arranged for the film to be made.

(b) In respect of the music on the advertisement film sound track, the author will be the composer of the music. There may be more than one author in a work which has both music and lyrics. The author's moral rights are not affected by the fact that the copyright in the music will be owned by a music publishing company, which granted the synchronisation licence to the agency.

ASSERTION OF MORAL RIGHTS

Positive action required

5.48.1   The author must have "asserted" his moral rights where he is entitled to do so, in order to exercise the right of being identified upon any of his creative work. In the absence of such assertion, his moral rights will not be infringed by any person who omits the author's name from being displayed on the relevant work.

General assertion

5.48.2   Where the author of a work wishes to protect his right to exercise his moral rights they may be asserted generally, such as by being included as one of the author's terms and conditions of doing business. For the assertion to be effective, the terms and conditions must be part of the contract for the work which is being done by the author, and the other party to the contract must be aware of the assertion when the work is commissioned.

Specific assertion

5.48.3   Moral rights may also be asserted in a specific instance by being part of the terms which are applied by the author to the artwork commission agreement, the assignment of the copyright in the work, or to the licence which is granted by the author to the agency or to the advertiser to use the work. No specific form of wording is required to assert moral rights under the Act. A clear and unambiguous reference in the commission agreement to the author "hereby exercising" his moral rights will be sufficient. The agency should agree with the author upon the wording of his asserted credit.

MORAL RIGHT OF IDENTIFICATION

Musical works

5.49.1   The author of a musical work, which would include the jingle on a TV advertisement's sound track, has the right to be identified with his work whenever:

(a) the work is published commercially, which for a TV jingle means when it is broadcast within the sound track of a TV advertisement;
(b) it is printed and sold as sheet music (a TV advertisement sound track is most unlikely to be published as printed sheet music unless it is expanded to being the music of a successful, commercially released, full-length recording on a single or an album);
(c) copies of a sound recording of the work are sold to the public; or
(d) a film whose sound track contains the work is shown in public—this includes a TV advertisement.

Artistic works

5.49.2   The author of an artistic work, such as an advertising poster or a printed media advertisement, has the right to be identified with his work whenever:

(a) the work is published commercially or is exhibited in public, or when a visual image of it is broadcast, or it is included in a cable TV programme service; or
(b) a film which includes a visual image of the work is shown in public.

Film directors

5.49.3   The director of a film (which includes a TV advertisement) has the right to be identified with his work whenever the film is shown in public.

Clear and prominent identification

5.49.4   Whenever an author's moral rights are exercised, his identification on the work must be in a manner which is likely to bring his identity to the attention of a person reading or seeing or hearing the showing or broadcast of the work, and the identification must be clear and reasonably prominent. Any form of identification which is chosen by the author may be used, including a pseudonym.

Where credits are not customers

5.49.5   There are many areas of creative activity (including all advertising material) where, by custom or because of the nature of the use of the work, it is not practical or intended that the person who created the work should get a publicised credit for having done so. In the designing of advertisements it is unlikely that the individuals involved will be entitled to exercise moral rights. It is more likely to occur where a photograph or painting is licenced for use in an advertisement, in which case paragraph 5.50.2 will apply.

WHERE MORAL RIGHTS DO NOT APPLY

Full time employee

5.50.1 The author of a copyright work does not have the benefit of the moral rights provisions of the Act where he is employed full time, and where the work he creates is done during the course of his employment. Any agency or any client which has an in-house advertising department should ensure that the terms of employment of anybody who may be involved in producing creative or filmed advertising or promotion material state a wide enough job specification, and it is a prudent precaution for those terms of employment to contain a waiver by the employee of his moral rights in the material which is created by him.

By agreement

5.50.2 Any person who is entitled to exercise his moral rights can waive those rights by a specific written agreement. Therefore an agency's standard terms and conditions for the commissioning of any original work from an independent contractor should include a waiver of his moral rights.

DEROGATORY TREATMENT OF COPYRIGHT WORKS

Right of objection

5.51.1 Under the Act in certain circumstances an author of a copyright work, or the director of a copyright film, can object to and prevent the treatment of his work by a third party in a "derogatory fashion". The relevance for the advertising industry of the derogatory treatment provisions of the Act is that an agency may wish to adapt, modify or lampoon original material to create an interesting advertisement. The agency may have obtained the written consent of the copyright owner to make the agreed modifications to the artwork, but if the derogatory treatment provisions of the Act would also apply to those modifications, the agency will have to get the written consent of the author to have them done, or the agency will have to get him to do the modifications. Where the author is also the copyright owner of the work the different written consents can be dealt with in the same document. (See paragraph 5.52.)

What is derogatory treatment?

5.51.2   Under the Act "treatment" of a work means any addition to, deletion from, alteration to or adaptation of the work. For this purpose it does not include a translation of a literary work, or an arrangement or transcription of a musical work involving no more than a change of key or register. The treatment of a work is "derogatory" if it amounts to a distortion or a mutilation of the work, or if it is otherwise prejudicial to the honour or to the reputation of the author or the director of the work. There is no explanatory definition in the Act of what constitutes a distortion or mutilation of a work, so it will be a matter of judgment in each case. The Act does not use words like "substantially" or "unreasonably" in connection with derogatory treatment. The usual connotation of distortion or mutilation implies that the work is changed in a manner whereby people will think the less of it, either aesthetically or artistically. The test is objective. If even minor modifications change the essential character or representation of the work, they could be a derogatory treatment. An oversensitive artist may be wholly out of step in his own opinion of what is derogatory in comparison with the opinions of advertising agency executives. So far there have not been any court decisions to give a legal guideline on what would be considered as derogatory.

Applies to all versions

5.51.3   The derogatory treatment provisions of the Act apply to the mutilation or distortion of any representation in any medium of an original work. If a copyright painting is reproduced in an advertisement after it has gone through a satirical modification by photography without the consent of the artist, his moral rights may have been infringed.

DIFFERENCES BETWEEN MORAL RIGHTS AND COPYRIGHT

Two separate rights

5.52.1   Breach of the moral rights of the author in his work, and infringement of his copyright in the work, are two different proprietary right infringements under the Act. (See also paragraph 5.61). A separate right of action exists in respect of each of these infringements even though they might arise from the same set of circumstances. Differences between the two rights include:

    (a) The moral right is retained by the author irrespective of whether he retains or sells the copyright in the work which is claimed by him to have been published without attribution or treated in a derogatory manner. The assignment of the copyright in the work by the author means that he stops having any ownership proprietary right in the work.

That assignment will not transfer the author's moral rights with the proprietary rights.

(b) The moral rights of the author are also exercisable by him irrespective of who has possession of the original work. So, from both a copyright and a moral rights points of view, the possessor of the original work (unless he is also the author of it) cannot make or authorise the making of modifications to it, such as for use as an advertisement. The derogatory treatment does not have to be perpetrated against the original work to be actionable (see paragraph 5.51.3). It is the derogatory use of any representation of the work which creates the liability for the person who makes that derogatory treatment.

Approvals to obtain

5.52.2 If the artist who created a painting sells the original artwork together with the copyright in it to another party, that party is not entirely free thereafter to modify the work, or a representation of it. As that party is the owner of the copyright, a modification which he does to the work will not be a copyright infringement. It would however be a moral right infringement if it was derogatory and unauthorised by the artist. If the artist has sold the original painting to one party, and the copyright in it to another, the agency will have two people to approach (the artist and the copyright owner) to authorise its modification in a potentially derogatory manner. If the modification will not carry any risk of being "derogatory", the agency only has to obtain the copyright owner's consent. If the agency gets the consents from the artist and the copyright owner, but if the original artwork has never been copied, the agency would have to get the consent of the owner of that artwork for a copy to be made if it is not otherwise accessible for that purpose. (See paragraph 5.26.) In this case the owner who is neither the artist nor the copyright owner has no proprietary rights in the artwork, but without the owner's consent the agency cannot get access to the artwork to make a copy of it. Two points arise from this example:

(a) neither the author nor the copyright owner can force the owner of the artwork to make it available for copying by the agency;

(b) once the owner has allowed access to the artwork for copies to be made, he has no control over what is done with them in the absence of making a watertight contract with whoever made the copies. Any such control is only contractual, and not proprietary.

FALSE ATTRIBUTION OF WORK

Incorrect attribution

5.53.1 Another of the moral rights under the Act (section 84) is that a person has the right in the circumstances set out in paragraph 5.56 below:

(a) not to have a literary, musical or artistic work falsely attributed to him as its author, or

(b) not to have a film falsely attributed to him as its director.

Rightful attribution

5.53.2   There do not appear to be any provisions under the Act whereby the author of a work, or the director of a film, can demand to have his name removed from the credits if he is the author or the director and if the relevant work has not suffered from any derogatory treatment, or has not been modified without his approval. This position might arise where an artist who has created artwork, and who subsequently thinks it is not up to his usual standard and wishes to be dissociated from it, is asking to have his credit as the author of the work removed from it.

Attribution defined

5.53.3   For the purposes of the Act an "attribution" in relation to such a work means an express or implied statement as to who is the author or director of the work. If the author is properly credited as the author of the work, and if the work is entirely his, that credit cannot be a false attribution. It can give a significant value or credibility to the relevant work to publicise it as having originated from the author. Nobody but the author can sign his name on the work (such as a painting), as that would be forgery. Referring to the author as being the author of the work is not actionable if it is true.

Attribution of photographer

5.53.4   If a famous photographer has a studio where assistant photographers are employed full time to do some of the routine work, and it is these assistants who do the photography for the advertisement artwork, it would be an infringement of the famous photographer's moral rights to attribute the advertisement photography to the famous name personally, rather than to the studio. If the names of the studio and the famous photographer are synonymous, the agency would have to be careful about how it words the attribution of the artwork to the studio, to avoid both an incorrect attribution and a misleading advertisement or statement.

RIGHTS RELATING TO FALSE ATTRIBUTION

Deceptive attribution

5.54.1   To attribute falsely the authorship of a work to another person who had nothing to do with its creation would give a fraudulent or deceptive provenance to the origin of the work. If the falsely attributed work is of poor quality, or if it is nothing like the attributed author's usual style or work, the attributed author's reputation will suffer as a result. The attribution may also be a defamatory imputation or statement which is actionable by the real author and by the attributed author.

Attribution infringement

5.54.2   The right of any person not to have a false attribution made to him in respect of any work is infringed by a person who:

(a) issues to the public copies of a work to which there is a false attribution of the authorship of the work (this will include printed media advertisements, and other printed material such as posters); or

(b) exhibits in public an artistic work, or a copy of an artistic work, to which there is a false attribution of the authorship of the work.

Double infringement

5.54.3   If an advertisement or any other published promotional material gives a credit to a person as being the creator of it, and that is not the case, then (where they are assertable) the moral rights of both the wrongly credited person and the person who should have been credited are infringed. The "person" who commits the infringement will be the manufacturer whose product is being advertised, not the agency, although the agency will have prepared all of the advertising material to which the false attribution attaches.

Attribution of concept authorship

5.54.4   Having been consulted by an agency, a well known artist may provide it with a brief description of an exciting new printed advertisement concept. The agency then decides to have the originating and the final artwork depicting that new concept done by an artwork house, because the well known artist is expensive and cannot do it in time. If the concept of the final artwork is credited by the agency to the famous artist who suggested the original idea for it, what is the attribution position? As there is no copyright in a concept, and as the famous artist provided only that concept and was not the author of the artwork, he would not be entitled to claim any authorship attribution for the artwork which embodies that concept. Neither is the agency entitled to credit the artwork, as an embodiment of the concept, as being the work of the famous artist. The agency might want to publicise that the artwork "is based upon a concept submitted by [famous artist]". Any objections to this accreditation are likely to be:

(a) from the famous artist to the effect that the artwork does not represent his concept as he saw it, or as he would have produced it artistically, and the attribution is false and misleading; or

(b) from the artist who did produce it to the effect that the concept of the final artwork was his original work, although it may slightly resemble the rough idea of the famous artist.

Using a Wrongly Attributed Work

Infringing performance

5.55.1   The right of a person not to have a false attribution made to him in respect of a work of which he is not the author is also infringed by a person who knowing, or having reason to believe, that the attribution is false:

(a) in the case of a literary, or musical work, performs the wrongly attributed work in public, broadcasts it or includes it in a cable programme service and does so as being the work of the complaining person, or

(b) in the case of a film, shows the wrongly attributed work in public, broadcasts it or includes it in a cable programme service as being directed by the complaining person.

Reasons for awareness test

5.55.2   The awareness test is applied to the above infringements of the moral right of attribution because those persons who perform or exhibit the work would not have been connected with the decision to create the work, nor would they have been involved in the creation of the advertisement which uses that work. Therefore they would not know whether the attributions are correct or false, and it would not be normal for them even to consider the point. It is reasonable for them to assume that the attributions are correct unless and until for any reason they are made aware of the potential offence. Once they are aware of what appears to be a valid complaint by a person who has been wrongly attributed as the author of the work, and if they continue to perform or broadcast the material complained about, then they will be committing an offence.

Dealing in Wrongly Attributed Works

Commercial dealing is an infringement

5.56.1   The right of a person not to have a false attribution made to him as the author of a work is also infringed by a person who in the course of a business, knowing that, or having reason to believe that, the authorship is false:

(a) possesses or deals with a copy of a work on which there is a false attribution, or

(b) in the case of an artistic work, possesses or deals with the work itself when there is a false attribution on it.

Private dealing is not infringement

5.56.2 "In the course of a business" means dealing commercially in the items which are being complained about. If a press advertisement is turned into a poster and is publicly merchandised containing a wrongful attribution, any party which stocks and sells the posters knowing of the wrongful attribution would be committing an infringement. A person who bought a stock of the poster and gave them to friends for Christmas would not.

DEALING WITH ALTERED WORKS

Artistic works misrepresentation

5.57 In the case of an artistic work the moral rights of the author are also infringed by a person who, in the course of a business, and knowing or having reason to believe that such is the case:

(a) deals with a work which has been altered after the author has parted with possession of it and represents it as being the unaltered work of the author, or

(b) deals with a copy of such a work which is represented as being a copy of the unaltered work of the author.

Printed advertising material and posters can infringe this moral right. An example would be where a work has been modified by superimposing an impression of the advertised product on it, so that it gives the impression of being part of the original work as produced by the author.

FURTHER MORAL RIGHT INFRINGEMENTS

5.58 The moral right provisions of the Act also apply where:

(a) a literary or a musical work is falsely represented as being an adaptation of the work of a person, or

(b) a copy of an artistic work is falsely represented as being a copy made by the author of the artistic work.

These activities may also be an infringement of copyright, and they may also constitute misleading advertising.

PRIVACY OF PHOTOGRAPHS AND FILMS

No general law of privacy

5.59.1 There is no general law in the U.K. which gives any individual the broad right of privacy as such, so that (subject to paragraph 5.59.2 below) a photograph or film which is taken of him can be sold or broadcast without him having any legal recourse in a claim for breach of copyright or breach of privacy. A personality has a right of action against an advertiser which is using his image without his authority to sell products, but only where the advertisement represents a recommendation or endorsement of the product by that personality without his consent. (See Chapter Six). That would also be contrary to section B17 of the Code of Sales Promotion Practice.

Enforceable privacy rights

5.59.2 An important exception to the above is that by section 85 of the Act a person who for private and domestic purposes commissions the taking of a photograph or the making of a film has, where copyright subsists in the resulting work, the right not to have:

(a) copies of the work issued to the public,
(b) the work exhibited or shown in public, or
(c) the work broadcast or included in a cable programme service.

Privacy only protects commissioner

5.59.3 It is only the private and domestic commissioner of the work who has the section 85 privacy rights in it. If other people feature in the photograph or the film, they do not have a privacy right to assert. The boundaries of what are "private and domestic purposes" are not defined, but it would clearly cover wedding photographs and family or holiday snaps. The commissioner does not have to own the copyright in the photograph or the film or their negatives to be entitled to exercise his privacy rights under the Act. The Act does not define what it means by "commissioning", so its normal definition of being a commercial transaction for the payment of money will apply. In contrast, if Mr. A asks Mr. B (who is a guest) to bring his stills or video camera to the party to record the celebrations for posterity, that is not a commission, and privacy rights would not apply to that film.

Spontaneous private film

5.59.4 A home video film of spontaneous family or personal humorous disaster or embarrassment, can be much more original and entertaining than a "set-up", scripted film. Some TV programmes consist of showing clips from private films, as do some TV advertisements. The privacy moral rights will only apply to these films if they were commissioned and if they fit the "private and domestic" test. If they were not commissioned then the moral right of privacy does not apply to them. If a passer-by happens to film or photograph a funny or embarrassing family event, the privacy rules will not apply. In that case the only restraints on their use commercially in advertisements are copyright clearance and the Code of Advertising Practice. The consents which are needed for the inclusion of privately commissioned films or photographs as part of a TV programme or a press or TV advertisement will therefore be from:

(a) the owner of the copyright in the photograph or videofilm, usually the photographer,
(b) (where applicable) the person who commissioned the photograph or videofilm, and
(c) (for advertisements) any prominently visible person under section B 17 of the ASA Code of Advertising Practice.

APPLICATION OF PRIVACY RIGHT TO ADVERTISEMENTS

Check for privacy risk

5.60.1 Because of the privacy right granted to individuals under section 85 of the Act, any photographic or filmed material, whether or not it was produced professionally, which has been commissioned for private and domestic purposes must not be used in advertisements without first checking whether the privacy rules apply. If they do apply, the consent of the individual who commissioned the work must be obtained. One possible source of material which might infringe this right is a photographic library, unless it makes sure that any photograph or film it has of unknown origin, but which may not be a professional production, has been checked and cleared. The agency should ask the library or any other source of such material to confirm in writing that all copyright and moral rights have been cleared for its intended use by the agency.

Incidental use

5.60.2 The moral right of privacy is not infringed by the incidental inclusion of the work in an artistic work, film, broadcast or cable programme. This exemption would not apply to a casual but essential inclusion of the work in an advertisement which is deliberately done to give it a greater impact. What is meant by "incidental" depends on the actual use which is being examined.

MORAL RIGHTS ARE PERSONAL

Non assignable

5.61 The moral rights which are granted under the Act are personal to the author; they cannot be assigned by him in any circumstances to any other party, even with the assignment of the copyright in the work. Any purported assignment of moral rights by the author while he is alive is wholly ineffective. He can nominate his successor to the right under his will. Failing that, it follows the copyright after his death.

USE OF MUSIC IN ADVERTISING

MOOD MUSIC

Anonymous music

5.62   Where a TV advertisement wants bland, evocative or soothing anonymous background music to suit the mood of the advertisement, the producer of the commercial looks for "mood music". Where copyright mood music is required, there are many sources, such as specialist studios, which have libraries of recordings of different kinds of background music. The appropriate music is found by the agency, the relevant forms are signed for the Mechanical Copyright Protection Society (MCPS), the appropriate fee is paid to MCPS on behalf of the copyright owner of the recording, and then it can be used in the soundtrack of the TV advertisement.

COMMISSIONING TV ADVERTISING JINGLES

Signature tunes

5.63.1   Alternatively original music may be commissioned by an agency for a TV advertisement from companies which specialise in the production of TV soundtrack jingles. The jingle company will be given a specific brief, the object being to produce what could be a signature tune for the advertised product. Like some artwork, which is suitable for further commercial possibilities, a piece of original music can be adapted to make it into a commercial recording with the possibility of becoming a financial success.

Copyright retention

5.63.2   Under their standard terms and conditions jingle companies always retain the copyright in the music which they create, and they will only grant a limited licence to the agency for the use of the music in the soundtrack of that TV advertisement. The jingle company retains the absolute right to adapt and to make any other use of that music without any further reference to the agency, and without having to get the consent of the client whose advertisement first publicised the music, and which originally paid for the music to be composed. The agency should negotiate a written agreement with the jingle company defining the extent of the authorised use of the music, and any restrictions imposed on that use by the jingle company.

PRS Income

5.63.3   The jingle music which is used in the TV advertisement will be registered with the Performing Rights Society Ltd. in the name of the jingle company as its copyright owner. The PRS will collect performance fees whenever the music is broadcast on TV as part of the advertisement, or over the radio. PRS also collects fees through its licensing of shops, restaurants and other public places where copyright music is played. Where the music is broadcast outside the U.K., the local affiliate society of PRS will collect the relevant performance income. If any of these public performance fees can be attributed by the PRS to a commercial recording of the jingle music only the jingle company will be paid—not the agency or the advertiser client.

Commercial recording

5.63.4   The 30-second concentrated jingle music which is used in the TV advertisement may be expanded into the music for a commercial recording to be made by an artist with words written especially for it. These will not be the words which are used in the soundtrack of the TV advertisement. The TV advertising version of the jingle may not have had any words at all. The sales of a record based upon the TV jingle increases the sources of income from that music for the owner of its copyright, which is the jingle company. The advertiser will not receive any payment for this use of "its jingle", and will not receive any part of the additional income generated from its commercial exploitation.

CLIENT PARTICIPATION IN JINGLE MUSIC EXPLOITATION

Jingle company independence

5.64.1   In relation to the agency and to the advertiser client the position of the jingle company is no different from that of an independent artwork contractor, except that there is a greater scope for lateral exploitation of a piece of music than there is for a piece of artwork. In different circumstances, where original music is commissioned from a composer, the commissioning party can negotiate a benefit for itself from the exploitation of the music, particularly if it has paid a generous commercial rate of fee for its creation. The benefit would be a share in the income which is generated by that exploitation.

Film scores

5.64.2   When a feature film company commissions a musical score from a composer for the sound track, it may demand that the music is published through its own music publishing company, to which the composer assigns the copyright in the music, so it derives its own share of income. The composer is paid a separate fee for creating the music, and the composer and the film company share in agreed proportions the copyright income which is derived from its commercial exploitation.

TV use income share

5.64.3 The music for the 30-second advertisement would not have been created but for the agency commission, and for which the jingle company has been well paid by the advertiser client. Why should the client not be entitled in certain circumstances to share in the income which is derived from other uses of that music? The jingle commissioning fee could take that possibility into account if the client would like to participate in exploiting the music. There may never be any further exploitation of the music which generates income, but successful lateral uses and adaptations of the music can be very profitable. Jingle companies will consider this suggestion as unacceptable heresy, but for major TV advertisers it is worth considering.

Share both cost and income

5.64.4 If a jingle company agrees to share any income from the commercial use and exploitation of the music with the client advertiser, then it would be reasonable for the client to share in any cost which may be incurred by the jingle company in the process of creating the source of such additional income. This would not apply to the production costs of making a record, as the record company takes over that cost because its artist is making the recording. The jingle company (being the copyright owner) licences the use of the music for the recording after extending the composition to a full-length song, and collects the copyright-related income which is derived from the sale of records and the public performances of the recorded composition. This applies to any recording of the composition which is released commercially. The agreement between the client and the jingle company could contain a provision that if the advertiser did not want to share in the cost of any form of exploitation (but it would have the choice), then neither would it share in the income which is created by that form of exploitation.

Free additional advertising

5.64.5 Since there is a close association between the recording of the expanded jingle music and the version of it on the TV advertisement sound track, the client's advertised product should get considerable additional exposure benefits at no extra cost from the commercial exploitation of the record. The recorded and broadcast version will help to promote the TV advertising, at a modest initial cost to the advertiser in comparison with the cost of producing the TV advertisement which contains the jingle.

USE OF EXISTING POPULAR RECORDING

Original hit recordings

5.65.1 As an alternative to having an original jingle or mood music used as the soundtrack music for the TV advertisement, the agency may prefer to use a clip from an existing popular song as performed by the original hit record artist. The song's title or its words may be appropriate to the product which is being advertised or to the scenario in which it is being presented. For any recording which will be used in the soundtrack of a TV advertisement there are two sets of rights which have to be cleared:

(a) the copyright in the music, which normally will be owned by its publisher; and
(b) the copyright in the recording of the music, which normally will be owned by the record comapny which made it.

Each of them will be clearly identified on (for an album) the central record label, and on the album sleeve or CD or tape insert.

Public domain music

5.65.2 If the recording to be used is of a public domain work for which no music copyright credit is claimed by a music publisher, no copyright consent will be required for the use of the music. As copyright is usually claimed by a composer or publisher of an original arrangement of a public domain work, the agency should check which version of the music will be used. The album label or the CD or cassette insert will indicate whether any copyright is claimed for the original arrangement, and if so, the name of the publishing company which is claiming it. If there is no indication in the record credits that copyright is being claimed for the public domain work, the agency should also check whether the arrangement has been registered with The Performing Right Society Ltd. as a copyright work. The use of an existing recording of a public domain work, such as a popular classical work, will still need consent from the record company.

Central clearance and fees

5.65.3 The written clearances can be obtained from the publisher of the music and the record company as the owners of those respective copyrights. The separate consent of the composer of the music or of the artist who recorded the song is not required for the use of the song or the recording in the advertisement, as they do not own any proprietary rights in those circumstances. Because the consents of the music publisher and the record company relate to different copyrights, there will be a different fee payable to each of them. Each fee is freely negotiable, depending on the perceived value of the relevant rights to each of the copyright owners and to the advertiser client. There is no scale of fee which can be forced upon any copyright owner for TV advertisement use of the music. Where the composition which is being cleared for TV advertising use consists of both words and music, there may be one copyright owner for the music, and a separate copyright owner for the words. If only the music is to be used, only that copyright owner's consent will be needed. If both the words and music are to be used, then consent is required from both copyright owners. The words and the music may be owned jointly by two publishers, when consent will be required from both of them.

Consent can be refused

5.65.4 If either the music publisher or the record company refuses to grant a licence to the agency to clear its own rights in the music or the recording for that TV advertisement soundtrack use, then that effectively prevents those rights from being used. There is no means of forcing either copyright owner to give its consent to the use of its rights in the music or the recording.

Music clearance is essential

5.65.5 If the music publisher refuses to allow the use of the music in the advertisement, then there is no point in contacting the record company, and neither can the advertiser get the music re-recorded. If the music publisher agrees to the use of the music, but the record company will not allow its artist's recording of that music to be used, the agency can go to the expense of having any other artist make a new recording of the segment of the song which is required for the advertisement.

Modifying the words

5.65.6 One benefit of re-recording the music is that it can be re-arranged to suit the imagery of the advertisement, and new words for the TV jingle can be written to be appropriate for the product which is being advertised. From the consent point of view several implications follow.

(1) The composing and recording of a new arrangement of the music will need the written consent of the music publisher. The publisher will also require the copyright in the new arrangement to be assigned to it by the arranger, so as not to dilute the copyright of the original music.

(2) If the original words of the song are going to be modified to refer to the advertised product, that will also need the consent of the music publisher. If a separate music publisher owns the copyright in the words, then only its consent is required for that modification.

(3) If totally new words are to be written to go with the music, then:
    (a) the consent of the publisher of the music is required for the use of the new words in conjunction with the music;

(b) if the copyrights in the music and the words are separate, consent is not required from the owner of the copyright in the original words, as they are not being used;

(c) if two music publishers own jointly both the words and the music, then consent will be required from both of them;

(d) the agency should make sure that the copyright in the new words is assigned by their author either to the music publisher or to the agency, depending on the publisher's terms of consent to use of the music.

CONSENT FOR USE OF NAME OR IMAGE

Personal rights

5.66.1 If the agency wants to use the name or image of the artist who recorded the song which is being used in the advertisement sound track in any promotional material for the TV advertisement, it must receive the artist's written consent. Making use of any personality rights of the artist as a performer in connection with the making, broadcasting, and publishing of the TV advertisement is nothing to do with the proprietary rights of the music publisher in the composition or of the recording company in the recording. The record company's right to use and to licence the use of the artist's name and likeness commercially will be limited to the marketing of the record company's audio and audio-visual products which contain the performances of the artist.

Endorsement implications

5.66.2 The use in the TV advertisement of the recording featuring the artist does not imply that the artist is endorsing or approving the advertised product. However, the use of his name and/or likeness independently in connection with the advertisement may be interpreted as an implied endorsement, depending on the presentation. Any such implication would have to be agreed with the artist, and he may request a fee for doing so.

RE-RECORDING BY THE ORIGINAL ARTIST

When re-recording is necessary

5.67.1 If the agency wants to use an existing recording of a hit song by a popular artist, the record company which owns it may refuse, or may charge too high a fee, for its consent. In that case the agency has no alternative but to ask the artist to re-record the appropriate section of that hit song if it wishes to continue with the same concept.

Re-recording restrictions

5.67.2 The legal ability of the artist to re-record the original hit song will be subject to any contractual restriction on him doing so contained in his recording contract. The re-recording restriction will (or should) be limited to the artist making a commercial recording for sale to the public. This is to prevent unfair competition with the original recording during its useful life, and to prevent the artist breaching his exclusive recording contract.

Validity of restriction

5.67.3 If the re-recording restriction upon the artist is still effective, and if the wording of the relevant clause covers a TV advertisement soundtrack recording, the consent of the record company will be required. This will be the case even if the re-recording has totally different words referring to the product. If the recording only ends up as thirty seconds of the artist's performance for the limited use in the soundtrack for the TV advertisement, the re-recording restriction in his recording contract should not apply. If it does, it may be too wide and unenforceable as representing an unreasonable restraint of trade upon the artist, in which case it could be challenged.

COMPARATIVE ADVERTISING

REASON FOR COMPARISONS

Demonstrating product differences

5.68.1 The basis of comparative advertising is that the manufacturer of the advertised product is publicising its claim that its product is better quality, better value for money, or otherwise is a better purchase than the similar product of a competing manufacturer. This is done by comparing the advertised product with similar product which is made by a competitor, in which the competing product is alleged to be inferior within the scope of the points of comparison which are examined in the advertisement. Comparative advertising is widely used for motor cars, as there are so many different features which can be compared between a wide choice of models. The fundamental rule is that the comparison, at whatever level and in respect of whatever characteristics, must be on a fair "like for like" basis, which is not derogatory of the product being compared, and which is not misleading.

Private comparisons

5.68.2 If a buyer wants to purchase a motor car in a price-range he can afford, but he has not yet chosen what to buy, he can make his own comparative chart by listing what he considers to be the good features and the disadvantages of different manufacturer's models within his price range. The personal preferences of the buyer may override what may seem to be a technically correct choice on an impartial basis. For example, he may only be interested in selected features, such as speed and acceleration. Whether his private research results in a fair comparison being made is only material to him.

Commercial approach

5.68.3   Conversely, the advertiser of a product is seeking to influence buyers to purchase that product, so in its advertising it will emphasise its good qualities and will not refer to its disadvantages. Taking the example of a motor car, what one manufacturer will consider to be the top priority selling points which appeal to a discerning motorist may not coincide precisely with those which are considered to be important by another manufacturer.

Exploiting buyer's priorities

5.68.4   Is a car which can travel at 150 mph but which suffers from terminal rust after two years better than a car which can do only 100 mph but which has a six-year rust-free warranty? The qualities which are important to a prospective car buyer depend on whether he is looking at a supersonic sports car, a modest family saloon, or an expensive but beautiful-to-look-at, top-brand-name vehicle. Is the car to be for everyday use about town, or is it to be a status symbol to be used for posing with only on weekends? Whatever the choice of vehicle, in any form of comparative advertising the comparisons must be made between approximately equal competing vehicles in order to be fair to each of them, and to reduce the risk of the advertising being misleading or in contravention of the ASA Code of Advertising Practice, or the E.C. Directive on comparative advertising.

ASA CODE OF ADVERTISING PRACTICE

5.69   Relevant extracts from sections 21 to 24 of Part B of the ASA Code of Advertising Practice are:

Fair dealing
Advertisements containing comparisons should deal fairly with any competitors involved and should be so designed that there is no likelihood of a consumer being misled. In particular:
—it should be clear with what the advertised product is being compared, and upon what basis;
—the subject-matter of the comparison and the terms in which it is expressed should not be such as to confer any artificial advantage upon one product as against another (this is of especial importance in comparisons

between branded and unbranded products and between natural products and substitutes for them);

—claims to objectively superior or superlative status should be expressed in terms which accurately reflect the extent and the nature of the evidence available to substantiate them; and

—no claim that a competitive product is generally unsatisfactory should be based on the highlighting of selected advantages only of the advertised product.

Prices

(1) When a price for a product is quoted in a way which may suggest that the product concerned is a bargain, and particularly when one price is compared directly with another, there should be no exaggeration of the extent to which a purchaser may benefit by buying at that price.

(2) Specifically, comparisons may be regarded as unfair when one (or both) of the elements in the comparison have been artificially selected or manipulated so as to maximise any apparent saving.

(See also Appendix 2 for the DTI Price Indication Code of Practice).

Denigration

Advertisers should not seek to discredit the products of their competitors by any unfair means.

In particular, no advertisement should contain inaccurate or irrelevant comments on the person, character or actions of a competitor.

Nor should an advertisement describe or show the products of a competitor as broken or defaced, inoperative or ineffective. The only exception to this rule is where the description or depiction is based upon the outcome of fair comparative tests to which the advertiser's product also has been subject and the results of such tests are stated.

Exploitation of goodwill

Advertisements should not exploit the goodwill attached to the trade name or mark of another, or his advertising campaign, in any fashion which may unfairly prejudice his interests.

Imitation

No advertisement should so closely resemble another advertisement as to be likely to mislead or confuse.

MISLEADING ADVERTISING

Voluntary product descriptions

5.70.1 There is no law which compels a manufacturer to state all of the good points about its product in its advertisements. Nor is an advertiser obliged to describe, or to warn the buyer about, any bad points relating to the product, such as high fuel consumption and expensive servicing costs. These disadvantages are not the same as the car having dangerous defects. What is considered to be an acceptable compromise of good and bad points is a matter of personal opinion, otherwise everybody would buy the same car.

Subjective quality opinions

5.70.2 Low fuel consumption for a car is a good point, but to compare the fuel consumption of a Mini with that of a Rolls Royce is not comparing like with like. To achieve a fair comparison, all of the factors which influence petrol consumption must be taken into account when choosing the car which will be compared with the advertised car.

Stretching the truth

5.70.3 Straightforward advertising can be selective about the product description, providing that the overall impression which is given by the advertisement is not misleading. It is misleading to state or to imply that the product has a certain attractive attribute which can only be achieved in circumstances which are so artificial that it cannot be reproduced in real life. The car can be shown to be capable of achieving a certain speed, or certain fuel consumption figures in carefully controlled tests, which are conducted in ideal road conditions, or which are done in simulated conditions, with the car being in tip top factory condition. But are those capabilities likely to be matched by the ordinary driver in normal road conditions, driving a car which is not likely to be in factory condition? The advertisement will be misleading where the attribute in real life conditions cannot reach within a reasonable margin the standard which is stated or implied in the advertisement, or where crucial qualifying information about the attribute is deliberately omitted from the advertisement, or is fudged in the advertised statement. Car performance data is therefore stated (often in very small print) to be according to a quoted road test, or to be as achieved in simulated conditions, or as estimated by the manufacturer's as a result of their own testing procedures.

Anonymous comparisons

5.70.4 Comparing a domestic washing powder with "Brand X" is common practice among detergent manufacturers. While the anonymity of the compared product prevents a claim of the advertisement being defamatory, nevertheless Brand X must be a readily available brand of soap powder for there to be a genuine comparison. In addition, since different brands of washing powder state how they should be used for the most beneficial results, the two products must have similar characteristics for the comparison to be fair.

COMPARISON GUIDELINES

Must be on a fair basis

5.71.1 It is permissible for one manufacturer to compare its product with another manufacturer's product in advertising provided that (using the example of a motor car):

(a) *The comparisons are on a "like-for-like" basis.* This means that the comparisons must be fair, taking into account individual differences such as size, price and intended function. A particular model of car may have a range of prices, engine sizes and additional features to suit the different tastes and purchasing powers of a variety of buyers. Comparing the acceleration and speed of a six cylinder turbo charged fuel injected two litre car with those of a four cylinder two litre family car with one economical carburettor is not a valid exercise, although they have engines of the same capacity.

(b) *The advertiser does not infringe the trade mark rights of the manufacturer whose product is being held up as being the inferior comparison.* If manufacturer A is advertising one of its cars in comparison with a similar car which is sold by manufacturer B, to what extent can the advertisement refer to the B car? A simple side-by-side listing headed as "A Car" and "B Car" will not be a trade mark infringement. If the advertisement contains a picture of Car B, its logo and stylised brand name, the advertisement could constitute a trademark infringement. The Car B trade mark can reasonably be alleged to have been used in the advertisement as promoting Car A, not Car B. How the trade marks are used will be the deciding factor, because they have to be used in a trade mark sense. Use in advertising is normally presented in a trade mark sense, i.e., it is being publicised in association with the advertised product so as to use its valuable reputation and goodwill for a commercial purpose.

(c) *The advertisement does not constitute a trade libel on Car B and its manufacturer.* A manufacturer is entitled to claim that its products are better than those of another manufacturer if it has a reasonable and justifiable basis for saying so. Provided that the claim does not make any false representation as to the quality or character of that other manufacturer's goods, there will be no trade libel even if the latter suffers damage. If Car B vehicles generally are renowned for excessive rust after 18 months, or having a history of faulty gearboxes, Car B's reputation will suffer if these serious and consistent faults are publicised. Substantiating such claims may be difficult, as such faults in the occasional car are not sufficient grounds for making much wider generalised disparaging and critical claims. If the statements are demonstrably true, they can be referred to in the advertisement comparing Car A with Car B without incurring legal liability provided that there is no exaggeration or no damaging unsubstantiated innuendo. If the advertisement goes further than a simple statement, and makes untrue disparaging comments or implications about the other product, there is a high risk of committing a trade libel in respect of Car B, which will probably result in immediate legal action.

Trade libel

5.71.2 In the case of a badly misleading comparative advertisement where the facts are distorted or false, and the impression which is given about the compared product is unjustifiably damaging to its name and reputation, its manufacturer may have a claim against the advertiser for trade libel. To succeed in an action for trade libel the plaintiff must prove that all of the following have occurred:

(a) the statement complained of relating to its products was false, and
(b) it was published maliciously, *i.e.* with a dishonest or improper motive, and
(c) the plaintiff has suffered special damage. The damage must be capable of being calculated in money terms, such as a proved loss of business. In the absence of an actual loss being proved, no claim can be made for this kind of attack even though the statement complained of was false and was made maliciously. By section 3(1) of the Defamation Act 1952 special damage need not be proved where the words complained of are calculated to cause pecuniary damage to the plaintiff and where they are published in writing or some other permanent form.

Personal libel

5.71.3 A disparaging statement in a comparative advertisement relating to the compared product may be libellous to the manufacturer, even though it is a company. Therefore there is a risk of two legal actions being brought against the advertiser; one for a trade libel against the compared product, and one for the personal libel against the manufacturer of that product.

EUROPEAN COMMUNITY RULES

E.C. DIRECTIVE 84/450 ON MISLEADING ADVERTISING

Harmonising national laws

5.72.1 This E.C. Directive on misleading advertising came into force in September 1984 and an amending proposal to include comparative advertising was submitted by the Commission in May 1991. The 1984 Directive and the

1991 amending Directive are paraphrased in the following paragraphs in respect of those items which relate to advertisements. For research on specific instances in greater detail the full text of the Directives should be examined. Pan-European advertising, despite the different languages, is becoming a reality for international manufacturers in the Economic Community. The E.C. Directive deals with harmonising the national laws on misleading advertising and sets out as a preamble the reasons for the Directive, some of which are:

(a) Misleading advertising can lead to distortion of competition within the common market.
(b) Advertising affects the welfare of consumers.
(c) Misleading advertising may cause a consumer to take decisions prejudicial to his interests when accepting goods or other property, or using services.
(d) There should be an effective and speedy judicial system to protect those who are damaged by unlawful advertising.
(e) The advertiser should be able to prove the material accuracy of the factual claims he makes in his advertising, and may in appropriate cases be required to do so by the court or an administrative authority.

Key elements of the Directive

5.72.2 Key elements which will govern the acceptability of comparative advertising in the E.C. will be that:

(a) only material elements or features should be compared;
(b) points of comparison must be chosen fairly;
(c) the essence of the comparison must be verifiable;
(d) comparisons should not mislead;
(e) the comparison should not cause confusion in the market place;
(f) comparisons must not be used to capitalise on the reputation of the compared product, its brand name, or its trademark;
(g) the comparison does not discredit, denigrate or bring contempt on a competitor or his trade marks, trade names, goods, services or activities;
(h) reference to or reproduction of the results of comparative tests on goods or services carried out by third parties shall be permitted in advertising only if the person who has carried out the test gives his express consent. In such cases the advertiser shall accept responsibility for the test as if it had been performed by himself or under his direction.

Setting the scene

5.72.3 Most of the Directive relates to establishing a legal administrative framework, but articles 2 and 3 set the scene in advertising terms.

Article 2 deals with four important definitions for the Directive:

(a) Advertising means the making of a representation in any form in connection with a trade, business, craft or profession in order to promote the supply of goods or services, including immovable property, rights and obligations.
(b) "Misleading advertising" means any advertising which in any way, including its presentation, deceives or is likely to deceive the persons to whom it is addressed, or whom it reaches and which by reason of its deceptive nature, is likely to affect their economic behaviour or which, for those reasons, injures or is likely to injure a competitor.
(c) "Comparative advertising" means any advertising which explicitly or by implication identifies a competitor or goods or services of the same kind offered by a competitor.
(d) "Person" means any natural or legal person.

Article 3 states that in determining whether advertising is misleading, account shall be taken of all its features, and in particular of any information it contains concerning:

(a) the characteristics, such as their availability, nature, execution, composition, method and date of manufacture and provision, fitness for purpose, uses, quantity, specification, geographical or commercial origin, or the results to be expected from their use, or the results and material features of tests or checks carried out on the goods or services;
(b) the price or the manner in which the price is calculated, and the conditions on which the goods are supplied or the services provided;
(c) the nature, attributes and rights of the advertiser, such as his identity and assets, his qualifications and ownership of industrial, commercial or intellectual property rights or his awards and distinctions.

Implementation

5.72.4 The rest of the Directive deals with the legal framework which is to be operated in member countries to protect those who may be damaged by misleading advertisements. This is not reviewed here, but the first paragraph of article 4 states that:

"Member States shall ensure that adequate and effective means exist for the control of misleading advertising in the interest of consumers as well as competitors and the general public."

In the U.K. the Directive has been implemented partly through the functioning of the Advertising Standards Authority and partly through the legal controls in the Trade Descriptions Act 1968 and Consumer Protection Act 1987.

MISLEADING STATEMENTS

STATMENTS IN ADVERTISEMENTS

Descriptions and price

5.73.1 The two main areas where the creators of advertising copy tend to make misleading statements are as to the description of the product being advertised, and the purchase price of that product. By statement or implication the advertiser wants to describe its product in the best light, and it also wants to make the price to the consumer sound attractive. The principal legislation is the Consumer Protection Act 1987 in respect of price indications, and the Trade Descriptions Act 1968 in respect of product descriptions.

CONSUMER PROTECTION ACT 1987

Application of sections 20 and 21

5.74.1 Section 20 of the 1987 Act defines the offence of giving a misleading price indication, and the main features of that section are:

(a) by section 20(1) a person shall be guilty of an offence if, in the course of his business, he gives by any means to any consumers an indication which is misleading as to the price at which any goods are available. See para. 5.76.1 for the meaning of "in the course of his business";

(b) by section 20(2) a trader will also be guilty of an offence if he has given a price indication to consumers which has only become misleading after he gave it, and consumers might reasonably be expected to rely on that price indication after it has become misleading, and the trader fails to take all such steps as are reasonable to prevent those consumers from relying on that price indication.

Meaning of consumer price and misleading

5.74.2 By section 20(*b*) in relation to any goods:

(a) "consumer" means any person who might wish to be supplied with the goods for his own private use or consumption;

(b) "price" means the aggregate of the sums required to be paid by a consumer for the supply of the goods, or any method which will be or has been applied for the purpose of determining that aggregate.

Misleading price indication

5.74.3 By section 21 a price indication given to consumers is misleading if by indication or omission from the indication:

(a) the indicated price is less than the actual price;

(b) the actual price is dependent on facts or circumstances which are not visible;

(c) the indicated price covers matters in respect of which an additional charge is in fact made;

(d) a person who in fact has no such expectation expects the price to be increased or reduced at a particular time or by a particular amount, or to be maintained;

(e) the facts or circumstances by reference to which consumers might reasonably be expected to judge the validity of any relevant comparison made or implied by the indication are not what in fact they are.

R. v. Warwickshire CC, ex p. Johnson, The Times, December 16, 1992

5.75.1   In December 1992 the above important House of Lords case clarified a grey area in defining what can constitute a misleading statement. A notice outside a High Street retailer in Stratford upon Avon stated "We will beat any TV, Hi-fi, Video price by £20 on the spot". A consumer saw that a TV set which was on sale in that shop at £179.95 was also on sale at another local shop for £159.95. On the strength of the High Street retailer's advertisement, the consumer sought to purchase from it the advertised product for £139.95, *i.e.* at "£20.00 off". The High Street retailer refused to sell its TV set to that consumer for £139.95, but offered to sell it at £159.95, thus matching its competitor's price. The consumer complained to his Trading Standards Department, and the High Street retailer was prosecuted for making a misleading statement. The case went from the Magistrates Court to the Divisional Court and then to the House of Lords. The Divisional Court certified the two following questions for consideration by the House of Lords:

(a) "Whether for the purposes of section 20(1) of the Consumer Protection Act 1987 a statement which in itself is not misleading on the face of it, can be rendered misleading by virtue of the fact that, even in the absence of evidence to show a general practice or intention to dishonour the offer contained therein, on one occasion the person making the statement declined to enter into a contract within the terms of that statement".

Their Lordships decided that the statement could be misleading because the notice was a continuing offer, and whether it was misleading or not could only be tested by somebody taking up the offer. It was misleading in that instance because the shop did not in accordance with the terms of the notice "beat any TV, Hi- fi, Video price by £20 on the spot".

(b) "Whether for the purposes of section 20(2)(a) of the Consumer Protection Act 1987 an employed branch manager who fails to comply with a price indication so that the same is to be regarded as misleading does so "in the course of any business of his".

Their Lordships decided that the words "in the course of a business of his" must mean any business in which the defendant is either the owner or in which he has a controlling interest. Therefore the employee manager of a store at which an offence is committed under section 20 of the Consumer Protection Act 1987 is not personally liable, even though he may have been the person who devised the offending promotion.

TRADE DESCRIPTIONS ACT 1968

Offence by supplier

5.76.1 By section 1 of the Trade Descriptions Act 1968 any person who in the course of a trade or business applies a false trade description to any goods, or who supplies or offers to supply any goods to which a false trade description is applied, shall be guilty of an offence. By section 6 of the Act, a person who exposes goods for supply, or who has goods in his possession for supply, shall be deemed to offer to supply them. By section 3 of the Act a false trade description is a trade description which is false to a material degree. Therefore there is a distinction between an inconsequential misdescription which does not affect the judgment of the consumer when purchasing the product, and one which is of a fundamental nature. This flexibility enables advertisements to contain language describing the product in glowing terms which do not amount to an intentional misdescription.

TRADE DESCRIPTION

5.76.2 By section 2 of the Act a trade description is defined as a direct or indirect indication by whatever means with respect to goods of any of;

(a) their quantity or size;
(b) their method of manufacture;
(c) their composition;
(d) their fitness for purpose, strength, performance, behaviour or accuracy;
(e) any other physical characteristics;
(f) any testing and its results;
(g) any type approval or similar conformity;
(h) the place or date of manufacture;
(i) the person by whom it is manufactured; and
(j) any other relevant history.

Applying a trade description

5.76.3 By section 4 of the Act a person applies a trade description to goods if he attaches it to or in any manner marks it on or incorporates it with the goods themselves, or anything in, on or with which the goods are supplied; or if he uses the trade description in any manner likely to be taken as referring to the goods.

6

Personality Endorsement and Advertising

PERSONALITIES INFLUENCE ADVERTISING

PURPOSE OF USING PERSONALITIES IN ADVERTISING

Advertising promotes the product

6.1.1 Advertising is said to be the art of influencing the public to purchase the manufacturer's products. Although the advertisement is a statement of all or some of the good features of the product, each member of the public is left to decide whether he should buy the product. Advertisements have one of two effects on those who read or see them:

(a) either they assume that everything which is stated in them must be true, otherwise it would not have been asserted; or
(b) they are more cynical and take the view that "You can't believe everything you read", they suspect that advertised products cannot be as perfect as they claim to be.

Personalities provide credibility

6.1.2 Most members of the public need to be convinced that the advertising claims represent a fair statement of the quality and value of the advertised product. They may be more likely to accept the validity of claims made in the advertisement if a person whom they recognise and admire persuades them that they can have confidence in the product.

Reference for convenience to sporting personalities

6.1.3 This chapter deals with legal and contractual aspects of personality endorsement which are relevant to product advertising. The first part briefly describes the use of personalities for endorsement advertising to set the scene for the discussion of the legal aspects which follows. For simplicity and convenience most references and examples relate to sporting personalities, as they tend to have a large public following and they easily demonstrate the principles which are being discussed.

259

WHAT IS ENDORSEMENT?

Personalities' recommendation

6.2.1 Endorsement is the advertising and promotion of a product by using the positive recommendation of a well known public personality. The choice of the personality to match the product involves skill, and the personality must have audience appeal. To be successful in endorsing and advertising products he will have to be sufficiently well known and popular to influence the purchasing pattern of a significant sector of the consumer public. Endorsement can also enable a personality to extend his own programme of self-promotion and increase his earning capacity.

Product association

6.2.2 The basic concept of the advertisement centres around the personality extolling the virtues of the product. The more subtle advertising presentations do not need a script as the visual story says it all. If there is a specific connection between the personality and the product, such as a golfer promoting a set of golf clubs, an association is created which is stronger than, say, the relevance to an advertisement of an opera star endorsing a new brand of lawnmower. The latter would be incongruous, except where it becomes a memorable spoof advertisement.

PSYCHOLOGY OF ENDORSEMENT

Belief in personality

6.3.1 The psychological basis of personality advertising is that if (say) a top athlete uses a manufacturer's special running shoes as his personal choice, there is a presumption that he believes they are the best shoes available. If he actively endorses and recommends that brand of running shoe in an advertisement for them, then both budding and experienced athletes might be influenced to purchase them. The advertised recommendation is intended to persuade athletes that the personality's secret of success lies partly in the use by him of that advertised brand of running shoes.

Matching personality with product

6.3.2 Whatever the product is which is being recommended by a personality, the personality and product must be compatible and a credible combination. The manufacturer must match correctly the product with the popularity and charisma of the advertising personality. After that it is up to the agency to make the most of the available material and to create a successful advertising campaign around that personality.

WHAT IS MERCHANDISING?

Product added value

6.4 In the case of a personality, and in the context of consumer product advertising, merchandising is the use of the personality's public recognition factor to promote and sell a product by having the name or features of the personality printed prominently on the product or its packaging. The distinction between merchandising and endorsement is that an endorsement is a positive recommendation of the product by the personality, whereas using his face or name on (say) clothing only gives an added value attraction to buyers. In the case of merchandising, it is unlikely that the public will believe that the passive representation of the personality on the product is in any way an implication that he is recommending it. The personality who grants merchandising rights does not want to be directly connected with recommendation or promotion of the product. For this reason, the merchandising contract must ensure that the use of the face or name of the personality is not presented as advertising or as otherwise recommending the products.

ADVERTISING VALUE OF PERSONALITY

Public recognition

6.5.1 A personality with a national or international public status has a valuable asset in his name, image and reputation. This marketable asset can be used as a means of promoting and advertising products and services. The value of the personality to an advertising campaign which is being considered by a manufacturer for one of its branded products depends on the public perception of the personality, and how established he has become in the "recognition factor" stakes. There are many people who are familiar to the public through TV music or sport, but who are "short-term" recollection personalities. However, not everybody who is known to the public can sell products to it. If the personality cannot make people's minds focus on the advertisement and encourage them to buy the product, there is little point in using him to endorse the product.

Established goodwill value

6.5.2 When a manufacturer finds a winning personality and it produces an expensive and extensive advertising campaign for its product featuring that personality, the manufacturer may be reluctant to change what has been a winning combination and style. A personality may be used to advertise one brand of product for so long that he becomes inseparable from it in the mind of the public, and that association between them can have a significant goodwill value to the product manufacturer. The advertising is intended to create the position where the mere sight of that personality in the advertisement or in any other context will subconsciously trigger the recollection of the product and its brand name in the mind of the viewer.

Slogan power

6.5.3 A product slogan which is associated exclusively with a personality can become a regular feature of advertising campaigns for the product, and is a good basis for promotional posters and roadside advertising hoardings. Some slogans can even outlive the memory of the personality who starred in the advertisement.

VALUE OF PERSONALITY FOR ENDORSEMENT

MONETARY AND STATUS VALUE

Relates to product prestige

6.6.1 Where a personality is charismatic and nationally known for whatever he does, his personal endorsement value extends to almost anything else which itself has a status or reputation which is consistent with that of the personality. A top personality may not want to be associated with recommending some mundane household product, on the basis that it is "down market" and his personal prestige can be damaged. "Is that the best he can do?" might be an implied question. Conversely, the manufacturer of an expensive prestige product may not want to rely on a personality with less status recommending it.

Personality enhances value

6.6.2 If the personality is advertising products which are related to his recognised activity or sport, then the value of his participation in the advertisement depends substantially upon his being, or having been, a champion or a top player. In competitive sports the personality should stay at or around the top of his sport during the period for which the advertisements will be running, to give maximum current exposure and credibility to his recommendation of the product. This is not an absolute rule, as a highly respected star of yesteryear who is still in the public eye can be equally marketable.

262

Marketable value

6.6.3   The advertising value of the personality in terms of exposure increases if he wins the next title, but decreases if he ceases to be involved competitively within the activity for which he is famous. The staying power of a personality's popularity is a key factor of his endorsement value. If there is no long lasting marketable substance, then he is not a likely candidate for endorsement advertising.

ASSESSMENT OF VALUE BY ADVERTISER

Additional sales potential

6.7.1   The value of the advertised recommendation by a personality to the manufacturer of the advertised product is limited to the extent that there is an unsaturated market for the product. There is no point in having a total marketing expenditure overkill where additional sales potential for the product does not exist. However, the manufacturer of a market leader product may still use a personality to endorse it in advertising to help to *maintain* its popularity and its market share.

Measure of personality's success

6.7.2   What is the measure of success of an advertising campaign which makes use of a personality? There may be no dramatic surge of sales of the product during the advertising campaign which can be identified as being the result of it. At worst it will have helped to maintain a steady level of sales in a period of intense competition. Personality advertising will usually be an additional promotion for the product, such as at Christmas, or when the personality is competing in a major event, and it will be complementary to all other normal media advertising of that product. If the normal advertising is kept to schedule, then any significant uplift in sales during the personality advertisement campaign period can be attributed largely to its influence upon the public awareness of the product at that time.

Effective support of advertising

6.7.3   The value of using a personality to advertise a product can be enhanced by extending the ways in which he becomes involved in the promotion of the product. These would need the consent of the personality, which would be easier to negotiate at the time of the endorsement deal. For instance, a substantial TV advertising campaign can be backed up by special product packaging containing his photograph which is linked with the TV advertising; a sales promotion scheme can be run which refers to the personality; and a mailshot or instore leaflets can follow to get the message fully across. If the product is suitable, part of the deal with the personality may be that he makes personal appearances at special promotional events such as new product launch parties or sponsored exhibitions to promote the product.

ENDORSEMENT AGREEMENTS

AGREEMENT WITH ADVERTISER

Reduces misunderstandings

6.8   Even if the personality is only going to be used for a short-term printed advertisement, there should be a written agreement between him and the manufacturer of the advertised product. This reduces the risk of misunderstandings which can occur when the deal is inadequately documented. The preparation of a detailed agreement addresses the minds of the parties to what should be negotiated between them. There is no standard format for an endorsement agreement. There will be clause headings which will be common to most agreements, but there is total flexibility for drafting the clauses dealing with individual commitments.

REASONS FOR WRITTEN AGREEMENT

Licence of rights

6.9   The essence of the agreement between the manufacturer of the advertised product and the personality is that the personality grants to the manufacturer a licence to use his name and likeness in advertisements for the products, together with the agreed text of a recommendation to be attributed to the personality. The agreement sets out their respective commercial, financial and intellectual property rights. A comprehensive agreement in writing between them is desirable because:

(a) An oral agreement or even a short heads of agreement is an inadequate substitute for a detailed legal agreement and the protection it provides.
(b) The right to use the name, image and reputation of the personality in advertisements is a clear matter of contract, so (for example) there must be no risk of the manufacturer being accused of breach of Section B paragraph 17.3 of the Advertising Standards Authority Code of Advertising Practice, which prohibits such use without the personality's permission.
(c) The commercial and financial terms of the deal should be properly documented. In the absence of a detailed agreement it is not safe to

assume that what one party considers to be an essential term of the agreement will necessarily be acceptable to or understood in the same manner by the other party. The advertiser has the most to lose by not having a carefully drafted agreement, because he has to incur the production and media costs of the advertising campaign. The agency owes the advertiser a strong duty of care if it is negotiating the deal with the personality and drafting the contract for it.

(d) Although it is unlikely, the personality may be involved in the advertising and endorsement of several different products over a period of time, such as in different territories. A proper agreement in each case will enable him to make sure that in arranging different advertising deals he does not inadvertently find himself in breach of any of them.

ENDORSEMENT CONTRACT PERIOD

Personality's availability and commitment

6.10.1   The period of the advertising agreement with the personality depends on the kind of advertising to be used. There are two possible contract periods:

(a) The period during which the personality will be available to be photographed or filmed, such as for a series of advertisements. This period will also cover any personal appearance commitments.

(b) The period during which the advertiser can use approval advertisements which contain the personality's endorsement.

Simple printed media use of name and photograph

6.10.2   The use of the personality may simply consist of a head-and-shoulders photograph of him in a leaflet or magazine advertisement saying why he thinks the promoted product is the best of its kind. Alternatively, there may only be a photograph, without any quoted words of recommendation. A well-known personality who is simply looking out of an open double-glazed window in a picturesque thatched cottage may be all the endorsement required for that product. If that is all there is to the advertising, the personality is not put under a time contract; the advertiser is given a licence to use that previously agreed photograph plus approved quotations within that advertisement for a limited period of time, in specified media, and in the same format only.

Continuous series use

6.10.3   A common use is where the personality features in a continuous series of TV or press advertisements for the same product over the years, with the result that the product and the personality become closely associated. The advertiser may want the right to resurrect previous advertising in the future as a nostalgic review of the role of the personality during the period of his advertising the product, such as in a "then and now" sequence. In this case, the contract between the personality and the manufacturer should require a long-term priority commitment by the personality in return for a schedule of commensurate payments. The agreement may also contain an option for the manufacturer to extend it if the long-term campaign continues to be successful.

Creating a personality

6.10.4 Personality advertising extends to the creation of a fictional person by an actor. The fictional character can then himself become a personality in the course of broadcasting a series of different but linked advertisements. British Telecom did this successfully with "Beattie". Some manufacturers of instant coffee and the producers of some liqueurs have got this form of advertising down to a fine art, because:

(a) It creates continuity in an advertising theme, which enables the advertiser to monitor its public reception and to extend the "serial" to the next campaign "instalment".
(b) The personal on-screen chemistry between the characters is as important as the product, as it generates press coverage and public interest—which extends public awareness of the advertisement and thus of the product.
(c) Unknown actors who are chosen to be the characters in the advertisement can become personalities as a result.

Ownership of character

6.10.5 What happens where a TV advertisement uses a personality to create a long-term fictional character to promote the product, and where the character becomes famous, and consequently becomes embodied in the personality who portrays the character? Are any proprietary rights created in the character, who is the original invention of the advertiser, and if so, who owns them? The personality, who is only employed by the advertiser to represent the character in the advertisements for a specific product, could not use the character to promote the products of other manufacturers, whether or not they are competitive. If being known as the character makes the personality a popular choice for opening supermarkets and making other personal appearances in his own persona, the advertiser who owns the character could not object. Whether the goodwill in the character will belong to the advertiser of the product with which it is so closely associated, or to the personality, will depend on how the character was evolved, and on the terms of the contract between the advertiser (or its agency) and the personality. If it is a "product character" which has been devised by the manufacturer's agency to symbolise the product, the personality who has become associated publicly with the character in the advertisements has no right to use "the character" outside the advertisements for the product. Nor can he insist on being retained by the manufacturer to represent the character in all future advertising of the product which uses the character. The personality would have no rights in any book, comic strip, poster or other commercial exploitation of the character, but any visual representation of the character could not use the image of the personality without his consent.

Useful life of advertisement

6.10.6 The rights of the manufacturer to broadcast and/or publish the personality advertisements should not be for less than one year if it it for a consumer related product. This period will enable the advertisements to catch both regular and seasonal trade during the year. The likely useful life of the advertisement or series of advertisements featuring the personality should be assessed, and a use period for the advertising should be negotiated accordingly. The advertising contract period should be long enough for the manufacturer to get the most out of the advertising campaign. If a sporting personality advertises products which he uses in his sporting activity, the advertising agreement should be terminable by either party if he stops using those products.

Useful life of personality

6.10.7 A regular "public figure" personality is not subject to a seasonal activity. Sporting, athletic and other competitive activities are seasonal, so the contract period for such a personality should be calculated to cover the active season in each of the years for which the advertiser's rights can be exercised. How important this consideration is will depend on:

(a) how well known the personality is outside the followers of his activity;
(b) whether the product which is being advertised is itself seasonal, such as ski wear and equipment, and
(c) for how long the product should be advertised with the personality's endorsement prior to the impact of the season which determines its main selling period.

PERSONALITY'S PERFORMANCE OBLIGATION

Cannot be absolute

6.11.1 If the golfer or athlete who is the endorsing personality has an "off" period, such as for injury or illness, there is no need for the manufacturer to terminate the advertising agreement. The ups and downs of sporting and competitive life are an accepted feature of endorsement contracts, and this should be documented in the contract. The initial obligations of the personality will have been completed when all the filming and photography for the advertising material has been completed, and the attributed quotations of the personality have been agreed. The question then is whether the personality should have any subsequent obligations to the advertiser during the advertisement use period such as not being convicted of drug abuse. Personal restrictions of this nature are not appropriate or enforceable, but the adverse effects of their occurrence can be dealt with in the contract for the protection of the advertiser. If the contract is made terminable by the advertiser due to the happening of an event caused by the personality which reasonably makes the advertiser withdraw the advertising to avoid embarrassment or ridicule for itself and its products, it should also be entitled to retain, or to have repaid some or all of the agreed fees, depending on the value (if any) it has already received from the campaign before the event which triggered the termination.

Contract period adjustment

6.11.2 If the rights of the advertiser, and therefore the endorsement contract period, are dependent on the personality being available and professionally active, what happens when circumstances prevent him from fulfilling those commitments? A spoilt season can be recompensed for by the advertiser being able to extend the period of agreement with the personality until the end of the next season, but this right will have to be set out in the agreement. It will not be assumed to be an implied right if the personality at that time does not wish to extend the agreement amicably. Because of the legal difficulties inherent in trying to enforce or control personal service contracts, any such condition should be made "of the essence" of the contract for any fee-reduction purposes, and for any contract period extension purposes.

EXCLUSIVITY OF PERSONALITY'S SERVICES

EXCLUSIVITY IS NECESSARY

Product category

6.12 Where a sporting personality is endorsing and advertising a brand of product which he uses for his activity (such as a brand of tennis racket), and where he is being highly paid for the endorsement, then the agreement should be exclusive to the product manufacturer for the product category. During the exclusivity period the personality should not be allowed to advertise or endorse any directly competitive products. These restrictions should be well defined and reasonable, so that the condition of exclusivity is not unacceptably oppressive to the personality. The restrictions could extend to indirectly competing products where they are reasonably connected with the endorsed product. For example, tennis balls are reasonably related to tennis rackets. If the advertiser makes both but the personality is only endorsing the racket, it would be reasonable to restrict him from endorsing the tennis balls of another manufacturer. It would not be reasonable to prevent him from endorsing other people's tennis courts or tennis clothing without him receiving an adequate compensation for accepting that restriction.

ADVERTISER'S MINIMUM OBLIGATIONS

Exposure for personality

6.13 Part of the benefit of the deal to the personality will be the broadcasting or the publication during the contract period of the advertisements which contain the agreed endorsement. The advertiser will never commit itself contractually to making any minimum public use of any advertisement which contains the personality's recommendation of the product. That must remain solely the advertiser's commercial decision. Neither will it commit itself to using the advertisement for specific campaigns because of many factors which can affect its schedule or its budget. It the advertising which contains the endorsement is never used by the advertiser, the personality loses an active outlet for the enhancement of his marketable value because:

(a) Appearing in the advertisements would give the personality enhanced publicity, and may give him opportunities for further personal promotion.
(b) Total failure of the manufacturer to use the advertising within a specified period after the advertisements have been completed the endorsement contract should allow the personality to end the restriction of exclusivity in TV and other advertising. In practice the advertiser will use expensive advertising, but there may be good reasons for not using it immediately.
(c) The personality may have chosen to work for this advertiser rather than for others which had made him product endorsement offers, and no use or inadequate use of the advertising may reflect badly on the personality. There may be an implication that either the personality or the advertising material had not been satisfactory to the advertiser. If the advertiser makes minimal or no use of the advertisement there may come a time when the personality should have the opportunity to resurrect other offers of endorsement which he turned down in favour of the advertiser. This right would have to be set out specifically in the endorsement contract.

269

Limitations on choice of personality

Avoid over exposure

6.14 A product manufacturer is not likely to use in a proposed heavy weight advertising campaign a personality who has recently featured in extensive national advertising for a major brand product of another manufacturer, whether or not it was competitive. The reasons are that:

(a) The background voice of an invisible personality can be used for numerous advertised products because it does not distract the viewer's attention, and it allows the advertisement to concentrate more on the product which is being advertised. However, in the case of endorsement advertising, the personality is prominently visible to the viewer while he is promoting the product and the emphasis of the advertisement is divided between them for its effect.

(b) Part of the value of the personality to the manufacturer will be because he does not endorse any other products. If his face is already familiar to the public as an endorsing personality, the novelty impact of having him in the new advertisement for this product is reduced.

(c) Consumers may be confused, having become used to seeing the personality advertising the previous product, and associating him with it. Intensive exposure over a period of time by a TV advertisement can leave a subliminal retention of it in the consumer's mind. When he sees the personality next time round advertising a different product, the subliminal memory may take time to accept the association of the personality with the new product that is being advertised. Some personalities are still renowned for having advertised a product long after the advertisement has stopped being shown or publicised. How long is it since Henry Cooper advertised Brut, or William Franklin advertised "Sssch. . . . you known who"? Many viewers of that era remember those advertisements vividly even now.

RESTRICTIONS ON THE PERSONALITY

Competing products

Personality's protection

6.15.1 Whether the personality is being used to promote the corporate image of the advertiser without any emphasis on a specific product, or whether the endorsement is of specific products, the extent of the exclusivity restrictions on the personality should be reasonable or they risk being unenforceable.

The personality should insist that the restrictions only relate to ranges of products which are specified at the time the endorsement agreement is signed. The advertiser's exclusivity should not extend to "any other product which the Company may manufacture or distribute during the period of this Agreement", unless the personality will be actually endorsing them. Even then the restriction can only apply to those specific products. This is because:

(a) that would enable the manufacturer arbitrarily to extend the restrictions upon the personality without his being able to object;
(b) the fee payable to the personality may take into account only the specific product restrictions he accepted under the endorsement contract;
(c) that quoted extension of restrictions on the personality does not refer to the "other products" necessarily being of a similar nature to those for which the advertiser already has exclusivity under the endorsement contract.

The personality should never accept any exclusivity restriction relating to the products which are made or distributed by any associated or subsidiary company of the advertiser unless they are specifically identified in the contract. Even then, they should be the kind of products for which the restrictions would have been reasonable if they had been produced by the advertiser.

Legal position

6.15.2   The general rule is that a restriction on any person which relates to or inhibits his ability to carry on any business activity so as to earn his living will not be enforceable unless it is reasonable and necessary to protect the legitimate interests of the party which claims the benefit of that restriction. In each case whether any restriction is fair, reasonable and legally justifiable depends on the circumstances in which it is demanded. The personality should only accept a restriction if it is reasonable to ensure that the advertiser gets proper value from the exclusivity of the personality's advertising services during his endorsement contract period.

ENFORCEABILITY OF PERSONALITY'S OBLIGATIONS

Legal practicability

6.16.1   There is a legal conflict between it being reasonable to expect the courts to enforce against a contracting party the obligations he took on willingly and knowingly and for good recompense, and the reluctance of the courts to enforce obligations by way of performance of personal services. The reason is that there is no practical means whereby the court can enforce positive personal commitments if the personality refuses to perform them. For example, if the endorsing personality agrees to use the manufacturer's advertised product, and during the period of restriction he uses the competing product of another manufacturer, that will be a breach of contract. Even so, the court will not order him to fulfil his contractual commitment by using the advertised product. Other personal obligations, which are of a negative nature, such as undertaking not to advertise a competitor's product, may be enforceable. The personality does not escape however if he breaches unenforceable obligations; the courts will, in the proper circumstances, award the manufacturer damages to compensate for the financial loss he has suffered as a result of the personality's breach.

Financial considerations

6.16.2 The obligations and restrictions which are accepted by the personality will be in consideration for the payment of money to him by the manufacturer of the advertised products. The payment schedule of the fee can be spread over the contract period, so that there is every incentive for the personality to complete his obligations fully and on time. So far as it is practical to do so, the contract should protect the manufacturer against a breach by the personality of his obligations to the manufacturer. For example, there may be circumstances in which the failure of performance by the personality should entitle the manufacturer to cease making payments to him, or to suspend or reduce them, or even to claim them back, depending on the seriousness of the breach. In the absence of a contractual right to control payments in that manner, the advertiser will have to take legal action and make a claim against the personality for breach of contract.

RESTRICTION AFTER CONTRACT PERIOD

Applies to competing products only

6.17 If the agreement makes it a reasonable requirement, for a stated period after the expiry of the exclusive endorsement advertising period granted to the advertiser, there could also be a restriction on the personality advertising any other product which is directly competitive with the advertised product. This restriction period should not be excessive, and should not prevent him from following his career. It should only be for a period which is reasonably required to enable the product manufacturer to wind down its promotional operations based on the personality advertising. Where it is relevant, the advertiser must also have time to dispose of remaining stock of "personality products".

ANALYSIS OF RESTRICTIONS

Use not endorsement

6.18.1   The following example relates to an advertising deal for the endorsement by a well-known golfer of a manufacturer's clubs, which he uses successfully and exclusively. He has also agreed to a six-month restriction after the end of the exclusive endorsement period on endorsing, recommending or advertising the clubs of any other manufacturer. This should not prevent the personality from *playing* with those competitive products immediately following termination of the endorsement agreement. He cannot be prevented from carrying on his career, and whilst he may start to endorse his new clubs in media advertising after his restriction period has expired, he has a contractual obligation to respect the restriction until then. In practical terms the use of new clubs is tantamount to endorsing them tacitly.

Extent of restriction

6.18.2   The restriction will refer to the contracted personality not doing those activities which are set out in the endorsement contract. A restrictive clause is always interpreted giving the benefit of any doubt to the personality, and it is interpreted strictly against the party claiming to benefit from it. As a result the following points are material:

(a) No restriction on the personality will be implied if it is not specifically included in the wording of the contract, and the effects of the restriction will not be extended beyond what the contract clearly states, irrespective of what the manufacturer intended to apply.
(b) The restriction will only apply to the personality; it cannot bind any other person who is not a party to the contract. What then is to prevent the golfer's new club manufacturer from itself advertising the fact that the personality is now using (during the restricted period) its clubs, and not the ones he had been endorsing previously? If the restrictive clause had a provision whereby the personality must procure that any other party would not use his name for the advertising of his new clubs during the restriction period, that may not be too remote, and could be enforceable. The restriction does not adversely affect his ability to play with the clubs and to earn a living, and it is within his control.

Effectiveness of restrictions

6.18.3   What would happen if the golfer started to use the new brand of competitive clubs during the endorsement contract period? A manufacturer would not be able to obtain a court order to force the golfer to use the manufacturer's clubs during the contract period rather than a competitor's products, even though to use those competing products would be a breach of contract. This breach of the rights of the manufacturer would be compensated by a suitable award of damages.

Enforcing personal performance

6.18.4 Because the choice of clubs he uses is a personal decision by a professional golfer, that use is not something which can be controlled by an impersonal contract or by the courts by way of specific performance. This is still the case where the manufacturer pays a personality to use the manufacturer's products for his sport by way of sponsorship. Any contract which is based upon the provision by one party of his personal services to the other has an inherent weakness in that the courts will not usually grant an order for specific performance by that person of obligations which relate to personal activities such as playing golf, or using a specified club. Neither would the court usually grant an injunction to stop him from using any other make of clubs as it would have the same effect, because such an order would ensure indirectly that he either uses the manufacturer's make of club or he does not play.

LOSS OF CONFIDENCE

Reason for change of clubs

6.19.1 A potential danger for personal endorsement agreements for sport-related products can arise in circumstances such as where a top golfer loses form in major tournaments. As a result he loses all confidence in himself, and all confidence in the manufacturer's clubs which he has been using and endorsing. In frustration, having tried all else to cure the cause of his disastrous form, he borrows and uses a friend's clubs which result in him regaining his winning form and self confidence. In the absence of any other explanation, the personality is convinced that the cure of his problem lies with his friend's clubs which happen to be made by a competitor of the manufacturer of the clubs he is currently advertising and recommending under a contract with say, six months to run.

Contractual clash

6.19.2 An "of the essence" clause in his advertising contract with the club manufacturer states that the personality must enter a minimum number of national or international tournaments to justify the endorsement fees he is receiving. He must also use the advertised clubs at all tournaments which he enters during the contract period. What is he to do in his dilemma about the new clubs? The problems the golfer faces are:

(a) Supreme confidence in the equipment he uses is psychologically essential to his tournament success in the future. He has lost all confidence in the advertised product which he previously used so successfully. Should he cease to compete in tournaments for the balance of his contract period because he no longer wants to use his previous equipment? That would be a breach of his contract. Should he continue using the advertised product for the rest of the contract period and hope for the best, to see whether his bad form is only temporary? Or should he disregard his contractual commitments and play with the new clubs in which he has such confidence? He should approach the manufacturer of the currently endorsed product and explain the problem as soon as it is evident. The manufacturer might be able and willing to analyse the apparent properties of the other clubs, and (without any infringement of patent or other proprietary rights in them) might agree to design and make a new range of clubs to the golfer's own specification. They could even be marketed as "personality clubs", with his name stamped upon them.

(b) If the endorsement agreement with the product manufacturer has just expired when the golfer discovers new-found confidence, he would be able to openly use the new clubs in tournaments. This could result in the manufacturer of the new clubs wanting to sign the personality immediately to an endorsement and advertising agreement for those clubs. The golfer would have to comply with a reasonable competitive endorsement and advertising restriction for a period of time after the expiry of his previous exclusive endorsement agreement.

BALANCE BETWEEN SAFEGUARDS

What is a fair deal?

6.20 An athlete or sportsman should make sure that any agreement which he signs for the use of products which he currently advertises will not unreasonably inhibit his freedom of choice of a permanent change to new products, and his ability to advertise them, should the need arise from a career point of view (not merely from a business point of view). The restrictions which should reasonably be accepted by the personality will depend on the deal which he does with the product manufacturer. The advertiser needs reasonable safeguards for its investment in the promotion of products which the personality endorses and the value of the goodwill which is generated for those products through the endorsement. If the deal is that the personality is prepared to advertise the manufacturer's products only for so long as he uses them, with no contractual commitment to use them for a specified period, then there should be no restriction on his subsequent use and endorsement of other products, even if they are competitive. (The fee structure should take into account this inherent weakness in the deal from the manufacturer's point of view.) Ultimately the deal has to be fair to both sides. The manufacturer should be entitled to reasonable protection by imposing sensible restrictions on the personality during and for a reasonable time after the contract period because:

(a) The reputation of the manufacturer and of the advertised products could be damaged by the manufacturer having to stop its advertisements prematurely, which would become misleading if they cannot be withdrawn and they are not true any more.

(b) The manufacturer will pay a significant fee to the personality to cover all of the rights granted to it for the contract period.

(c) There is also a significant cost to the manufacturer of creating, publishing and broadcasting the advertising campaign for the products based upon the endorsement by the personality.

INFRINGEMENT OF PERSONALITY'S RIGHTS

HIS PROFILE IS PUBLIC PROPERTY

No right of privacy

6.21.1 In the U.K. a personality has only a limited right to prevent the use and publication of his name and likeness. There is no statutory proprietary right in his name and likeness in the sense that he could always control their use however casual it may be, but in certain circumstances he can control them under common law as marketable assets. For example, there is no copyright in his name, and the ownership of copyright in any photograph featuring him is governed by sections 9 and 11 of the Copyright Patents and Designs Act 1988. A personality, such as a top motor car racing driver, has to accept that he is subject to publicity in the context of his racing activities, and that his name and image will appear whenever he or his sport is reviewed or discussed. It is this high personal profile which creates his marketability as a personality.

What can be infringed

6.21.2 A personality's common law rights will be infringed if, without his authority, his name or image is used specifically to endorse or to recommend a product. Whether the use of his name or image will be an infringement of his rights will depend on the context of the presentation in which he features. For an infringement to occur the unauthorised use of the personality's name or image must be in the course of trade as an advertisement or promotion of the relevant product, with the purpose of exploiting his marketability. It is a form of "passing-off", in that the advertiser passes off the purported endorsement as being genuine. If contained in an advertisement it would also constitute a misleading statement. His marketability is a commercial asset which is of value to him due to his public status and reputation. There is a form of protection under Part B.17 of the Code of Advertising Practice, but that is only an industry guideline and does not have statutory force.

Non-endorsing use

6.21.3 "Happiness is a cigar called Hamlet", T.V. advertisements are no longer broadcast due to the restrictions on advertising tobacco products. They were clever and imaginative and became one of the cult forms of advertising. Their press advertisements would consist of the photograph of a prominent person who had hit the headlines for suffering an unfortunate or unlucky experience, with the above slogan attached to it. The juxtaposition was always apt, the photograph highlighted that person's depressed or distressed state, and in many cases infuriated the person appearing in the advertisement. But it was always clear that the objectors were not claimed to be recommending the cigars. They had no legal right of privacy as such and there was no legal mechanism to prevent that use of their image, or to get compensation for that use, although it added a substantial value to the Hamlet advertisements.

ILLUSTRATION OF PUBLICITY PROBLEMS

6.22.1 If a film star is photographed in a casual moment drinking from a can of Coca-Cola, and the photograph is printed in a newspaper as part of a news item of general interest concerning that personality, that use of the photograph is not an infringement of any right the film star has in his personal marketability. Neither will it be an infringement of the Coca-Cola trade mark. The use of the photograph is not in the course of trade, and it is not an advertisement put out by Coca-Cola. If Coca-Cola uses the same photo in any context for the clear purpose of advertising and promoting their product, such as by implying an endorsement of it by the personality, that would infringe the personality's rights in his own marketability. This would also be in contravention of Paragraph B.17 of the ASA Code of Advertising Practice, by incorrectly purporting to be an authorised endorsement of the product by the personality. There is a fine line between using the photograph to make a statement of fact of general public interest, and using it as an advertisement.

This case can be distinguished from the above Hamlet example. In the Hamlet photograph there is nothing to connect the photographed person with the cigar; whereas the actor is holding the can of Coca-Cola, which can be used to create an association between them. If a "Hamlet person" were photographed smoking a cigar, then the cases would be the same in the absence of a contract validating the use of the photograph in the advertisement.

Tennis illustration

6.22.2   Another example would be where a top tennis player, who is famous for always using a known brand of tennis racket, is photographed unwittingly playing in a casual practice prior to a big tournament with a racket of another make. The photograph shows the racket poised at the top of the tennis player's serve, so that the manufacturer's logo on the racket strings is clearly shown. The manufacturer of that racket would be using that photograph as an implied endorsement by the personality of its product at its peril. Using a racket and recommending it are two different things, especially if the personality is already contracted to endorse and advertise exclusively the brand of racket with which he is professionally associated. Publication of the photograph by the press with some comment could not be prevented by the tennis player, in the absence of the comment being defamatory.

AVOIDING PERSONALITY MARKETING INFRINGEMENTS

What is an advertisement?

6.23.1   A manufacturer who has not obtained the consent of the personality to advertise its products in association with his name or image may try to do so in a manner which may not appear to be an advertisement. Would it be possible for the manufacturer of the "practice racket" referred to in paragraph 6.22.2 to publish the photograph ostensibly as a statement of fact, rather than as an advertisement? What would be the legal position if the manufacturer of the practice racket bought the copyright in that photograph, and published and sold large posters of it without any text or comment? The following rules would be relevant:

   (a) An advertiser must not publish any paid for advertising material under the deceptive guise that it is not an advertisement, but a news item or an item of general comment, or a genuine editorial or other article. Where it is not obvious that such a publication is an advertisement for a product, it must be clearly qualified by a reasonably prominent statement that it is an advertisement. Section B.11 of the British Advertising Code of Practice states that an advertisement should always be so designed and presented that anyone who looks at it can see, without having to study it closely, that it is an advertisement.
   (b) If the "practice racket" manufacturer buys the copyright in the photograph and publishes the posters, or licences a specialist poster publishing company to do so, could the featured personality obtain:
      (i) an injunction to present such publication, or
      (ii) damages against the poster company for infringing the marketable value of the personality's character and image?

Unless the personality owns the copyright in the photograph, because of the "no privacy" position he has no legal cause of action on which to have either an injunction or a claim for damages. These remedies may be available if it is decided judicially that the poster was an endorsement advertisement. If the logo on the racket is a registered trademark the manufacturer may have a claim for infringement against the poster publisher.

(c) If the advertiser or the poster publisher reproduces the photograph of the personality without the consent of the owner of the copyright in the photograph, that copyright owner would have a claim against the advertiser or the publisher (or both) for infringement of his copyright in the photograph. The personality, on the other hand, has no control over the photograph, or any claim to the copyright in the photograph, although it features only him.

Implied endorsement

6.23.2   There can also be an implied endorsement where the advertisement consists of a photograph which prominently features the personality together with the apparently incidental presence of the product which is being advertised. An advertisement for an exotic motor car, publicised with nothing else in the picture but the personality casually leaning against the car exuding an air of proud ownership, could give the impression of being implied endorsement of the car by the personality. That implication is not an automatic consequence; it would depend on how the photograph is shot and the wording of any accompanying text. This is similar to the example in paragraph 6.22.1

Obvious intention

6.23.3   The purpose of having the personality as a feature of the implied endorsement advertisement must be to give it "added value ", in the same way as if the advertisement had been authorised by the personality. Any "trade use" of the image of a personality creates a risk that he will object to it, but he has to prove the infringment of a legal right. The advertiser could arrange a belated agreement with the personality to legitimise the use, but the advertiser would be in a weak position when negotiating both the consent and the fee.

DEFAMATION OF PERSONALITY

Untrue implications believed

6.24.1   An advertisement which is not authorised by the personality who features in it and who apparently endorses the advertised product could be defamatory of him if it is advertising a product which is personally sensitive, controversial or contrary to the known attributes of the personality. The danger is that it would be reasonable for people to believe from the advertisement that the personality is using or recommending that product.

Damage to reputation

6.24.2   The circumstances would have to be such that his personal standing, integrity and his professional reputation would be substantially damaged in the eyes of those who reasonably assumed that the advertisement is genuine. An example might be an advertisement of a brand of spirits which features a teetotal personality without his consent, or where the advertisement represents an implied approval by an athlete of legally available body-building performance-enhancing drugs, the use of which is prohibited within the sport.

Fictitious infringement

6.24.3   The depiction of the personality does not have to be photographic. The unauthorised use of personalities can also be the basis of a legal action where creative artwork for advertising or promotional material for a product is based on a sport such as football and contains a recognisable drawing of the personality. To prevent this from happening the agency must make sure that:

(a) none of the players featured in the advertisement bear even a passing resemblance to real players without their written consent;

(b) none of the team shirts are in the colours of a known team, unless consent has been obtained; and

(c) a well known personality footballer who plays for Club A and who has agreed to be drawn in the advertisement, must not be erroneously depicted in the playing colours of Club B. The "strip" of Club A can only be used with its consent.

Allowable factual statements

6.24.4   What would be the unlikely position where a top tennis player, who always uses one manufacturer's brand of racket, does not want to endorse it for the manufacturer? Could the racket manufacturer nevertheless publicise that player's use of that racket? Without the consent of the personality, the racket manufacturer would not be able to use his name and image as a means of endorsing the racket. An advertisement simply stating a fact, if neutrally worded, and not using a photograph of the player, should not give the impression that the player is positively recommending the product, and so it would not be actionable. "X won Wimbledon using the Y racket" as a true statement does not infringe the personality's marketable image. But the manufacturer is still using the name of the personality without his consent to promote and sell that brand of racket. Section B.17 of the ASA Code of Advertising Practice would apply, even if an alleged marketable reputation infringement claim made by the tennis player against the racket manufacturer failed. Section B.17 states that, with certain exceptions, advertisements should not portray or refer to any living person unless his express prior permission has been obtained. A response to any complaint to the ASA by the tennis player would be the fact that, as the tennis player plays with that racket, it is self-evident that he considers it to be a very good racket. As he has a strong public profile it would be unreasonable for him to complain if the racket manufacturer comments on that fact. Nevertheless that does not allow the racket manufacturer to assume an advertised endorsement by the player.

ADVERTISING FEES

DIFFERENT FEE STRUCTURES

Printed media

6.25.1 A simple licence may be granted by a personality to the product manufacturer to use an agreed selection of photographs of him and quotations attributed to him in printed media advertising for the product over an agreed period of time, and limited to an agreed territory. This could be on a non-exclusive basis, and usually a one-off fee will be paid at the time the agreement is signed between the personality and the manufacturer. There is no active participation by the personality in producing or acting in the advertising, which will be reflected in the level of the licence fee. There may be options for extended use of the advertisements for further fees.

TV advertisements

6.25.2 The personality will be actively involved in the filming of the TV advertisements and any other supporting photography for printed media versions of the advertisement. The advertiser will have a limited period within which to broadcast the advertisements, or there will be a maximum number of authorised screenings of the advertisement during a total period. There will also be a territorial limitation for the broadcast use of the advertisement, so satellite T.V. Stations will have to be taken into account. The fee will be based upon the number of advertisements to be made by the personality, the extent of the broadcasting rights and the perceived market value of the personality.

Personality brand products

6.25.3 Where the personality endorses a product which is marketed as the "personality product" such as the X snooker cue or the Y golf club, he will get a royalty on sales of that personalised brand-name product. He will also receive a payment on signing the agreement, which could partly or wholly be treated as an advance against the royalties payable on sales of the "personalised" product under the contract.

Endorsement fee not based on product sales

6.25.4 The endorsement advertising fee for standard products will be a fixed amount and will be paid to the personality irrespective of whether or not the endorsement campaign is successful in increasing the sales of the endorsed product. The advertising personality has provided his services as per the contract; how effectively the manufacturer uses the marketing opportunity is beyond his control. A significant portion of an endorsement fee will be payable as an advance on signing the agreement between the personality and the manufacturer. The balance will be paid by the time the personality has finished doing the filming, or the still media photography, and whatever else he is obliged to do, such as to approve the references to his quoted recommendations to be contained in the promotional material. Additional fees may be payable to the personality when options are exercised to extend the use of the endorsement advertising, either locally or internationally, or beyond the first contract year which has already been paid for.

NO ROYALTY FOR ADVERTISED PRODUCT SALES

Sales not directly related

6.26 While using the personality to recommend the product in advertisements may be beneficial it may not result in extra sales of the product which can be identified as being directly and solely due to the personality's presence. Therefore a per-unit royalty on the increased sales of endorsed products (excluding "personality products") is never paid to the personality because it would be wholly unjustified, impractical and uneconomical for the manufacturer. It could also result in excessive remuneration to the personality. The sales of the advertised product are not dependent on the endorsement by the personality in the same way as if the product was being sold and promoted as the "personality brand product" in paragraph 6.25.3 with the name of the personality attached to it. His advertising endorsement is intended to increase sales by developing a greater public awareness of the product. The product has a substantial volume of sales before the personality was involved, and it will continue to sell in the same way after the expiry of the personality advertising period.

GENERAL CONTRACTUAL CONSIDERATIONS

TERRITORIAL LIMITS FOR ADVERTISING USE

Personality's rights affected

6.27   The endorsement agreement should state whether the rights granted by the personality to the manufacturer are in respect of the U.K. only, or whether they are European or even worldwide. That will depend on what the product is, whether the product is available in enough major countries throughout the world, and whether the personality is sufficiently well known in those countries to support an advertising campaign for the product. The most likely candidates for such extensive endorsement are internationally known sportsmen. If the rights are to be exerciseable by the manufacturer outside the U.K. the personality should ensure that his endorsement agreement deals with the following matters:

(a) How is the fee to be calculated for use of the endorsement advertisements in other countries, and who is to be responsible for paying it? The contracting manufacturer may be the U.K. subsidiary or the distributor of an international company. If international rights are granted, how does the U.K. company ensure that the terms of the agreement will be fully observed and performed in those countries where the U.K. company has no control?

(b) What contract period will be needed by the manufacturer to enable the other countries within the contracted territory to fit in their own advertising and promotion plans for the product, using the material created by the contracting manufacturer featuring the personality? For the tennis or golfing circuit within any country there may be increased and special local advertising campaigns containing the endorsement for the product when the personality plays there in a major tournament.

(c) Will photographs and quotations which have been agreed between the personality and the manufacturer need to be modified or translated to cater for different markets? A range of photographs and quotations will be approved by the personality or by his agent for use as the manufacturer chooses. The manufacturer should be able to make language translations to get the same message across without having to obtain further approval from the personality. If a recommending quotation of the personality cannot be translated literally, the manufacturer should ensure that the translation is as close to the essence of the original quotation as possible.

(d) The personality or his agent should also give approval to a range of presentations of the personality within several advertising scenarios, which can then be used by the manufacturer as he thinks best. The personality will have to give a responsible manufacturer a reasonable amount of discretion and freedom of expression when creating advertising material which refers to the personality. The manufacturer must be relied upon not to do something which may cause concern or embarrassment to the personality. To do so would reflect adversely upon both the advertised product and the image and reputation of the manufacturer, as well as the personality.

APPROVAL OF MATERIAL

Protection of personality

6.28.1 The personality or his agent should be entitled to approve all basic promotional and advertising material which features or which refers to the personality, to ensure that it is reasonable, accurate and truthful. The product's advertising agency must also comply with the contractual obligations of the manufacturer to use only approved photographs and quotations. Therefore the agency should have a copy of that contract to refer to when necessary. If the advertising material in which he is quoted or in which he appears infringes any third-party rights or legal requirements, or if it contravenes any relevant code of practice, the personality will be affected by any consequent criticism or liability. Whether he will have any personal liability will depend on what is wrong with the advertisement. Therefore the personality must be careful in what he approves as statements of recommendation for the advertised product. If there is any question over the accuracy of any claims or opinions to be attributed to him which recommend the products, the agency should be required by him to get satisfactory documentary back-up and justification before his approval is given.

Withholding approval

6.28.2 The endorsement agreement should give the personality the right to withhold or to withdraw his approval of the use of his name or photographs of him or any other reference to him in an advertisement which he reasonably considers (after taking legal advice if necessary) to be illegal, misleading, contrary to the Code of Advertising Practice, infringing any third-party rights or in breach of the terms of his endorsement agreement. This right to withhold approval should be subject to the advertiser being entitled to resolve the problems by modifying the advertisements to the personality's reasonable satisfaction. The precise wording of any direct or indirect quotation, must be checked and agreed, to ensure that it reflects accurately what the personality is prepared to say by way of positive recommendation, as opposed to only urging the consumer to buy the product.

CONFIDENCE IN THE PRODUCT

Endorsement responsibility

6.29 Compared with ordinary media advertising, an endorsement of a product by a personality in an advertisement is a much more personal and direct appeal from him to the buying public. He is assumed by all those who respond to the appeal by purchasing the advertised product to have good grounds for recommending the purchase of the product which he endorses. Therefore the personality must be careful in the choice of products which he is prepared to advertise and recommend. He should have personal experience of, and real confidence in, the product he is asked to promote.

ADVERTISEMENT REPRESENTATIONS

Product liability

6.30.1 A personality who advertises and recommends a product is not connected with the design, manufacture and sale of the product, and therefore he is not responsible for any items of the product which are defective or dangerous. With the current trend of consumer protection legislation, it is possible in due course that a consumer who has been injured by a defective or dangerous product, which he only bought on the strength of the recommendation of the personality, may have a claim against the personality for negligently recommending the purchase of something which turned out to be defective or dangerous. The prospect of such a claim being sustainable would depend on whether it could be proved by the injured consumer that the product is inherently defective or dangerous due to a design or manufacturing defect and that the personality could or should have known of the defect. If the injury was caused by an isolated faulty item of the product which slipped through quality control, that of itself may not be a good basis for suing the personality.

Negligence by the personality

6.30.2 If the quotation by the personality which is used in the advertisement is given negligently and is a positive assurance and representation by the personality as to the safety, structure and quality of the product, and if the injured consumer genuinely believed and relied on that representation, it would be worth the consumer joining the personality as a co-defendant to an action for damages against the product manufacturer or its distributor. The quotation complained of would have to be a statement of fact, not of opinion, and the claimant would have to show that it was reasonable for him to rely on the statement. As the statement could not be a contractual representation the claimant would have to prove that it was a tortious and negligent representation. Proving negligence may be difficult, as to be negligent means that the statement must be made recklessly and without any prudent research being done on the recommended product by the personality or by somebody on his behalf. This risk is only likely to apply to newly marketed product which could be inherently dangerous, and where its research and development prior to commercial sales was not sufficiently thorough to guarantee a safe product design or manufacturing process.

Precautionary research

6.30.3 The personality's defence to such a claim would be that the representation was made by him in good faith based upon the facts as he believed them to be after making reasonable enquiries about the product, or having been a satisfied user of it for a considerable time. He will have to show that he took reasonable care in getting verification of any representation he was asked to make about the product, and that it was reasonable for him to assume that the information he was given about the product was correct, complete and reliable. However, in reality the personality would not normally make such enquiries about a well-known brand of product which he is asked to advertise and which has no history of being defective. Although the risk of legal action referred to above is slight, it shows that the personality must take care in approving the exact wording of any statement which is attributable to him in the advertisement regarding the quality or function of the product.

Manufacturer's indemnity

Personality relies on advertiser

6.31 The endorsement agreement should contain a warranty and an indemnity from the manufacturer to the personality in respect of the legality and veracity of all advertising and other material which refers to the personality and which contains his recommendation of the product. A warranty and an indemnity should also be given by the manufacturer to the personality in respect of the advertised product should it be defective and should any consumer make a claim against the personality in connection with the product or his endorsement advertising of it.

Assignment of personality's contract

Control by personality

6.32.1 The manufacturer should be prohibited from assigning the benefit and obligation of the endorsement agreement, except (for example) to an associated company which deals with all advertising for the group of companies, without the prior consent of the personality. This should not be unreasonably withheld in normal circumstances.

Necessary transfer of rights

6.32.2 Where the endorsement agreement relates to a specific product, the only circumstances in which it should be possible for the manufacturer to assign the agreement would be if he sold the whole of its rights to the manufacturer, distribution and sale of the advertised product to a third party. Part of the value of the sale price may be the manufacturer's right to use the endorsement of the personality in advertising the product. The identity of the new manufacturer may not concern the personality, provided that the assignee is substantial and reputable, and that it performs and observes all of the previous manufacturer's obligations under the endorsement agreement.

VOICEOVERS

A FORM OF RECOMMENDATION

Personality recognition

6.33.1 It may be said that "voiceovers" which are used to back TV advertisements for products are a remote form of implied recommendation, although the personalities who are speaking are not visible and are not named. They are chosen for the distinctive quality of their voice, the idea being that subliminally the familiar voice recommends that product, and the script together with the voice over urges the listener or viewer to buy it. However, because of the visual anonymity of the personality behind the voice, the use of a voiceover in a TV advertisement is not considered to be recommendation of the advertised product by the personality whose voice is being used. When his voice is recognised, there is no implication in the advertisement that the personality is actively recommending the product which is being advertised.

Character of the voice

6.33.2 In choosing the personality to fit both the product which is to be advertised and the style of advertisement, it is necessary to assess the "character" of the voice of the personality. Is he a zany character or a serious one? Is he humorous or deadpan? Can his voice be stylised so as to appeal to a younger audience or can it be adapted to sound like the archetypal senior statesman? Instantly recognisable voices produce a mental image of the personality whose voice is being heard. Distinctive voices and the personalities who have then can become synonymous with the advertised product, although some personalities derive a lot of money from being the anonymous voiceover on an endless number of advertisements for different products.

IMITATION VOICEOVERS

Rights of voice "owner"

6.34.1 Part of the interest in watching TV advertisements is guessing the identity of the personality who is being used for the voiceover. But what about "copycat" voiceovers, where the listener believes that the voice belongs to a well known personality, but in fact it is the voice of an imitator? Does a personality have any proprietary rights in his voice? As he is anonymous in the advertisement and is given no credit for being the owner of the voice, does it matter to him whether or not it is his voice in the advertisement or that of an imitator?

What is the legal principle?

6.34.2 An imitator can only be claimed to infringe the rights of the personality if the latter can find a legal principle which will uphold his right to reproduce and to make commercial use of his voice exclusively, and to prevent others from breaching those rights by copying it. A famous voice is a marketable commodity, but is it as definable and protectable as a name or a face? There is no copyright in a voice, so the exclusive right to reproduce it, and the moral rights, set out in the Copyright, Designs & Patents Act 1988 cannot apply to a voice. The imitation of a voice does not come strictly within the established test for passing off although it is a reasonable analogy. If the passing-off test could be adapted to protect an active voiceover personality from a damaging imitator, that would result in a legal right being attached to the commercial use of a famous and instantly recognisable voice in the same way as a trade mark. A famous voice may be thought of as a human form of branding, in that it instantly identifies its owner, but it does not come within the strict definition of a trade mark.

Misleading advertising

6.34.3 Recording voiceovers for TV advertisements is a lucrative business for famous voices, and an imitator is falsely representing his voice to the viewing (and product-purchasing) public as being the (easily recognisable) voice of the personality. Does that make the advertisement misleading? It does not in so far as the advertised product is concerned. The agency which is responsible for creating the TV advertisement and for using a voiceover imitator will have deliberately set out to find a voice which sounds like the personality it wants the viewer to recognise; it will not have been just coincidence. The advertisement features the product, and there is no representation in it by the advertiser that the voiceover belongs to any named personality. Would it make any difference to the consumer whether the voice is genuine or not, and would that difference affect the consumer's decision whether to buy the advertised product? There may be a form of technical misrepresentation but it would not be a criminal offence under the misleading advertising regulations.

DAMAGE SUFFERED THROUGH IMITATION

Loss of income

6.35.1   The unauthorised use of "his" voice deprives the personality of the fee which he would have charged for doing the work had he been asked to do so, as it was "his" voice which was apparently required by the advertiser. The personality also loses the repeat fees which are payable whenever the advertisement is broadcast. The unauthorised use of "his voice" also falsely attributes to the personality an association with the advertised product, as viewers who recognise it will assume that the voice belongs to the personality. The advertised product also gets an added benefit for which the manufacturer has not paid the personality, which is the recognition factor value of his distinctive voice. If the use of the imitation voice is not legally actionable by the "real" personality, then there is no claim for loss of income either.

Damage to name

6.35.2   If the public believes that the voice belongs to the imitated personality, then where the advertisement is criticised for being in bad taste, or if it is for a product which is contrary to his public image, his reputation can be damaged. For example, if a renowned teetotaller is apparently heard as, and is believed to be, the voiceover for an alcoholic drink, that would make him appear to be hypocritical. Such an imitation use of his voice could be defamatory of the personality in extreme circumstances, although the defence would be that the voice is not that of the personality, and it is not recommending the alcoholic drink.

THE PERSONALITY WHO DOES NOT DO "VOICEOVERS"

No loss or damage

6.36.1   Would the position be different if the personality never does voiceovers, and so has no business in that area? Is he being deprived of money and of personal public exposure by a ghost professional "voice"? Is there any infringement by the imitator of a potential business asset which the personality has never developed or used? In those circumstances is there an actionable infringement by the professional voice, or is it just an encroachment on personal privacy, which is not actionable. In the absence of loss or damage, there cannot be an equivalent right of action for "passing-off" should such a course of action be available.

Code of practice

6.36.2   A TV advertisement which deliberately uses a professional imitator's voice so successfully that all viewers believe it to be the voice of a well known personality may infringe section 17.3 of the Advertising Standards Authority's Code of Advertising Practice, on the basis that the distinctive voice of a well known personality is as much a representation of him as his photograph, or at least is part of his commercially exploitable reputation.

Natural similarity

6.36.3   It may be possible for an agency which would like to commission a reluctant personality (such as a politician) to do a voiceover to find someone whose natural voice is the same as the voice of the personality. There is no actual imitation, in the sense of mimicry, although it would be an imitation in the sense that people would think that it is the voice of the politician. That transparent device won't work; the end result will still be a misrepresentation to the public, and the possibility of a claim from the imitated personality.

7 Product Branding

PROPRIETARY RIGHTS IN BRAND NAMES

LEGAL RIGHTS AND RESTRICTIONS

Knowledge of brand names

7.1.1 A good working knowledge of what brand names are, how they are created, how they are protected and how they can be infringed is fundamental to the promotion and advertising industries because:

(a) All promotions and advertising are based on publicising the brand name of the product.

(b) The brand names of all well known products have taken a good deal of time, effort and cost to devise and to make popular, and it is a serious matter to infringe the proprietary rights in them. It is not always obvious when the use of a brand name constitutes an infringement of its proprietor's right, or when one brand name is so similar to, or confusing with, another brand name, that there is a risk of infringement.

(c) The goodwill value of a successful brand name can be very substantial. This is built up through extensive use and publicity, resulting in a high recognition factor with the public.

(d) Brand names are protected by law, as trademarks.

Forms of legal protection

7.1.2 The means of protecting the proprietary rights of the owners of brand names are listed below.

(a) Brand names and logos which are original and distinctive can be protected by trademark registration, providing they comply with the strict criteria which are applied to the granting of a trademark.

(b) In the absence of registration, they can be protected as unregistered trademarks under the common law and infringers can be stopped by a legal action for passing off (see paragraph 7.30 onwards).

(c) Brand logos and devices of an artistic nature can also be protected by the law of copyright if they are original and come within the operation of the Copyright, Designs and Patents Act 1988.

(d) Branding which is represented by the artwork, design and "get up" of the packaging of the product may be protected by the law of copyright if it is sufficiently distinctive and original to be an artistic work. Distinctive designs in the package artwork could become forms of trademarks if they are used consistently for the product package, so that they become a regular means of identifying the product.

Marketing structure

7.1.3   Because product branding, advertising campaigns and promotions are such closely related marketing functions, and because any illegality or third-party proprietary right infringement within any of them affects all of the others, this chapter deals first with the broad concepts of product brand creation and related legal considerations.

USE OF BRAND NAMES

WHY BRANDING IS NECESSARY

Marketing base

7.2.1   The promotion of the product helps to raise the brand name profile by attracting the buyer's attention to the product. TV and printed media advertising are the normal means of keeping the public aware of the product, by emphasising its brand name, its advantages over competitive products, and (where appropriate) its distinctive physical shape and any other unique or visually attractive characteristics. A package shape can become a form of branding, such as the Coca-Cola bottle or the Jif lemon.

Public recognition

7.2.2   Any product manufacturer, or supplier of services, has two primary means of being recognised by the public; they are by its corporate identity and by its product brand names. Both of these are trademarks in the broad sense, and they can be a combination of logos, devices, words, slogans or the design of product packaging, which attach to and identify the product. These forms of identification enable the public to distinguish that brand of product from all the other similar types of product which are on the market. (See paragraph 7.45 for the standard accounting recognition criteria for branding.)

GENERIC BRAND NAMES

Product categories

7.3.1   One of the greatest disadvantages of success in creating and publicising a brand name for a major, internationally available product is the risk that the brand name will become so well known that it evolves into a generic identity, definition or description of the whole of the relevant range of similar products, irrespective of the fact that they come from different manufacturers. The brand name for that product becomes so successful that it is used by the public to represent any product of a similar nature. This has happened to Hoover, Sellotape, Biro and to many others.

Two-tier brand names

7.3.2   Some ranges of product, such as cosmetics and perfumes, have two brand names which gives the manufacturer scope for flexibility in product line design, as well as in marketing. There is an overall product identity which is used for the whole range, with a subsidiary brand name for each specific product within that range. The range brand name may be based upon the manufacturer's corporate name, and the product brand name is something which is evocative of the product. If there are several products within that range, such as for cosmetic products, they will each have names which are distinctive and different from the brand names of the other products within that range.

In-house brand names

7.3.3   Most major chains of stores have their "own brand" of certain universally popular products, such as tinned or packaged foods and drinks. The brand name may not always use the chain store's own name, but that name will be prominently displayed on the product's label, to associate the chain store with what would otherwise be an unknown brand name. The chain store will not necessarily be the manufacturer of the products, but will have an agreement with their manufacturers to package and supply the products with the chain store's own labelling.

BRANDS WHICH IDENTIFY THE MANUFACTURER

Brand and corporate name connection

7.4.1   The brand name of a product may be connected with the name of its manufacturer, and so it also serves to promote its corporate identity. The identification can be made by association, such as with the ICI logo being placed prominently on the packaging of its products, whatever their brand names may be, or directly such as by the Heinz range of products using the company name as the brand name.

Brand names identify product quality

7.4.2   The manufacturer can extoll the virtues of its product in advertising material, but if widely held rumour or impartial testing by a consumer watchdog body indicates otherwise, the public will tend to believe the lowest general estimate of quality for that product. Quality in a product is mainly a matter of public perception, as it means different things to different people. Quality can mean image prestige, a certain taste in the case of consumable goods, or reliability of construction and performance for non-perishable products. Brand names are therefore associated with a perceived level of quality for their product, irrespective of any marketing which is done by the manufacturer to publicise the product.

Disparagement can be beneficial

7.4.3 The reverse can also apply. However well made, or however efficient, comfortable and reliable they may actually be, certain East European manu-factured motor cars are assumed by many people to be of bad quality. This is because of the extensive use of jokes and semi-serious disparaging comments. It has been said that all publicity is good publicity, and the amount of free publicity which is gained for such cars by the wide range of jocular comment must have a significant value.

Brand names identify price ranges

7.4.4 The public perception of the brand name of the product, its quality and its price are firmly linked, although it is not always true that you get what you pay for. The achievement of genuine quality will have an inevitable cost, but a high price does not necessarily mean that such achievement has even been attempted by the product manufacturer. Stella Artois lager has been advertised as being "reassuringly expensive", but then it is a top product and it is recognised as such by the drinking public, as it is a brand leader.

Deceptive branding

7.4.5 Where the origin of the product is of concern to a buyer, the manufacturer may intend to deceive the public, such as into believing that the product originates from an "acceptable" country. This can be done by choosing for the product an aristocratic-sounding English name, or a French or Italian-sounding name, and with a packaging design to match the image it is trying to project for the product. For instance, the packaging design artwork may have a picture of an old castle, or of something else uniquely English, so that the visual image is consistent with the "old English" brand name.

BRAND SLOGANS

SLOGANS BECOME BRANDING

Equivalent identity

7.5.1 Some advertising slogans become so well known, and become so firmly associated with the products which they advertise, that they can be considered as "brand slogans". Slogans do not necessarily contain the brand name of the product which they help to advertise. Consider the slogans "Snap Crackle and Pop", and "Put a tiger in your tank" (and its recent derivatives). Slogans can become as well known as the brand names of the products for which they are used, to the extent that merely to mention the slogans brings the brand name to mind immediately. As marketing developments change over the years, and as the image of product brands is updated to keep in touch with changing consumer fashions, so brand slogans are suitably modified or changed.

Slogan characters

7.5.2 The characterised brand slogan may be an image without any words, or it may be an image which is supported by a catch-phrase. The personified slogan is not the established brand logo of the advertised product, but it becomes an equally well known visual element which is uniquely associated with the product. Well-known examples were the Guinness toucan and the Esso tiger, where the slogans, such as "Guinness is good for you" and "Put a tiger in your tank" become more memorable due to the associated imagery.

Outdated but memorable slogans

7.5.3 Motoring connoisseurs may remember "Safety Fast" as being synonymous with early MG sports cars, and that "Space, Pace and Grace" once epitomised early Jaguars. These brand slogans do not contain the name of the product; "Ssch . . . you know who" nearly does, and "Guiness is good for you" certainly does. These brand slogans are static, in the sense that in their day they were always used in the same context, and have not been re-vamped and modernised over the years. Classic slogans do not take kindly to being updated, and quite often the modern derivative is not so successful as the original version.

BRAND PACKAGING

PRODUCT PACKAGING

Packaging as branding

7.6.1 Distinctive product packaging has become as much a form of brand identity as the name of the product itself. The outline of an original glass bottle of Coca-Cola instantly identifies the product, as it is very distinctive and has featured heavily in advertising of the product. A very distinctive shape of package design which is retained in the same form for a substantial period could become a form of unregistered trademark for the product, as it can have the same recognition factor value as a brand name or a logo.

Visual recognition

7.6.2 Designing an original and distinctive "get up" for the artistic design of a product's packaging can create as great a visual impression as that which is produced by a brand name. Products may be asked for by their brand name, but at a distance, or among an array of different products on a shelf, it is the visual recognition of the distinctive design of package shape or artwork that symbolises the brand name of the product.

Reliance on advertising

7.6.3 That mental association between the product, its brand name and its packaging design has been created by successful advertising. A good example of this power of package identity is the chevron-shaped red and white colour scheme used for the package and advertising of Marlborough cigarettes. A glimpse of the distinctive colour scheme representation of that package, whether it is on a racing car or on a roadside hoarding or on the back of a promotional windcheater, instantly identifies that product.

Package identity

7.6.4 Package branding is based upon a distinctive package shape, or a colour scheme, or a label layout. Vast sums of money are spent by major product manufacturers in designing and publicising the package of their products. The Jif lemon juice container, being a yellow plastic lemon, convinced the House of Lords in *Reckitt & Colman Products* v. *Borden Inc.* [1990] 1 All E.R. 873 of the value of its visual goodwill and brand identity. Not all unique package designs become world-famous; it is not an automatic result of creating them—many other factors are relevant. Some forms of package become art objects in their own right, and can eclipse the product which they represent: Dimple Haig bottles or long twist-stemmed Chianti bottles are used as the base of designer table lamps, and so may be bought as much for the bottle as for its contents.

Misleading packaging

7.6.5   A grand-sounding name which is used as a brand identity for a product which is of mediocre quality, especially when such a brand name is combined with a "quality" style package, will be a persuasive product purchase reason for some buyers who are impressed by outward appearances. They will assume that the product has the quality which equates to the impression of quality which is given by the brand name and the packaging of the product. A good example of the persuasive power of packaging is the vivid or lurid covers on many modern paperback fiction books. This most affects "browsers", who are spoilt for choice and who want something to read on a long flight, or on holiday. Unless they are looking for a specific book, the odds are that the book they choose at random is chosen because of its cover.

Modification for licensed products

7.6.6   The products may be manufactured under licence in foreign territories rather than being exported there from the originating country. In that case it will be the responsibility of the licensees to comply with local legal and commercial proprietary and consumer protection requirements in respect of the branding and packaging of the product, so that the original versions may have to be modified accordingly.

BRAND NAME CHARACTERISTICS

BRAND NAMES MUST BE CAPABLE OF PROTECTION

Legal availability

7.7   The creative aspects of devising a new brand name for a product must be subject to commercial and legal investigations into the market-wide availability and the public acceptability of the chosen brand name. As far as the brand name is concerned, legal checking means that in all the countries where the products bearing it may be sold a search must be made for any registered or the use of any unregistered brand name or logo trademark within the same trademark class or the same product category which is remotely similar to the one which is being considered for the new product. Doing these searches is a specialised job and takes time, and can be expensive, so on an international basis it is not undertaken lightly.

BRAND NAMES MUST BE APPROPRIATE

Product identity

7.8   The brand name must be appropriate for the product, so that it and the product image should be synonymous in the buyer's mind. Suitability of brand names may also be divided into various categories such as:

(a) a catchy, phonetically-spelt word which tends to indicate some form of gadget or a process of a practical nature;

(b) evocative French or Italian words which denote something personal or sensual, like cosmetics, clothes and body-care items;

(c) macho, ambitious or stylish brand names, which are intended to appeal to the male ego, and which are used for items such as aftershave lotion and motor cars.

BRAND NAMES MUST BE DISTINCTIVE

Marketing necessity

7.9   Designing a brand identity for a product by way of name, logo and packaging is intended to make both the brand name and the product distinctive. This will enable the product to be easily identified, and to have a marketing image and a visual character which will be attractive to buyers, and will enable them to distinguish it easily from competitive products. Distinctiveness also enables the branding to be protected as a trademark or by copyright. It is this feature of individuality which gives a "hook" to effective advertising and sales promotion for the product.

BRAND NAMES MUST BE ORIGINAL

To avoid infringement

7.10.1   Originality in a brand name, logo or package design is necessary to avoid a confusing and actionable similarity to the brand name of an already existing product. Otherwise there is the risk of infringing the proprietary rights of third parties, whether of a trademark or of a copyright nature. Being distinctive and being original are not necessarily the same thing. A name or a design can be distinctive without being original, such as where its concept is based upon something which already exists in the public domain.

Concept or expression?

7.10.2   It is difficult to be wholly original in designing a brand name, logo, or packaging artwork, so originality in branding is a matter of degree. When a manufacturer commissions a specialist designer to create a brand name or logo, or to design new artwork for packaging or labelling material for a new product, in the commission agreement the designer must undertake to ensure that whatever it produces for the manufacturer is sufficiently original that it will not infringe any third-party proprietary rights. This undertaking should be supported by an indemnity from the designer against the consequences of a successful infringement action being brought against the manufacturer in respect of the designer's work.

BRAND NAMES MUST BE MEMORABLE

Appeal to the senses

7.11 The manufacturer will have to maintain a substantial advertising campaign to get the public used to a new product brand name. There is no guaranteed formula to ensure that a new brand name, or a revised or new brand package artwork design, will achieve lasting public recognition. To be memorable the brand name must have visual appeal and must be distinctive. For visual appeal, the brand name can be connected with a logo or an artistic device, so that the whole logo may be visually identifiable even before the brand name is seen. The more distinctive it is, the more likely it is that a similar logo which is used for new competing product will be an infringement.

THE BRAND NAME SHOULD BE ENDURABLE

Lifetime of product

7.12 Trendy brand names, or those which are evocative of the transient fancy of the time, may not be suitable after the trend or fancy has been forgotten. Every effort should be made to ensure that the brand name which is chosen for a product which has a long term future will be endurable because of:

(a) the cost of developing a new brand name,
(b) the value of the goodwill which can be generated in it, and
(c) the time it takes to get that new brand of product established in the market.

BRAND NAMES SHOULD SUIT THE PRODUCT

Implied personality

7.13.1 Whether the potential market for the new product is national or international, the brand name and the package artwork design should be suitable for the image of that kind of product. Brand name creators and package designers should categorise the product with a personality, as part of its image-building process, to suit the product and to give structure to its advertising.

Masculine or feminine

7.13.2 Aftershave lotion tends to be given a male personality, whereas perfume tends to exude the essence of femininity. Branding a soap powder often assumes that the majority of purchasers are women. Different petrol manufacturers attribute different characteristics to their products, and confectionery manufacturers produce snappy, neutral advertising for their products so that they can aim at all sections of the public. Those confectionery products which are intended for the "young" market will have brand names which are designed especially to be attuned to that generation.

Technology-related

7.13.3 High-technology products need brand names which demonstrate that the product is the latest available gadget. There is a custom of using letters and numbers for technological hardware, which sound scientific while also being useful as grading identifications for the product manufacturer. The brand identity is usually the name of the manufacturer, and a combination of numbers and letters is useful to denote different capacity or function models. Numbers and letters do not date, and changes to them are not so dramatic as name changes. They also eliminate the need for costly searching for similar existing brand names.

CHOOSING BRAND NAMES

MARKET RESEARCH

Existing competition

7.14 Where comparative information relating to brand names and logos for the market sector of the new product is not already available, an appropriate market research study should be commissioned within the countries where the product will be marketed. The objectives of the research would be to establish how many competing products there are in the target territory, what their brand names are, and what their package get-up looks like. The brand name chosen for the new product and its package artwork design must not be sufficiently similar to anything which already exists so that there is a risk of infringement. The brand name may be available in some countries but not in others.

NEW BRAND IDENTITY

Preliminary assessment

7.15.1 There are two preliminary areas of assessment which should be considered when choosing a brand name for a new product:

(a)   public awareness of brand identity for the category in which the new product will be competing;

(b) the costs and benefits of creating a new brand image.

Forward planning

7.15.2   Because of the time lapse between thinking of a good original brand name and getting it cleared and protected internationally, some manufacturers set up a bank of usable brand names well in advance. This will ensure that the development of a new model or product is not delayed by the choosing and protecting of a suitable brand name. It also means that associated or similar brand names can be "booked" to cover a range of products (see paragraph 7.21.2).

High value for a short period

7.15.3   Major international trade exhibitions or conventions, and every Olympic Games or World Cup Football competitions, have new logos and their equivalent of "brand names". These are used extensively for commercial purposes to provide income to the promoters of the event, and to publicise the event. These brand names and logos have a limited life, and therefore a limited commercial value, which peaks when the event is held.

INTERNATIONAL BRAND NAME COMPATIBILITY

Foreign language embarrassment

7.16.1   There may be foreign brand names which require a knowledge of the originating language to understand what the brand name means. The danger is that the brand name will not "travel" well internationally. Alternatively, an innocuous word in one language which is used as the brand name of a product originating in that country may have a totally different, and possibly a disparaging or vulgar, meaning when used in another country. Changes in language, especially in the evolution of trendy slang words, may inadvertently make the brand name undesirable or embarrassing by associating it with connotations which were not dreamed of at the time the brand name was created.

International adaptability

7.16.2 Is the brand name adaptable, so that for international use its spelling or its logo version can be modified if necessary to suit different cultures or languages, while retaining the essence of the international association between the brand name and the product? Any modification of a registered trademark brand name to suit territorial requirements will require an application for registration of that modification in the countries where it is to be used.

Corporate or brand identity

7.16.3 The broad difference between product brand identity and corporate brand identity is that where there is a mix of brand identity between them, the branding emphasis in advertising material may be changed. For example:

(a) Where the corporate name and image has priority, the product may be marketed as the "Whizzo Corporation Inter-Galactic Gizmo", which competes with all other gizmos of a like nature.
(b) Where the product name of Widget has priority over the corporate trademark, it will be promoted as the Widget. The fact that it consists of a gizmo is self-evident, and anybody wanting one just asks for "the Widget" and gets what he expects.
(c) A balance between the corporate image and the product brand identity can be struck by marketing the gizmo as "the Whizzo Corporation Widget". This closely associates the product brand name with the name of its manufacturer.

PROMOTIONAL FEATURES AFFECTING BRAND NAME CHOICE

Market share objective

7.17 Consumer brand products may reach the saturation point at which it becomes difficult to create, present and establish at a commercially profitable level yet another product within that category. The measure of success for consumer products is "market share". The manufacturer can decide to rejuvenate a product which, despite all its efforts to retain sales levels, is losing its market share. This may need an updating of its brand name or its marketing image as a "hook" for new promotions. Any significant change to an accepted and established branding presentation should be made only after carefully considering the following questions.

(a) What is the overpowering reason making it necessary to change what has so far been a successful approach?
(b) How is the replacement brand name or image an improvement, and why is that so?

(c) What will be the cost of effecting the change?
(d) What is the current market value of the goodwill attaching to the intangible asset which is being modified, and will that value transfer to the new identity without incurring a loss?

BRAND NAMES AS TRADEMARKS

LEGAL PROTECTION

Trademark registration

7.18 If the proposed brand name is potentially registrable as a trademark, then an application for registration in each country where it is likely to be sold is the best initial form of protection. This should be done as soon as possible, even though the brand name may not be used there for some time. The technicalities of trademark law and practice are outside the scope of this book, and the manufacturer or agency should seek expert professional advice on the subject. However, in broad terms some of the aspects of trademarks as brand names are discussed in this section to explain brand name protectability.

DEFINITION OF A TRADEMARK

Statutory definition

7.19.1 A trademark is essentially a brand name, and a trademark is defined by section 68(1) of the Trade Marks Act 1938 as:

"a mark used or proposed to be used in relation to goods for the purpose of indicating, or so as to indicate, a connection in the course of trade between the goods and some person having the right either as registered proprietor or as registered user, to use the mark, whether with or without any indication of the identity of that person."

For the purposes of the above definition a "mark" also includes a device, brand, heading, label, ticket, name, signature, word, letter, number or any combination of them. Anything of an original nature which is used consistently to identify and publicise the product as its "name" will be considered to be a trademark. Section 68(1) refers to registered trademarks, but the definition applies equally well to unregistered brand names and logos.

Labels

7.19.2 A distinctive label design, although it may consist of many different things such as the brand name, logo, and some surrounding artwork, if it is used widely enough will become a form of trademark for that product. A trademark must be used in conjunction with the product with which it is associated, such as on its container and in advertising material relating to it. The product may have several distinct and well known trademarks, such as its brand name, its logo and its label; but they do not all have to be used at the same time to advertise the product, and they may not all be registered trademarks.

Brand names

7.19.3 The definition of a trademark covers any brand name, whether that is an invented word, logo or device. The relevance of a brand name coming within the trademark legislation is that it is capable of being registered as a trademark, provided that it fulfils the criteria for registrability.

TRADEMARK LEGISLATION

International application

7.20.1 Trademark legislation has evolved internationally, so that all countries have internal laws to protect trademarks originating within the relevant country. The Paris International Convention enables a trademark owner in one signatory country to have the right of priority in applying for the registration of its trademark in other Convention member countries within a period of six months from the date of the first trademark registration application in a member country.

Schedule of product classes

7.20.2 There is a common international schedule of classes of trademarks, divided into distinctive groups of products and services. The trademark registration application is made in the class or classes which may be applicable to protect all trademark uses which are relevant to the branded product. Registration of a trademark in one class gives an exclusivity of use only within that class.

Dates of effect and priority

7.20.3 The making of a trademark application does not give any statutory rights in that trademark until the registration is granted. The protection then becomes retrospective to the date when the application was made. Meanwhile the applied-for trademark will be treated as an unregistered mark, with only common law protection. If the registration application fails, the status of an unregistered trademark is not affected.

Restrictions on protection granted

Limited exclusivity

7.21.1 Registered trademark exclusivity for its proprietor is limited to use of the brand name in a trademark sense within the registration class in connection with goods sold in the course of trade, as a means of product identification. The fact that a manufacturer has registered the trademark of "Whizzo" for its consumer products in a certain class of goods does not entitle that manufacturer to a statutory right to stop anybody else from using the word "Whizzo" in different classes for different kinds of goods. If the other manufacturer is using "Whizzo" as a trademark for its products in a way which implies some connection with the first registered proprietor, which suffers damage or loss as a result, it may have a claim against the second user for passing off.

Trademarks must be used

7.21.2 The exclusivity of use which is given to a registered trademark within its class of goods can also be further limited to a specific category of goods within that class. The proprietor of the trademark has control over its use in connection with goods within its registered class and category. To prevent entrepreneurs from permanently blocking the commercial use of interesting brand names, the U.K. legislation states that if a registered trademark has not been used in connection with its goods for five years, and if there is reasonable evidence of total non-use or of abandonment of the trademark, then anybody can apply to the Registrar of Trade Marks to cancel that registration. Therefore, if a manufacturer has created a "bank" of registered brand names for future use, failure to do so within that time puts them at risk.

Protecting unregistered trademarks

Common law remedy

7.22.1 Not all brand names will be registrable, and those which are not registrable (or which are not registered although they may be registrable) will have to rely in the United Kingdom on the English common law concept of "passing off", or upon the law of copyright in the case of artistic device trademarks or logos, to obtain protection from infringement by third parties. A registered trademark artistic logo will also be protected as a copyright work if it is original and sufficiently substantial. Other legal jurisdictions will have to be examined to see how they protect unregistered trademarks which are infringed in their territories.

Create reputation and goodwill

7.22.2   The best form of protection for an unregistered brand name is to get the product on sale in significant commercial quantities as soon as possible. The sales of the product should be supported by extensive and continuous advertising and sales promotions, to generate as wide a public awareness of the brand name as possible, and to deter infringing imitators. Not being registered does not reduce the effectiveness of a brand name; all that is affected is its capacity for legal protection. That depends upon how widely it is used, how well it is known publicly, and the extent of the reputation it has acquired. Therefore, with the investment which is needed to create and establish a new brand name, it would be foolish not to choose one which will be registrable as a trademark.

CONSEQUENCES OF NOT REGISTERING

Conflicting trademarks

7.23.1   If the manufacturer makes no trademark registration to safeguard the future use of the brand name in any significant market territory, it will risk not having any right of priority to claim trademark rights over the unregistered brand name in one country just because it uses the brand name by selling the product in another country. The proposed new brand name may be registered as a trademark in that class of goods by a third party in countries where that branded product is not yet available, and where it has not yet been promoted or advertised. This may be done with the intention of selling that trademark registration to the manufacturer of the new product at an extortionate price, the registration having been made speculatively and only for that purpose. In the absence of such a deal the manufacturer may find itself legally prohibited from selling its product under its usual brand name in that country.

In addition, a local third party may never have heard of the foreign product manufacturer or of its intention to launch a new product using that brand name in that country. By coincidence the third party may genuinely intend to manufacture and distribute its own product using that brand name or something very similar to it locally where it has made its own trademark applications.

Effect on brand name value

7.23.2   The market value of the manufacturer's new brand of product will be reduced in corporate asset terms if the manufacturer does not have effective trademark protection for the brand name in all of its active product sales territories. For a truly international product that means the world. Part of the strategic thinking of the management of the manufacturer must be that if the company were to be sold by the present shareholders a significant part of the company's value would be the goodwill of the brand names of its products.

INFRINGEMENT OF TRADEMARKS

TRADEMARKS AND ADVERTISING

Correct use of trademarks

7.24.1 An agency has to be careful about the depiction of trademarks, including logos and packaging design, in advertising and in promotions. A brand name or a logo may be carefully thought out for trademark registration application purposes, but it may be modified for convenience when it is used. For example, a brand name may be shortened to make it sound punchy, especially where it is more than one word, or a logo device may be changed to suit the new design of the packaging of the product. An excessive or careless use of "artistic licence" in its representation can cause a trademark modification. For example:

(a) The correct use of the trademark must be made whenever it appears in advertising material. This will not prevent puns and other deliberate misapplications of the trademark from being used occasionally by the advertiser to catch the eye of the public and to make the advertising amusing and interesting. However, a distortion or modification of the trademark of the product should not be used so frequently that the use of the registered version is in danger of being abandoned or diluted. (See paragraph 7.21.2). A modified version can be the subject of a separate trademark application.

(b) If the agency is producing material for a sales promotion, where the competition prize or the redemption gift is a third party branded product with the authority of the proprietor, the correct trademark of that brand must be used in accordance with its registration wherever it appears. The advertiser should also give the correct credits in the promotion material to the proprietor of that trademark.

(c) The possible infringement risk of third-party trademarks in the use of comparative advertising must be avoided.

(d) There is a trademark infringement risk in "reflected glory" advertising where the manufacturer makes intentional and prominent use of top quality and reputable third party products in the advertising of its own product in order to imply that they have the same level of quality, performance or reputation.

"COPYCAT" TRADEMARKS

Registered or unregistered

7.25 When the manufacturer has acquired a registered brand name as a trademark which has a high goodwill value, it can become the target of an imitator. If any other party tries to use a brand name with a similar style or spelling, or with a slightly different spelling but with a similar phonetic expression, at what point will that use become an infringement of the manufacturer's registration and of its rights of exclusivity in the use of the trademark? To be an infringement of the manufacturer's registered trademark, the use of the same or of a similar brand name must be in relation to goods within the same trademark class. In the case of a registered trademark the proprietor does not have to prove confusion or damage to substantiate an infringement, whereas that proof is necessary for a passing off claim.

STATUTORY DEFINITIONS OF CERTAIN INFRINGEMENTS

By authorised user

7.26.1 Section 6(1) of the Trade Marks Act 1938 sets out what could constitute infringement of a trademark, notwithstanding that the infringer has been authorised by the proprietor of the trademark to use it. This will happen where the third party has been granted a licence to make and sell the trademark owner's goods and has also been granted a trademark licence for use of the brand name or logo with those goods. The effect of this sub-section is that an authorised user of a trademark can become an infringer of that trademark if he uses the trademark in any manner which is specifically prohibited by the terms of the trademark licence agreement, or if it is used in any manner which is not specifically permitted under the licence agreement. This section is particularly relevant to any advertisement or sales promotion for the product which uses a modified form of the correct brand name trademark without the consent of the trademark proprietor. This can happen where the advertisement is humorous, or relies on a pun to get its message across.

Unauthorised alteration of product

7.26.2 The third-party licensee will also infringe the trademark if it:

(a) Applies the trademark to the licensed product after the product has been altered in any manner from its specification as described in the licence agreement. The specification will include a description of the quality of the licensed product and the design of its packaging.
(b) Alters or removes or partly obliterates the trademark or any other wording which is attached to or is part of the product and which

connects the licensing manufacturer with those goods. The result of doing so is that an unauthorised, modified or different trademark is used with that product, which will be an infringement of the original trademark.

(c) Applies any other trademark to the product. The licensee may have his own corporate logo, or a logo relating to similar goods of his own. If, without the authority of the trademark owner, the licensee includes any of his own logos or trademarks on the product or its packaging, that will give a false impression to consumers and will be prejudicial to the trademarks which are properly associated with the product.

(d) Incorporates onto the product any other matter in writing or graphics which is likely to injure the reputation of the trademark.

NON-INFRINGING SIMILARITY

Similar but not confusing

7.27.1 There are many different trademarks or brand names which have some similarity to each other, and which are capable of being used by their owners without any of them being entitled to claim against the others for infringement. This will depend on whether the goods to which they relate are also similar, and on whether the similarity of the trademarks is sufficiently close to cause confusion between the products or to be deceptive due to their origin and reputation. Anybody trying to use the words "Rolls Royce" in connection with anything at all may discover that the car company will object to such use, although it does not make (for example) potato crisps. A brand name such as "Rolls Crisps" or "Roller Crisps" may not be a trademark infringement provided that the advertising, promotion and packaging of the product does not have any direct or clearly implied association with Rolls Royce cars.

Copyright compared with trademarks

7.27.2 One fundamental difference between the rights of the proprietors of similar trademarks and similar copyrights is that:

(a) Two identical copyright items will not infringe each other, and can co-exist, if they originate entirely independently, so that neither of them is a copy of the other. This would not apply to the trademark aspect of artistic logos which are trademarks and which are also copyright protected.

(b) Even if two identical trademarks originate entirely independently for the same kind of product, the basic rule is that they cannot co-exist on commercially available products, and:

(i) if one of them is an existing registered trademark, then the other (which would not be registered) cannot be used, even if the registered one is not yet being promoted commercially.

(ii) if neither of them is a registered trademark, the first one to be used commercially in a substantial way will have a common law priority over the one which has not yet been commercialised. The owner of the prior use trademark would also have a priority of right to make an application for registration of that trademark.

Thematic brand names

7.28   It is possible for different manufacturers of similar kinds of product to use thematic words in their brand names. These may be modified by suitable prefixes or suffixes to be associated with their product whilst still giving the overall impression for which the theme brand description is recognised. This refers to common words which may be used by a number of products within their different brand names, where the words themselves in isolation are not protectable or exclusive. The words tend to be descriptive of the category of product to which they relate for example, mini, maxi and magnum.

VERSIONS OF BRAND NAMES

Different interpretations

7.29.1   New brand names which are the linguistic translation of an existing brand name or a visual device do not necessarily constitute an infringement. If a thistle device is the trademark logo of a brand of product without any "Thistle" word to support the brand name, it may be possible to have a brand name "Thistle" as a word but without using the illustrated thistle. In the case of a registered trademark device, the Registrar may block a word application as effectively being too similar. It does not matter that "Thistle" may not be registrable by itself as an ordinary word unless the criteria of long established use in connection with the goods can be proved. Because of its lack of distinctiveness, for the thistle word to be a trademark which does not infringe the thistle device it would have to be used in conjunction with other words. This would also distinguish between different "thistle" word trademark uses.

Confusing versions

7.29.2   There could be confusion where the brand name is a device, such as a thistle, which can only be described in speech by using the word "thistle". This could depend on whether the first product's brand name is "Whizzo" plus a prominent thistle device (in which case it would be known as "Whizzo"), or whether the product does not have a word brand name, but has just a large thistle on the packaging. In that case the product would be known by consumers as "thistle", because that would be the only natural way of asking for the product. Inevitably there would be confusion when consumers ask for "Thistle" where the products are similar and one product's brand name trademark is the device, and the other product's name trademark is the word. There would be no confusion where the two products have no connection, and are not of a similar nature, and are promoted in a different way.

PASSING OFF

THE CONCEPT OF FAIRNESS

Equitable principle

7.30.1 The unauthorised use and infringement of a registered trademark is actionable by its proprietor as a breach of its statutory trademark right. A copy of an original artistic logo will be a breach of copyright, and if the logo is also a registered trademark the copy will be an infringement of that also. Where a brand name is an unregistered trademark, or where a much-used logo is not protected by copyright because it is a public domain design, the proprietor does not have any statutory protection for it. The English law of equity has evolved an additional "fair play" concept called "passing off" whereby the copying of unregistered trademarks (including substantial similarity) will be actionable by their proprietors against infringers in certain circumstances.

Passing off defined

7.30.2 The judgments in the leading cases confirm that the necessary elements which have to be proved by the plaintiff in establishing a good basis for a passing off action against an infringing defendant are that:

(a) there is a misrepresentation;
(b) which is made by a trader (the defendant) in the course of its business;
(c) to prospective customers or to customers doing business with it;
(d) which is calculated to injure the business of another trader (the plaintiff), in that the injury is a reasonably foreseeable consequence of doing so;
(e) and which causes actual damage to the business of that trader (the plaintiff). Confusion without damage will not be enough to justify a passing off legal action.

Origin of passing off

7.30.3 A simple means of passing off is by manufacturer B making unauthorised use for its own product of manufacturer A's unregistered logo, brand name or packaging get-up, without any modification, and with the intention of deceiving the public. A more subtle approach is to have a "look alike" brand name, or even one which is sufficiently different to avoid being an infringement, but being strongly reminiscent of the established brand name. A reduced similarity also reduces the risk of a legal action for passing off, but exactly where the risk of infringement ceases is a matter of judgment, ultimately being that of a court.

Effects of passing off

7.30.4   In the above example manufacturer A will have spent a good deal of time, money and expertise in creating and developing the product brand name or logo trademark for its product. By promoting and advertising the product with that brand name manufacturer A will also have built up a considerable goodwill value in it. Manufacturer B is damaging the business of manufacturer A because manufacturer B is shortcutting the time and effort which he would otherwise have to spend in creating his own original brand name, so he benefits from not having to go through all those development processes and expenses. This gives manufacturer B an unfair commercial advantage over manufacturer A as well as infringing his trademark.

Manufacturer B is immediately getting an unfair reflected product recognition, market acceptance and goodwill value for the product which uses the infringing trademark. Since trademark B is confusingly similar to trademark A, it is already familiar to consumers through the marketing efforts of manufacturer A for its own products. This gives manufacturer B another unfair advantage over manufacturer A.

Manufacturer B is causing manufacturer A economic loss, as consumers are being deceived into buying the products of manufacturer B in the belief that they are the products of manufacturer A, or that the products are related to each other as originating from manufacturer A. Manufacturer B's action will undoubtedly cause damage to the reputation of manufacturer A if the infringing goods are shoddy or overpriced, or if the marketing activities of manufacturer B are seen by consumers as being dishonest or misleading.

DIFFERENCE BETWEEN REGISTERED AND UNREGISTERED TRADEMARKS

Registered trademarks

7.31.1   The benefit of being able to obtain a registration for a brand name or logo as a trademark is that legal action can be taken against an infringer by the registered proprietor of the brand name on the grounds of similarity without having to prove consumer confusion between the infringed and the infringing brand names. The proprietor of the registered trademark does not have to prove any intention on the part of the defendant to deceive the public, or that the proprietor has suffered, or will suffer, economic loss or damage as a result of the infringement.

Unregistered trademarks

7.31.2 The disadvantage of trying to protect an unregistered brand name is that a passing off of it can only be claimed if the similarity of the infringing brand name is confusing, and if the proprietor of the first brand name has actually suffered economic loss or damage as a result of the use of the similar brand name. Similarity without confusion and loss will not be sufficient grounds for a passing off action.

OEM PRODUCTS

Misrepresentation

7.32.1 For a passing off infringement, there must be a misrepresentation which amounts to a deception of the public. An OEM (Original Equipment of Manufacturer) product originates from a branded product manufacturer, which supplies it as wholesale anonymous unbranded merchandise to retailers, who put their own brand name upon it, and advertise and sell it as their own range. In bulk quantity this is done by the OEM manufacturer producing an "own brand" range of its products for the retailer.

Representations to the public

7.32.2 Where products are made by manufacturer A, which under a supply agreement delivers them to company B with an "own label" brand name showing them as being the ostensible product of company B, does this constitute a deception of the public? Not all suppliers are manufacturers, and the authorised attachment of a "B" brand name to an "A" product is not necessarily misleading. The B brand product is of exactly the same quality and design as the A brand product, but probably sells at a lower price to a different market. It may be evident that an "own brand" product cannot have been made by company B, because it not in that business.

Exclusion of brand name references

7.32.3 Manufacturer A is not being damaged through the sale of OEM versions of its product because that is its authorised deal with company B, although in a sense company B is passing off the product of manufacturer A as being its own product. The brand name of company B is being promoted on a product which was not made by Company B, so the advertising material must be carefully drafted so as not to be misleading as to the origin of the product.

Leaving aside the agreement between the two companies, what would be the position if company B started to advertise its OEM products as originating from manufacturer A? It may be a breach of contract and a breach of confidentiality but the statement would be technically correct and not deceptive or misleading in advertising terms. Is the revelation by company B an infringement of the brand name trademark of manufacturer A? A true statement such as "manufactured by A" would not be an infringement. Applying manufacturer A's brand name trademark, such as by stating that the OEM product "is equivalent to" manufacturer A's X brand, could be an infringement, as company B's goods were not authorised by manufacturer A to be sold with its own brand name.

ASSESSMENT OF BRAND VALUE

INTANGIBLE ASSETS

Valuable rights

7.33.1   In the world of consumer goods and their advertising and promotion, there is a major preoccupation with evaluating the market worth of brand names. The brand names of products and other intangible intellectual property rights such as know how, copyright and product design rights are assets of the manufacturer. Their perceived value may well exceed the value of the ordinary net tangible assets of the manufacturer, such as property, stock and tools for product manufacture.

Asset and share value

7.33.2   The manufacturer's share price will be affected by what is considered to be the market value of the brand names and the goodwill and reputation of its products. If the manufacturer is subject to a takeover bid for its shares, or if there is a willing seller and a willing buyer for at least a controlling interest in its share capital, an immediate question is, what market value can be attributed to the intangible assets? The same question applies where the manufacturer is just selling certain assets, such as all of the proprietary and manufacturing rights in a well known brand product. How do you assess the balance between what would be a fair value offer by the buyer and an excessive valuation which is made by seller? Brand valuation is not a simple exercise, and there are experts in this field.

SECURITY FOR FINANCING

Conservative valuation

7.34 The manufacturer may want to borrow large sums of money during a period of expansion and investment to develop existing brands of products, and to launch new brands, rather than raise the medium-term finance required by increasing the company's share capital. Any institution which provides substantial funding will require adequate security for its repayment. For calculating what is adequate security on a sell-off basis, if the need arises, the value of the manufacturer's intangible assets will be set conservatively at much less than their value is when the manufacturer's business is a going concern.

BASIS OF BRAND NAME VALUATION

No fixed basis

7.35.1 Apart from agreeing upon an acceptable multiplier of the annual net sales profitability of the branded product, or calculating the whole of the historical cost of creating and developing the brand name, there is no customary scale by which the value of a brand name for an established product can be calculated. There are many factors which have to be taken into account when valuing intangible assets, and it is difficult to get a "like for like" comparative table with similar products from other manufacturers. Each brand name has to be assessed and evaluated in its own right.

Market capacity

7.35.2 The size and sales potential of the overall market in which the branded product is distributed must be known. An assessment can be made of whether there is an excess sales capacity which is available to absorb greater quantities of the product if the production levels and marketing efforts were both increased. A leading question is whether there is a market demand for the product category which is not being fully met, and which could be fulfilled by the branded product if enough of it were available. Market saturation for the product category and market saturation for that brand of product are not the same; a judgment on the latter is made by looking at its market share in relation to the manufacturing capacity.

Brand product range expansion

7.35.3 The valuation of the brand name may include the possibility of future marketing expansion of the range of products covered by the brand name. If the brand name of a popular plain chocolate bar is extended to cover a milk chocolate bar with similar packaging, it will increase the market range, the sales potential and therefore the brand name value for those products.

Brand value influences

7.35.4 If the owner of the brand name wants to sell it together with the product manufacturing rights, it must agree with the purchaser on the method of calculating the value which is put upon the brand name. The following points may be relevant:

(a) The value which is put upon the brand name by the purchaser may be influenced by whether the brand product will be the first one in its category to be acquired and marketed by the purchaser, or whether it is an additional brand which extends an existing presence by the purchaser in that product category.

(b) There may be special know-how in the design or processing of the product, or its ingredients, which gives it an edge over other competitive products by way of consumer appeal, quality or price.

(c) If the brand product already has a major share of the market, a purchaser of the brand name and the manufacturing rights may be prepared to pay a premium to get them. The fact that it is the acknowledged brand leader in the product category can give the product a value to the purchaser which is greater than, say, the value of it to any other interested party.

(d) The value of a brand name is ultimately what somebody will be prepared to pay for it. When no sale or purchase of the brand name is contemplated, but a valuation of it is required for commercial or accounting reasons, a realistic assessment as a benchmark has to be made of what a suitable willing purchaser might be prepared to pay.

DEVELOPMENT COSTS

Historical cost or current cost

7.36.1 Another method of valuing a brand name is by calculating the overall cost to date of creating it, and adding a premium to represent the "profit" of that investment. A prospective purchaser may get the feel of what the value to him of that brand name may be by calculating what the current likely cost would be of trying to establish the product with that brand name from scratch up to the present level of sales and market share.

Costs which count

7.36.2 For a house-hold name, high-volume-sale branded product, the establishment and promotion of its new brand name would be very expensive, and the time it would take to achieve the objective would also be considerable. Expenditure of executive time within the manufacturer's organisation is invisible, but it is a substantial overhead. There is also the ongoing investment

316

of promoting, publicising and supporting that branded product to consolidate and increase its market share.

ANNUAL SALES GROWTH

Commercial measure of success

7.37.1 Whatever the cost of having developed the branded product has been, a current valuation of it is influenced by the sales and market share pattern of the brand over the last three or five years, together with its anticipated growth. The current sales value to the manufacturer will be multiplied by a figure to take account of future years' anticipated sales value. The purchaser must have some prospect of profitability after recouping the purchase price, so the multiplier has to be negotiated.

Comparative sales

7.37.2 Increased sales of the branded product over the past years is not of itself a wholly reliable indicator, because competitive products may have attained an even grater sales level increase. The major concern of a prospective purchaser of the brand name is to check the public interest in the brand product. Diminishing interest by consumers in the product, as shown by static or falling sales figures or market share, acts as a warning and affects the value of the brand name.

MARKETING AFFECTS VALUATION

Sales depend upon marketing

7.38.1 Advertising campaigns, sales promotions and all other marketing activities are vital to the popularity of the branded product. The question is whether the product sells consistently well because consumers know, like and want it; or because the high profile and pressure of its advertising and marketing maintain its sales momentum in an almost artificial way. The test would be to see what happens if the marketing effort is reduced. Therefore a proposed purchaser of the brand name should also look at the aspects of the marketing activities for the branded product discussed below.

Marketing costs and profits

7.38.2 Is the cost of all marketing activities which are used to promote the product excessive in relation to the potential profitability from the sales of the product? High sales levels of the product sound good in isolation, but if the marketing and associated costs which are incurred to achieve impressive sales

317

are so great that the product profitability becomes uneconomically low, then something is wrong. This is a good example of where a valuation of the brand name which is based upon insufficient information or inadequate research can be significantly misleading and incorrect.

Effects of marketing strategy

7.38.3 The purchaser of the brand name and product manufacturing rights should research the potential adverse effects of a change in marketing strategy. Is the consumer public responding more to the advertising for the product that it is to the product itself? That distinction can be difficult to make but occasionally a branded product does not live up to the promise of the advertising which promotes it. This is more likely to happen to newly launched products, before they become recognised and accepted by consumers.

Inadequate marketing

7.38.4 On the other hand, the marketing for the branded product may not be wholly effective or appropriate either for the brand name or for the image of the product. The result would be that the product's sales potential is not fully realised. If that is the case, then with an update or change of marketing style the product sales may increase at a greater rate than would be anticipated as a result of only continuing the current promotion activities.

ACCOUNTING FOR BRAND VALUE

MARKET VALUE

Updating assessment

7.39 The manufacturer of the branded product has the difficult task of maintaining an up to date calculation of the realistic value of the brand name, and (where it is entitled to do so) of reflecting this value in its balance sheet fairly and in a manner consistent with accepted accounting practice.

BALANCE SHEET REGULATIONS

Third-party protection

7.40.1 The regulations which determine if, and to what extent, a brand name can be stated as an individual asset in the balance sheet of the manufacturer's accounts, or even if it can be identified as an asset in the accounts, exist because:

(a) the company should not be able to give a misleading value of itself by the expedient of stating an arbitrary value for an intangible asset where that value is not verifiable; and

(b) there must be some protection for people who deal with the company, or who make secured loans to the company, or who wish to buy shares in the company, based upon an assessment of what the company is worth.

Subject to accounting standards

7.40.2 If a brand name has a value in monetary terms in excess of its historic cost, that value can only be a "goodwill value", because the brand name is intangible, and is incapable of being transferred by physical delivery. The accounting guidelines which should be observed are set out by the Accounting Standards Committee (ASC) of CCAB Ltd., a company whose members consist of the following bodies:

(a) Institute of Chartered Accountants in England and Wales;

(b) Institute of Chartered Accountants in Scotland;

(c) Institute of Chartered Accountants in Ireland;

(d) Chartered Association of Certified Accountants;

(e) Chartered Institute of Management Accountants; and

(f) Chartered Institute of Public Finance and Accountancy.

STATEMENTS OF STANDARD ACCOUNTING PRACTICES

Proposals

7.41.1 The ASC has issued two Exposure Drafts (ED), proposed Statements of Standard Accounting Practice (SSAP), which are consultative documents, and which deal with the question of brand name status in a company's balance sheet. These two documents are "Accounting for goodwill" ED47, (February 1990) and "Accounting for intangible fixed assets" ED 52, (May 1990).

Subject to amendment

7.41.2 As at March 1993 there had been no directives by the ASC following the consultative procedures carried out on either of the two above documents, and so the comments in this section are subject to amendment when the ASC issues standard accounting practice directives based upon ED 47 and ED 52. These two publications, and all directives which are issued, should be read in their entirety. The following comments on each of them only highlight certain points made in them.

ED 52: ACCOUNTING FOR INTANGIBLE FIXED ASSETS

External financial reporting

7.42.1 ED 52 is intended to establish the most appropriate method of accounting for brand names for the purpose of external financial reporting. By paragraph 37 of ED 52 an intangible fixed asset is defined as a fixed asset that is non-monetary in nature and without physical substance. This definition encompasses a brand name.

Balance sheet requirements

7.42.2 All assets of a company have to be declared in the balance sheet to the company's annual accounts, which are filed at the Companies Registry, and which are publicly available documents. Schedule 4 to the Companies Act 1985 deals with the contents of a company's accounts. Paragraph 47 of ED 52 explains that "intangible assets" which can be set out in the balance sheet include development costs, concessions, patents, licences, trademarks and similar rights, assets and goodwill.

Ascertainable value of intangible assets

7.42.3 Paragraph 48 of ED 52 states that intangible assets can only be separately identified if they were acquired for valuable consideration, and if they are not required to be shown as an unidentified part of a global goodwill value.

INTANGIBLE FIXED ASSET RECOGNITION CRITERIA

7.43 By Part III of ED 52, in paragraph 38, the accounting status of a brand name as an intangible fixed asset is put forward as a proposed Standard Accounting Practice. Paragraph 38 states that an intangible fixed asset should be recognised in the balance sheet (*i.e.* separately identified) only if all of the following recognition criteria can be satisfied:

(a) either the historical costs incurred in creating it are known, or it can be clearly demonstrated that they are readily ascertainable; and

(b) its characteristics can be clearly distinguished from those of goodwill and other assets; and

(c) its costs can be measured independently of goodwill, and of other assets, and of the earnings of the relevant business or business segment.

ASSESSMENT OF PARAGRAPH 38 OF ED 52

Brand names fail

7.44.1 A brand name is an intangible fixed asset; so can it come within the recognition criteria set out in paragraph 38 of ED 52 (see paragraph 7.43 above) to enable it to be separately identified in a balance sheet? It is possible that subparagraph (a) can be achieved by demonstrating the identifiable historical costs incurred in creating the brand name, but it is not practical to apply the requirements of subparagraphs (b) and (c) to a brand name. Consequently the present thinking is that the value of a brand name must be included in the balance sheet as part of goodwill, and not as an independent intangible asset.

Historical cost defined

7.44.2 The historical cost of a brand name can be either the purchase price of the acquisition of the brand name and manufacturing rights of a product, or it can be the expenditure-related cost of devising and protecting an original brand name. If the brand name has been purchased by the company, it may be eligible for treatment as "purchased goodwill", the accounting treatment for which is set out in ED 47.

APPLICATION OF RECOGNITION CRITERIA TO BRAND NAMES

Explanatory reasoning

7.45 Paragraphs 19 to 25 of ED 52 explain how the recognition criteria set out in paragraph 38 of ED 52 are to be applied to brand names. These paragraphs are relevant to determining what method of accounting should be applied to brand names which have an intrinsic value. Whether that value is modest or significant in commercial terms does not of itself dictate what accounting method should be applied to it. The significance of paragraphs 19 to 25 is that they set out the studied reasoning behind the conclusion which is referred to at the end of paragraph 23 of ED 52. Because they are important, and because they cannot be summarised and should be reviewed in their correct context, paragraphs 19 to 25 of ED 52 are quoted in full.

Paragraph 19
There is no doubt that brands and branding under skillful management can add significant value to commercial operations and are a major force in modern commercial practice. Significant commercial value, however, does not in itself assist in determining the method of accounting for brands to which this value attaches. The aim of this Statement of Standard Accounting Practice in relation to brands is to establish the most appropriate method of accounting for them for the purpose of external financial reporting.

321

Paragraph 20
The term "brand", undefined as it is, is generally used with a meaning significantly different from, and wider than, a trade name. Whilst every recognised brand has a trade name, the name is not synonymous with the brand. Branding connotes a continuous process of assembling, developing and exploiting all the tangible and intangible elements of the product to achieve commercial advantage over competitors. The term brand is thus generally used to mean a conjunction of characteristics which, operated in combination, offer the expectation of a stream of future benefits exceeding in aggregate what the constituent items could produce separately or without brand differentiation.

Paragraph 21
It is not practicable to identify or list all the typical constituents of a brand, but they normally include some or all of the following: a recognised name, a product or range of products, an established operation and market position, marketing and other specialist know-how, and trading connections. The characteristics described are expected, in conjunction and skillfully exploited, to generate enhanced future earnings.

Paragraph 22
In practice, brands are seldom sold and acquired as bare rights to trade names. If they were, their correct description would be trade names or trademarks. Brand acquisitions, however, normally involve all or part of the integrated set of supporting functions discussed above.

Paragraph 23
In all these senses, the term brand is used to describe what is generally regarded for accounting purposes as goodwill: that is, a combination of factors which is expected to produce enhanced earnings in the future; often the expectation of enhanced future earnings is based on a past history of such earnings. This interpretation is confirmed by the fact that the most commonly used methods of evaluating both goodwill and brands involve the use of multiples or present values of projected future earnings. It has therefore been concluded that for accounting purposes brands are subsumed within goodwill and should be accounted for accordingly.

Paragraph 24
This is not to say that it is considered that financial information about brands is not important to the users of financial statements. It obviously is, and reporting enterprises are encouraged to provide relevant information about brands that will help users to evaluate them. Some enterprises may wish to indicate, probably in a note to the financial statements, the amount of purchased goodwill being carried in the balance sheet which they consider is attributable to brand names. If this is done, sufficient information should be given about the identity of major individual brands, the method adopted to determine the amount apportioned to them and other

details to enable users to understand the valuation process and the nature of the uncertainties surrounding the valuation.

Paragraph 25
While this Statement of Standard Accounting Practice requires that brands should be treated as part of goodwill and not carried in the balance sheet as independent intangible fixed assets, the amounts concerned will, in the case of brands acquired through business combinations, often be eligible to be treated as purchased goodwill and capitalised and amortised in accordance with the provisions of ED 47 "Accounting for goodwill".

ED 47: ACCOUNTING FOR GOODWILL

Asset definition

7.46   In paragraph 4 of ED 47 an asset is defined as "a resource controlled by the enterprise as a result of past events and from which future economic benefits are expected to flow", and it is accepted that goodwill comes within this definition. The argument for having goodwill, and particularly purchased goodwill, included in the balance sheet is set out clearly in the following paragraph 9 of the Appendix to ED47.

Paragraph 9
An asset should be recorded in the balance sheet of an enterprise where that asset passes the recognition criteria of the system under which the accounts are prepared. Recognition criteria are designed to distinguish between those assets whose inclusion as an amount in the balance sheet gives useful and relevant information and other assets which it is not considered useful to enter in the balance sheet. The IASC Framework state that an asset should be recognised if (a) it is probable that any future economic benefits associated with the item will flow to or from the enterprise, and (b) the item has a cost or value that can be measured with reliability. These criteria are broadly in line with the main criteria developed by other frameworks. Goodwill fulfils criterion (a) for recognition under the IASC Framework. The interpretation and application of criterion (b) is therefore key to determining which goodwill if any, should be recognised and recorded as an amount in the balance sheet.

AMORTISATION OF INTANGIBLE FIXED ASSETS

7.47   Amortisation of intangible fixed assets has been a matter of some debate, and paragraph 40 of ED 52 puts the argument as follows:

Paragraph 40
This Statement of Standard Accounting Practice requires that intangible fixed assets, if recognised in the balance sheet, should not be treated as

having an infinite life. It is considered that it cannot be predicted with reasonable certainty that economic benefits will continue to flow to the reporting enterprise indefinitely from the asset in the form in which it was acquired or created. Given the rate of technological change and the dynamic nature of modern consumer fashions and tastes, a long past life does not afford a sufficient basis for a prediction of similar longevity in the future. Furthermore, many intangible assets which have existed over a number of generations have undergone profound change during this time such that the characteristics of the present asset are totally different from those of the original one.

CONCLUSION

Brand name goodwill

7.48.1   As ED 47 and ED 52 currently represent only proposed Standard Accounting Practices, it is possible that changes may be made as a result of the consultation procedures prior to their becoming established Statements of Standard Accounting Practices. The proposals are that the value of brand names will not be placed in a balance sheet as a separate item, but their valuation will be included in a goodwill asset provision.

Different accounting and commercial values

7.48.2   Irrespective of the goodwill provision in the balance sheet, because on a commercial basis the market value which is attributable to the brand name of a successful product may exceed the accounting value placed upon it, the assessment of a realistic free market value will not be inhibited by any negotiations based upon normal criteria for other matters for the purchase of the shares in the company, or for the purchase of just the brand name and the rights to make and sell the product to which the brand name is attached.

8 Promotion Rules

RULES GOVERN PROMOTIONS

PROMOTION AS A LEGAL CONTRACT

Contract terms

8.1.1 As set out in Chapter 1, a promotion can be seen as a legal contract between the product manufacturer (the promoter) and the participant in the promotion. A commercial contract consists broadly of two sections:

(a) those clauses which describe what the contract is intended to achieve. In the case of a promotion these are equivalent to the mechanic; and

(b) those clauses which set out the rights and the obligations of each of the parties. In the case of a promotion the parties are the manufacturer and the participant, and these clauses are represented by the rules of the promotion.

Risk of misrepresentation

8.1.2 The terms of a badly drafted and badly presented promotion can constitute contractual misrepresentations, and these could cause the manufacturer to be in breach of contract in respect of that promotion. This chapter deals with the legal side of some promotion rules which can cause problems, by explaining what they do and how they can go wrong. Because it is more convenient to do so, certain rules have also been dealt with in Chapter 5 because they can best be explained in the context of the relevant mechanic which they govern.

Sufficient prominence

8.1.3 Any fundamental requirement or restriction in the rules affecting a consumer's participation in the promotion must be placed prominently on the outside of the product package and in any other explanatory material. In this context "prominently" means easily visible, and highlighted if necessary to draw attention to essential matters. The main ones are:

(a) The description of who are eligible or ineligible participants.

(b) The promotion closing date.

(c) The main conditions of participation, such as:
  (i)   participation procedures
  (ii) redemption application limits for gifts or money off vouchers
  (iii) the number of proofs of purchase required.

PUBLIC PERCEPTION OF PROMOTIONS

Entertainment

8.2.1 It is unlikely that members of the public who participate in promotions think of them in legal terms. Although promotions do not seem to be litigated upon, they can be the subject of enquiries or disputes between the promoter and participants where the rules are not clear, or where they do not cover the point in question. For example, the three main prizes in a competition may be a "holiday in the sun" to be taken through a specified tour operator, although that last fact is not publicised in the promotion rules. Suppose the winners receive a tour operator's brochures from which they can choose their holiday, but the tour operator chosen by the promoter goes bust. By this time one winner has booked the holiday (but has not yet taken it) and the other two winners have not even booked their holiday yet. The rules of a promotion never deal with such a possibility, even by having a *force majeure* rule to cover any performance failure through no fault of the promoter. It is uncertain whether a "subject to availability" rule would cover this event to protect the promoter. What is the legal position of the competition promoter?

Problem resolution

8.2.2 The promotion rules must be examined first to see whether such a possibility is dealt with. In the absence of any rule which deals specifically with the situation, the promoter still has an obligation to provide the prizes to the winners, and must arrange to do so through another tour operator. The bankrupt tour operator is only the facility chosen by the promoter through which the holiday prizes were to be provided. Failure by the tour operator does not remove the obligation of the promoter to provide the prizes. Any promoter would be sensitive to the likely adverse publicity it would get if it declined to provide the winners with their prizes. Therefore the resolution of all promotion problems which are not covered by the rules is achieved by a mixture of tact and common sense, with probably some cost to the promoter.

RELEVANCE OF PROMOTION RULES

PARTICIPATION GUIDANCE

8.3.1 The essence of a promotion is the combination of the instructions for the operation of the mechanic of the promotion, and the rules which govern the participation of product buyers in the promotion. Different kinds of promotion need different rules, although there is a "core" of basic rules which will be applicable to most promotions.

Irrelevant rules are dangerous

8.3.2 Irrelevant rules and a total mismatch of the promotion mechanic and its rules can make the promotion meaningless, and possibly illegal. If the rules for a free prize draw contain a rule referring to there being a tiebreaker system to decide upon who is the ultimate winner of all the correct entrants, that would be a contradiction. There is no entry to be correct about, because there is no exercise of skill in a free prize draw and there is only one first prizewinner which is drawn at random for that purpose. This example would indicate that the free prize draw rules had been carelessly based upon a selection of competition rules.

Rules will not be implied

8.3.3 The shortage of space on the promotion package may be so acute that some rules may be omitted because the agency considers that they are self-evident. There is a risk if, due to a shortage of space on the package, the agency omits any rules on the basis that such "obvious" rules should be deemed to be included. Any "off pack" rules must be obtainable from the handling house free of charge, and there must be an "on pack" statement to that effect. If there is a set of stated rules which govern the operation of a promotion, those contract terms are set at the promotion launch, and neither the promoter nor the participant can imply into them unilaterally any other rule for convenience or for any other reason.

Only stated rules apply

8.3.4 If rules could be implied unilaterally, a new rule would have to be included for every promotion to the effect that the printed rules are final, and that no additional rules will be implied under any circumstances. If the rules are incomplete or inadequate, and if the shortcoming could easily be resolved by the promoter implying into them something which would be recognised by all participants as self evident, it will probably do so and it is unlikely that any complaints would be made unless a participant considers that his rights under the promotion rules as they stand will be prejudiced by the operation of any such implied rule.

Risk of misleading promotions

8.3.5 A promotion is a form of advertising for the product, so it has to comply with the relevant legislation against misleading advertising, and it must comply with the Advertising Standards Authority Code of Sales Promotion Practice. A promotion may be misleading if its rules:

(a) are confusing about the number of proofs of purchase which are needed for a valid application for a redemption gift;

(b) contradict the promotion mechanic, or do not refer to something vital relating to the mechanic;

(c) are not all applicable or suitable to the promotion mechanic; or

(d) are so skimpy that the promotion terms are not clear.

Basic rules structure

8.3.6 The final selection of rules must be appropriate to the promotion, and even for similar promotions each mechanic may differ from others in detail. In the process of producing rules for promotions, the agency can split them into two categories:

(a) Those which will normally be included in all promotions, which can be set out in a standard form. A comprehensive "mix and match" selection of common rules can be made for any promotion. They can be modified if necessary to fit in with any special factor of the individual promotion mechanic.

(b) For promotions with an unusual mechanic the agency must consider what specifically applicable rules are needed to deal with the mechanic details. The chosen selection of standard rules must be amended where necessary to be compatible with the individually drafted rules.

All promotions need rules

8.3.7 Promotions for consumer products and which are governed by promotion rules will fall into one of the following categories:

(a) a non-competitive, proof-of-purchase collection to be redeemed for a voucher for value, which may be set against the price of a subsequent purchase of the product;

(b) a non-competitive, proof-of-purchase collection, which by itself or together with an additional cash balance may be used for the redemption of a gift;

(c) a free prize draw;

(d) a lawful competition;

(e) a lawful lottery; or

(f) a trade promotion for the benefit of retailers or cash and carry outlets.

328

INADEQUATE RULES

EFFECT OF INADEQUATE RULES

What is inadequate?

8.4.1 The inclusion of inadequate or inappropriate rules, or the omission of a vital rule, can make the administration of a competition style of promotion difficult. Rules can be inadequate for the following reasons:

(a) they do not deal with elementary but essential points of the promotion mechanic;
(b) they can be so badly worded that they are meaningless in the context of the promotion, or they are ambiguous;
(c) if rules which are only relevant for a competition appear in the rules for a free prize draw, or vice versa, they are wholly inappropriate;
(d) through carelessness, such as by adapting a set of rules from a selection of other promotion rules, there can be two rules on the same subject but which are differently worded and which contradict each other.

Effect of inadequacy

8.4.2 The effect of inadequate rules is that it may not be possible to resolve unequivocally a problem or a query in the operation of the promotion. Some possible consequences of that are:

(a) inadequate rules may have the effect of turning a basically legal competition concept into an illegal lottery. A classic example is to have a competition mechanic with skill, but to have rules which allow the winners to be established purely by chance;
(b) if the promotion is a competition with one or more major prizes, an inadequate means of narrowing down and deciding the winners from all the correct entries could create a greater than expected commitment for the promoter to provide prizes to all of the correct entrants. It can be extremely expensive for the promoter if entitlement to the competition prize is not defined precisely. For example, if all the correct entrants are intended to share equally between them the prize of £1,000, an inadequate prize entitlement definition in the rules could result in each correct entrant being entitled to claim the full £1,000;
(c) it may not be clear as to what a participant has to do, or what restrictions there are on his doing it.

Conformity

8.4.3 If a full set of rules is being drafted from scratch for a promotion, they should be similar in style, and should deal with the mechanic in a logical manner. If, to save time, different rules are being taken from different existing sources, they will need modifying to make them conform with each other in the new rules structure. Each rule should be relevant and should have a purpose: there is no benefit in having any rules which are redundant to the promotion.

CAREFUL PREPARATION ESSENTIAL

8.5 The agency may consider that drafting a set of rules especially for each promotion is unnecessary where it is dealing with several different promotions which have much the same mechanic. It may only be necessary in each case to make superficial modifications to the rules of a previous successful promotion of a similar nature, but the revised rules should still be checked carefully to ensure that they are complete and appropriate to the promotion to which they apply. If anything goes wrong with the promotion, or if its legality is challenged, the first step for the promoter and the legal authorities is to check the text of the promotion and the rules.

PROMOTION DEVELOPMENT TIME PRESSURE

Timetable deadlines

8.6.1 When time is of the essence to meet any deadlines set by the manufacturer and agency for each development stage of the promotion the timetable for the promotion must include the time it takes to prepare and finalise the draft rules. That timetable must allow for the possibility of the original storyboard being substantially different from the final promotion, and so the rules may have to be compiled at a very late stage. At that point deadlines may be very pressing, and the risk is that they are compiled in a hurry and without enough thought, which can cause important points to be missed. Alternatively the timetable may have to include room for the previously drafted rules to be reviewed and sufficiently modified to accord with the final form of the promotion.

CHARACTERISTICS OF RULES

COMPLIANCE WITH LEGAL REQUIREMENTS

Promotion validity

8.7.1 The rules of the promotion must comply with the relevant legal and Code of Practice requirements which apply to the style of promotion for which they are being drafted. If the mechanic of the promotion is intended to be a lawful competition or a legitimate free prize draw, then carelessly drafted mechanic instructions and rules can invalidate the essential requirements for the legality of the promotion. When reviewing the final version of the rules against the promotion mechanic, the following questions should be asked:

(a) If the promotion is intended to be a free prize draw:
    (i) Is there any connection between the draw ticket (or chance) availability and the purchase of any product?
    (ii) Is there a "no purchase necessary" rule and does it work in practice? If the obtaining of an entry to the free prize draw is primarily through the purchase of a product, is there a "saving grace" rule which enables any person, without buying the product, to apply to the handling house for a free entry?
    (iii) Is there any direct or indirect "contribution" which has to be made by the person who gets the draw ticket? If so, what is it, and is it sufficiently direct and of a compulsory nature that it could be deemed to be a form of purchase price for the ticket? If so, the promotion will be an illegal lottery.

(b) If the promotion is intended to be a competition:
    (i) Is there a reasonable skill element for the mechanic?
    (ii) Is the procedure of elimination of correct entries down to the final winner also based on skill and not on chance? This is particularly relevant for a two stage elimination competition, as reliance on chance for the second stage will make the whole competition illegal.

UNAMBIGUOUS AND UNDERSTANDABLE RULES

Benefit of participants

8.8 The rules must be clear, complete, unambiguous and concise, and they should be worded in language which is understandable by an ordinary consumer. If the promotion is only open to limited sectors of the public, or if there are other restrictions upon how the promotion is entered or run, then these restrictions must be included in the rules. They must also be placed prominently on the promoted product packaging. This is important where the attraction of the promotion may have been the main reason for the buyer purchasing the product, but where he may not be eligible to participate in the promotion.

ACCESSIBLE AND VISIBLE PROMOTION TEXT

Keep related text together

8.9.1 All related statements, whether they are mechanic directions or promotion rules, should be together on the packaging. If the promotion rules are separated so that they are not all in the same field of vision, and if the immediately visible rules reasonably make the buyer believe something which is incorrect or out of the context of the full set of rules, that will be misleading and therefore illegal. The essential promotion rules must be easily visible on the package or label without having to remove it from the product. When reviewing the promotion text on the packaging for visibility and prominence, the promotion package artwork (including the text) should be viewed in whatever folded or other configuration it will be in when it is used by the product. Flat artwork as produced by the agency will not always show whether any vital part of the promotion text will comply with the above guidelines.

Separately available rules

8.9.2 The minor promotion rules need not be contained on the product package, provided that a complete set of rules does exist, and that prominent reference is made on the package to their existence, and how to obtain them. Any participant who wants a copy of the full promotion rules should be required to send a stamped addressed envelope together with the written request to the handling house which should provide them promptly and without charge.

ELIGIBILITY RULES

SAMPLE ELIGIBILITY RULE

8.10 A suggested wording is:

"This promotion will only be open to persons who are aged 18 or over and who are resident in the UK and who are not employees or contractors (including their immediate family) who are, directly or indirectly, connected with [the promoted product manufacturer] or [the manufacturer's sales promotion agency] or [the gift redemption handling house]."

PROHIBITED PARTICIPANTS

Compliance with the law

8.11.1 The first promotion rule is to define who is, and who is not, eligible to participate in the promotion. In the case of promotions for products which have a legal minimum purchase age, such as alcoholic drink, the eligibility rule must exclude all persons below that age since participation in the promotion is conditional upon the buyer providing proofs of purchase of the product.

Free prize draws and redemption

8.11.2 In the case of a free prize draw, where no special advantage can be gained by anyone who is directly connected with the promotion because the result is by random chance, and where there is no inside information to benefit from, it is safe for the rules to say that (subject to paragraph 8.11.1) anyone may be eligible. Sometimes the promotion may be limited to distinct classes of persons, such as the members of a club. Where the promotion is a simple gift redemption, except for any minimum age legal qualification, there is no need to have an eligibility rule. For consumable products there should be a "for bona fide home consumption" eligibility rule to disqualify traders from participating in the promotion if it is intended to be limited to consumers.

Competitions

8.11.3 Where the eligibility rule applies to a competition, it is wise to ensure that any person who, through his position with the manufacturer or with the agency, or through any other connection with the creation or administration of the promotion, might have the opportunity to make unfair use of inside information relating to the correct competition answer, is excluded from participation. How wide this exclusion should be is discussed in the following paragraphs.

EXTENT OF PROHIBITION FROM PARTICIPATION

Access to inside information

8.12.1 The wording of the eligibility rule in defining those classes of persons who are prohibited from participating in the promotion should be limited so as to cover only the normal reasonable circumstances in which such an unfair advantage might be available to those persons. The eligibility rule helps to prevent the possibility of a complaint being made that a winner of a competition won because of his ability to get an inside advantage, however unrealistic that claim may be, and whether or not any such advantage was taken.

Reasonable definition

8.12.2 The wording of the eligibility restriction should not be so wide and general as to make the rule invalid and unenforceable in law as being too uncertain. This could happen where the rule does not specify reasonably precisely who is eligible and who is prohibited, so that it may not be possible to ascertain from the rule who exactly should be prohibited from participating in the promotion. The example rule set out in paragraph 8.10 is the common style for all promotions, although it does not follow the advice which is given in this paragraph.

Applicable to certain employees

8.12.3 While employees of the manufacturer or the agency may purchase the product in their normal day-to-day life, promotions are run for the purpose of developing sales of those products to the wider public. In their private capacity all of those persons are part of that wider public. But if in the course of their employment they are actively connected with the development or management of the promotion, the real or potential conflict of interest must be resolved by making them ineligible to participate in the promotion. This precaution is for the benefit and protection of all other participants, although it can operate unfairly to most of those who are excluded.

Inapplicable employees

8.12.4 Is it fair or reasonable to prohibit *all* employees, including the manufacturer's office junior, from participating in the competition? The answer must be "no", because he would never have access to such marketing or confidential information. He would not be aware of the promotion until he saw it on the promotion package of the product. Nevertheless, technically he would come within the normal exclusion set by the wording of an ineligibility rule. Because the only reason for the participation prohibition is to be fair to other participants and to prevent cheating, the court might rule that the office junior would be exempt from the restriction. In this case the limitation may be deemed in law to be excessive and therefore invalid. However, it would be impractical to draft a short and sensible rule which addresses itself to being fair to all potential classes of employee, from those who may be absolutely ineligible to participate in the promotion, through to those whose risk to security and fairness is illusory.

Assessment of applicability

8.12.5 It is possible, for example, that the office junior in a sales promotion agency could become aware of confidential information about the promotion which gives him an inside unfair advantage. The agency may have open-plan office areas, and internally there is normally no need for security of promotion artwork visibility. For this reason the office junior of any agency is much more likely than his counterpart at the manufacturer to see the material for the promotion as it is developed.

INAPPROPRIATE RESTRICTIONS

Examples of application

8.13.1 There are some promotions where a rule which restricts any participation in the promotion would not be appropriate. It is a matter of practical judgment, but the following examples illustrate the point.

(a) A simple "50p off" the next product purchase voucher should have no eligibility limitation, with obvious exceptions such as people under 18 being barred from an alcohol-related promotion.

(b) A lawful competition where the answer is not predetermined by the exercise of logic or skill need not have any blanket eligibility restriction (except for the under age one). If the competition is an individual creative one, such as write a short story or design a new logo, insider information cannot help. In this case the competition entries are being assessed by a panel of judges after all entries have been received and the closing date has passed, so the result of the competition cannot be rigged by a person who has any connection with the promotion.

EFFECTIVENESS OF ELIGIBILITY RESTRICTION RULE

Example of wife of agency executive

8.14.1 Whenever a restrictive eligibility rule is applied to a promotion, how effective is it, and can it be enforced? It appears that the question has never been tested in court, and so any answer must be largely speculative. The necessity to apply and enforce the rule would only exist in circumstances such as where, for example, the winner of a valuable first prize in a lawful competition is discovered to be the wife of the agency executive who devised and planned it.

Effect of independent achievement

8.14.2 The executive may have been the soul of discretion, and his wife may have worked out the answer to the competition entirely without reference to her husband. But if the connection becomes known, there would almost certainly be accusations of cheating. Under the sample rule given in paragraph 8.10 wives of employees of any party which is directly connected with the promotion are stated to be ineligible to participate in it, so the agency executive's wife could not retain the prize if her eligibility was challenged. The question of whether "immediate families" should be excluded would depend on how serious the competition is, and upon the value of the first prize. Even that expression is not clear and precise.

EMPLOYEE NOT CONNECTED WITH PROMOTION

Relevance of employee status

8.15.1 Would the position be different if a secretary who works in the warehouse of the manufacturer was the winner of the first prize, as she would technically be within the class of prohibited participants? It would appear to be even more unfair to apply the eligibility exclusion rule to her if the warehouse is in Manchester, and the manufacturer's marketing department is in its London head office. In those circumstances she would not know of the existence of the competition until she saw it on the promotion package on the supermarket shelf.

Subsequent eligibility challenge

8.15.2 If no objection is made at the time the winner is announced, either by the manufacturer, or by the agency which is running the competition, what would happen if a contestant, who may be a "runner up" with a much more modest consolation prize, becomes aware of the facts, remembers the ineligibility rule, and objects to the secretary being entitled to retain the first prize? This is an extremely unlikely scenario, but it is an interesting point. Relevant factors would include:

(a) at what point in time it would be unfair even to investigate the alleged disqualification;
(b) whether the prize has already been used, be it a holiday abroad or a dinner for two at the Savoy;
(c) on the basis that a promotion is a form of contract when a person participates in it, whether the manufacturer would be in breach of it. If it is, then it would run the risk of having to compensate the displaced winner to the extent of what he would have won if the eligibility rule had been applied strictly to the award of the valuable first prize.

Enforcing the rule

8.15.3 The complaint will be valid if the ineligibility rule has been infringed by the secretary's participation in the promotion. What should the manufacturer do? The alternatives are:

(a) to disallow the award of the first prize to the unhappy secretary, and to award it to the runner-up. However, if there was one main prize and ten equal runners-up prizewinners, without any means stated in the rules of choosing a new first prize winner, another dilemma would arise.
(b) to leave the prize with the secretary and to get another identical prize for the technically eligible and upgraded runner-up. This could be dressed up as awarding the first prize to the runner-up, and, as an *ex gratia* gesture, giving the secretary a comparable consolation prize.

Can the exclusion be challenged?

8.15.4 If the secretary's employer declares the secretary to be ineligible to have entered the competition and thus not entitled to win the first or any other prize, can the secretary object to that decision? An objection may be sustainable on the basis that the exclusion rule as drafted is not legally enforceable. By entering the competition the secretary is deemed to have accepted the rule, but it is possible that a court may decide that it is drawn so widely that it is excessive and indiscriminate, and so cannot have any meaning or effect in the case of the secretary. Alternatively, by the manufacturer (or the handling house on its behalf) accepting the secretary's entry and awarding her the first prize, can it be deemed to have waived the rule? Awareness of the infringement of the rule would be necessary for a waiver of it to operate. On balance, an unnecessarily wide rule would be judged ineffective.

ALCOHOLIC DRINKS

Compliance with the law

8.16.1   When the promotion is run by a producer or supplier of alcoholic drinks, there must be a rule which states that no person under the age of 18 is eligible to participate in the promotion. This is because the conditions of entry to the competition, or of making a redemption application for a gift, will require the purchase of a specified quantity of the alcoholic product to provide the participant with the proofs of purchase required to enter the competition, or to enable him to make an application to redeem the gift.

Purchase not essential for consumption

8.16.2   Persons under the age of 18 are not permitted to purchase alcoholic products, but they are allowed to drink them, and it is not illegal for a person under the age of 18 to be in possession of bottle labels or coupons which came from the package or containers of alcoholic drinks. It could be argued that, providing the parent bought the alcoholic product, why should the under age child not be entitled to apply for the gift when the gift itself is not an alcoholic product?

Purchaser and participant may be different people

8.16.3   The eligibility rule never stipulates that the competition entrant or the gift redemption applicant has to be the actual purchaser of the promoted alcoholic product from which the proofs of purchase are taken. Wherever they come from, all the participant has to do is send in to the handling house the proofs of purchase in compliance with the rules and directions which govern the redemption of the promotion gift. On a strict interpretation of the terms and rules of the promotion, who bought the alcoholic product from which the proofs of purchase are taken is not material to eligibility for participation.

Social responsibility

8.16.4   The under 18 prohibition rule is included so that the producer of the alcoholic drink is not seen to encourage through the promotion the illegal purchase or even the drinking of alcohol by persons who are under the age of 18. This rule follows the requirements of paragraph 5.6.3 of the Code of Sales Promotion Practice. The social awareness factor behind the rule is widely disregarded in respect of drinking, but the law against under-age sale of alcoholic products is strictly enforced. Even then, redemption applications and competition entries are made by post, so the likelihood of discovery of an applicant's true age and thus of a breach of the rule is remote. There is never any requirement in the rules of the applicant's age.

MOTOR VEHICLE COMPETITION PRIZES

Licence-holder restriction

8.17.1   If the first prize in a lawful competition is a motor bike or a motor car, and as the riding or driving of these in public is legally restricted to those persons who are over a specified age and who have an appropriate valid driving licence, should there be a rule restricting entry to the competition to those classes of people? This would be consistent with the over-18 rule for alcoholic drinks promotions.

Ownership and use

8.17.2   Even if a 12-year-old boy completed the entry to the competition and won it, he would not personally be able to take away the prize, but his father could if he had a valid driving licence. A 20-year-old man who does not have a valid driving licence but who wins the car is in the same position as the 12-year-old boy, in that he cannot legally drive it away. It is not illegal to purchase or to possess a motor bike or a car without having a valid driving licence; it is only illegal for that owner to ride or to drive it in public. To that extent it is not the same as the over-18 rule for alcoholic product promotions. By omitting to apply such a rule to the competition, the manufacturer could not reasonably be accused of conniving in, or of encouraging, illegal under-age driving.

PARTICIPANTS MUST BE IN THE U.K.

A practical limitation

8.18.1   There is a common eligibility rule stating that competition entries or gift redemption applications will be valid only if they are made by participants or applicants who live within the United Kingdom. The product in its promotion package may only be available in the U.K. (this acts as an automatic restriction), and the promotion is intended to encourage U.K. buyers of the product. The territorial limitation is a practical safeguard for the manufacturer where the promotion is a gift redemption and the participant is not charged for the cost of postage and packaging for the delivery of the gift. If deliveries of the promotion gift have to be made to any country outside the U.K., the cost of doing so could be prohibitive within the budgeting for the whole promotion.

Insurance considerations

8.18.2 In the absence of a territorial limitation of eligibility, the level of redemption estimates made by the manufacturer or its agency as information required by the insurer of the excess redemptions could be at risk as being too conservative. The conditions which are usually imposed by the insurer may be exceeded or breached, causing the insurance policy to be invalidated. If those insurance conditions did not specify that the promotion should only be U.K. based, and if the proposal form which is accepted by the insurance company simply appended the promotion rules for identification as being incorporated into the terms of the insurance contract, the omission of a territorial limit for the eligibility of applicants would not invalidate the policy.

Competitions

8.18.3 In the case of a competition the excessive cost risks of a redemption promotion do not apply provided that the prize (if it is a large physical object) does not have to be delivered to the winner outside the U.K. If the winner must attend a presentation of the prize at an organised occasion, the fact that he lives outside the U.K. would not adversely affect the competition promoter, although it might seriously detract from the value of the prize to the winner. There is no legal restriction on a competition having to be limited to U.K. participation, but in practice seldom is it likely that an entry will be received from overseas.

PROOF OF PURCHASE RULES

Sample proof of purchase rule

8.19 A typical wording is:

"Send three of these special coupons together with the completed entry form to the address set out below to arrive not later than the [ ]. [This entry form is part of the coupon and all you need to do is complete it and send to the address below together with two other similar coupons.] [Only original coupons will be valid]."

USE OF PROOF OF PURCHASE

Essence of the promotion

8.20.1 As eligibility for participation in the promotion (except in the case of a free prize draw) is normally conditional upon the purchase of the promoted product, every competition entry or gift redemption application requires the inclusion of a specified number of proofs of purchase of those items. What has to be sent in by the participant as a proof of purchase must be easily identifiable from the promotion package and the rules. It will be a clearly marked section of the package, or a label or some other device which can be detached from the package of the product, or it may be an identifiable form of receipt evidencing its purchase.

Redemption rates and proofs of purchase

8.20.2 The proof of purchase may be of a type that can conveniently be detached from the package without disturbing the contents, or alternatively the package may need to be empty to do so. That difference can affect the rate of redemption of the gift, particularly during the early part of the promotion period. The reason is that with an easily detachable proof of purchase the buyer can make a redemption application before he even opens the package. If the product has to be used or decanted before the proof of purchase can be detached from the package, there will be a greater time interval between the product purchase and the application for redemption after use of the product.

Proof of purchase design

8.20.3 The proof of purchase should be so designed that, on removal from the package, it does not contain (and therefore remove) any part of the instructions or the rules to which the participant may want to refer afterwards. The redemption application form may also represent the proof of purchase for that package.

Product consumption rate

8.20.4 Where the proof of purchase is an integral part of the package, the difference in time between the purchase of the product and the proof of purchase being used for a redemption application becomes more apparent if the redemption requirements need two or more proofs of purchase. This is especially so if the package is the kind which take a while to be emptied, and where normally only one package is used at a time.

340

IN-STORE PROMOTIONS

Based on till receipt

8.21 A voucher by mail promotion which is run internally by a chain of stores in conjunction with a manufacturer for its promoted product will require as part of the redemption validation procedure proof that the product was actually purchased in one of its stores The proof of purchase must be accompanied by a till receipt which shows that the product has been purchased, and from which branch of the chain of stores running the promotion the purchase was made. Special rules as to redemption validity will be needed for such in-store promotions. The promotion offer flash must refer prominently to retaining and submitting the till receipt as being a condition of validity for the redemption application, otherwise the purchaser might discard it.

MISSING PROOFS OF PURCHASE

Make tamper proof

8.22 The proof of purchase, as a part of the product package, must be tamper-proof. An easily detachable label, such as one which is loosely attached to the neck of a bottle, may be easily removed at any time before its retail sale. If a consumer buys the package specially to participate in the promotion, only to find on inspecting it at home that the proof of purchase had already been removed, he could complain to the retail outlet, demanding a replacement proof of purchase. What is the position of the retail outlet?

(a) The buyer may have difficulty in proving to the reasonable satisfaction of the outlet that the originally attached proof of purchase was missing from the package when he bought it.

(b) The retailer will say that it makes no representation that the proof of purchase will be attached to the product. It will be the responsibility of the buyer to make sure that it is attached before he buys the product.

(c) The retailer is not the promoter of the competition or the redemption offer or his agent, and it will have no obligation to the dissatisfied buyer to replace the missing proof of purchase, or to take the "defective" product back. The retailer will not have any spare proofs of purchase to replace missing ones.

(d) As the outlet is offering the promoted product for sale, would the failure of the promoted product package to comply with the promotion offer terms in this instance be deemed to be a form of misleading advertising by the outlet or by the manufacturer? The product as advertised and sold does not comply with the promotion offer terms if there is no proof of purchase attached to it, and the purchaser is not able to participate in the promotion. That may be technically misleading.

REQUIRED NUMBER OF PROOFS OF PURCHASE

Prominent statement

8.23 The number of proofs of purchase of the product which have to be submitted with the redemption application form or the competition entry must be stated clearly in the promotion rules. If the promotion requires the participant to purchase more than one package of the promoted product in order to collect the requisite number of proofs of purchase, that fact must be explained prominently and clearly on the package. Where only two proofs of purchase are required, "Send in this application form together with two proofs of purchase" is ambiguous unless there is a separate proof of purchase section of the product packaging. If the application form is the proof of purchase, "Send in this application form plus one from another [packet]" makes it clear.

LIMITS ON MULTIPLE APPLICATIONS

SAMPLE LIMIT ON APPLICATIONS RULE

8.24 An example is:

"Only three applications for the redemption of a [gift] may be made [per person] [per household]."

PURPOSE OF LIMIT

Limit discount costs

8.25 The limit normally applies to the number of applications which can be made for the redemption of gifts, or to applications for "money-off" vouchers to be set against the price of the next purchase of the product. That is because each gift redemption, or each "money-off" voucher applied for, represents an additional discount cost to the manufacturer which is incurred after it has sold the promoted product to wholesalers. The cost of a redemption gift promotion to the manufacturer can become excessive where the redemption level is greater than the one which it has anticipated and budgeted for.

TICKETS FOR FREE PRIZE DRAWS

Limit on numbers

8.26.1   If a free prize draw is being held legally in limited circumstances, such as in a pub, club or restaurant, while the "no purchase necessary" rule must still apply, there is no obligation on the proprietor of the premises to allow it to be a free-for-all, mass application for tickets. The limitation rule may be that only one draw ticket will be issued per request, and perhaps with a further limit of one ticket being issued per person during each opening hours session. If a free prize draw ticket is being handed out as a matter of courtesy with each purchase of a particular brand of drink which is being promoted in a pub, a random request for tickets for the draw by a person must be honoured (subject to application limits) whether or not he has purchased, or shows any indication of purchasing, any of the promoted product. This is to comply with the "no purchase necessary" rule.

Advertising the limits

8.26.2   The rule containing the limit on the number of free draw tickets which can be taken must be prominently set out on all the advertising material for the promotion which is displayed on the premises. The point of sale advertising should be displayed wherever the free draw tickets can be obtained.

LIMITATIONS PER HOUSEHOLD

Clear definition

8.27.1   The promotion rule may be expressed as limiting gift redemption applications to a number per person, or per household. The rule must not confuse the issue by making the limit "per person *or* per household" —it must be one or the other. The computerised checklist of redemption applications which is maintained by the handling house will list each redemption applicant by name and address, so it is not difficult to find those persons who make an excessive number of redemption applications. (See paragraph 2.19 of Chapter 2).

Excessive applications

8.27.2   Where a participant makes redemption applications for a gift in excess of the maximum limit allowed under the promotion rules, the excess applications are not valid. If the first or only application is for too many gifts according to the rules, the handling house should process the maximum which is allowed, and reject the rest. Any subsequent application from the same household should be rejected. The handling house has no obligation under the rules to notify the applicant of that rejection, unless it is an "added cash" redemption for a significant gift.

Two-family households

8.27.3 The "household" limitation rule will not apply to different people from a block of flats who make separate applications, provided that each flat has its own postal address. Where one address, being a family house, actually contains two related but separate families, the rule will be applied in the absence of a waiver of it by the handling house if it is satisfied about the "two-family" explanation. If the two families send their separate maximum number of redemption applications in the same envelope for convenience, that is less likely to indicate a fraudulent intent, because anybody who is deliberately trying to bypass the limitation rule would take care to separate the applications by sending them from different addresses. The combined applications would however still be invalidated by the limit rule. Therefore the word "household" should be interpreted sensibly by the handling house.

OTHER MULTIPLE APPLICATIONS

Discretionary view

8.28 There are other legitimate reasons for multiple redemption applications which could be looked at sympathetically, even though the rule would be breached by allowing them. An example is where the members of a School's scout troop have saved up all their proofs of purchase to get a large number of the gifts or additional products for distribution to, say, an old people's home. The scoutmaster making one redemption application for all of them would be substantially in breach of the application limitation rule. The alternative approaches are for him to send a covering letter to the handling house explaining the position, or for each scout to make his own individual maximum number of applications from his own address. To avoid disappointment after a major effort, the scoutmaster could try to get a clearance in principle for the project from the handling house or the manufacturer before collecting the proofs of purchase.

SPLIT GIFT PROMOTIONS

Clarify choice

8.29 A split gift promotion is where there are two gifts on offer for redemption. The offer is split because Gift A can be obtained for X proofs of purchase, while Gift B can be obtained for Y proofs of purchase. A split gift promotion limitation rule should specify whether the limit on applications applies to both of the gifts, or whether only one of them can be chosen, or whether the limit can be made up from a mix of the two gifts. The rule would also have to explain clearly the different numbers of proofs of purchase which will be required with the redemption application for each combination of gift.

PARTICIPATION IN PROMOTION

INFORMATION REQUIRED FROM PARTICIPANT

Personal information

8.30.1 The competition entry form or the redemption application form should be simple and should require only the minimum necessary amount of information about the participant. In the case of a competition the information is needed to check whether the entry is correct, and to provide a sufficient identity of the participant for contact purposes should he be a winner. If the competition contains a tie-breaker, it will also be set out in the entry form, and must be completed by the entrant. In the case of a redemption application all that is needed is the name and address of the applicant and any reference to the proofs of purchase and/or cash which are necessary for the redemption application to be valid.

Participant's privacy

8.30.2 On voucher or gift redemption applications it is a common practice to include questions about the purchasing or consumption habits of the redeemer which are pertinent to the promoted product, or to the promoter (such as if it is a High Street store). A "privacy selector" question should be included, so the participant can block any further mailing by the promoter. Manufacturers get valuable "trend" information from the "habits" questions, which go into a marketing data base for future use and analysis. Section CV1 of the ASA Code of Advertising Practice deals with this area in detail.

INVALID ENTRIES OR APPLICATIONS

Rejection by handling house

8.31.1 The promotion rules must cover those circumstances in which a competition entry or a redemption application will be rejected by the handling house as not being valid. As examples of what should be contained in the invalidity rule, a redemption application or a competition entry form should be declared to be invalid in each of the following circumstances.

Failure to meet the closing date

8.31.2 A rule must be included to state that all entries or applications must be received by the handling house on or before the stated closing date. Where the competition entry or the redemption application is received after the closing date for the promotion it should not be accepted. As the rule never states that the entry or application should be sent by "prepaid post", where there is an excess postage to pay on receipt by the handling house due to it having no stamp, should it be accepted as valid? It will have been received according to the rules, and should be accepted.

Posting is not delivery

8.31.3 To cover the position of where what would otherwise have been a competition winning entry goes astray in the post, or where a gift redemption application is never received by the handling house, or where it is posted in good time but is received after the closing date, there should be a rule to state that proof of posting of the application or entry will not be deemed to be proof of receipt.

Mutilated or illegible entries

8.31.4 There should be a rule to state that where a competition entry form is mutilated or illegible in respect of essential information, or where it does not otherwise comply with the rules, it shall be deemed to be invalid. The rule is intended to eliminate those entries which are deliberately illegible in an effort to get an each-way bet in the confusion upon having a correct answer among all of those which are contained in the entry. There is no definition of what may be considered to represent mutilation, but any amendments to the answer given on the entry form will be treated as invalid. The entrant may have changed a first incorrect answer to the correct answer very clearly and legibly; but that might also have been done by an "insider". The entrant may also claim that he did not make the alteration if the scratched out answer turned out to be correct. In the case of a scratchcard promotion, a misprinted or insufficiently latexed card which makes the correct answer visible should be invalidated.

ORIGINAL PROOF OF PURCHASE

Prevents cheating

8.32 The obvious purpose of requiring an original proof of purchase is to show that it comes from a purchased product. A photocopy of the proof of purchase will not be accepted as being valid, because it cannot have come from a purchased item of that product and it would open the possibility of numerous fraudulent applications from the one original proof of purchase. A rule invalidating a copy for use as an application form should not be necessary if the participation directions and rules are clear, such as "Complete this application form".

INCOMPLETE COMPETITION ENTRIES

Interpretation of rule

8.33.1 If the competition entry form is incomplete, or if it is incorrectly completed, so that the conditions of entry are not fulfilled according to the rules, it should be invalid. A sensible interpretation of what is incomplete must be applied. Omitting the postcode from the entrant's address should not make it incomplete for this purpose. But having more than the maximum number of words in a tie-breaker makes the entry incorrectly completed and so does the omission of completing the tie breaker section. What would be the status if such an entry was the only correct entry, and therefore was the winner, so the tie-breaker is not operated? The tie-breaker rule has not been complied with, but is therefore the whole entry invalid? It depends upon the wording of the rule, but the invalidation should only apply if the tie-breaker procedure is actually operated. The tie-breaker is not a part of the main competition itself, as it is not related to the competition response. It is only a legal means of finding the winner if there should be several all correct entries, and therefore represents a secondary and distinct competition.

No investigation obligation

8.33.2 While the handling house should make a reasonable effort to decipher the competition entry or the redemption application, it has no obligation to spend time in doing so, and it should take a strict view as to whether the promotion rules have been complied with. Each participant must study the terms of the competition or promotion, and the applicable rules, and must complete the entry or application form properly.

INSUFFICIENT PROOFS OF PURCHASE

Depends on application

8.34 A gift redemption application will be invalid where the number of proofs of purchase sent with it is less than the number which is required under the rules to obtain the gift. If there is a discrepancy between the number of proofs of purchase which is stated in the application form and the number actually enclosed, the handling house can accept the number of applications (within the limit) which is validly suported by the enclosed proofs of purchase.

If the rule clearly states that for an in-store promotion the till receipt is required as well as the promoted product proofs of purchase for a valid redemption, failure to send it in will invalidate the application. Therefore the wording of such a rule must be easily visible and printed in bold or large letters.

MONEY-OFF VOUCHERS

One at a time

8.35.1   In the case of a money-off voucher which can be used against the price of the next purchase of the product, the rules should state that only one voucher may be used for each purchase. It must also be made clear on the package whether the consumer can use the voucher immediately against the next purchase, or whether the consumer has to send off one or more coupons from packages to receive a "money-off" voucher by mail.

No cash value

8.35.2   There should also be a rule stating that the "money-off" voucher has no cash value, or any usable value other than as a price discount off the purchase price of the promoted product. The voucher should also have a "use by" date on it after which it is invalid.

Applicable to next purchase

8.35.3   The wording of the on-pack text or of the promotion rules should not imply that the voucher which is contained on that package may be used in reduction of the purchase price of that package; it must only be used against the purchase price of another purchase of that product. Use of words such as "only this purchase necessary" on the package to activate the voucher use will be confusing in the absence of an equally prominent and clear explanation of what that statement represents. The instructions contained on an immediately usable "off next purchase" voucher do not state when that "next purchase" has to occur, only the last date by which it must be made. Therefore if two of the promotion packs are bought at the same time, unless the rules state otherwise, the voucher on each of them can be used against the purchase price of the other of them if they are detachable at the point of sale.

OVERLAPPING PROMOTIONS

Achieving separation of entries

8.36.1   For a short period the manufacturer may be running two different promotions at the same time for the same product due to the overlap of different promotion periods. Proper timing schedules for the separation of consecutive promotions for the same product should prevent such an overlap, but this may happen where there are residual promotion packages still available from the existing (but about to expire) promotion for that product, and there are recently distributed packages containing the new promotion which has just started.

Specification of voucher use

8.36.2 One promotion may be a "10 per cent. extra free" additional amount of product package, and the other promotion may be a "£1 off next purchase" voucher contained on the package. The rules of the second promotion should state that (in this case) the £1 voucher cannot validly be used towards the purchase price of any other unconnected specially promoted package of the product. The rule could state that the £1 voucher can only be used against the purchase price of the product packages which are subject to the same voucher promotion. If the £1 voucher can be used in reduction of the purchase price of the "10 per cent. extra free" offer package, that is causing the manufacturer to incur a double promotional discount on them. If the product is continuously subject to one relatively short lived promotion after another, and where "standard packages" (*i.e.*, not being subject to any form of promotion) are seldom on sale, such a rule may not be practical. Also, the validity life of vouchers normally extends well beyond the date by which those same promotion packages are totally sold out to consumers.

GIFT DELIVERY PERIOD

Customary 28 days

8.37 For a gift or voucher redemption application there should be a rule stating that the gift or voucher will be delivered within 28 days after receipt by the handling house of the valid redemption application. It may be done sooner, but that period gives the handling house adequate time within which to process the mass of redemption applications which it receives for the promotion. In the case of a "while stocks last" promotion, delivery should be qualified by a subject-to-availability rule.

LIST OF WINNERS

Must be published

8.38.1 In the case of a competition, there must be a rule which states that anyone can find out who the prize winners were by writing to the handling house with an SAE within 28 days after the date by which the winners were to have been notified of their success. As handling houses are computerised, and as compliance with this rule will mean that personal information will be divulged to total strangers, the handling house's Data Protection Act 1984 Registration must enable it to do so. For security or privacy reasons the identity of the winner or winners should be just their names, or their names and the name of the town or county where they live. Precise private addresses should never be given. Alternatively an enquirer will be told whether or not he has won anything, so that the winners' identities are kept confidential.

Date of availability of information

8.38.2 If the competition is in a magazine, the winner's details can be published in the next available issue after the results become known, and the promotion rule can be worded accordingly. In this case, due to the lead time which is required by a monthly magazine to produce print before publication, the results may not appear until the second issue of the magazine after the promotion closing date. The rule covering publication of the results should be worded accordingly.

9 Public Relations

LEGAL CONSTRAINTS ON PUBLIC RELATIONS

DEFINITION OF PR

Communication

9.1.1   Public Relations (PR) is the art of communication; it is the propaganda side of the battle to promote the public profile of a product or its manufacturer. Of the several definitions which exist for PR the simplest to understand is the one which was put forward by the Institute of Public Relations when it began; "Public Relations practice is the planned and sustained effort to establish and maintain goodwill and mutual understanding between an organisation and its publics".

"Publics" defined

9.1.2   In this context "publics" means whatever sectors of the public the PR campaign is aimed at, and which could be the purchasers or users of that product for which the PR activities are being undertaken. Generation of public perception of the product can only be achieved by effective communication by or on behalf of the product manufacturer. This is done through advertising, promotions and PR. These communicate to the public and to other important elements of its market all relevant and current information about either the company or its products. The information may relate to the launch of a new product, or to the publicising of a new development of it, or to any other feature or event affecting the company or its products which is reasonably newsworthy.

Overlap of PR and advertising

9.1.3   When dealing with customer requirements there may be many areas where the role of the PR department and the role of the advertising agency overlap. Where that happens, the input required from each of them, and their areas of responsibility, should be defined in order to avoid unnecessary duplication of effort and to ensure that the advertising and PR are co-ordinated. Where there is collaboration between them, the wording and presentation of the end product to be released for publication should be approved by all those who have been involved in creating it, and who are responsible for it, so as to get a balanced opinion.

PR IS NOT A LEGAL SUBJECT IN ITSELF

No specific legal framework

9.2.1 This chapter deals with certain legal issues which affect how PR activities are carried out. There are no specific statutes or regulations which create PR as a legal subject, or which state that the conduct of the business of PR must be within a specified legal framework. The Institute of Public Relations has a Code of Practice as a voluntary conduct guideline, but it does not have the force of law behind it. In this way PR is much less formally regulated than advertising and certain aspects of sales promotion.

Activities with legal content

9.2.2 In the course of creating and publicising any PR campaign or project, there will be a variety of features which themselves are subject to legal rights or restrictions. Providing that these areas of concern are identified at an early stage, and that they are dealt with in accordance with the appropriate legal principles, the carrying out of any reasonable PR activity should not cause any legal problems that have not already been discussed in previous chapters.

Advisability of legal checking

9.2.3 Everyone has their own idea of what constitutes good PR practice for their business; but they should review what they do in legal terms. There are occasions when an intended public statement of a sensitive nature should be given legal clearance independently of the PR objective.

PR USE OF COPYRIGHT MATERIAL

Photographs

9.3.1 The most likely use of photographs as part of the PR effort will be in the company's annual report, in press releases or in promotional brochures or other publications which are used to support a new product launch. The ownership of the copyright in photographs, whether they are loaned for use or whether they are commissioned specifically for the publication, has been dealt with in Chapter 5, but the two rules are listed below:

(a) If a photographer is commissioned by the company or by the PR agency to take the photographs, they must make sure that as part of the agreement for the commission there is a specific assignment of the copyright in the photographs to the company. Unless the photographer is used frequently by the company and is well known to it, at the end of the commission the company should also be given the negatives.

(b) If the photograph is provided from any other source, the company must make sure that it has the written consent of the owner of the copyright in the photograph for its required use.

Press releases

9.3.2 The text of a press release which is created entirely by the PR agency is copyright material, and may not be reproduced by anybody else without the copyright owner's prior permission. While most press releases are of no lasting interest, there may be a particularly noteworthy occasion for the company which makes the press release about it a special event document. The company should have an assignment of copyright in all PR releases and documentation from the PR agency, so that it owns and controls all such material. Unless it owns the copyright in its PR material, if the company ever wants to reproduce it, such as in a "company history", it would need the written consent of the agency, and this could create difficulties.

Use of PR material

9.3.3 The purpose of making the press release is to get it publicised as widely as possible within the appropriate media. If it is reproduced by appropriate publications accurately, or even in a fair edited form, and in the right context, no copyright infringement complaint could be made by the PR agency, as this was the object of sending out the press release in the first place. A publication which receives the press release from the agency will be deemed to have been granted an implied licence to publish it in the precise form in which it is submitted. It is recognised that all publications retain editorial control over what they publish, and a fair and representative edited version of the press release will be acceptable to the agency and the company. If the press release is reproduced in a substantially distorted and edited form, with the result of wholly misrepresenting the contents of the press release and of making a mockery of the company, that unauthorised form of publication might be actionable.

Third-party material

9.3.4 The text of a PR statement must not contain any third-party copyright material without the consent of the owner of the copyright in it, otherwise that use will be an infringement. As the copying must be of a "substantial" amount of the copyright material to be an infringement, an exception is that a brief relevant quotation from the copyright work may be acceptable, such as a favourable comment which is contained in a financial review article about the company. The other exception is where the copyright material is to be the subject of a bona fide review within the press release, when the "fair dealing" provisions of the Copyright, Designs and Patents Act 1988 could apply. If the use is not authorised by the copyright owner or under the Act, even paraphrasing copyright material can be an infringement if the changes to it are superficial and the "substance" of the copyright material has been reproduced. If any copyright material is reproduced in the press release, an acknowledgment should be given to the copyright owner.

DEFAMATORY MATERIAL

Defamation

9.4.1   A defamatory statement can be defined as one which is published to a third party, and which contains an untrue statement or an imputation which damages the reputation of another person. Financial loss or damage by him does not have to be proved. A false imputation which tends to lower the plaintiff in the estimation of right-thinking members of society, or which exposes him to hatred, ridicule or contempt can be defamatory of him; fair criticism of any person is allowed, but a defamatory statement is not.

Careful wording

9.4.2   The risk of a defamatory statement being made in PR terms can exist where untrue allegations or damaging insinuations have been made in an article, or in a spoken statement concerning the company, or any of its executives. Whether or not those allegations or insinuations are defamatory, any response which is made by the company upon the advice of its PR agency must not itself refer in a defamatory manner to the originator of the offensive material which is being complained of, however tempting it may be to cast aspersions on his sanity, credibility or parentage.

CONSUMER PROTECTION

Misleading statements

9.5.1   Any PR-based statement which is released *to the public* referring to the company's products has to comply with any relevant consumer protection legislation and the Code of Advertising Practice in respect of deception of the public, or of making any misleading statement as to the quality, performance or price of the product which is being publicised. PR statements are not advertisements in the normal sense, but they can be used to advertise and promote the company and its products in different ways.

Responsibility for deception

9.5.2 Who is responsible where a press release contains misleading or deceptive statements, or if (where applicable) a Code of Practice has been breached? A PR agency is in much the same position as an advertising agency, except that it does not act as a principal. The responsibility as between the agency and the company will depend on the circumstances in which the press release was drafted and approved. For example:

(a) If the company drafts the press release, but the PR agency modifies it without authority to make a snappy statement out of a boring one, the agency will be responsible to the company for the consequences attributable to those alterations. As the publisher of the press statement, the company will be liable to injured third parties.

(b) If the agency incorrectly interprets information which is correct and which is supplied to it by the company, and the incorrect interpretation causes a misleading inference or statement to be included in the press release, there are two possibilities:

(i) The agency distributes the press release without getting it checked and approved by the company. In this case the PR agency will be liable to the company for any adverse consequences which are attributable to the incorrect interpretation.

(ii) The company checks the press release, but does not spot the misleading or incorrect inference or statement, and approves the press release for publication. The company may criticise the agency for the misinterpretation, but it is the company which will be liable for having approved the press release for publication.

Legally controlled statements

9.5.3 In PR terms, the more mundane contacts between the company and the media relate to announcements by the company in the financial sections of national newspapers, or responding to normal financial comments on the company's performance which affect its share value. Public and quoted company financial statements have to comply with strict regulations (outside the scope of this book), which limit the scope of a PR department to be creative in minimising or emphasising some trading or financial feature.

CONFIDENTIALITY

Confidentiality of information sources

9.6.1 Where the company's PR department or agency has to put together a public statement which relates to sensitive issues of an internal nature, it may have to be given access to confidential information where that is necessary in order to ensure that the statement is correct and in the right context. The executives in the PR department or the agency will have to maintain confidential any such information, because that will be part of their legal obligations as the employees of the company or of the PR agency, and because it will be a contractual requirement in the agreement between the PR agency and its client. This is one occasion when the company may prefer its internal PR department to handle the announcement, as it may be reluctant to give really sensitive information to an outside agency, despite good confidentiality restraints.

Premature publication of press release

9.6.2 Press releases are usually subject to an embargo date, so they can be distributed to the publication sources earlier, with the intention of having an overall simultaneous publication date. The more sensitive the press release details are, the shorter should be the embargo period. The consequences of the premature publication of a press release depends on the sensitivity of its contents. If a premature publication causes the company actual loss, damage or liability, it could only claim against the publisher if there has been a breach of a contractual obligation not to publish prematurely. It would be difficult to argue that a contract exists between the company and the publisher. Although the press release is offered for publication, and accepted for publication, there is no "consideration" or tangible benefit passing from one party to the other to constitute a legally binding agreement. Acceptance for publication does not mean that the press release has to be published or if it is published, that the publisher must comply with the condition imposed by the company, namely the embargo date. A right cannot be exercised contrary to any obligation which is attached to that exercise, and premature publication would be a breach of the embargo condition which is placed upon the publication right. If a court should decide that such a contract exists, the company could claim for what it has lost in direct quantifiable terms.

Breach of copyright licence

9.6.3 The premature release could also be held to be a breach of the implied licence to publish copyright material, as an implied condition of the licence is that publication will not take place before the embargo date. That implied condition could be an additional, though weak, support for a claim by the company for any damage it has incurred as a result of premature publication of the press release.

10 Promotions and Tax

INTRODUCTION

10.1 This chapter covers the main taxation aspects of typical business promotion schemes and is, of necessity, more technical in its content and treatment than the rest of this book. Detailed advice should, of course, be taken in respect of any particular scheme. As will be seen it is usually value added tax (VAT) which is the principal or only tax concerned. Because of this a general introduction to VAT is given as well as a VAT analysis of typical schemes. There will be other tax considerations in operating a business promotion scheme, but it is unlikely these will give rise to problems. For the most part non-VAT considerations should be routine, although some areas of difficulty are mentioned, where appropriate.

The Customs and Excise leaflet on "Business Promotion Schemes" (VAT leaflet No. 700/7/81) was issued in November 1981 and has been due to be revised and re-issued in a much more comprehensive form. Much of the current edition is now out of date and it should therefore be viewed with caution. This means that there is now considerable uncertainty regarding the correct treatment of many schemes. Traders should try to reach an agreement with Customs and Excise before introducing a new scheme, to ensure that problems do not arise at a later stage.

VAT: GENERAL PRINCIPLES

10.2 VAT is charged in accordance with the provisions of the Value Added Tax Act 1983 ("VAT Act 1983") on the supply of goods and services in the United Kingdom and on the importation of goods into the United Kingdom. (The use of the expression "importation", in this context, refers to goods arriving in the U.K. from outside the European Community ("E.C."). Goods arriving from another E.C. member state are subject to special rules which are beyond the scope of this chapter). It is usually the consumer of such supplies who bears the cost. As businesses are not usually the ultimate consumer, they should not bear the burden of VAT. The following explains certain aspects of the VAT system in more detail, in particular those aspects which are helpful in understanding the VAT treatment of business promotion schemes.

CHARGEABLE SUPPLIES

10.2.1 Section 2(1), VAT Act 1983 states as follows:

> "Tax shall be charged on any *supply of goods or services made in the UK* where it is a *taxable supply* made by a *taxable person in the course or furtherance of any business* carried on by him." (emphasis added)

Each of the elements in this definition is now considered in turn.

(a) Supply

Section 3(2)(*a*), VAT Act 1983 states as follows:

> "Supply" in this Act includes all forms of supply, but not anything done otherwise than for a consideration."

In the context of sales promotions, examples of supplies include all goods and services sold for consideration.

(b) Taxable supply

Section 2(2), VAT Act 1983 states as follows:

> " . . . a taxable supply is a supply of goods or services made in the United Kingdom other than an exempt supply." (See paragraph 10.2.7 on exempt supplies).

(c) Taxable person

Section 2C(1), VAT Act 1983 states as follows:

> "A person is a taxable person for the purposes of this Act while he is, or is required to be, registered under this Act."

(d) Classification—goods or services

Usually this will be straightforward. There are detailed rules in Schedule 2, VAT Act 1983 which deal with particular supplies. The following are examples of supplies of goods:

1. Power, heat, refrigeration or ventilation.
2. Grants and assignments of major interests in land.

The following are examples of supplies of services:

1. Transfers and issues of shares and securities.
2. Hiring of goods.
3. Grant or assignment of minor interests in land.

The following are neither a supply of goods nor services (supplies "outside the scope" of VAT):

1. Business assets transferred as a going concern—S.I. 1992 No. 3129, Regulation 5.

2. Supplies made between companies registered as a group under section 29, VAT Act 1983.

(e) Consideration

(i) *Services.* In general, if there is no consideration (such as payment of money or the foregoing of something valuable) in respect of the services, then for VAT purposes no supply is deemed to take place. Therefore there is no VAT charged on a gift of services.

(ii) *Goods.* Even if there is no consideration for the transfer of goods, Schedule 2, para. 5, VAT Act 1983 deems there to a be supply for VAT purposes in the case of a gift of goods (See paragraph 10.9.1).

(f) Made in the U.K. (sections 6 and 8 VAT Act 1983)

For VAT purposes goods are supplied at the place where they are situated at the time of their supply. The basic rule is that services are supplied from the location of the business establishment of the supplier most closely connected with the supply. Certain categories of services, however, are deemed to be supplied where the recipient belongs.

(g) Course of furtherance of a business

In most cases it will be clear whether or not a supply is made in the course or furtherance of a business. Section 47(2), VAT Act 1983 extends the definition to include grant of club memberships, admission to premises and a professional person accepting an office in his professional capacity. An employee does not make a supply in the course of furtherance of a business to his employer—see the case of *Rickarby* v. *Customs and Excise* [1973] V.A.T.T.R. 186.

REGISTRATION

10.2.2 Schedule 1, paragraph 1(1), VAT Act 1983 states as follows:

" . . . a person who makes taxable supplies . . . becomes liable to be registered . . .

(a) at the end of any month, if the value of his taxable supplies in the period of one year then ending has exceeded £37,600; or
(b) at any time, if there are reasonable grounds for believing that the value of his taxable supplies in the period of 30 days then beginning will exceed £37,600."

The registration limit (£37,600 at the time of writing) is reviewed annually. A person who makes principally zero-rated supplies (see paragraph 10.2.6) is entitled to apply for exemption from registration (Schedule 1, paragraph 11,

VAT Act 1983). On the other hand, a person making supplies below the VAT registration threshold or who has not yet started trading can register voluntarily (Schedule 1, paragraph 5, VAT Act 1983).

OUTPUT TAX

10.2.3   (1) Time of supply

The time at which a supply takes place is known as the tax point. The basic tax point is determined as follows:

   (a) in the case of goods—when the goods are made available (section 4(2), VAT Act 1983);
   (b) in the case of services—when they are performed (section 4(3), VAT Act 1983).

The basic tax point is varied in the following situations:

   (a) Where a tax invoice is issued or payment is received before a basic tax point, then the date of the issue of the tax invoice or the receipt of the payment becomes the tax point (section 5(1), VAT Act 1983).
   (b) Where a tax invoice is issued within 14 days after the basic tax point, the invoice date becomes the tax point (section 5(2) VAT Act 1983).

Continuous supplies of goods (*e.g.* power) and of services lead to the creation of a tax point whenever cash is paid or an invoice is issued.

Once a tax point has occurred, this creates a liability to account for VAT even if the customer has not paid.

10.2.3   (2) Value of a supply

The value of a supply is the tax-exclusive price on which VAT is paid. Contract law determines that the price agreed for a supply will be treated as a VAT-inclusive price if no specific reference is made to VAT. The supplier will have to account for VAT out of the total price paid. This, however, does not apply if the supply has become liable to VAT due to a change in the law (for example, the removal of zero rating for a particular supply)—in this case the contract price will be deemed to be varied by the change in VAT unless the contract states to the contrary (section 42, VAT Act 1983).

Where the consideration is wholly monetary, the value is such amount as with the addition of VAT is equal to the consideration, reduced by any discount for prompt payment even if not taken (section 10(2) and Schedule 4, paragraph 4, VAT Act 1983) (see further on this point at paragraph 10.7.2). Where the consideration is not wholly monetary, the value is now taken to be such amount in money as, with the addition of the tax chargeable, is equivalent to the consideration (section 10(3) VAT Act 1983). This rule applies as from August 1, 1992. Prior to that date, VAT was calculated on the open market value in this situation. In most cases, where the parties are at arm's length, this will not alter the value of the supply for VAT purposes. There would only be a difference if the total consideration was clearly of a different amount to the open market value of the supply.

VAT can be calculated on the open market value if HM Customs & Excise so direct in the case of supplies between connected parties (Schedule 4, paragraph 1, VAT Act 1983).

10.2.3 (3) Tax invoices

Tax invoices must be issued within 30 days of the tax point (S.I. 1985 No. 886, Regulation 12(5)). The tax invoice must contain the following information:

(a) an identifying number;
(b) the tax point;
(c) the supplier's name, address and registration number;
(d) the customer's name and address;
(e) the type of supply (sale, hire, etc.);
(f) a description of the goods or services supplied;
(g) the value of the supply;
(h) the rate of tax and the amount of tax;
(i) the rate of any cash discount offered.

Retailers need only issue a tax invoice if requested by a taxable person. If the supply is for not more than £100, the tax invoice can be less detailed (S.I. 1985 No. 886 Regulation 15).

Input tax

10.2.4 Input tax is VAT incurred by a taxable person on his purchases, imports and acquisitions from other EC member states. Input tax is refundable or offset against output tax. The conditions necessary for input tax credit to be available are as follows:

(1) The goods and services must have been received by the taxable person;
(2) He must use them for business purposes; and
(3) He must possess the specified evidence (i.e. invoice or certificates supplied to importers by HM Customs & Excise).

It should be noted that it is not a condition that the taxable person has paid for the supply.

Certain forms of input tax are not available for credit, for example, input tax incurred on business entertaining (see paragraph 10.12).

ADMINISTRATION

10.2.5   Taxable persons are allocated prescribed accounting periods, usually lasting three months. Within one month of the end of the prescribed accounting period they must file a VAT return at Central Unit and pay any VAT due.

ZERO RATING

10.2.6   Zero-rated supplies are treated as taxable supplies for all purposes except that the rate of VAT charged on the supply is zero. This enables any input tax incurred in order to be able to make the zero-rated supplies to be recovered in the same way as in input tax attributable to the making of standard rated supplies. Zero-rated supplies include all exports of goods (section 16, VAT Act 1983) and those supplies set out in Schedule 5, VAT Act 1983. Examples of zero-rated supplies, relevant to business promotion schemes, are books and cold take-away food.

EXEMPTION

10.2.7   A person who makes only exempt supplies will not be registered for VAT (except possibly as part of a group registration) but a person who makes both exempt supplies and taxable supplies is likely to be registered for VAT and is known as partially exempt. Input VAT is recoverable only if *attributable to a taxable supply*. There is a standard method of working out what input tax is attributable to a taxable supply although it is possible to obtain the agreement of Customs and Excise to use a special method in appropriate cases. The categories of exempt supplies are set out in Schedule 6, VAT Act 1983. Examples of such supplies include certain financial, insurance and land supplies.

DISCOUNTS

10.3   The VAT treatment of business promotion schemes involving unconditional discounts is usually straightforward. As explained above, where a cash price only is paid for a product, VAT is calculated by reference to that cash price. A consumer paying £23.50 for a product will currently (with VAT at 17.5 per cent.) be paying £3.50 in VAT included in that price. If the product is sold at a "50 per cent. discount" (£11.75) then the VAT due will be halved (£1.75 instead of £3.50). If instead the product is sold at the same price but the contents of the package are increased ("50 per cent. extra free") there will be no change in the VAT due. The product price will still be £23.50, of which £3.50 will still be the VAT element. Such schemes should not therefore give rise to VAT complications.

Discounts might also be offered for prompt payment or subject to fulfilling some other condition. These are considered at paragraphs 10.7.2 to 10.7.4 in relation to trade promotion schemes. In some schemes it may not be clear whether or not a discount, as recognised for VAT purposes, is involved.

A discount scheme may involve a manufacturer in, for example, greater expenditure on packaging. There should be no difficulty in obtaining a credit for any extra input tax incurred. It is clear that the extra expenditure is referable to the manufacturer's business activities, so an input tax credit should be available (see paragraph 10.2.4).

REVISED DESIGNS

10.4 It is unlikely that a scheme merely involving revised designs would give rise to any particular VAT concerns. A change in the wording on a package or revising its size or colour is unlikely to have VAT consequences, although it is just conceivable that by changing the description of a product it may move from one VAT category to another. Children's painting and picture books are currently zero-rated for VAT purposes. A promotion scheme which involves removing all references to children from such books could change this classification: painting and similar books which are intended primarily for use by adults are standard rated. Any VAT incurred in creating such new designs (for example on consultants' fees) should be recoverable without any difficulty.

COUPONS

10.5 Schemes involving coupons (including vouchers, tokens and wrappers of any kind) are likely to require careful consideration of their VAT aspects. The VAT treatment of such schemes in the past may now be incorrect following the decision of the European Court of Justice in the case of *Boots Co. plc* v. *Customs & Excise Commissioners* [1990] S.T.C. 387. It is possible that VAT has in fact been overpaid on some business promotion schemes involving coupons, in which case there is scope to recover overpayments made in error (see paragraph 10.6).

Boots involved a "money-off" coupon. This involved a customer obtaining a voucher which allowed him to buy sun-tan lotion at 25p less than the normal retail price. On purchasing the sun-tan lotion the customer would pay the reduced cash consideration and hand over the money-off coupon. The basic question for the courts was, what consideration was given for the supply of the sun-tan lotion? Customs and Excise contended that the sun-tan lotion was supplied in return for consideration consisting not only of the cash the consumer paid but also of the coupon. This conclusion would have led to VAT being due on the normal retail selling price notwithstanding the 25p reduction, on the basis of Section 10(3), VAT Act as it was before August 1, 1992 (see paragraph 10.2.3(2)). The European Court of Justice delivered its Judgment on March 27, 1990. It decided that money-off coupons, obtained by consumers when they buy goods, do not amount to consideration when they are used to purchase other goods. The coupon is merely evidence of an entitlement to purchase goods at a discounted price. VAT is therefore only due on the actual amount paid by the consumer. Following delivery of the judgment, Customs and Excise issued a news release in which they stated that they accepted the judgment of the European Court and explained that the decision would affect the VAT treatment of a wide range of business promotion schemes involving coupons and vouchers. The following paragraphs set out comments on various coupon based schemes and include, as far as possible, the current views of Customs and Excise.

COUPON-ONLY SCHEMES

10.5.1 These are schemes in which coupons are supplied with products which can then be redeemed for either more of the product or a gift, in either case without further payment. The products supplied with coupons may be known as the premium goods and the items received for the coupons as the redemption goods.

The VAT position on the sale of the premium goods should be clear. The coupons and the premium goods are usually regarded as being sold together in a combined supply. VAT is accounted for in the normal way on the cash amount received from the customer. It is the rate of tax applicable to the premium goods which is used for this purpose. The premium goods may, for example, be standard rated. If they are sold for £10 (excluding VAT) then the VAT due in addition is £1.75.

It is now the view of Customs and Excise that the supply of the redemption goods does not give rise to the need for a VAT adjustment but if the *cost* of the redemption goods exceeds £10 and they are standard-rated goods, VAT will have to be accounted for in the same way as applies to business gifts (see paragraph 10.9.1). This would appear to be technically incorrect as it is difficult to see how the supply of the redemption goods can be seen to be a genuine gift without strings attached.

COUPON AND CASH SCHEMES

10.5.2 These are schemes in which payment is made by a customer for the product as well as the presentation of one or more coupons. The coupons may have been collected from magazines or from the packaging on products. Such schemes usually involve the purchase of premium goods, giving access to the coupons. However, Customs and Excise do not require VAT to be accounted for on the redemption goods until they are actually supplied to the customer. VAT is calculated at the relevant rate at the time the redemption goods are supplied. The promoter of this scheme is expected to charge VAT on the price paid by the customer (including any charge for postage and packing).

In the past, when a retailer has obtained reimbursement of the face value of a voucher from a manufacturer, this has been considered outside the scope of VAT. Customs and Excise now regard the reimbursement as part of the consideration for the supply of the redemption goods to the customer on which VAT is due. This has the effect of increasing the output tax of the retailer, without a corresponding increase in the recoverable input tax of the manufacturer (as the supply of the redemption goods is not made to the manufacturer but to the customer). Careful wording of an agreement between the retailer and the manufacturer may avoid this result. For example, it may be possible to devise an agreement whereby the reimbursement is, instead, described as a fee payable by the manufacturer to the retailer in return for the retailer operating a business promotion scheme on behalf of the manufacturer, thus giving rise to recoverable input tax on the fee for the manufacturer. Alternatively, the agreement could provide that the reimbursement is in respect of a discount in the price charged for the redemption goods by the manufacturer to the retailer. If this type of planning is carried out, it is vital that the agreement should be carefully presented to Customs and Excise, in advance.

JOINT PROMOTION SCHEMES

10.5.3 These are schemes in which two or more manufacturers jointly promote their respective products. Such schemes may involve vouchers, as an example, the manufacturers of, say, cricket jerseys may distribute a voucher with each jersey bought entitling the holder to a "pocket-radio" from a named manufacturer of pocket radios. The jersey manufacturers account for VAT on the sale of jerseys as normal, calculated on the cash consideration received. The pocket radio manufacturers receive the vouchers and account for VAT on the amount paid by the customer for the radio (or treat them as business gifts, if the vouchers entitle the customers to a free radio (see paragraph 10.9.1)). In this scheme, the jersey manufacturers may have agreed to reimburse the pocket radio manufacturers part of the cost of any "radios" claimed by their customers. Again, Customs and Excise now regard this as consideration for the pocket radios and therefore subject to VAT.

If, instead of the vouchers entitling the customers to a pocket radio, they entitle them to goods or services which would normally be zero-rated (such as air flights), the payment made by the jersey manufacturer in return for the vouchers will be consideration for a zero-rated supply. This follows from the decision in the case of *Facthaven Incentive Marketing Ltd.* v. *Customs and Excise Commissioners* (LON/90/1340Z) in which Customs & Excise argued, unsuccessfully, that what in fact was being supplied was a standard-rated business promotion services.

TRADING STAMP SCHEMES

10.5.4 Trading stamp schemes involve a form of coupon for which there are special VAT rules. The purchase of trading stamps from the promoter is outside the scope of VAT under S.I. 1973 No. 325 unless the purchaser is a taxable person who manufacturers goods or makes up such goods for wholesale and the delivery is subject to a condition that the trading stamps will be enclosed in packages of the goods sold retail. Any charge made for the services of the promoter, over and above the charge for the stamps is, however, taxable at the standard rate.

The delivery of the trading stamps to customers of the retailer, in conjunction with supplies of goods and services, is also outside the scope of VAT unless they are packaged with the goods. Paragraph 78 of Customs and Excise Notice 727 describes in detail the method of apportioning the selling price between the goods and the stamps for the retail scheme calculation. Where the retailer subsequently exchanges goods or cash for trading stamps, any payments he receives from the promoter for the goods or cash are added to the daily gross takings.

GIFT VOUCHERS

10.5.5 Gift vouchers are mentioned only for completeness, as they are not business promotion schemes in themselves. A typical example of such a voucher is a book or record token. This will have a face value and will be accepted as if it is cash by a record shop or bookseller as the case may be. If a gift token is purchased for its face value, then no VAT will be due on that sale. VAT is only due in respect of any excess over the face value (Schedule 4, paragraph 6, VAT Act 1983). When the token is exchanged for goods, then VAT will be due at that time on the face value of the token (if the goods are not zero-rated). *Boots* did not affect the treatment of such tokens.

The use of more elaborate schemes involving gift vouchers has given rise to difficulties. The case of *High Street Vouchers Ltd* v. *Customs and Excise Commissioners* ([1990] S.T.C. 575) concerned a method of promoting sales by means of a gift voucher scheme. The facts of this case (in outline) were that HSV sold vouchers to trading companies at a discount. (This sale is disregarded for VAT purposes because of Schedule 4, paragraph 6, VAT Act 1983, see above). The trading company sold the vouchers to the public, who used them to purchase goods from retailers. HSV then paid the retailers, in exchange for the vouchers, their face value less a discount. It was held by the

High Court that the services provided by HSV to the retailers (of allowing them to participate in its scheme) were supplied for consideration equal to the discount. It would appear that HSV should therefore have been entitled to issue an invoice to the retailers and that they, in turn, should have been able to claim credit for the input tax arising on such invoices. This would have removed the VAT cost of the promotion.

The treatment of gift vouchers has been extended to "Premier Cheques" in the case of *Showmarch Marketing Ltd* v. *Customs and Excise Commissioners* (LON/90/1096Y). These had a face value but could not be exchanged for cash. Instead they entitled the holder to benefits such as a free meal or a free night in a hotel but only after something had been purchased from the provider of the "free" goods or services. The Premier Cheques were sold by the promoters to the appellant which sold them on to retailers for 10 per cent. of their face value. The Tribunal accepted that the onward sale of Premier Cheques amounted to the granting of a right to receive goods or services for an amount stated on a token, stamp or voucher (as required by Schedule 4, paragraph 6, VAT Act 1983) so no VAT was due on the sale. The fact that the scheme could be described as a discount scheme did not prevent this treatment from applying. It is understood that this decision may be the subject of an appeal.

REPAYMENTS OF EXCESS VAT

10.6 In cases where too much VAT was paid in the past it may be possible to obtain a repayment from Customs and Excise. The Finance Act 1989 gives statutory effect to such a right (section 24).

However Customs and Excise will not repay amounts (unless the claim was made or notified before January 1, 1990) if the repayment would "unjustly enrich" a claimant. A trader would be considered unjustly enriched if he does not pass on the benefit of the repayment to his customers. The practicalities of achieving this mean that few claims have been made. Also, as a general rule, an amount may only be reclaimed under the Finance Act 1989 provision before the expiry of six years from the date on which it was paid. There is an exception where an amount has been paid by mistake. In this case the period for recovery expires six years from the date on which the claimant discovered the mistake or could with reasonable diligence have discovered it.

Section 38A, VAT Act 1983 gives the taxpayer a statutory right to interest on overpayments of VAT resulting from an error of Customs and Excise. Again, no claim will be permitted after six years from the date the taxpayer discovered the error or could, with reasonable diligence, have discovered it.

TRADE PROMOTIONS

10.7 Schemes for "the trade" could very well include unconditional discounts or coupons. This paragraph however concentrates mainly on "dealer loader" schemes (not involving coupons) and other schemes which are particularly aimed at obtaining increased trade orders.

DEALER LOADER PROMOTIONAL SCHEMES

10.7.1 Customs and Excise issued a leaflet on these schemes in July 1988 (VAT Leaflet No. 700/36/88). For the most part its contents are unaffected by the decision in *Boots*. A dealer loader scheme involves the supply of both main and reward goods. The main goods are those for which the trade order would usually be placed. The reward goods are those offered under the terms of the scheme. Typically the scheme will set a condition that a trade order of a particular size must be made before the reward goods are made available.

The reward goods are clearly not being given away. The retailer must buy the main goods in order to qualify for the reward goods. So as well as paying the usual price for the main goods the retailer must fulfil a condition. According to Customs and Excise, this introduces an important distinction from ordinary bulk purchase discounts. Under a dealer loader scheme a retailer may be told that if he places an order for 1000 products next month at the usual price of £1000 he will get a further 100 products free of further charge. This is a different arrangement from being told that where the usual product price is £1 per item a retailer can buy 1100 items for £1000. In this latter case VAT will be calculated on the cash price. If a condition has to be fulfilled, Customs and Excise take the view that in law, this introduces non-cash consideration (see paragraph 10.2.3(2)). In the former case this would probably mean the manufacturer accounting for VAT as if he had received £1100 for the 1100 products (although he actually only received £1000).

Customs and Excise do however allow an important "concession" in respect of certain dealer loader schemes. The concession is explained in the dealer loader promotional schemes VAT Leaflet No. 700/36/88. It provides that a promoter need not account for VAT on the open market value of the reward goods (or presumably, more correctly now, the value of the non-cash consideration provided—see paragraph 10.2.3(2)) if the following conditions are met:

   (a) the reward goods are not intended for the personal use of the person receiving them;
   (b) the reward goods are either similar to the main goods supplied or of a kind used in that person's business; and
   (c) a person does not have to make a number of orders or reach a specified level of purchases over a period of time to qualify for the reward goods.

If the reward goods are the same as the main goods, then conditions (a) and (b) above are likely to be met. If a single order is required in a particular period or by a particular date, then (c) above should also be met. In introducing any dealer loader promotion scheme a promoter would usually try to come within the above conditions, so as to avoid creating an extra VAT liability.

The dealer loader promotional scheme leaflet also includes a further condition. This is that the concession cannot be used in schemes where vouchers, points or coupons are issued with the goods to trade customers. (This is likely to change in the light of *Boots*.)

If a promoter supplies both the main and reward goods direct to the retailer, then it must show them both on its tax invoice. If both the main and reward goods are standard rated, then only one price need be shown on the invoice. In this way the retailer will not see a value for the reward goods. HM Customs and Excise announced in News Release No. 1136 of August 20, 1986 that, as an alternative, the reward goods could be shown as being supplied free of charge. Previously this was not permitted.

If the main goods and the reward goods are taxable at different rates, then a fair apportionment must be made so that VAT is correctly accounted for on the reward goods.

It may be that the promoter supplies the main goods and an administrator or handling house supplies the reward goods. In this case the concession is modified. If the main goods and reward goods are again both standard rated, then no additional tax is due on the supply by the administrator of the reward goods. An administrator must not issue a tax invoice to the retailer for the reward goods. If the administrator's accounting procedures require an invoice to be issued, then it must not be a tax invoice. It should be clearly endorsed: **"No VAT charged—Business promotion Scheme, VAT Leaflet 700/36/88 paragraph 4 refers"**. The administrator must keep a record of such goods supplied so that it can explain the situation to Customs and Excise if an enquiry is made.

If instead the main goods are zero-rated and the reward goods are standard rated, then the supplier of the reward goods must account for VAT. This VAT is calculated on the value of the reward goods. A tax invoice should then be issued.

The problem identified for a promoter in the case of *Customs and Excise Commissioners* v. *Sooner Foods Ltd.* [1983] S.T.C. 376 is that having an administrator in a promotion scheme may lead to a loss of input tax for the promoter. This meant the promoter was not maximising the offset of input tax against output tax, the difficulty in the case being that the administrator bought in the reward goods and passed these directly to the relevant retailers on receipt of coupons. There would be an input tax credit for the promoter on the administrator's charge for its services. However, the promoter could not claim an input tax credit in respect of the reward goods because at no time were these supplied to the promoter. So, the contractual arrangements in schemes involving administrators or handling houses must be considered carefully, especially where the concession does not apply.

PROMPT PAYMENT DISCOUNT SCHEMES

10.7.2 Such discounts are so prevalent that they do not really amount to business promotion schemes. If a customer is offered a discount on condition he pays within a specified time, then VAT is calculated on the discounted amount. This rule applies even if the customer does not qualify for and therefore does not obtain the discount by actually paying within that specified time.

OTHER CONTINGENT DISCOUNT SCHEMES

10.7.3 The customer may be offered a discount on condition that something happens subsequently, such as the customer making a further order. In this case VAT is calculated in the first instance on the actual amount paid. If the discount is later earned, then a credit note can be issued. As well as adjusting the amount paid this will adjust, correspondingly, the amount of output tax.

This treatment may not apply to more complicated discount schemes in which other conditions are attached to obtaining the discount. It could be that the retailer is in fact supplying valuable services to the wholesaler (in fulfilling the extra conditions) which are additional consideration for the products. This would mean the wholesaler would have to account for VAT on the full wholesale price of the products under section 10(3), VAT Act 1983 (see paragraph 10.2.3(2)). This was the position in the case of *Naturally Yours Cosmetics Ltd.* v. *Customs and Excise Commissioners* [1988] S.T.C. 879, where a pot of cream was sold by the company to retailers at a discount, on the basis that the retailers would use this item as a gift to "hostesses" who organised parties in their own homes at which the company's other goods were sold. It was held by the European Court of Justice that the company had to account for VAT on the normal wholesale price of the pot of cream because the retailers had provided the valuable services of arranging the parties.

LINKED GOODS SCHEMES

10.8 These schemes involve the sale of two or more types of goods at a single price. A customer may, for example, be able to buy a toothbrush with a tube of toothpaste for one price. For practical reasons the goods are usually physically linked, although this is not essential from a VAT point of view. If goods are linked together in a promotion scheme then they may be treated as a combined supply sold at an inclusive price.

The VAT analysis becomes more interesting if the linked goods are liable to different rates of tax. In this case, an apportionment of the price must be made to the different items. If a standard rated promotional item is attached to a magazine (which is zero-rated), this could cause practical problems, particularly if the promotion is only short term. This difficulty is recognised by Customs and Excise who offer a concession. The concession is set out in VAT Leaflets Nos. 700/7/81 and 701/10/85. The conditions to be met are:

(a) The promotion scheme is for a limited duration (in the case of magazines the promotional items are not included as a regular feature).
(b) The minor article is not charged at a separate price.
(c) The minor article costs no more than 15 per cent. of the total cost (excluding VAT) of the combined supply (or in the case of magazines the total cost of all the promotional items included in issues during the year does not exceed 15 per cent. of the total selling price of all those issues).
(d) The minor article costs no more than 25p (excluding VAT) if included with goods intended for retail sale (or 75p (excluding VAT) otherwise).
(e) In the case of a magazine, it is sold at the same price as issues that do not contain the minor article.

If the concession applies, then it is only necessary to account for tax on the minor article at the same rate as the article with which it is supplied and so no apportionment will be necessary.

This type of concession covers the type of goods included with, for example, cereal packets as part of a promotion scheme. The promoter of the scheme should take care to ensure that the contracts for the supply of the minor articles keep the costs of such items below the limits of the concession.

If a linked scheme is used to promote trade orders, then the promoter will be involved in issuing a tax invoice. The directions on tax invoicing which apply in relation to dealer loader schemes (see paragraph 10.7.1) will therefore usually apply. However, if the minor article comes within the concession, then it does not need to be detailed separately on the invoice.

Where goods are linked as part of a manufacturer's promotion and are supplied to the retailer already linked, the retailer cannot use the concession if the supplier showed separate prices and amounts of tax on his invoice to the retailer.

The above examples, in which the linked goods are liable to different rates of VAT, both involve zero-rated main goods and standard-rated minor goods. If the position were reversed, then it is unlikely a trader would want to claim the benefit of the concession. To do so would involve the promoter in accounting for VAT on goods which would otherwise be zero-rated.

GIFTS AND SAMPLES

GIFTS

10.9.1 A business promotion scheme might involve genuine business gifts. If there are any "strings" attached, then it is unlikely that there will be a genuine gift. If there is a genuine gift of a business asset then there will be no consideration (whether cash or non-cash). However, this does not mean the gift falls outside the scope of VAT. There are special rules to charge VAT on the cost of the business asset given away. It is likely that input tax will have been incurred (and claimed as a credit) by the promoter on purchasing or manufacturing the business gifts. It is perhaps not surprising that output tax should then be due on any supply of those gifts. This is achieved by Schedule 2, para. 5(1) VAT Act 1983 which deems there to be a supply of goods in this situation. However, there is an important statutory exception (Schedule 2, para. 5(2), VAT Act 1983). This applies to goods which cost the donor less than a specified amount. The detailed conditions are that the item must:

(a) cost the donor no more than £10 (excluding VAT);
(b) be given for business reasons; and
(c) not be part of a series or succession of gifts to the same person (if this happens simply by chance then this is not a series or succession of gifts).

With regard to the first condition, it is interesting to note that this test should enable a company which receives goods valued at more than £10 by way of gift (perhaps from a related company) to make an ongoing gift of the goods without having to account for VAT on the gift as the cost to the company of those goods would be nil. If the test had been based on the value of the goods, as laid down in the E.C. Sixth Directive Article 5(6), this would not be the case. The test may eventually change to this basis, particularly as it would correspond to the basis of the charge where the conditions are not satisfied (see below).

With regard to the third condition, this prevents the exception applying even where the cost of all the gifts in the series put together does not exceed £10. So two separate gifts of, say, a pint of beer to the same retailer would not qualify.

In the event of the conditions not being met then Customs and Excise have often agreed to an alternative arrangement. This involves the donor not claiming input tax on acquiring the business gifts, in which case Customs and Excise may agree to not to assess output tax on the later gift of those assets. This arrangement has now been given statutory effect by Schedule 2, para. 5(3A), VAT Act 1983 (inserted by The Finance Act 1993).

If VAT is due, then the amount of tax must be based on the current purchase price of the goods (Schedule 4, para. 7, VAT Act 1983). This basis enables any depreciation in value, since the goods were acquired by the donor, to be taken into account.

Additionally, if VAT is due, the invoicing arrangements must be considered. It is not possible to issue a tax invoice. However, the donor can provide the recipient of a gift with a certificate to the effect that output tax has been accounted for on the supply. This will enable the recipient of the gift to claim credit for input tax if he is a taxable person. The suggestion made in the Customs and Excise leaflet on business gifts is that the normal invoicing documentation can be overwritten with the following statement: "**Tax Certificate—no payment is necessary for these goods. Output tax has been accounted for on the supply**." The documentation must show full details of the goods supplied and the amount of the tax.

The question of whether there was in fact consideration for a supply was considered by the House of Lords in the case of *Customs and Excise Commissioners* v. *Professional Footballers' Association* [1993] S.T.C. 86. The Association had arranged an annual dinner for its members who voted for "Player of the Year" awards. These awards were presented at the dinner and consisted of cups and medals purchased by the Association. The Association accounted for output tax on the ticket sales to the dinner but Customs and Excise argued that the supply of awards was a separate supply for no consideration on which output tax was also due. The House of Lords held, however, that there was consideration which was included in the price paid for the tickets.

One possible method for avoiding the rules for VAT on gifts is to sell the goods for a nominal amount (say, 1p) and account for VAT on just this amount. It is understood that Customs and Excise accept that they have no mechanism for attacking such a scheme (unless the recipient is a connected person which would enable Customs and Excise to treat the sale as having been made for the market value of the goods (Schedule 4, para. 1, VAT Act 1983)). Care must be taken that no other conditions are attached, which would invoke the rules which apply where the consideration is not wholly monetary (see paragraph 10.2.3 (2)).

SAMPLES

10.9.2 Schemes involving samples may very well involve a gift of business assets, in which case, if the cost of the sample is less than £10, the above treatment would apply. If it is not applicable, then other arrangements may be possible to avoid the need to charge output tax. These include the following:

(a) Trade samples

No output tax need be accounted for if there is no charge made for the samples. It used to be the case that the samples had to be in a form which was not ordinarily available for sale to the general public. This usually involved marking the product with words such as "not for resale". This marking had to be indelible so a removable label would not have sufficed.

There has recently been a relaxation in this regime which has been achieved by Schedule 2, para. 5 (2A), VAT Act 1983 (inserted by The Finance Act 1993). In future, samples supplied to an actual or potential customer will not give rise to the need to account for output tax even if they are not marked. The relief will not be given where two or more identical samples are supplied to the same person. The main beneficiaries of this relaxation are expected, by Customs and Excise, to be producers of compact discs and tapes who send samples to TV and radio stations or to reviewers.

(b) Market research samples

The business promotion scheme might be based, in part, around market research. Again, no output tax need be accounted for provided certain conditions are met. These are:

(i)   The products are supplied only for the purpose of market research.
(ii) Results are required which are reported to the promoter.
(iii) No charge is made for the research samples.
(iv) The research samples must remain the property of the promoter (so that any samples not used in the course of research must be returned or destroyed).

(c) Other samples

Samples might also be distributed in other ways, for example as linked goods (see paragraph 10.8).

DIRECT TAXATION

10.9.3   Expenses incurred on the provision of gifts are disallowed in computing profits chargeable to income or corporation tax under Schedule A or Schedule D by section 577(8) of the Income and Corporation Taxes Act 1988, (I.C.T.A. 1988). A limited exception applies where the gift is of an article bearing a conspicuous advertisement for the donor if the cost of the article and other such articles given to the same person do not exceed £10. Articles of food, drink, tobacco or coupons exchangeable for goods are not within the exception.

The above restriction does not apply to expenses incurred on the provision of samples (regardless of their cost and even if they are articles such as, for example, food and drink) of the type which it is the supplier's trade to provide and which are provided gratuitously with the object of advertising to the public generally (section 577(10), I.C.T.A. 1988). An example would be the provision by a drinks manufacturer of samples of his product to the press.

COMPETITIONS

10.10 Competition prizes (where the winner does not have to do something in return for the reward of the prize) are considered business gifts. The business gift rules will therefore apply, so VAT has to be accounted for if the cost to the promoter of the individual prizes is more than £10 (see paragraph 10.9.1). As a general rule, VAT is not due on a gift of services (rather than goods). It may therefore be better to offer services as prizes rather than goods. Another possibility is that the retailer buys tickets in a lottery run by someone else and gives these away to customers, in which case the gifts of tickets are considered outside the scope of VAT. Any payment received by way of commission for the tickets given away is treated as payment for an exempt supply.

EXCHANGES

10.11 Business promotion schemes based around, for example, the exchange of an old product for a new one involve careful consideration of the VAT aspects. In some circumstances the arrangements are treated as if a discount had been offered. This is usually the case where there are fixed trade-in allowances (such as £10 "for your old iron"), although this is not the case in relation to motor car part exchanges. In other cases, products taken in part exchange will be considered to be non-cash consideration (see paragraph 10.2.3(2)).

BUSINESS ENTERTAINMENT

10.12 Business promotion schemes based on the entertainment of customers is, unfortunately, inefficient from a taxation point of view. Credit for input tax incurred on goods or services used for the provision of business entertainment is prohibited by Regulation (1) of S.I. 1981 No. 1741. Business entertainment is defined in Regulation 2 of S.I. 1981 No. 1741 to include entertainment and hospitality of any kind provided by a taxable person but does not include the provision of anything for employees unless the provision is incidental to its provision for others. Therefore credit for input tax is available for entertaining members of staff unless they are acting as hosts for customers of the business. The position regarding entertainment of directors is uncertain. There are good arguments for treating these in the same way as other employees but this is not necessarily accepted by Customs and Excise. If the business is run as a partnership, however, entertainment of the partners will clearly not give rise to credit for input tax since partners are not employees (unlike directors).

Credit will still be available, however, if the partner eats at restaurants or stays at hotels when away from his normal place of work on a business trip (see Customs and Excise Notice 700 paragraph 40). The provision of entertainment under a contractual obligation (for example the provision of accommodation by hotels) is not business entertainment. In this case there is no restriction on credit for input tax, although output tax must be accounted for on the amount charged.

The direct tax rules largely mirror those for VAT. Section 577(1), I.C.T.A. 1988 prohibits a deduction from being made in computing profits chargeable to tax under Schedule A or Schedule D for any expenses incurred in providing business entertainment. Assets used in providing entertainment are disqualified from capital allowances (section 577(1)(c), I.C.T.A. 1988). Business entertainment is defined in similar terms by section 577(5), I.C.T.A. 1988 as under Regulation 2 of S.I. 1981 No. 1741. Once again, the rules do not apply to the provision of entertainment in the ordinary course of trade by a person whose trade consists of the provision of that entertainment (section 577(10), I.C.T.A. 1988).

APPENDICES

APPENDICES

A1   Model Promotion Rules

Promotion rules have been dealt with in Chapters 5 and 8, which explained that the rules to be applied to any form of promotion should be drafted to be comprehensive and suitable to the relevant promotion. The limiting factor is space on the packaging available for the rules. If virtually no space is available, the packaging should at least contain a prominent statement to the effect: "Send SAE to XYZ of [ ] for a copy of the full rules applying to this promotion." Copies should be sent by return post. Nevertheless any crucial rule which could affect a consumer's judgment on the promotion must be included on the package. (See Section 5.8 of the British Code of Sales Promotion Practice.)

Set out in this Appendix is a selection of rules which may be applicable to different kinds of promotion. They are expressive rules, not "shorthand", so that the reader can see what they are covering. A sales promotion agency can use them as ideas upon which to base whatever rules it needs, which can be drafted by it with economy of language. The mechanic of each promotion will also involve drafting other rules necessary to deal with its individual needs.

ELIGIBILITY

(a) [*For a competition or other elimination type of promotion*]. Any person who is under 18 or who is an employee or their immediate family of [the manufacturer] or of [the agency] or of [the handling house] or any other person who is directly connected with this [promotion] [competition] will be ineligible to [enter] [participate].

(b) [*For unlimited money-off voucher for extra quantity of alcoholic product promotion*]. Any person who is aged 18 or over may [enter this promotion].

(c) [*Local club or other restricted entry*]. Any person aged 18 or over who is a [paid up member of the club at the closing date of this promotion] may enter [this promotion].

(d) These rules will be deemed to include the instructions set out in the [promotion terms].

(e) By entering this competition [participating in this promotion] the entrant [consumer] will be deemed to have read and understood these rules, and to be bound by them.

(f) This promotion is only available to *bona fide* registered retail traders who must complete the section in the application form requiring the

name and address of the wholesaler with whom the applicant is registered and its registration number. XYZ reserves the right to reject as
invalid any application which it reasonably believes not to be *bona fide* or
in compliance with this rule.

(g) [Entry to the competition] [application for the gift] may only be made
by persons who have bought [the product] from a [retail outlet] for
personal home consumption.

(h) Notwithstanding that the winner has been declared, if [the promoter]
discovers before the delivery of the prize that for any reason under these
Rules the winner should have been ineligible to [enter the competition]
or if the entry should have been declared invalid, [the promoter]
reserves the right to determine that the winner is disqualified.

CLOSING DATE

All [competition entries] [redemption applications] must be sent by prepaid
post and received by XYZ on or before the [ ] 199[ ] irrespective of the date of
posting. Proof of posting will not be deemed to be proof of delivery.

DEFECTIVE APPLICATIONS

(a) Any [entry] [application] which is damaged, defaced, illegible or incomplete, or which otherwise does not comply with these rules, may be
deemed to be invalid in the sole discretion of XYZ.

(b) Only this original [label] [entry form] [application form] will be valid
and any [entry] [application] which is not [on] [accompanied by] this
[and X other] original [ ] will be rejected.

REDEMPTION OF VOUCHERS OR GIFTS

(a) Send [this coupon plus [two] further similar coupons from promotion
packs of X product] together with the completed [entry form] [application
form] to XYZ at the address given below.

(b) Allow 28 days for delivery of the [voucher] [gift].

(c) If the gift is found to be defective or damaged on delivery, XYZ must be
notified in writing within [7] days after receipt otherwise the gift shall be
deemed to have been accepted as delivered.

(d) XYZ will not be liable to the applicant if the gift is defective in materials
and workmanship except to the extent that such liability cannot be
contracted out of by law.

(e) [*For "while stocks last" promotions where there is a cash balance payment*].
If there are no [gifts] available to satisfy the application then XYZ will
return the applicant's cheque within 28 days of receiving the
application.

(f) Only the original [proof of purchase] [application form] will be accepted as a valid application.

(g) [*For limited availability gift promotion with no cash balance*]. If there are no [gifts] available to satisfy the application, in the absolute discretion of XYZ it may substitute another gift in satisfaction of the application.

(h) [*For gift and voucher redemption applications*]. Only [three] applications may be made [per person] [per household].

(i) [*For limited competition entries*]. Only [three] entries may be made by each entrant. [Breach of this rule will invalidate all entries.]

(j) [*For retailers—a trade promotion*]. Only [three] applications may be made by each registered trader irrespective of the number of retail outlets which are operated by that trader under the same registration.

(k) [*Where the gift is two-tiered—e.g. 4 coupons for gift A and 8 coupons for gift B*]. The applicant may only make [two] applications for each of A and B [for a combination of A or B gifts].

(l) [*Money-off voucher redeemable against next purchase of promoted product*]. Only one voucher may be used toward the purchase price of each [product item].

COMPETITION RULES

(a) The winner will be the entrant with the correct answer. If there is more than one correct entry the winner will be the entrant who, in the sole opinion of the panel of judges appointed by XYZ, has submitted the most [apt] [witty] [original] tiebreaker.

(b) [*Tiebreaker*]. In no more than [12] extra words complete the following sentence [in the form of an original advertising slogan]: "Whizzo Gadgets are the greatest because . . . . . . "

(c) The copyright in the completed tiebreaker slogan is hereby assigned by the entrant to XYZ in consideration of the entrant having the opportunity to enter the competition.

(d) [*Where the competition is to design a new logo for the promoted product*]. The copyright in the logo and the copyright in the tiebreaker [slogan] is hereby assigned . . . [as per (c) above.].

(e) All decisions of the panel of judges will be final and binding on the entrants and no correspondence will be entered into.

(f) There is no cash alternative to any of the competition prizes.

(g) Winners of prizes will be notified in writing within 28 days after the winner(s) have been ascertained. [The prize(s) will be despatched to the winner(s) promptly thereafter] [The winner of the first prize motor car will be invited to a presentation ceremony].

(h) [*For third-party-provided prizes*]. The winner of the [holiday for two in Spain] will be required to complete all booking formalities direct with ABC and XYZ will have no responsibility for the acts or defaults of ABC or the holiday hotel, or the accuracy of the holiday brochure. [The winner will be entitled to nominate any other person to book the holiday in his place.] [Full details of the prize will be provided to the winner at the time of notification.]

(i) The "Free holiday for two" first prize consists of two weeks at Hotel X [half board], being package holiday No. 123 as published in ABC's current catalogue. [Travel to and from the airport will be paid by XYZ up to a maximum of £.)

(j) The "Free holiday for two" first prize must be booked so as to commence within the period of [ ] to [ ] 199[ ]. [If the winner fails to make a booking in time to comply with those dates, he may book a holiday to commence within [ ] months of the last date, provided that if the cost of the holiday as booked is greater than the cost of the holiday would have been if taken between the stated dates, the winner must pay the excess at the time of making the booking.

(k) The first prize of "two best seats on men's finals day at Wimbledon and a champagne lunch" means [ ].

(l) The winner of the "two tickets for the inaugural passenger flight to the moon" first prize must contact XYZ on or before the [ ] to confirm that the tickets will be used and to collect them from XYZ. If the winner does not do so, XYZ reserves the right to withdraw the award of the prize to the winner and to award it to the runner up.

(m) [*Where winner has left the premises*]. If the winner of any prize cannot be traced after reasonable efforts have been made by [the Promoter] then [the Promoter] will be entitled to dispose of the prize as it thinks fit without any liability to the winner for having done so.

(n) The list of winners will be available for [ ] weeks following the 28-day period and can be obtained by sending an SAE to XYZ.

(o) There is no limit on the number of entries which can be made but any entrant can only win one prize.

(p) [*Where there are several prizes*]. The winner of any prize may not elect to accept a lesser prize in substitution except with the consent of [the Promoter] and of the winner of that lesser prize.

Free prize draw rules

(Additional to any of the above which are applicable).

(a) No purchase is necessary for the receipt of this [prize draw ticket]. Complete your name and address in the box provided and place this entry form in the collection box. [There is no limit to the number of entries which can be made.]

Withdrawal of promotion

XYZ will be entitled to terminate or modify the [promotion] [competition] or to modify these rules prior to the Closing Date [by an advertisement in the [nominated] national newspaper].

Availability of separate rules

These rules are not complete. To obtain a complete set of rules send a request plus an SAE to XYZ.

Scratchcard promotion rules

(a) [*For skill-based scratchcards*]. Using your skill and judgement, answer the question by carefully scratching off the covering on the box which you consider to be the correct answer.

(b) If you have correctly answered all [three] questions please scratch off the covering of the box marked "prize". You may claim your prize from this [or any other XYZ shop] by the close of business on the [ ] by handing in the card in a valid state and with all answers correctly scratched.

(c) On no account are you to scratch the cover off the marked "security" area even if you have answered all of the questions correctly, as to do so will invalidate this card.

(d) If more than one answer box for any question is scratched off or tampered with or if this card is otherwise mutilated or if there is any other breach of these rules, this card will be invalid. This card will be deemed to be mutilated if for any other reason any of the [symbols] are not invisible when the card is received by the participant.

(e) [*For "chance" scratchcards*]. Scratch any one of the boxes on this card to see if you have won a prize. The prize must be claimed by the [ ] by handing in this card in a valid state and with the prize box only scratched.

(f) This card is valid for the claiming of any prize until the [ ].

Promotion gift rules

(a) All [gifts] supplied to valid redeemers will be subject to the warranty provisions of the manufacturer of the [gift] and any complaints about the [gift] should be made to [supplier] in writing promptly after discovery of any defect or deficiency. Its name and address is [ ].

(b) The prize [tickets to Wembley] are provided subject to the terms and conditions upon which they are issued. The prize is offered subject to the [event] taking place as advertised and [the promoter] will not be responsible for anything affecting the issue or use of the prize tickets which is not within its absolute control.

A2 DTI Code of Practice for Traders on Price Indications

In November 1988 the Department of Trade and Industry issued a Code of Practice for Traders on Price Indications for the purpose of giving guidance in respect of the requirements of section 20 of the Consumer Protection Act 1987. Sections of the code which are relevant to consumer product promotions are set out below. For any other purpose the complete text of the Code should be used.

DEFINITIONS

In this code:

Accommodation

includes hotel and other holiday accommodation and new homes for sale freehold or on a lease of over 21 years but does not include rented homes.

Consumer

means anyone who might want the goods, services, accommodation or facilities, other than for business use.

Price

means both the total amount the consumer will have to pay to get the goods, services, accommodation or facilities and any method which has been or will be used to calculate that amount.

Price Comparison

means any indication given to consumers that the price at which something is offered to consumers is less than or equal to some other price.

Produce

means goods, services, accommodation and facilities (but not credit facilities, except where otherwise specified).

Services and Facilities

means any services or facilities whatever (including credit, banking and insurance services, purchase or sale of foreign currency, supply of electricity, off-street car parking and caravan sites) except those provided by a person or appointed representative under the Financial Services Act 1986 in the course of an investment business, services provided by an employee to his employer and facilities for a caravan which is the occupier's main or only home.

Shop

means any shop, store, stall or other place (including a vehicle or the consumer's home) at which goods, services, accommodation or facilities are offered to consumers.

Trader

means anyone (retailers, manufacturers, agents, service providers and others) who is acting in the course of a business.

PRICE COMPARISONS

1.1 PRICE COMPARISONS GENERALLY

1.1.1 Always make the meaning of price indications clear. Do not leave consumers to guess whether or not a price comparison is being made. If no price comparison is intended, do not use words or phrases which, in their normal, everyday use and in the context in which they are used, are likely to give your customers the impression that a price comparison is being made.

1.1.2 Price comparisons should always state the higher price as well as the price you intend to charge for the product (goods, services, accommodation or facilities). Do not make statements like "sale price £5" or "reduced to £39" without quoting the higher price to which they refer.

1.1.3 It should be clear what sort of price the higher price is. For example, comparisons with something described by words like "regular price", "usual price" or "normal price" should say whose regular, usual or normal price it is (*e.g.* "our normal price").

Descriptions like "reduced from" and crossed out higher prices should be used only if they refer to your own previous price. Words should not be used in price indications other than with their normal everyday meanings.

1.1.4 Do not use initials or abbreviations to describe the higher price in a comparison, except for the initials "RRP" to describe a recommended retail price or the abbreviation "man. rec. price" (see paragraph 1.6.2 below).

1.1.5 Follow the part of the code (sections 1.2 to 1.6 as appropriate) which applies to the type of comparison you intend to make.

1.2 COMPARISONS WITH THE TRADER'S OWN PREVIOUS PRICE

General

1.2.1 In any comparison between your present selling price and another price at which you have in the past offered the product, you should state the previous price as well as the new lower price.

1.2.2 In any comparison with your own previous price:

(a) the previous price should be the last price at which the product was available to consumers in the previous 6 months;

(b) the product should have been available to consumers at that price for at least 28 consecutive days in the previous 6 months; and

(c) the previous price should have applied (as above) for that period at the same shop where the reduced price is now being offered.

The 28 days at (b) above may include bank holidays, Sundays or other days of religious observance when the shop was closed; and up to 4 days when, for reasons beyond your control, the product was not available for supply. The product must not have been offered at a different price between that 28 days period and the day when the reduced price is first offered.

1.2.3 If the previous price in a comparison does not meet one or more of the conditions set out in paragraph 1.2.2 above, the comparison should:

(i) be fair and meaningful; and

(ii) give a clear and positive explanation of the period for which and the circumstances in which that higher price applied, for example "These goods were on sale here at the higher price from February 1 to February 26" or "These goods were on sale at the higher price in 10 of our 95 stores only". Display the explanation clearly, and as prominently as the price indication. You should not use general disclaimers saying for example that the higher price used in comparisons have not necessarily applied to 28 consecutive days.

Food, drink and perishable goods

1.2.4 For any food and drink, you need not give a positive explanation if the previous price in a comparison has not applied for 28 consecutive days, provided it was the last price at which the goods were on sale in the previous 6 months and applied in the same shop where the reduced price is now being offered. This also applies to non-food perishables, if they have a shelf-life of less than 6 weeks.

Catalogue and mail order traders

1.2.5 Where products are sold only through a catalogue, advertisement or leaflet, any comparison with a previous price should be with the price in your own last catalogue, advertisement or leaflet. If you sell the same products both in shops and through catalogues etc, the previous price should be the last price at which you offered the product. You should also follow the guidance in paragraphs 1.2.2 (a) and (b). If your price comparison does not meet these conditions, you should follow the guidance in paragraph 1.2.3.

Making a series of reductions

1.2.6 If you advertise a price reduction and then want to reduce the price further during the same sale or special offer period, the intervening price (or prices) need not have applied for 28 days. In these circumstances unless you use a positive explanation (paragraph 1.2.3):

- the highest price in the series must have applied for 28 consecutive days in the last 6 months at the same shop; and
- you must show the highest selling price, the intervening price(s) and the current selling price (*e.g.* "£40, £20, £10, £5").

1.3 INTRODUCTORY OFFERS, AFTER-SALE OR AFTER-PROMOTION PRICES

Introductory offers

1.3.1 Do not call a promotion an introductory offer unless you intend to continue to offer the product for sale after the offer period is over and to do so at a higher price.
1.3.2 Do not allow an offer to run on so long that it becomes misleading to describe it as an introductory or other special offer. What is a reasonable period will depend on the circumstances (but, depending on the shelf-life of the product, it is likely to be a matter of weeks, not months). An offer is unlikely to be misleading if you state the date the offer will end and keep to it. If you then extend the offer period, make it clear that you have done so.

Quoting a future price

1.3.3 If you indicate an after-sale or after-promotion price, do so only if you are certain that, subject only to circumstances beyond your control, you will continue to offer identical products at that price for at least 28 days in the 3 months after the end of the offer period or after the stocks run out.
1.3.4 If you decide to quote a future price, write what you mean in full. Do not use initials to describe it (*e.g.* "ASP", "APP"). The description should be clearly and prominently displayed, with the price indication.

1.4 COMPARISONS WITH PRICE RELATED TO DIFFERENT CIRCUMSTANCES

1.4.1 This section covers comparisons with prices:

(a) for different quantities (*e.g.* "15p each, 4 for 50p");
(b) for goods in a different condition (*e.g.* "seconds £20, when perfect £30");
(c) for a different availability (*e.g.* "price £50, price when ordered specially £60");
(d) for goods in a totally different state (*e.g.* "price in kit form £50, price ready-assembled £70"); or
(e) For special groups of people (*e.g.* "senior citizens' price £2.50, others £5").

General

1.4.2 Do not make such comparisons unless the product is available in the different quantity, conditions etc. at the price you quote. Make clear to consumers the different circumstances which apply and show them prominently with the price indication. Do not use initials (*e.g.* "RAP" for "ready-assembled price") to describe the different circumstances, but write what you mean in full.

"When perfect" comparisons

1.4.3 If you do not have the perfect goods on sale in the same shop:

(a) follow section 1.2 if the "when perfect" price is your own previous price for the goods;
(b) follow section 1.5 if the "when perfect" price is another trader's price; or
(c) follow section 1.6 if the "when perfect" price is one recommended by the manufacturer or supplier.

Goods in a different state

1.4.4 Only make comparisons with goods in a totally different state if:

(a) a reasonable proportion (say a third (by quantity)) of your stock of those goods is readily available for sale to consumers in that different state (for example, ready assembled) at the quoted price and from the shop where the price comparison is made; or
(b) another trader is offering those goods in that state at the quoted price and you follow section 1.5 below.

Prices for special groups of people

1.4.5 If you want to compare different prices which you charge to different groups of people (*e.g.* one price for existing customers and another for new customers, or one price for people who are members of a named organisation (other than the trader) and another for those who are not), do not use words like "our normal" or "our regular" to describe the higher price, unless it applies to at least half your customers.

1.5 COMPARISONS WITH ANOTHER TRADER'S PRICES

1.5.1 Only compare your prices with another trader's price if:

(a) you know that his price which you quote is accurate and up-to-date;
(b) you give the name of the other trader clearly and prominently, with the price comparison;
(c) you identify the shop where the other trader's price applies, if that other trader is a retailer; and
(d) the other trader's price which you quote applies to the same products–or to substantially similar products and you state any differences clearly.

1.5.2 Do not make statements like "If you can buy this product elsewhere for less, we will refund the difference" about your "own brand" products which other traders do not stock, unless your offer will also apply to other trader's equivalent goods. If there are any conditions attached to the offer (*e.g.* it only applies to goods on sale in the same town) you should show them clearly and prominently, with the statement.

1.6 COMPARISONS WITH "RECOMMENDED RETAIL PRICE" OR SIMILAR

General

1.6.1 This section covers comparisons with recommended retail prices, manufacturers' recommended prices, suggested retail prices, suppliers' suggested retail prices and similar descriptions. It also covers prices given to co-operative and voluntary group organisations by their wholesalers or head-quarters organisations.

1.6.2 Do not use initials or abbreviations to describe the higher price in a comparison unless:

(a) you use the initials "RRP" to describe a recommended retail price; or
(b) you use the abbreviation "man. rec. price" to describe a manufacturer's recommended retail price.

Write all other descriptions out in full and show them clearly and prominently with the price indication.

1.6.3   Do not use a recommended price in a comparison unless:

(a) it has been recommended to you by the manufacturer or supplier as a price at which the product might be sold to consumers;
(b) you deal with that manufacturer or supplier on normal commercial terms. (This will generally be the case for members of cooperation or voluntary group organisations in relation to their wholesalers or head-quarters organisations); and
(c) the price is not significantly higher than prices at which the product is generally sold at the time you first make the comparison.

1.7 PRE-PRINTED PRICES

1.7.1   Make sure you pass on to consumers any reduction stated on the manufacturer's packaging (*e.g.* "flash packs" such as "10p off RRP").

1.7.2   You are making a price comparison if goods have a clearly visible price already printed on the packaging which is higher than the price you will charge for them. Such pre-printed prices are, in effect, recommended prices (except for the retailer's own label goods) and you should follow paragraph 1.6.1 to 1.6.4. You need not state that the price is a recommended price.

1.8 REFERENCES TO VALUE OR WORTH

1.8.1   Do not compare your prices with an amount described only as "worth" or "value".

1.8.2   Do not present general advertising slogans which refer to "value" or "worth" in a way which is likely to be seen by customers as a price comparison.

1.9 SALES OR SPECIAL EVENTS

1.9.1   If you have bought in items specially for a sale, and you make this clear, you should not quote a higher price when indicating that they are special purchases. Otherwise, your price indications for individual items in the sale which are reduced should comply with section 1.1. of the code and whichever of section 1.2 to 1.6 applies to the type of comparison you are making.

1.9.2   If you just have a general notice saying, for example, that all products are at "half marked price", the marked price on the individual items should be your own previous price and you should follow section 1.2 of the code.

1.9.3 Do not use general notices saying *e.g.* "up to 50% off" unless the maximum reduction quoted applies to at least 10% (by quantity) of the range of products on offer.

1.10 FREE OFFERS

1.10.1 Make clear to consumers, at the same time of the offer for sale, exactly what they will have to buy to get the "free offer".

1.10.2 If you give any indication of the monetary value of the "free offer", and that sum is not your own present price for the product, follow whichever of sections 1.2 to 1.6 cover the type of price it is.

1.10.3 If there are any conditions attached to the "free offer", give at least the main points of those conditions with the price indication and make clear to consumers where, before they are committed to buy, they can get full details of the conditions.

1.10.4 Do not claim that an offer is free if:

(a) you have imposed additional charges that you would not normally make;

(b) you have inflated the price of any product the consumer must buy or the incidental charges (for example, postage) the consumer must pay to get the "free offer"; or

(c) you will reduce the price to consumers who do not take it up.

ACTUAL PRICE TO CONSUMER

2.1 INDICATING TWO DIFFERENT PRICES

2.1.1 The Consumer Protection Act makes it an offence to indicate a price for goods or services which is lower than the one that actually applies, for example, showing one price in an advertisement, window display, shelf marking or on the item itself, and then charging a higher price at the point of sale or checkout.

2.2 INCOMPLETE INFORMATION AND NON-OPTIONAL EXTRAS

2.1.1 Make clear in your price indications the full price consumers will have to pay for the product. Some examples of how to do so in particular circumstances are set out below.

Limited availability of product

2.2.2 Where the price you are quoting for products only applies to a limited number of, say, orders, sizes or colours, you should make this clear in your price indication (*e.g.* "available in other colours or sizes at additional cost").

Prices relating to differing forms of products

2.2.3 If the price you are quoting for particular products does not apply to the products in the form they are displayed or advertised, say so clearly in your price indication. For example, advertisements for self-assembly furniture and the like should make it clear that the price refers to a kit of parts.

Postage, packing and delivery charges

2.2.4 If you sell by mail order, make clear any additional charges for postage, packing or delivery on the order form or similar document, so that consumers are fully aware of them before being committed to buying. Where you cannot determine these charges in advance, show clearly on the order form how they will be calculated (*e.g.* "Post Office rates apply"), or the place in the catalogue etc where the information is given.

2.2.5 If you sell goods from a shop and offer a delivery service for certain items, make it clear whether there are any separate delivery charges (*e.g.* for delivery outside a particular area) and what those charges are, before the consumer is committed to buying.

VALUE ADDED TAX

(i) Price indications to non-business customers

2.2.6 All price indications you give to private consumers, by whatever means, should include VAT.

(ii) Price indications to business customers

2.2.7 Prices may be indicated exclusive of VAT in shops where or advertisements from which most of your business is with business customers. If you also carry out business with private customers at those shops or from those advertisements you should make clear that the prices exclude VAT and;

  (i)   display VAT-inclusive prices with equal prominence; or
  (ii) display prominent statements that on top of the quoted price customers will also have to pay VAT at the current rate.

(iii) Professional fees

2.2.8 Where you indicate a price (including estimates) for a professional fee, make clear what it covers. The price should generally include VAT. In cases where the fee is based on an as-yet unknown sum of money (for example, the sale price of a house), either:

(i) quote a fee which includes VAT; or
(ii) make it clear that in addition to your fee the consumer would have to pay VAT at the current rate (*e.g.* "fee of $1\frac{1}{2}$% of purchase price, plus VAT at 17.5%")
Make sure that whichever method you choose is used for both estimates and final bills.

(iv) Building work

2.2.9 In estimates for building work, either include VAT in the price indication or indicate with equal prominence the amount or rate of VAT payable in addition to your basic figure. If you give a separate amount for VAT, make it clear that if any provisional sums in estimates vary them the amount of VAT payable would also vary.

Service, cover and minimum charges in hotels, restaurants and similar establishments

2.2.10 If your customers in hotels, restaurants or similar places must pay a non-optional extra charge, *e.g.* "service charge".

(i) incorporate the charge within fully inclusive prices wherever practicable; and
(ii) display the fact clearly on any price list or priced menu, whether displayed inside or outside (*e.g.* by using statements like "all prices include service").

Do not include suggested optional sums, whether for service or any other item, in the bill presented to the customer.

2.2.11 It will not be practicable to include some non-optional extra charges in a quoted price; for instance, if you make a flat charge per person or per table in a restaurant (often referred to as a "cover charge") or a minimum charge. In such cases the charge should be shown as prominently as other prices on any list or menu, whether displayed inside or outside.

Holiday and travel prices

2.2.12 If you offer a variety of prices to give consumers a choice, (for example, paying more or less for a holiday depending on the time of year or the standard of accommodation), make clear in your brochure–or any other price indication–what the basic price is and what it covers. Give details of any optional additional charges and what those charges cover, or of the place where this information can be found, clearly and close to the basic price.

2.2.13 Any non-optional charges which are for fixed amounts should be included in the basic price and not shown as additions, unless they are only payable by some consumers. In that case you should specify, near to the details of the basic price, either what the amounts are and the circumstances in which they are payable, or where in the brochure etc the information is given.

2.2.14 Details of non-optional extra charges which may vary (such as holiday insurance) or of where in the brochure etc the information is given should be made clear to consumers near to the basic price.

2.2.15 If you reserve the right to increase prices after consumers have made their booking, state this clearly with all indication of prices, and include prominently in your brochure full information on the circumstances in which a surcharge is payable.

Ticket prices

2.2.16 If you sell tickets, whether for sporting events, cinemas, theatres etc, and your prices are higher than the regular price that would be charged to the public at the box office, *i.e.* higher than the "face value", you should make clear in any price indication what the "face value" of the ticket is.

Call-out charges

2.2.17 If you make a minimum call-out charge or other flat-rate charge (for example, for plumbing, gas or electrical equipment repairs etc carried out in consumer's homes), ensure that the consumer is made aware of the charge and whether the actual price may be higher (*e.g.* if work takes longer than a specific time) before being committed to using your services.

Credit facilities

2.2.18 Price indications about consumer credit should comply with the relevant requirements of regulations under the Consumer Credit Act 1974 governing the form and content of advertisements.

Insurance

2.2.19 Where actual premium rates for a particular consumer or the availability of insurance cover depend on an individual assessment, this should be made clear when any indication of the premium or the method of determining it is given to consumers.

PRICE INDICATIONS WHICH BECOME MISLEADING AFTER THEY HAVE BEEN GIVEN

3.1 General

3.1.1 The Consumer Protection Act makes it an offence to give a price indication which, although correct at the time, becomes misleading after you have given it, if:

(i) consumers could reasonably be expected still to be relying on it; and
(ii) you do not take reasonable steps to prevent them doing so. Clearly it will not be necessary or even possible in many instances to inform all those who may have been given the misleading price indication. However, you should always make sure consumers are given the correct information before they are committed to buying a product and be prepared to cancel any transaction which a consumer has entered into on the basis of a price indication which has become misleading.

3.1.2 Do not give price indications which you know or intend will only apply for a limited period, without making this fact clear in the advertisement or price indication.

3.1.3 The following paragraphs set out what you should do in some particular circumstances.

Newspaper and magazine advertisements

3.2.1 If the advertisement does not say otherwise, the price indication should apply for a reasonable period (as a general guide, at least 7 days or until the next issue of the newspaper or magazine in which the advertisement was published, whichever is longer). If the price indication becomes misleading within this period make sure consumers are given the correct information before they are committed to buying the product.

Mail order advertisements, catalogues and leaflets

3.3.1 Paragraph 3.2.1 above also applies to the time for which price indications in mail order advertisements and in regularly published catalogues or brochures should apply. If a price indication becomes misleading within this period, make the correct price indication clear to anyone who orders the product to which it relates. Do so before the consumer is committed to buying the product and, wherever practicable, before the goods are sent to the consumer.

Changes in the rate of value added tax

3.4.1   If your price indications become misleading because of a change in the general rate of VAT, or other taxes paid at point of sale, make the correct price indication clear to any consumers who order products. Do so before the consumer is committed to buying the product and, wherever practicable, before the goods are sent to the consumer.

A3 Example Agreements

This Appendix contains some example agreements which will commonly be negotiated in respect of any dealings within the advertising, sales promotion and related businesses. As with most industries, the various agencies or product manufacturers tend to have their own versions of whichever agreements are relevant to their activity. Sometimes they are short and simple, being understandable but not sufficiently comprehensive to cover all the necessary commercial and financial aspects adequately. Other companies use agreements which are convoluted, complicated and difficult to understand.

The essential qualities of any commercial agreement are that it must be:

(a) understandable by anybody reading it, and so where possible it should be "user friendly". This is helped by setting out its terms in a logical sequence, and by avoiding unnecessary legal mumbo-jumbo.
(b) sufficiently comprehensive to deal with all the major points which are relevant to that industry, and their material ramifications. It may not be possible or practical to try to cover every conceivable contingency, but it is an error not to deal with significant matters just for the sake of reducing the length of the document.
(c) unambiguous and clear in what it says. The style and layout of the document is a great help in making it clear, and careful use of the English language will reduce the risk of the agreement containing confusing or contradictory terms.

It is generally better to have a longer agreement which meets the above criteria than a shorter one which does not. The agreement governs the legal and commercial relationships between the parties, and it should be good enough to stand up to hostile litigation.

The example agreements set out in this Appendix are not put forward as representing the ideal, comprehensive format and content. Every deal is different, and the example agreements are only there to give some guidance as to what should be considered by the parties as being relevant to the subject. Some of the clauses may not be relevant to every deal, but any form of drafting of agreements is essentially a thought-provoking process. The different drafting of similar clauses is indicated in square brackets, to show that a rigid approach to wording is not necessary, providing the clause achieves the meaning intended for it.

There are good industry association models for some of these example agreements which will obviously be different. Therefore the example agreements are designed to show that there are alternatives.

ADVERTISING AGENCY AGREEMENT

THIS AGREEMENT is made the   day of   19 BETWEEN
MARVOSUDS LIMITED of [   ]
(hereinafter called the Client) of the one part and CREATIVE ACME-ADS
LIMITED of [   ] (hereinafter called the Agency) of the other part

WHEREAS The Client is the manufacturer in the United Kingdom (the
Territory) of the products set out in the Schedule hereto (the Products) [which
will include such other products which are manufactured by the Client during
the period of this Agreement.]

NOW IT IS HEREBY AGREED as follows

Appointment

1. (a) Subject to and upon the terms and conditions herein set out the Client
hereby appoints the Agency and the Agency accepts the appointment to be the
sole and exclusive advertising agency of the Client within the Territory for the
Products in respect of [TV, Cinema, radio and printed media] advertising (the
Rights Media).

(b) For so long as this Agreement remains in force the Client agrees not to
appoint any other party to act as an advertising agency for the Products within
the Rights Media within the Territory.

[(b) The exclusive appointment of the Agency will be in respect of [TV,
Cinema and national printed media] advertising (the Rights Media) and the
Agency is appointed on a non-exclusive basis in respect of [local commercial
radio advertising].]

[(c) The Agency agrees that it will not take on as a client another company
which has products which are competing directly with the Products and
business of the Client without prior written approval of the Client.]

Agency as principal

2. The basis of this Agreement is that in law the Agency acts in all matters
in connection with the Client and with third parties as a principal and
consequently the Agency is not authorised or entitled to make any representations on behalf of the Client or to make any commitment on behalf of the
Client unless the Client has first authorised and approved such action by the
Agency in writing.

Contract period

3. This Agreement will commence on the date hereof [will be deemed to
have commenced on the [   ] day of [   ]] [will commence on the [   ]
day of [   ]] and will be for an initial period of one year and will continue
thereafter until either party gives to the other party not less than [four] months
prior notice in writing.

4. During the period of this Agreement the Agency will provide to the Client the personal services of Mr [ ] who will be the Agency executive contact for liaison with the Client. He will supervise and co-ordinate all of the work done by the Agency for the client under this Agreement subject only to his absence on holiday, illness and for other good reasons, in which circumstances the Agency will appoint (if necessary) another executive [acceptable to the Client] to undertake the same responsibilities.

Obligations of Agency

5. The Agency agrees to create and to submit to the Client original advertising concepts in accordance with an agreed brief and upon approval thereof the Agency will prepare advertising material for the Products suitable for the Rights Media and in respect thereof the Agency will:

(a) advise the Client upon advertising strategies and concepts which will be suitable for the Products.

(b) prepare the design of all printed matter for press advertising campaigns which are approved by the Client.

(c) prepare, supervise and produce all filming for TV advertising including commissioning or licensing suitable music.

(d) contract directly with the relevant parties for the media placement of all press and TV advertising [in accordance with a Schedule of timings of broadcasts and/or publication] and to obtain the best discount and other terms available therefor.

6. (a) In respect of each printed media advertising project (whether proposed by the Agency or requested by the Client) the Agency will:

(i) submit to the Client for approval the preliminary sketches or other concept work and storyboard.

(ii) modify the preliminary sketches if required to do so by the Client and then produce finished artwork in accordance with the approved version and submit that to the Client for final approval.

(b) Whenever any approvals are required from the Client they will not be unreasonably delayed by the Client, and approval will not be unreasonably withheld by the Client if the material submitted by the Agency for approval is substantially according to instructions confirmed by the Client but the Client also reserves the right to approve the quality of the finished artwork.

(c) In the case of TV advertisements, the Agency will seek approval of the Client at the concept design, shooting script and the rough and final edited stages of the advertisement.

7. (a) The Agency warrants that all concepts, artwork, text, photography or other material which will be created by it or by its subcontractors for use in any advertising for the Products:

(i) will be original work entitled to copyright protection and will not be a copy of nor infringe the copyright of any other proprietary right of any third party;

(ii) will not be defamatory of any person or product and will not be otherwise actionable as being damaging to their or its name image reputation or business.

(iii) where the Agency designs a logo or brand name or packaging artwork for one of the Products it will not infringe any trademark (registered or unregistered) within the Territory nor will it constitute "passing off" or be a breach of copyright nor will it be otherwise actionable by a third party.

(iv) will not be subject to any moral rights obligation or claims.

(b) The Agency undertakes that it will not at any time design and develop for any other party any advertising concept or any advertising material which is confusingly similar to any of the advertising concepts and material which has been devised for the Client by the Agency under this Agreement and which has been or which will be used to advertise the Products.

Budgets

8. (a) The Agency and the Client will agree an annual budget for advertising to be undertaken for the Products and an annual schedule of proposed advertising campaigns for each Product.

(b) On a [monthly] basis the Agency will prepare a report on the expenditure during the previous [month] and the anticipated expenditure during the coming [month] with a comparative analysis of total expenditure against the annual budget with an explanation of the reason for any significant variation from the budget.

(c) The budget will be reviewed by the Client and the Agency on a [six monthly] basis to monitor the effectiveness of the advertising campaigns for the Product and to make any adjustments to proposed expenditure which appear to the Client to be appropriate at that time.

Legal clearance

9. (a) The Client will ensure that any facts or opinions or other material provided by it to the Agency which will be the basis of any representation or statement to be contained in any advertising material will be correct and (where appropriate) will be authorised to be available for public use in the advertising.

(b) The Client is relying on the expertise and experience of the Agency in creating the advertising material submitted to the Client and (with the

exception of material provided to it by the Client as referred to in Clause 9(a))
it will be the responsibility of the Agency to:

(i) obtain legal and copyright and trademark clearance of all advertising material produced by the Agency and (if requested by the
Client) to provide the Client with reasonable evidence of the legal
clearance advice which has been obtained by the Agency. If the
legal advice required there to be any modification or the scrapping
of the advertising material, then the Agency will [at its own cost]
make such advised modification, except that where the cause of the
illegality is the fault of the Client under 9(a) above the Client will
pay for the cost of the modifications.

(ii) ensure that the advertising material complies in all respects with the
appropriate sections of the ASA Code of Advertising Practice and if
necessary to obtain the ASA's advice on any element of a proposed
advertisement which either the Agency or the Client reasonably
considers may need investigation.

10. The Agency will be responsible for any act or default of any subcontractor of the Agency which causes the Agency to be in breach of any term of this
Agreement, whether or not that subcontractor acted within the instructions
given to it by the Agency.

11. The Agency will indemnify the Client from any claim, cost, damage or
loss (including legal costs or an indemnity basis) which the Client incurs as a
reasonably direct consequence of any breach by the Agency of any of its
obligations to the Client under this Agreement.

Intellectual property

12. (a) The Agency undertakes that whenever it commissions any original
photography or other creative material from a sub-contractor or an independent third party the Agency will have the world wide copyright in such original
material assigned to the Agency or that it will be entitled to call for an
assignment of the copyright unconditionally when all of that sub-contractor's
or third party's agreed fees have been paid and at the time the Agency will take
all necessary steps to obtain the copyright assignment. The Agency will also
ensure that in any case where moral rights may apply it will obtain all the
relevant waivers from authors.

(b) If the sub-contractor or third party is not prepared to assign the
copyright in whatever it produces for the Agency under this Agreement or if it
is only prepared to do so subject to a substantial additional fee being paid, then
the Agency will consult with the Client before commissioning the material
from that sub-contractor or third party.

13. The Client accepts that for musical soundtracks of TV advertising,
even where the composing of a new piece of music is specifically commissioned
by the Agency from a music publisher, normally the Agency will only be

granted a licence to use the music and only in the synchronised sound track of the TV advertisement for which the music has been commissioned.

14. (a) When the Agency has been paid in full by the Client for any advertising material, whether it was produced in house by the Agency or whether it was produced by a sub-contractor of the Agency or a third party, the Agency will promptly assign to the Client the worldwide copyright and all other rights in and to such material.

(b) The Client will be entitled to make unconditional use of all copyright material assigned to it under this Agreement without paying any additional fees to the Agency or to any sub-contractor or third party.

15. If a sub-contractor or third party is commissioned by the Agency to produce any artwork, notwithstanding that the sub-contractor or third party refuses to assign the copyright in the artwork, the Agency will ensure that the Agency (and therefore the Client) is granted an exclusive licence extensive enough to enable the Client to make unconditional use of the artwork to advertise and promote the Product.

16. If the subcontractor or third party is commissioned by the Agency to design a new logo or device to be used together with a Product brand name and for which the Client will make a trademark application, or will use it as an unregistered trademark then the commission will be conditional upon the assignment to the Agency of the copyright in the design of that logo to safeguard the trademark and other proprietary rights in the brand name for the benefit of the Client.

Financial arrangements

17. (a) The Agency will be responsible for making all payments to media suppliers and the Client will pay the Agency for such charges as herein set out.

(b) The Agency will invoice the Client [in advance] [in arrears] for all committed media transmissions and publication costs and the Client will pay the Agency for those invoices within [ ] days after receiving them.

(c) If the Client is late in paying the Agency for media costs resulting in the Agency incurring late payment penalties with the media suppliers, then the Client will reimburse the Agency for such surcharges.

18. [(a)] The Client will pay to the Agency a fee in consideration of its media related work being 17.65% (or such other fee level as they may agree) of all media charges for the broadcast and publication of all advertising created by the Agency for the Product.

[(b) If the Agency obtains advantageous discount terms on media charges to the Client by reason of the overall Agency purchasing power and which would not reasonably have been obtainable by the Agency for the Client by itself, then the Agency may retain [75%] of any such advantageous discount and the media charge payable by the Client will be calculated accordingly.]

19. (a) The Agency will invoice the Client monthly in arrears for all authorised sub-contractor or third party expenses and fees and the Agency will

be entitled to mark up those costs by [10%] to cover its own handling and administration overhead costs.

(b) Any other overhead costs which are chargeable to the Client as set out below will be charged at cost and these costs will be:

- packaging and courier costs in transporting artwork, proofs and other materials to the Client;
- video cassettes and audio cassettes for transferring copies of advertisements as required by the Client;
- taxi costs when attending the Client at the Client's request;
- presentation materials and the hire of viewing facilities and similar costs incurred in the course of developing advertisements or for demonstration purposes but only if requested by the Client;
- [any other agreed category of cost].

(c) The Client will not be charged with internal UK telephone charges and other normal overhead costs incurred by the Agency in the ordinary course of running its business.

(d) If the Client requests the Agency to commission a piece of work such as an independent market research survey where the cost is likely to be substantial, the Agency will be entitled to require that all or some of that ascertained third party expense is paid in advance by the Client before confirming the commission.

20. (a) If the client wishes to use any of the advertising material produced for it by the Agency in a country outside the United Kingdom for broadcast or published advertisements it will be entitled to do so, but it will pay the Agency an override commission of [%] of the media cost in doing so whether or not the Client owns the copyright in the material being used.

(b) If after the expiry or termination of this Agreement but within [ ] years the Client uses within the Territory any of the advertisements produced for it by the Agency then the Client will pay to the Agency a commission of [%] of the media cost.

(c) The Client will account to the Agency for any commission payable to it under this clause within [ ] days after the broadcast use if it was one-off and on a [monthly basis one month in arrears] if the use is intended to be regular.

21. If after the expiry or termination of this Agreement but within [ ] years the Client or the Client's new advertising agency produces new advertising material which is based upon or which utilises substantially any theme of advertisements produced by the Agency for the Client under this Agreement, then the Agency [will be paid a flat fee of £] [will receive no further fees or commissions in respect of that new advertising] [will receive a commission of [ ] of the media cost for a maximum period of [twelve] months].

STANDARD CLAUSES

NOTE: These clauses are "boiler plate" clauses which will be found in one form or another in all commercial agreements. They would be set out at the end of the preceding example agreement insofar as they are relevant and appropriate, and are not repeated in the subsequent example agreements. They may need modifying to fit into the context of any specific agreement, and they may not all be necessary or relevant to the agreement being drafted. Also ensure that there is no contradiction or conflict between the main clauses and any standard clauses being added to the end of the draft agreement.

Warranties

The [Agency] warrants to the [Company] as follows:

(a) That the [Agency] is entitled to enter into this Agreement and that there are no commitments or other circumstances which will inhibit the [Agency] from providing the services to the [Company] as set out herein.

(b) That any artwork or text or other creative services provided by the [Agency] to the [Company] will be original to the [Agency] and that it will not infringe the copyright, trademark or other proprietary rights of any other party nor will it be defamatory or contain any other actionable material.

(c) That the use by the [Agency] of any third part material has been approved by the owner of the copyright or other rights in it.

(d) That in respect of the [Agency's] other clients there is currently no conflict of interest between the [Agency] and the [Company] and if any such conflict of interest should arise the [Agency] will promptly notify the [Company] in writing and they will use their best endeavours to resolve any adverse effects.

Indemnity

(a) The [Agency] agrees to indemnify the [Company] from and hold it harmless against any and all claims, actions, damages, expenses, costs (including legal costs on an indemnity basis) and other liabilities which may be incurred by the [Company] as a result of the breach by the [Agency] of any of its warranties, undertakings and obligations set out in this Agreement.

(b) If the [Company] has any claim made against it (or becomes aware of the threat of such a claim) against which it is indemnified by the [Agency], it will promptly notify the [Agency] in writing, giving such details as are available, and the [Agency] will forthwith at its own expense take all such steps as may be necessary to defend or settle such a claim.

(c) The [Agency] will pay direct to the successful claimant or it will reimburse the [Company] (as the case may be) immediately upon demand the whole of any monetary award (including legal costs) and/or (as the case may be) the [Agency] will perform and observe any other relevant requirement of the award of the Court or the Arbitrator.

(d) If any claim for which the [Agency] is liable to indemnify the [Company] becomes the subject of litigation, the [Agency] may if it decides to do so take over the conduct of the litigation in the name of the [Company] and the [Company] will provide the [Agency] with all necessary assistance at the cost of the [Agency].

Termination

(a) Either party will be entitled to terminate this Agreement forthwith by written notice if the other party:

  (i) fails to remedy a material breach of this Agreement within [21] days after receiving a written notice specifying the breach and requiring its remedy, provided that if the breaching party is persistent in committing the same or a similar breach and remedying it each time within the said [21] days then on the [third] occasion the party giving the breach notice will be entitled to terminate this Agreement forthwith notwithstanding that the breach is again remedied in time on that [third] occasion;

  (ii) ceases permanently to trade;

  (iii) passes a resolution to wind up otherwise than for amalgamation or reconstruction or has a winding up petition made against it;

  (iv) enters into a composition with its creditors;

(b) Termination of this Agreement will not affect any rights of either party against the other which exist as at the termination date.

(c) Upon termination under this clause:

  (i) all finished and unfinished artwork, storyboard and other material belonging to the [Company] and in the possession or under the control of the [Agency] will promptly be delivered to the [Company];

  (ii) the [Company] will be entitled to appoint another [Agency] to complete any unfinished project and [the Agency] will have no further right therein for fees or otherwise;

  (iii) the [Agency] will on demand by the [Company] assign to the [Company] all outstanding copyrights in accordance with Clause [ ] in respect of original photography, artwork and any other original material received by or due to the [Company].

(d) A material breach of this Agreement by one of the parties will be deemed to have been accepted and waived by the other party if that other party does not make a formal written complaint about that breach to the breaching party within [ ] days after becoming fully aware of the existence of the breach.

(e) If either party waives any material breach of this Agreement committed by the other party, that will not be deemed to be waiver of any subsequent similar breach or of any other breach at any time.

(f) Termination of this Agreement will not release either party from its continuing obligations under Clauses [*confidentiality etc.*]

Confidentiality

(a) Each party undertakes to the other that it will not disclose to any unauthorised party any secret or confidential information relating to the other party or its business and neither will it make unauthorised use itself of any such information.

(b) For the purposes of this Agreement confidential information will be deemed to include any industry information, mailing lists, corporate strategy and any other information which is of commercial use and which is not readily available from any other public or authorised source.

(c) This restriction will not apply to any information which has been confidential but which becomes publicly available otherwise than through the breach of this restriction by the receiving party.

Force majeure

Neither party will be liable to the other for any default or breach of this Agreement which is caused directly by circumstances beyond its control provided that:

(a) the defaulting part will use its best endeavours to minimise the adverse effects of the enforced default or breach;

(b) the default or breach will be remedied as soon as the force majeure event has ceased to exist;

(c) if the force majeure event has affected a sub-contractor of the [Agency] and the Agency is dependent upon the work to be provided by the sub-contractor, the [Agency] and the [Company] will immediately consult to see whether the delayed work can be done or obtained elsewhere if necessary at no additional cost to the [Company].

Ostensible authority

Neither party will be entitled to pledge the credit of the other party or enter into any commitment on behalf of the other party or represent itself as having any authority to represent the other party or to act on its behalf as set out in this Agreement.

Assignment

(a) The [Agency] will not be entitled to assign any of its benefits or obligations under this Agreement to any other party but it will be entitled to sub-contract artwork and any other matters of a specialist nature which are sub-contracted by [agencies] in the ordinary course of their business.

(b) The [Agency] will be liable to the [Company] for any act or default of any of its sub-contractors as if it were the act or default of the [Agency].

(c) The [Agency] will ensure that any obligations of the [Agency] to the [Company] which are relevant to any work being done by a sub-contractor for the [Agency] will be accepted by the sub-contractor either under a written form of commission for each project or in accordance with the standard terms and conditions applied by the [Agency] to all sub-contractors.

Illegality

If any part of this Agreement is found to be illegal or unenforceable by a court of competent jurisdiction then:

(a) it will be deemed to be deleted from this Agreement and any affected clauses will be construed accordingly;

(b) any previous act or forebearance will remain in place and will not constitute a breach by that party;

(c) if any significant part of this Agreement is adversely affected by the illegality or unenforceability the parties will use their best endeavours in good faith to find a legal and enforceable means of achieving the objective of the adversely affected part;

(d) if the illegal or unenforceable part of this Agreement represents any essential requirements of this Agreement so that it cannot be proceeded with, then the parties will in good faith use their best endeavours to agree the terms of a termination which is fair to each of them.

Applicable law

This Agreement will be construed and enforced in accordance with the Laws of England and the High Court of Justice will be the court of competent jurisdiction. If both parties agree in writing upon the terms of doing so, a minor dispute may be settled in arbitration.

Complete agreement

(a) This Agreement [and its Schedules] constitutes the whole of the agreement between the parties and any matter previously referred to in meetings, correspondence, memoranda or elsewhere which is not set out in this Agreement will not be effective.

(b) This Agreement can only be amended by an instrument in writing setting out the whole of any modifications and signed by both parties. In this context subsequent correspondence between the parties on any contractual matter will not be effective unless it complies with this sub-clause.

(c) It is specifically agreed that any course of conduct between the parties which is not documented in accordance with this Clause will not be deemed to have become a contractual commitment.

(d) This Agreement supercedes any previous agreement made between the parties whether of a formal or an informal nature and if either party now or in the future has an established set of "terms and conditions" contained on or referred to in any transaction documentation they will not be effective unless they are specifically made part of this Agreement in accordance with this Clause.

Notices

(a) Any notice to be given by one party to the other must be in writing and delivered personally or sent by first class prepaid registered post or faxed with the original letter being posted on the same day and the effective date of the notice will be the date it is first received by the party to which it is addressed.

(b) Any notice will be sent to the party at its last known business address and will be marked to be for the attention of [ ] for the [Agency] and [ ] for the [Company].

Headings

The headings to the clauses set out in this Agreement are for convenience only and are not to be taken into account in the interpretation of any of the terms set out herein.

ARTWORK PROJECT AGREEMENT

From: :   Commissioning Agency
To   :   Artwork Company   [Date]
Dear—————,

Project X

We attach to this letter of agreement a synopsis [description] of the project entitled "X" which we are undertaking for our clients [ ] Ltd. Subject to the terms set out below we hereby commission you to design and produce artwork for project X (the Artwork).

1. We have provided you with a working concept theme [as attached hereto] and you will design and produce artwork utilising that concept primarily for use as printed media advertising.

2. We are proposing to develop an advertising theme for our clients brand product "Whizzo" based upon an imaginary character which is to be distinctive and who will be known as the "Whizzoman". You will design a character which will become the Whizzoman (the Character).

3. In consideration of the fees paid to you under this Agreement:

(a) You hereby assign to us the worldwide copyright and all other design and proprietary rights in all of the Artwork produced by you in respect of the advertising and of the Character and the goodwill, reputation and concept of the Character.

(b) You will deliver to us the original Artwork as produced by you.
[OR:

(a) In consideration of the fees paid to you under this Agreement you hereby grant us the exclusive licence in perpetuity to use the Artwork in the United Kingdom and for the purposes of [printed media advertising and display posters].

(b) If our clients wish to use the Artwork outside the United Kingdom for either of those licensed uses or if they wish to use the Artwork for any other purpose you agree to grant us a licence for such use upon payment of [£ to cover all uses] [a fee to be negotiated in good faith].]

4.(a) You will submit to us preliminary sketches of the proposed Artwork for approval.

(b) When the preliminary sketches have been approved you will proceed to produce final Artwork on that basis for final approval.

(c) All approvals will be given promptly and will not be unreasonably withheld but it is accepted by you that we and our clients are not bound to accept artwork which we reasonably consider not to be satisfactory.

(d) If, following submission by you of any Artwork for approval, we require modifications to be made to it to make it comply with our previously known requirements they will be done by you promptly at your cost and in accordance with our instructions.

5.(a) The Artwork is required for an advertising campaign starting on the [ ] and the agreed timetable for production of the Artwork is as follows which timetable is to be deemed "of the essence" of this Agreement.

    (i)   Delivery of preliminary sketches for approval by [ ];
    (ii) Approval and design or concept modification by [ ];
    (iii) Final artwork delivered for approval by [ ];
    (iv) Camera-ready artwork by [ ].

(b) If you fail to produce the camera-ready artwork by its due date (except due to our delay at any approval stage) and if we or our clients suffer a cost or loss as a reasonably direct consequence then you will reimburse that cost or loss on demand.

6.(a) You warrant that all of the Artwork and the Character will be original to you and that it will not infringe the copyright, trademark, design right or any other proprietary right of any third party nor will it be defamatory of any third party or derogatory of any third party products or services.

(b) If the Artwork includes any third party copyright or trademark or other protected rights it will be our responsibility to get legal clearance for its use if it is our requirement, and if it is your proposal then obtaining legal clearance will be your responsibility, and you will provide us with copies of such consents. Any third party fees for clearance will not be our responsibility in the second case unless they are first agreed by us.

(c) You will indemnify us and our clients from any claim, cost, loss, damage or expense incurred by us as a result of any breach by you of your warranties or commitments under this Agreement.

7. You undertake not to create for any other party any advertising or promotional material which is confusingly similar to or which could reasonably be considered as being connected with the Artwork or the Character.

8.(a) In consideration of the satisfactory production by you of the Artwork and an approved representation of the Character we agree to pay to you a fee as follows:

(i) £[ ] in respect of Artwork for the advertising;
(ii) £[ ] in respect of the Character.

(b) The fee will be paid as to [25% on the signing of this Agreement, 25% on the approval by us of the preliminary sketches and 50% on receipt by us of the complete approved camera-ready artwork].

(c) Payment will be made by us (as appropriate) on the signing of this Agreement and thereafter within [14] days after receipt from you of an invoice when you are entitled to render one under (b) above.

[Check for any advisable standard clauses]

COMMISSION OF PHOTOGRAPHS

To [Photographer]
From [Agency]
Dear [————————]

I am writing to confirm that we have commissioned you to be the photographer for the [   ] project (the Project) upon the following terms.

1. You will provide a suitable selection of photographs for us to consider and for the fee set out below we will be entitled to choose and have up to [ ] photographs which we will nominate.

2. Our artwork director will explain to you what kind of photographs we are looking for so that you can arrange the photographic sessions accordingly. [The artwork director will accompany you on the site so that you can consult with him on any artistic questions you may have].

3. The photographs which we choose (the Photographs) will be dealt with as follows:

(a) In consideration of the fee paid by us, you hereby assign to us the copyright in the Photographs unconditionally.

(b) Consequently we can make unconditional use of the Photographs within the Project but it is agreed that if we make commercial use of any of the Photographs which is not connected with the Project we will pay you an extra fee of [£] per Photograph as a once only fee to cover unlimited use for any purpose.

(c) At our request you will provide us with the negatives of the Photographs.

[(d) We may refer in promotional material to you as having been the photographer of the Photographs.] [You hereby waive your moral rights in respect of the Photographs].

[ALTERNATIVE CLAUSE 3.]

[3. The photographs which we choose (the Photographs) will be dealt with as follows:

(a) You hereby grant us an exclusive worldwide perpetual licence to use the photographs as we see fit but with a use related to the Project.

(b) You will not licence the use or publication of the Photographs to any other party for any purpose.

(c) If we wish to make commercial use of any of the Photographs outside the Project you will give us exclusive licence to do so for [a fee to be agreed for each such use] [a fixed fee of £ to cover all such commercial use.]]

4. In consideration of your undertaking the photography and assigning to us the copyright in the Photographs [granted to us the Licence] under Clause 3 we will pay you the following fee (plus VAT):

(a) the sum of £[ ] of which X% will be paid on your signing this letter and Y% will be paid when a satisfactory selection of photographs is presented to us from which to choose the Photographs;

(b) Your reasonable expenses of travel and accommodation on site, provided that the period of your stay is no longer than [ ] days, and any other reasonable expenses which we have first approved.

(c) Any additional use fees as set out in Clause 3.

[5. You agree to supply photographs to us no later than [ ] and for the purposes of this commission agreement time is of the essence [as the brochures for the product launch need final approval by the [ ]]. If you do not deliver the photographs to us by that date this agreement will be deemed to have been terminated and:

(a) we will have no obligation to accept the photographs for review and choice;

411

(b) no fee will be payable to you;

(c) you will immediately return to us the advance payment already made by us under Clause 4(a).]

6. You warrant that the Photographs will be your own original work and that in taking them or in our making commercial public use of them there is no breach of any third party right.

7. This commission agreement is personal to you.

8. This letter agreement is in complete substitution for any other terms and conditions which either of us apply in the course of our business.

[Include other terms, such as where and when the shoot is to take place].

[Check for any advisable standard clauses].

Please signify your acceptance of the above terms by countersigning the enclosed copy of this letter.

COPYRIGHT ASSIGNMENT

To: Advertising Agency

From: Artwork house [Date]

Dear ――――――――

Project X

In compliance with our obligations contained in Clause [ ] of the Artwork commission agreement between us dated the [ ] we hereby assign to you the worldwide copyright and all other proprietary rights in the Artwork as defined in the Agreement and delivered by us to you under the Agreement.

We confirm that we have full right and title to make this assignment and that there is no restriction upon us to do so.

Yours faithfully,

SALES PROMOTION AGENCY AGREEMENT

N.B. This example is exclusive for the U.K., but most sales promotion agencies are appointed non-exclusively for specific categories of brand promotions, and regionally.

THIS AGREEMENT is made the . . . . . day of . . . . .
BETWEEN MARVO SUDS LIMITED of ....
.... (hereinafter called the
Client) of the one part and INCREDIBLY EXCITING PROMOTIONS
LIMITED of ....
(hereinafter called the Agency) of the other part.

412

WHEREAS

(A) The Client is the manufacturer and supplier of the products set out in the schedule hereto (the Products) and
(B) The Agency is a sales promotion agency operating within the United Kingdom (the Territory) and concentrating on consumer related goods;

NOW IT IS AGREED as follows:

Appointment

1. (a) Subject to and upon the terms and conditions set out in this Agreement the Client hereby appoints the Agency to be the exclusive sales promotion agency for the Products within the Territory.

(b) During the period of this Agreement the Client agrees not to appoint any other party to undertake sales promotion projects for the Products within the Territory.

(c) The exclusive appointment of the Agency under this Agreement is in respect of national and regional sales promotion schemes for the Products but the Client reserves the right to authorise localised in-store sales promotion activities by wholesale or retail traders provided that the Client will not authorise any sales promotion activities which it reasonably considers would adversely affect or interfere with any existing or planned sales promotion scheme being operated by the Agency.

(d) The Agency agrees that it will not take on any new clients which are directly competitive with the business of the Client without the prior approval of the Client. If the Agency accepts a new client which is competitive with the Client then the Agency will notify the Client in writing and the Client will be entitled to terminate this Agreement forthwith by written notice provided that:

(i) the Agency will complete all of its obligations in respect of existing promotions which cannot be suspended or cancelled;
(ii) the Agency will transfer the storyboard and all rights in any current concept or project promotion to the Client together with all outstanding copyrights upon payment of the fees and other payments due to the Agency up to the date of transfer.

Agency obligations

2. (a) The Agency will propose and develop a range of sales promotion schemes for each of the Products projected on an [annual] basis and will submit to the Client a schedule of its proposals and a budget for the year relating to each of the Product's marketing programmes.

(b) The Agency will provide the Client on a [monthly] basis with a written report of progress of each of the promotions in being at the time and the results and analysis of each promotion which has been concluded during the previous [month].

(c) The Agency will hold contact report meetings as and when requested or agreed to by the Client so that the Agency can obtain the Client's approval referred to below and to enable the parties to make assessments of marketing trends and developments within the consumer and retail business and to make any adjustments to the planned promotions which they consider to be worth undertaking in the current budget year of the Client.

(d) On an ongoing basis the Agency will provide the Client with general advice on current trends in sales promotion concepts and upon whether the Schedule of Promotions established for any of the Products should be amended to avoid any significant marketing clashes;

(e) The Agency will appoint a senior account executive to be the primary contact between the Client and the Agency to ensure that there is proper communication between them.

Operation of promotions

3. In respect of each of the sales promotion schemes (herein called Promotions) to be undertaken by the Client for each of the Products the Agency will provide the following services:

(a) The Agency will provide a schedule of the proposed Promotions for the Product within the [current] budget year and the Agency will explain to the Client the reasoning behind the concept and mechanic of each of the Promotions so that the Client is in a position to approve the schedule in its presented or in any modified form and thereafter each of the stages set out below will apply to each of the approved Promotions.

(b) The Agency will submit to the Client for approval a concept storyboard of the Promotion including concept artwork and an explanation of the mechanic to be applied to the Promotion.

(c) At the time when the concept storyboard has been approved by the Client it will in consultation with the Agency agree upon a timetable for the production of all the necessary material for the Promotion depending on the lead time required by the Client to enable production of the promoted Product and the availability of printed and manufactured promoted Product packaging to be co-ordinated.

(d) The Agency will produce the intermediate and final artwork and text of the Promotion for approval by the Client by the date set out in the Promotion Timetable.

Promotion clearance procedures

4.1 The Agency will ensure that the basic concept of each Promotion and the artwork mechanic and presentation of it will not infringe the copyright, trademark or any other proprietary right of any third party.

4.2 The Agency will at its own cost take all such legal advice as it considers necessary to ensure that each Promotion will not infringe third party rights and that it will be legal and in compliance with the ASA Code of Sales Promotion Practice.

4.3 The approval by the Client of promotional material at each stage is limited to approving the layout and quality of the artwork and is not to be deemed to constitute acceptance or approval of the material as being legal or as not containing any third party's material infringement except in respect of any information or material which has been provided to the Agency by the Client.

4.4 If the Client becomes aware that there is a potential legal or proprietary problem in any Promotion it will promptly notify the Agency, and if the advisers to the Agency agree that is the case, then the Agency will make any modification which may be necessary to remedy that defect in the Promotion at its own cost.

5. The Agency will not have any liability to the Client in respect of any information given to the Agency by the Client which is incorrect or misleading or for any liability caused because the Client failed to give the Agency any material or relevant information affecting the Promotions.

Proprietary rights in artwork

6. It is agreed that the Client will be the owner of the copyright in all artwork or text contained in the Promotion material and including special photography which is commissioned from an independent party by the Agency and at the request of the Client the Agency will execute or obtain the execution of a specific confirmatory assignment of any such copyrights to the Client in consideration of the fees paid to the Agency for the Promotion to which the Copyright relates.

7.1 The Agency will ensure that if it commissions any artwork or photography or any other original work for the Promotion from a third party it will include in the commission agreement an assignment to the Agency of the copyright in all of such work including all preliminary and intermediate work.

7.2 The commission agreement will also make the Agency the owner of any original artistic work and of any photographic negatives produced by a third party, and these, together with any such material produced by the Agency, will belong to the Client.

8. If at the expiry or earlier termination of this Agreement there are any Promotions which are in the course of preparation or which are being run through the Agency then:

(a) All Promotions which have been launched or which are yet to be launched but where the Agency costs and/or fees for the launch and management of the promotion have been substantially paid in advance or where the third party commitments have been entered into by the Agency for that Promotion, then [the Agency will be entitled to retain the management of such Promotions] [the Client will inform the Agency whether or not it will continue to manage the Promotion];

(b) All promotions which are only in concept or storyboard stage or for which the Agency has not yet entered into any third party commitments (other than the creation and production of Promotion material), then the Client will be entitled to remove such Promotions from the Agency at no cost or condition other than the full settlement of all the Agency fees and costs incurred up to date for those Promotions.

Project management

9.1 The Agency will be responsible for the effective management of each Promotion in accordance with its agreed timetable and budget and the Client will provide the Agency with any information or assistance in connection with any Promotion which it reasonably requests.

9.2 The Agency will provide where necessary or where requested by the Client the following project management facilities or will ensure that they are provided by third parties in accordance with the Promotion timetable and the agreed budget for the relevant activity:

(a) the finalising and printing of point-of-sale and other material which is required to support the product packaging which contains the Promotion;

(b) the provision of a telephone answering service where the Promotion contains a phone-in function;

(c) surveys or research amongst the public during the Promotion period or immediately thereafter to ascertain the impact of the Promotion and the perception of the public of the benefits derived from participating in the Promotion;

(d) the services of a handling house in accordance with Clause 10;

(e) providing a terminal report on the Promotion within a reasonable time after the closing date;

(f) where the Promotion is a competition, an appropriate panel of judges where relevant. The Agency will provide and maintain secret the correct answer to the competition question and will organise any ceremony or presentation to the winners of the prizes offered in the competition and in the case of a free prize draw the Agency will organise and attend the drawing of the winning ticket;

(g) where the prize for a competition is a holiday or the attendance at a special sporting or other event the Agency will ensure that the prize tickets are purchased prior to the launch of the Promotion and where as part of the prize the Client is providing hospitality or any other benefit or activity, the Agency will ensue that it is properly organised.

Appointment of a handling house

10. Where the Promotion requires the services of a handling house to deal with the redemption of vouchers or merchandise gifts in response to applications from consumers, the Agency will appoint one.

11. The Agency will either obtain for the Client a copy of the standard terms and conditions of the handling house for approval or amendment or it will negotiate an agreement between the handling house and the Client to include the following matters:

(a) which of the parties will be responsible for ordering and paying initially for redemption merchandise gifts;

(b) the quantity of merchandise which will be reserved for supply to the handling house for the promotion gift with particular reference to whether availability of the gifts will be limited necessitating the promotion to make redemption of the gift subject to its availability.

(c) the unit cost of the merchandise gifts;

(d) the quality of the merchandise gifts and the back up by the supplier in the event of any of the merchandise being defective or dangerous.

12.1 If the redemption gift is a proprietary branded product the Agency will be responsible for negotiating the supply agreement for the product from its manufacturer or from an authorised supplier.

12.2. If the branded gift is provided by an authorised supplier the Agency will be responsible for obtaining clearance for the use of the product's brand name and logo (whether or not they are registered trademarks in the United Kingdom) in connection with describing the gift within the promotion advertising and publicity material for the Promotion.

Period of contract

13. Subject to earlier termination in accordance with the terms set out herein this Agreement will be for an initial period of [twelve] months from the date hereof.

14. [This Agreement will cease to be effective upon the expiry of the period of [twelve] months unless the parties have agreed a renewal period and terms no later than [21] days prior to the expiry date.] OR [The period of this Agreement will continue from the date hereof until not less than [three] months prior written notice of termination is given by one party to the other.]

Redemption insurance

15.1 The Client and the Agency will co-operate in assessing the likely redemption rate of a Promotion which offers vouchers by mail or merchandise gifts or any other redemption scheme based upon past experience and any factors in the Promotion which may make it unusually attractive for redemption.

15.2 If the Client wishes to take out redemption insurance in respect of the Promotion, then it may request the Agency to arrange such insurance after the Client has agreed upon the premium and upon any conditions which may be imposed by the insurers upon the Client in relation to the Promotion. [The Agency will obtain excess redemption insurance quotations for each Promotion for submission to the Client.]

Financial provisions

16.1 In consideration of the Agency undertaking all of its obligations hereunder it will be paid fees as follows:

(a) When the budgeting is done for each of the Promotions the man hours and other factors which will affect the charges to be made by the Agency will be estimated as closely as possible and a time schedule over the Promotion period will be agreed for periodic payments to be made to the Agency on account of the fees which will become due to it.

(b) Provided the Promotion is progressing as planned the scheduled fees will be paid and before the final payment is made the actual fee will be calculated from the information then available in respect of the whole Promotion and the final instalment will be paid accordingly.

[(c) A fixed fee will be agreed with the Agency on a Promotion by Promotion basis which will be paid as to [50%] on the commencement of the promotion and [50%] upon completion of the Promotion.]

[(d) Not less than [ ] months before the beginning of the Client's financial year the Promotions scheduled for each of the Products for that year will be agreed, and there shall be agreed an overall fee to the Agency for that year which will be paid in equal monthly instalments in arrears. This fee will be adjusted by mutual agreement if there is any material and substantial change in the schedule of Promotions.]

16.2 If a Promotion is withdrawn by the Client otherwise than by reason of a default attributed properly to the Agency then;

(a) all accrued fees for work done on the Promotion by the Agency to that date will become payable; and

(b) any authorised and irretrievable expense committed by the Agency will be paid as well as all properly accountable expenses already laid out by the Agency.

16.3 The authorised expenses incurred by the Agency in accordance with the budget for each Promotion will be paid monthly in arrears within [21] days after receipt by the Client of an invoice for those expenses supported by a copy of the relevant receipt or vouchers.

16.4 VAT will be charged by the Agency on all invoices which are properly subject to VAT.

[Check for any advisable standard clauses].

PUBLIC RELATIONS AGENCY AGREEMENT

THIS AGREEMENT is made the   day of
BETWEEN THE WHIZZO GADGET CORPORATION of
(hereinafter called the Client) of the one part and SOCK IT TO THEM
PUBLIC RELATIONS LTD of

(hereinafter called the Agency) of the other part.

WHEREAS
   (A) The Client is the international proprietor and manufacturer of the Whizzo Gadget (the Product) and it has established a subsidiary company of the same name in England for the purpose of commencing the manufacture and sale the Product within the UK:
   (B) The Agency is an established public relations agency which has marketing and publicity expertise in promoting consumer products and their manufacturers.
NOW IT IS AGREED as follows:

Appointment

1.(a) Subject to and upon the terms herein set out the Client hereby appoints the Agency to be the sole and exclusive public relations agency for the Client and the Product [for the Client and all its products] within the United Kingdom and the Agency hereby accepts such appointment.

(b) During the period of this Agreement the Client undertakes not to appoint any other independent agency to represent the Client as its public relations consultant or agent within the UK, but the Client reserves the right to exercise any or all such functions itself.

(c) The Agency confirms that it does not work for any other client which is in a business competitive with the business of the Client and in order to prevent there being a conflict of interest the Agency undertakes that during the period of this Agreement it will not provide P.R. services for any party which is competitive with the Client.

(d) In the context of (c) above "competitive" will mean that the other party is actively marketing products which are themselves directly competitive with those of the Client and will not be extended to mean parties who are only in a similar kind of business or who market the same category of product but where that product is not directly competitive with the Product of the Client.

(e) If during the period of this Agreement the Client extends its product range to include products competitive with those which are already marketed by existing clients of the Agency, then the restrictions accepted by the Agency under (c) and (d) above will not apply to those existing clients.

Period of Agreement

2. This agreement will commence on the date hereof and will continue until terminated by either party giving to the other not less than [one] months prior notice in writing.

Liaison Executive

3.(a) At all times during this Agreement the Agency will provide to the Client the personal services of Mr . . . or in his absence such other executive of the Agency as will be agreed by the Client to be the prime means of communication between the Client and the Agency (the Liaison Executive).

(b) The Liaison Executive will give priority of attention to the Client at all times subject to his non-availability being due only to reasonable circumstances.

Agency services

4. The Agency will provide the Client with customary PR and any other related services and in particular the Agency will:

(a) devise and provide the Client with a PR campaign strategy to publicise the Client and its international activities and its plans for establishment and development within the UK;

(b) produce a similar strategy plan for the launch in the UK of the Product;

(c) within each of the campaign plans referred to in (a) and (b) above the Agency will include a detailed proposed timetable of events and a detailed budget of costs which will be incurred by the Agency or by the Client.

(d) liaise with any market research organisation which may be commissioned by the Client to review the UK market in the Product and to advise on any strategy which may be required to maximise the sales and image impact of the Product;

(e) advise the Client if required to do so on the packaging and advertising, artwork and presentation concepts with regard to the Product to the extent that it is intended to be "user-friendly";

(f) organise, supervise and manage the PR-related activities of the Client such as customer hospitality and consumer and trade-related personal contact events to be staged for the promotion of the Client and the Product;

(g) obtain favourable press and specialist publication editorial comment about the Client and the Product and agree with the Client press statements relating to any newsworthy event or circumstance featuring the company.

(h) advise the Client generally upon all its PR needs and provide reports to the Client of any relevant press, trade or public comment of which the Agency becomes aware.

5. [...]

6. Additional services to be provided by the Agency to the Client will include:

(a) advising the Client on the layout and design of its corporate and Product brochures and other publications;

(b) liaising with the Client's internal marketing department as and when required to do so.

Client's obligations

7. The Client will provide the Agency with all information and assistance reasonably required by the Agency to enable it to provide the PR services to

the Client on an efficient and timely basis and the Client's obligation will include the following:

(a) giving the Agency full briefing on all specific PR projects which the Client requires to be undertaken by the Agency and which will be in writing or confirmed in writing.

(b) requiring the Client's marketing department to liaise with the Agency and to supply the Agency with all material which is relevant to any active project being dealt with by the Agency;

(c) providing its own liaison executive to manage all of the Agency activities with the Agency's Liaison Executive and through whom all project instructions to the Agency will come or from whom they will be authorised.

Contact reporting

8. The Client and the Agency will establish through their respective liaison officers an effective communication system and:

(a) formal meetings will be held between them when convenient but not less than once [fortnightly] to review completed and current projects and budgeting and expenditure and to plan and put into effect future PR projects and to deal with any other relevant business;

(b) contact reports or minutes of all significant matters dealt with at formal meetings will be prepared and circulated by the Agency and if there is any disagreement as to what is reported it will be resolved promptly and (if necessary) an amended accurate contact report will be issued.

Complaints procedure

9. If either of the Client of the Agency has any complaint about the other then:

(a) If it is a minor matter such as a personality clash or unsatisfactory working habits or environment then the two Liaison Officers will promptly discuss the problem and attempt to resolve it satisfactorily.

(b) If a problem under (a) cannot be resolved by the Liaison Officers or if the complaint is a material or persistent one then the Liaison Officers will refer the matter to their respective department heads for resolution.

(c) If the complaint is a material breach of this Agreement or if it cannot be resolved under (b) then subject to the termination rights set out herein the department heads must refer the matter to the Client or Agency director in charge of PR as the case may be.

Financial provisions

10. (a) The Agency will be paid:

    (i) a monthly fee of [£] payable in advance [arrear] on the [ ] day of each month to cover general PR activities of the Client as listed below; [*list of activities*]

    (ii) an additional fee to be agreed for special work to be undertaken on specific projects.

(b) At the end of each year of this Agreement the monthly fee level under (a)(i) above will be reviewed in the light of activity by the Agency in the previous year and the anticipated needs of the Client within the next year will be agreed and any necessary adjustment of the monthly fee will be made accordingly.

(c) The annual value of the monthly fee does not constitute a minimum annual guarantee so that if this Agreement is properly terminated the monthly fees will be payable only until the termination date of this Agreement.

11. The Agency will be reimbursed all of the following expenses, it being agreed that the Agency will not charge the Client for the Agency's ordinary day-to-day expenses incurred in attending to the business of the client;

(a) all expenses which have been incurred by the Agency of an unusual nature and which have been agreed previously with the Client.

(b) the following business-related specific expenses authorised or ratified by the Client in writing reasonably incurred by the Agency for providing the services to the Client and which are properly receipted or vouched for including but not limited to:

    (i)   travel and accommodation costs for Agency executives who need to attend to the Clients business;

    (ii) bulk photocopying of material for the Client;

    (iii) entertainment of third parties for the benefit of the Client.

    (iv) [*any other agreed categories of cost*]

12. All reimbursable expenses will be invoiced by the Agency monthly in arrears and will be paid within [14] days of receipt by the Client of the relevant invoice.

[Check for any advisable standard clauses]

SALES PROMOTION HANDLING HOUSE AGREEMENT

THIS AGREEMENT is made the   day of   199
BETWEEN   GUTROT   BOOZE   LIMITED   of   [   ]
(herein after called the Company) of the one part and SALES PROMOTION SUPPORT LIMITED of [   ]
(hereinafter called SPS) of the other part

WHEREAS
    (A) The Company is the manufacturer and distributor of the Product and SPS agrees to provide the merchandise supply services to the Company in respect of the Promotion for the Product as set out herein;

(B) The Agency as herein defined will represent the Company in connection with all matters relating to the Promotion;

NOW IT IS AGREED as follows;

Definitions

1. In this Agreement the following expressions shall have the meaning set against them:

"The Product" means the brand of product known as "Gutrot".

"The Promotion" means the sales promotion scheme (including the rules) as set out in the first Schedule hereto for identification.

"The Gift(s)" means the merchandise which is to be delivered to each purchaser of [four] bottles of the Product who completes the Application Form validly and which is received by SPS on or before the Closing Date.

"The Application Form" means the designated gift application form [which is part of the label on the product]

"The Applicant" means the person whose name and address is upon the completed Application Form.

"The Launch Date" means the date on which the Product in its promotion packaging will first be made publicly available.

"The Closing Date" means the date designated in the Promotion Rules as being the last date by which SPS is to receive Application Forms to make the Applicants eligible to claim the Gift.

"The Rules" means the rules governing the Promotion.

"The Specifications" means the description of the Gift.

"The Services" means the obligations of SPS as set out herein.

"Proofs of Purchase" means [four] original promotion labels from bottles of the Product.

"The Database" means the computer database which contains a complete record of all valid and invalid Application Forms received by SPS.

"The Agency" means [ ] being the sales promotion agency which is managing the Promotion on behalf of the Company.

Appointment

2. Subject to and upon the terms and conditions herein contained, the Company hereby appoints SPS to provide the Services to the Company in

connection with the Promotion and SPS agrees to accept the appointment accordingly.

Promotion terms

3. The terms of the Promotion which are relevant to the Services are as follows:

(a) A purchaser of [four] bottles of the Product and who retains the labels from each of those bottles will be entitled to complete the Application Form on one of them and send the [four] proofs of purchase to the SPS.

(b) Provided that the Applicant has sent in to SPS the correct proofs of purchase by the Closing Date and has correctly completed the Application Form, that Applicant is entitled to receive a Gift.

(c) In accordance with Rule [ ] of the Rules only [one] Application for a Gift may be made per household.

(d) In accordance with Rule [ ] of the Rules the Applicant will receive the Gift within 28 days after the receipt by SPS of the Application.

Supply of Gifts

4.(a) The Company confirms that according to the previous experience of the Company in running similar promotions for the Product it anticipates that the redemption level of applications for the Gift will be approximately [ ] but SPS acknowledges that such figure may fluctuate considerably.

(b) SPS warrants to the Company that it will be able to obtain unlimited quantities of the Gift to satisfy the full number of applications which are received by SPS prior to the Closing Date for the Promotion and that it has entered into an agreement with the manufacturers or suppliers of the Gift accordingly.

(c) SPS will maintain an adequate stock of Gifts to enable it at all times to despatch a Gift to each Applicant within [28] days.

(d) SPs warrants to the Company that all supplies of the Gift to Applicants will have the same specifications and quality, design and size as the sample Gift which has been supplied to and approved by the Company.

(e) SPS warrants to the Company that the Gift is not dangerous in its construction or contents and that it complies with any legal requirement or regulation relating to goods of that description.

[5. The Company has entered into an agreement with Brand Product Limited to enable the Company to use the branded Gift within the Promotion (a copy of which agreement is attached as the Second Schedule hereto for identification) and SPS undertakes that it will perform and observe all the obligations under that agreement.]

[6.(a) Only [ ] items of the Gift are obtainable for the Promotion and the promotion has been clearly made subject to a 'While stocks last' rule.

424

(b) After all the available stock of the Gift have been exhausted SPS will promptly send to each subsequent Applicant a letter in the form provided by the Agency explaining that the Gift is not available.

(c) In the event of (b) the Company will make available through SPS suitable alternative Gifts to satisfy valid redemption applications.]

Gift redemption procedures

7. SPS will create the Database into which it will record all Application Form details received by SPS with a separation of valid applications and invalid applications.

8.(a) SPS will check that each Application Form is correctly completed and that the Proofs of Purchase have been enclosed with it in accordance with the Rules.

(b) SPS will reject and keep a record of any Application Form which is not correctly completed or does not enclose the Proofs of Purchase or which does not otherwise comply with the Rules.

(c) SPS will check each Application Form it receives against the Database to ensure that there are no invalid multiple applications from any household. Any excess applications will be rejected.

(d) If the Applicant has omitted one or other of his name or address from the Application Form and if the Proofs of Purchase requirement has been fulfilled then SPS will use its discretion to try to complete the redemption of the Gift without incurring any cost or SPS may consult with the [Agency] as to what it should do for the proper maintenance of good customer relations on behalf of the Company notwithstanding that the application will be invalid under the Rules.

9.(a) SPS will despatch to each Applicant his Gift entitlement reasonably promptly and in any events within 28 days after receiving a valid Application Form.

(b) If for any reason the despatch of Gifts to Applicants will be delayed for longer than 28 days, then SPS will notify the Applicants in writing in an agreed form of letter.

10. SPS will ensure so far as possible that each Gift is undamaged and in good order before its despatch to an Applicant but in any event SPS will accept the return of any Gift which it is reasonably satisfied has been damaged in transit or which was damaged or defective prior to being despatched, and in this event SPS will provide the Applicant with a replacement Gift free of charge to the Applicant.

11. All Gifts will be despatched by an appropriate postal or delivery service and will be properly packaged and addressed to the Applicants, and if any despatched Gift is returned to SPS because the Applicant cannot be found at that address or if the address is found to have been incorrectly completed on the Application Form, then Clause 8(d) will apply.

12. SPS will provide the Agency with a [weekly] update of the numbers of valid Application Forms which have been received and the number of Gifts which have been despatched within the previous [week].

Complaints procedures

13.(a) If SPS receives any written complaint about the Promotion from a member of the public (whether or not he is an Applicant) or from any Trading Standards Authority it will immediately deliver it to the Agency to be dealt with, and if SPS receives any telephoned complaint it will refer the complainant to the Agency.

(b) SPS will make a complete record of the details of complaints received about the Gift or the Promotion and of how they were dealt with.

14.(a) If an Applicant complains that the Gift which was delivered to him was broken on delivery or if it apparently does not work properly or at all, SPS will ask the Applicant to return the broken or defective Gift safely to SPS [and SPS will refund the postage cost incurred by the complainant in doing so.]

(b) SPS will examine the Gift or will get the supplier of the Gift to examine it and:

(i) If it is reasonably satisfied that the complainant is correct, then Clause 10 will apply.

(ii) If it is reasonably clear that the complainant has caused the breakage, damage or defect in the Gift after he has received it, then SPS will consult with the Agency and if the Agency so requests SPS will either replace the Gift under Clause 10 or it will write an agreed form of letter to the complainant explaining why it will not accept the complaint and will not therefore replace the Gift.

Closing Date procedures

15.(a) All Application Forms received by SPS after the Closing Date will be invalid [but if any are received by SPS within a few days after the Closing Date and if there are still Gifts available for despatch, where the redemption rate for the promotion is below the excess redemption rate which has been insured against, SPS will consult with the Agency as to whether the Closing Date should be ignored].

(b) Any remaining stocks of the Gift will be returned to the supplier in accordance with the terms of supply agreed with SPS or (if they are not returnable) SPS will deliver them at the cost of the Company to whatever destination the Company will notify to SPS in writing.

(c) Within [14] days after the Closing Date SPS will at the request of the Agency supply the Agency with the Database and all the Application Forms it received during the Promotion Period separated into valid and invalid Application Forms and any other written records or correspondence relating to the Promotion, and if the Agency requests SPS to retain all of that material, it will do so for a period not exceeding [three] months, after which the Agency has the choice of taking those records or allowing SPS to destroy them.

Financial arrangements

16.(a) In consideration of SPS undertaking its obligations hereunder the Company will pay SPS a Promotion Gift handling fee of [£] (the Fee) which will be in respect of all activities of SPS under this Agreement with the only exception of the reimbursement of expenses. [The fee will be increased if . . .]

(b) The fee will be payable as to [£] on the signature hereof and [£] to be invoiced monthly by SPS [in advance] which will be paid on or before the [10th] day of the month in respect of which the invoice related and [£] will be paid one month after the Closing Date.

[17. Whether the Gifts are stocked by SPS from the supplier on a purchase basis or on a sale or return basis, the Company will pay SPS for them within [10] days after receiving an invoice for those which have already been paid for by SPS.]

18. All other expenses incurred by SPS and which the Company has agreed to pay, including but not limited to packaging and postage or delivery charges, will be paid monthly within [21] days after receiving an invoice from SPS in respect of the costs incurred within the previous month. [Within [ ] days of the launch Date the Company will pay SPS £[ ] on account of postal and delivery charges.]

19. VAT at the standard rate will be charged by SPS upon all invoices for service or goods to which VAT is applicable.

[20. SPS will be acting as a principal in its dealings with the supplier of the Gifts and with any other party supplying goods and services to SPS in connection with the Promotion and SPS will indemnify the Agency and the Company from any claim made by any such party for any reason.] [The Company will ensure that the Gift supplier will provide the quantities of Gifts agreed with SPS.]

21. SPS will only invoice and charge the Company with those quantities of Gifts which are despatched to Applicants in accordance with the Rules and with the authority of the Company or the Agency together with any excess stocks which are not returnable to the Supplier and which are delivered under Clause 15(b) to the Company or to the Agency.
[Check for any advisable standard clauses].

BRANDED PRODUCTS AS GIFTS AGREEMENT

THIS AGREEMENT is made the   day of   199
BETWEEN GUTROT BOOZE LIMITED of [   ]

(hereinafter called the Company) of the one part and
BRANDED PRODUCT LIMITED OF [   ]
(hereinafter called BPL) of the other part.

WHEREAS the Company is the manufacturer and distributor of the Product
and is proposing to launch the Promotion with effect from the Launch Date
and BPL has agreed to provide to the Handling House stocks of the Gift to be
redeemed under the promotion:
NOW IT IS AGREED as follows:

　　1. In this Agreement the following expressions shall have the meanings set
against them:

"The Product" means the brand of product known as 'Gutrot'.

"The promotion" means the Sales promotion Scheme set out in the
Schedule hereto.

"The Gift(s)" means the [ ] brand of BPL product.

"The Trademark" [means [ ] of which BPL is the registered proprietor in
the United Kingdom.] [means the device or logo a copy of which is set out
in Schedule [ ] hereto.]

"The Handling House" means [ ] which is supplying the Gift to valid
Applicants under the Promotion.

"The Applicant" means the person entitled to receive a Gift under the
promotion.

"The Launch Date" means the date on which the Product in its Promotion
Packaging will first be made publicly available.

"The Closing Date" means the last date on which valid applications for the
Gift must be received by the Handling House.

Grant of rights

　　2.(a) Subject to the terms and conditions set out in this Agreement BPL
authorises the Company to use the Gift as the merchandise redemption gift for
the Promotion.
　　(b) The Company will be entitled to advertise the Gift as being the
redemption Gift for the Promotion both on-pack and elsewhere and using any
advertising medium.

　　3. BPL herby grants to the Company a non-exclusive licence to use the
Trademark in connection with advertising the Gift as being available under
the Promotion.

　　4. The rights hereby granted by BPL will be exercisable for the period of
[30] days prior to the Launch Date to publicise Promotion through to [30]
days after the Closing Date to enable the Promotion to be wound down.

5. [The Company] [the Handling House] will purchase quantities of the Gift from BPL or from an authorised trade supplier of the Gifts upon such terms as they shall agree and if requested by the company BPL agrees to confirm to any such authorised supplier that the Handling House is authorised to purchase such quantities of the Gift for use within the Promotion.

The Company's obligation

[6. As a special one-off Gift for use in the Promotion BPL agrees that the Company may place upon a specified position on the Gifts the logo or brand name of the Product in a size and in the manner which will be agreed between them, provided that:

(a) The Company will provide BPL with a sample of the modified Gift for approval (which shall not be unreasonably withheld or delayed) and the approved version may not be modified in any other way without the prior written approval of BPL;

(b) The Company will not modify the Gift or remove or deface the Trademark and it will not attach to the Gift any other label, trademark or brand name (including that of the Product) without the prior consent in writing of BPL.]

7. The Company will not be entitled to dispose of any of the Gifts otherwise than under the terms of this Agreement or as individual gifts to employees of the Company and any Gifts which have not been redeemed validly hereunder will not be sold or otherwise disposed of to the public or any other third party.

8. The Company will not advertise or offer the Gifts otherwise than in accordance with the terms of the Promotion and the Company will not use the Trademark otherwise than in connection with the Gifts.

9. The Company will place on the Product Promotion packaging and wherever else on promotional material as agreed with BPL a credit of BPL being the owner of the Trademark.

[Check for any advisable standard clauses].

A4 Extracts from Copyright, Designs and Patents Act 1988

For easy reference for Chapter 5 this Appendix contains limited and sometimes abridged extracts from the Copyright, Designs and Patents Act 1988 which are pertinent to advertising. Where any section contains subsections or references which are inappropriate to advertising they have been omitted. For accuracy of reference the numbering of subsections is as in the Act, so missing numbers only mean that the author of this book considered the inclusion of that subsection not to be essential for the purposes of this Appendix. Where the Act is to be studied the full published text must be used.

PART I: COPYRIGHT CHAPTER I SUBSISTENCE, OWNERSHIP AND DURATION OF COPYRIGHT

INTRODUCTORY

Copyright and copyright works

1.–(1) Copyright is a property right which subsists in accordance this Part in the following descriptions of work–
   (a) original literary, dramatic, musical or artistic works,
   (b) sound recordings, films, broadcasts or cable programmes, and
   (c) the typographical arrangements of published editions.
   (2) In this Part 'copyright work' means a work of any of those descriptions in which copyright subsists.

DESCRIPTIONS OF WORK AND RELATED PROVISIONS

Literary, dramatic and musical works

3.–(1) In this part–
'literary work' means any work, other than a dramatic or musical work, which is written, spoken or sung.
   'dramatic work' includes a work of dance or mime; and
'musical work' means a work consisting of music, exclusive of any words or action intended to be sung, spoken or performed with the music.

(2) Copyright does not subsist in a literary, dramatic or musical work unless and until it is recorded, in writing or otherwise; and references in this Part to the time at which such a work is made are to be the time at which it is so recorded.

(3) It is immaterial for the purposes of subsection (2) whether the work is recorded by or with the permission of the author; and where is is not recorded by the author, nothing in that subsection affects the question whether copyright subsists in the record as distinct from the work recorded.

Artistic works

4.–(1) In this Part 'artistic work' means–
(a) a graphic work, photograph, sculpture or collage, irrespective of artistic quality,
(b) a work of architecture being a building or a model for a building, or
(c) a work of artistic craftsmanship.

(2) In this Part–
'building' includes any fixed structure, and a part of a building or fixed structure;
'graphic work' includes–
(a) any painting, drawing, diagram, map, chart of plan, and
(b) any engraving, etching, lithograph, woodcut or similar work;
'photograph' means a recording of light or other radiation on any medium on which an image is produced or from which an image may be produced by any means, and which is not part of a film;
'sculpture' includes a cast of a model made for purposes of sculpture.

Sound recording and films

5.–(1) In this Part–
'sound recording' means–
(a) a recording of sounds, from which the sounds may be reproduced, or
(b) a recording of the whole or any part of a literary, dramatic or musical work, from which sounds reproducing the work or part may be produced,
regardless of the medium on which the recording is made or the method by which the sounds are reproduced or produced; and
'film' means a recording on any medium from which a moving image may be produced by any means.

(2) Copyright does not subsist in a sound recording or film which is, or to the extent that it is, a copy taken from a previous sound recording or film.

Published editions

8.–(1) In this part 'published edition', in the context of copyright in the typographical arrangement of a published edition, means a published edition of the whole or any part of one or more literary, dramatic or musical works.

(2) Copyright does not subsist in the typographical arrangements of a published edition if, or to the extent that, it reproduces the typographical arrangement of a previous edition.

AUTHORSHIP AND OWNERSHIP OF COPYRIGHT

Authorship of work

9.–(1) In this part 'author', in relation to a work, means the person who creates it.

(2) That person shall be taken to be–

(a) in the case of a sound recording or film, the person by whom the arrangements necessary for the making of the recording or film are undertaken;

(b) in the case of the typographical arrangement of a published edition, the publisher.

Works of joint authorship

10.–(1) In this Part a 'work of joint authorship' means a work produced by the collaboration of two or more authors in which the contribution of each author is not distinct from that of the other author or authors.

First ownership of copyright

11.–(1) The author of a work is the first owner of any copyright in it, subject to the following provisions.

(2) Where a literary, dramatic, musical or artistic work is made by an employee in the course of his employment, his employer is the first owner of any copyright in the work subject to any agreement to the contrary.

CHAPTER II RIGHTS OF COPYRIGHT OWNER

THE ACTS RESTRICTED BY COPYRIGHT

The acts restricted by copyright in a work

16.–(1) The owner of the copyright in a work has, in accordance with the following provisions of this Chapter, the exclusive right to do the following acts in the United Kingdom–

(a) to copy the work (see section 17);

(b) to issue copies of the work to the public (see section 18);

(c) to perform, show or play the work in public (see section 19);

(d) to broadcast the work or include it in a cable programme service (see section 20);

(e) to make an adaptation of the work or do any of the above in relation to an adaptation (see section 21);

and those acts are referred to in this Part as the 'acts restricted by the copyright'.

(2) Copyright in a work is infringed by a person who without the licence of the copyright owner does, or authorises another to do, any of the acts restricted by the copyright

(3) References in this Part to the doing of an act restricted by the copyright in a work are to the doing of it–

(a) in relation to the work as a whole or any substantial part of it, and

(b) either directly or indirectly;

and it is immaterial whether any intervening acts themselves infringe copyright.

Infringement of copyright by copying

17.–(1) The copying of the work is an act restricted by the copyright in every description of copyright work; and references in this Part to copying and copies shall be construed as follows.

(2) Copying in relation to a literary, dramatic, musical or artistic work means reproducing the work in any material form.

(3) In relation to an artistic work copying includes the making of a copy in three dimensions of a two-dimensional work and the making of a copy in two dimensions of a three-dimensional work.

(4) Copying in relation to a film, television and broadcast or cable programme includes making a photograph of the whole or any substantial part of any image forming part of the film, broadcast or cable programme.

(5) Copying in relation to the typographical arrangement of a published edition means making a facsimile copy of the arrangement.

(6) Copying in relation to any description of work includes the making of copies which are transient or are incidental to some other use of the work.

Infringement by issue of copies to the public

18.–(1) The issue to the public of copies of the work is an act restricted by the copyright in every description of copyright work.

(2) References in this Part to the issue to the public of copies of a work are to the act of putting into circulation copies not previously put into circulation, in the United Kingdom or elsewhere, and not to–

(a) any subsequent distribution, sale, hiring or loan of those copies, or

(b) any subsequent importation of those copies into the United Kingdom;

. . .

Infringement by performance, showing or playing of work in public

19.–(1) The performance of the work in public is an act restricted by the copyright in a literary, dramatic or musical work.

(2) In the Part 'performance', in relation to a work–. . .

(b) in general, includes any mode of visual or acoustic presentation, including presentation by means of a sound recording, film, broadcast or cable programme of the work.

Infringement by broadcasting or inclusion in a cable programme service

20. The broadcasting of the work or its inclusion in a cable programme service is an act restricted by the copyright in–

(a) a literary, dramatic, musical or artistic work,

(b) a sound recording or film, or

(c) a broadcast or cable programme.

Infringement by making adaptation or act done in relation to adaptation

21.–(1)The making of an adaptation of the work is an act restricted by the copyright in a literary, dramatic or musical work.

For this purpose an adaptation is made when it is recorded, in writing or otherwise.

(2) The doing of any of the acts specified in sections 17 to 20, or subsection (1) above, in relation to an adaptation of the work is also an act restricted by the copyright in a literary, dramatic or musical work.

For this purpose it is immaterial whether the adaptation has been recorded, in writing or otherwise, at the time the act is done.

(3) In this Part 'adaptation'–

(a) in relation to a literary or dramatic work, means–

(i)   a translation of the work;

(ii) a version of a dramatic work in which it is converted into a non-dramatic work or, as the case may be, of a non-dramatic work in which it is converted into a dramatic work;

(iii) a version of the work in which the story or action is conveyed wholly or mainly by means of pictures in a form suitable for reproduction in a book, or in a newspaper, magazine or similar periodical;

(b) in relation to a musical work, means an arrangement or transcription of the work.

CHAPTER III ACTS PERMITTED IN RELATION TO COPYRIGHT WORKS

GENERAL

Research and private study

29.–(1) Fair dealing with a literary, dramatic, musical or artistic work for the purposes of research or private study does not infringe any copyright in the work or, in the case of a published edition in the typographical arrangement.

(2) Fair dealing with the typographical arrangement of a published edition for the purposes mentioned in subsection (1) does not infringe any copyright in the arrangement.

Criticism, review and news reporting

30.– Fair dealing with a work for the purpose of criticism or review, of that or another work or of a performance of a work, does not infringe any copyright in the work provided that it is accompanied by a sufficient acknowledgement.

Incidental inclusion of copyright material

31.–(1) Copyright in a work is not infringed by its incidental inclusion in an artistic work, sound recording, film, broadcast or cable programme.

(2) Nor is the copyright infringed by the issue to the public of copies, or the playing, showing, broadcasting or inclusion in a cable programme service, of anything whose making was, by virtue of subsection (1), not an infringement of the copyright.

Adaptations

76. An act which by virtue of this Chapter may be done without infringing copyright in a literary, dramatic or musical work does not, where that work is an adaptation, infringe any copyright in the work from which the adaptation was made.

CHAPTER IV MORAL RIGHTS

RIGHT TO BE IDENTIFIED AS AUTHOR OR DIRECTOR

77.–(1) The author of a copyright literary, dramatic, musical or artistic work, and the director of a copyright film, has the right to be identified as the author or director of the work in the circumstances mentioned in this section; but the right is not infringed unless it has been asserted in accordance with section 78.

(2) The author of a literary work (other than words intended to be sung or spoken with music) or a dramatic work has the right to be identified whenever–

(a) the work is published commercially, performed in public, broadcast or included in a cable programme service; or

(b) copies of a film or sound recording including the work are issued to the public;

and that right includes the right to be identified whenever any of those events occur in relation to an adaptation of the work as the author of the work from which the adaptation was made.

(3) The author of a musical work, or a literary work consisting or words intended to be sung or spoken with music, has the right to be identified whenever–

(a) the work is published commercially;

(b) copies of a sound recording of the work are issued to the public; or

(c) a film of which the sound-track includes the work is shown in public or copies of such a film are issued to the public;

and that right includes the right to be identified whenever any of those events occur in relation to an adaptation of the work as the author of the work from which the adaptation was made.

(4) The author of an artistic work has the right to be identified whenever–

(a) the work is published commercially or exhibited in public, or a visual image of it is broadcast or included in a cable programme service;

(b) a film including a visual image of the work is shown in public or copies of such a film are issued to the public; or

(c) in the case of a work of architecture in the form of a building or a model for a building, a sculpture or a work of artistic craftsmanship, copies of a graphic work representing it, or of a photograph of it, are issued to the public . . .

(6) The director of a film has the right to be identified whenever the film is shown in public, broadcast or included in a cable programme service or copies of the film are issued to the public.

(7) The right of the author or director under this section is–

(a) in the case of commercial publication or the issue to the public of copies of a film or sound recording, to be identified in or on each copy or, if that is not appropriate, in some other manner likely to bring his identity to the notice of a person acquiring a copy, . . .

(c) in any other case, to be identified in a manner likely to bring his identity to the attention of a person seeing or hearing the performance, exhibition, showing, broadcast or cable programme in question,

and the identification must in each case be clear and reasonably prominent.

(8) If the author or director in asserting his right to be identified specifies a pseudonym, initials or some other particular form of identification, that form shall be used; otherwise any reasonable form of identification may be used.

Requirement that right be asserted

78.–(1) A person does not infringe the right conferred by section 77 (right to be identified as author or director) by doing any of the acts mentioned in that section unless the right has been asserted in accordance with the following provisions so as to bind him in relation to that act.

(2) The right may be asserted generally, or in relation to any specified act or description of acts–

(a) on an assignment of copyright in the work, by including in the instrument effecting the assignment a statement that the author or director asserts in relation to the work his right to be identified, or

(b) by instrument in writing signed by the author or director.

Exceptions to right

79.–(1) The right conferred by section 77 (right to be identified as author or director) is subject to the following exceptions.

(3) The right does not apply to anything done by or with the authority of the copyright owner where copyright in the work originally vested–

(a) in the author's employer by virtue of section 11(2) (works produced in course of employment), or

(b) in the director's employer by virtue of section 9(2)(a) (person to be treated as author of film).

(4) The right is not infringed by an act which by virtue of any of the following provisions would not infringe copyright in the work–[under] . . .

(b) section 31 (incidental inclusion of work in an artistic work, sound recording, film, broadcast or cable programme) . . .

(6) The right does not apply in relation to the publication in–

(a) a newspaper, magazine or similar periodical, or

(b) an encyclopaedia, dictionary, yearbook or other collective work of reference,

of a literary, dramatic, musical or artistic work made for the purposes of such publication or made available with the consent of the author for the purposes of such publication.

RIGHT TO OBJECT TO DEROGATORY TREATMENT OF WORK

80.–(1) The author of a copyright literary, dramatic, musical or artistic work, and the director of a copyright film, has the right in the circumstances mentioned in this section not to have his work subjected to derogatory treatment.

(2) For the purposes of this section–

(a) 'treatment' of work means any addition to, deletion from or alteration to or adaptation of the work, other than–

(i) a translation of a literary or dramatic work, or

(ii) an arrangement or transcription of a musical work involving no more than a change of key or register; and

(b) the treatment of a work is derogatory if it amounts to distortion or mutilation of the work or is otherwise prejudicial to the honour or reputation of the author or director.;

and in the following provision of this section references to a derogatory treatment of a work shall be construed accordingly.

(3) In the case of a literary, dramatic or musical work the right is infringed by a person who–

(a) publishes commercially, performs in public, broadcasts or includes in a cable programme service a derogatory treatment of the work; or

(b) issues to the public copies of a film or sound recording of, or including, a derogatory treatment of the work.

(4) In the case of an artistic work the right is infringed by a person who–

(a) publishes commercially or exhibits in public a derogatory treatment of the work, or broadcasts or includes in a cable programme service a visual image of a derogatory treatment of the work.

(b) shows in public a film including a visual image of a derogatory treatment of the work or issues to the public copies of such a film, or

(c) in the case of–

(i) a work of architecture in the form of a model for a building,

(ii) a sculpture, or

(iii) a work of artistic craftsmanship.

issues to the public copies of a graphic work representing, or of a photograph of, a derogatory treatment of the work

(6) In the case of a film, the right is infringed by a person who–

(a) shows in public, broadcasts or includes in a cable programme service a derogatory treatment of the film; or

(b) issues to the public copies of a derogatory treatment of the film, or who, along with the film, plays in public, broadcasts or includes in a cable programme service, or issues to the public copies of, a derogatory treatment of the film sound-track.

FALSE ATTRIBUTION OF WORK

84.–(1) A person has the right in the circumstances mentioned in this section–

(a) not to have a literary, dramatic, musical or artistic work falsely attributed to him as author, and

(b) not to have a film falsely attributed to him as director;

and in this section an 'attribution', in relation to such a work, means a statement (express or implied) as to who is the author or director.

(2) The right is infringed by a person who–

(a) issues to the public copies of a work of any of those descriptions in or on which there is a false attribution, or

(b) exhibits in public an artistic work, or a copy of an artistic work, in or on which there is a false attribution.

439

(3) The right is also infringed by a person who–

(a) in the case of a literary, dramatic or musical work, performs the work in public, broadcasts it or includes it in a cable programme service as being the work of a person, or

(b) in the case of a film, shows it in public, broadcasts it or includes it in a cable programme service as being directed by a person, knowing or having reason to believe that the attribution is false.

(4) The right is also infringed by the issue to the public or public display of material containing a false attribution in connection with any of the acts mentioned in subsection (2) or (3).

(5) The right is also infringed by a person who in the course of business–

(a) possesses or deals with a copy of a work of any of the descriptions mentioned in subsection (1) in or on which there is a false attribution, or

(b) in the case of an artistic work, possesses or deals with the work itself when there is a false attribution in or on it,

knowing or having reason to believe that there is such an attribution and that it is false.

(6) In the case of an artistic work the right is also infringed by a person who in the course of a business–

(a) deals with a work which has been altered after the author parted with possession of it as being the unaltered work of the author, or

(b) deals with a copy of such work as being a copy of the unaltered work of the author, knowing or having reason to believe that that is not the case.

(7) References in this section to dealing are to selling or letting for hire, offering or exposing for sale or hire, exhibiting in public, or distributing.

(8) This section applies where, contrary to the fact–

(a) a literary, dramatic or musical work is falsely represented as being an adaptation of the work of a person, or

(b) a copy of an artistic work is falsely represented as being a copy made by the author of the artistic work,

as it applies where the work is falsely attributed to a person as author.

RIGHT TO PRIVACY OF CERTAIN PHOTOGRAPHS AND FILMS

85.–(1) A person who for private and domestic purposes commissions the taking of a photograph or the making of a film has, where copyright subsists in the resulting work, the right not to have–

(a) copies of the work issued to the public

(b) the work exhibited or shown in public, or

(c) the work broadcast or included in a cable programme service;

and except as mentioned in subsection (2), a person who does or authorises the doing of any of those acts infringes that right.

(2) The right is not infringed by an act which by virtue of any of the following provisions would not infringe copyright in the work–[under]

(a) section 31 (incidental inclusion of work in an artistic work film, broadcast or cable programme); . . .

SUPPLEMENTARY

Duration of rights

86.–(1) The rights conferred by section 77 (right to be identified as author or director), section 80 (right to object to derogatory treatment of work) and section 85 (right to privacy of certain photographs and films) continue to subsist so long as copyright subsists in the work.

(2) The right conferred by section 84 (false attribution) continues to subsist until 20 years after a person's death.

Consent and waiver of rights

87.–(1) It is not an infringement of any of the rights conferred by this chapter to do any act to which the person entitled to the right has consented.

(2) Any of those rights may be waived by instrument in writing signed by the person giving up the right.

(3) A waiver–
(a) may relate to a specific work, to works of a specified description or to works generally, and may relate to existing or future works, and
(b) may be conditional or unconditional and may be expressed to be subject to revocation;
and if made in favour of the owner or prospective owner of the copyright in the work or works to which it relates, it shall be presumed to extend to his licensees and successors in title unless a contrary intention is expressed.

(4) Nothing in this Chapter shall be construed as excluding the operation of the general law of contract or estoppel in relation to an informal waiver or other transaction in relation to any of the rights mentioned in subsection (1).

Application of provisions to joint works

88.–(1) The right conferred by section 77 (right to be identified as author or director) is, in the case of work of joint authorship, a right of each joint author to be identified as a joint author and must be asserted in accordance with section 78 by each joint author in relation to himself.

(2) The right conferred by section 80 (right to object to derogatory treatment of work) is, in the case of a work of joint authorship, a right of each joint author and his right is satisfied if he consents to the treatment in question.

(3) A waiver under section 87 of those rights by one joint author does not affect the rights of the other joint authors.

CHAPTER V DEALINGS WITH RIGHTS IN COPYRIGHT WORKS

Copyright

Assignment and licences

90.–(1) Copyright is transmissible by assignment, by testamentary disposition or by operations of law, as personal or movable property.

(2) An assignment or other transmission of copyright may be partial, that is limited so as to apply–

(a) to one or more, but not all, of the things the copyright owner has the exclusive right to do;

(b) to part, but not the whole, of the period for which the copyright is to subsist.

(3) An assignment of copyright is not effective unless it is in writing signed by or on behalf of the assignor.

(4) A licence granted by a copyright owner is binding on every successor in title to his interest in the copyright, except a purchaser in good faith for valuable consideration and without notice (actual or constructive) of the licence or a person deriving title from such a purchaser; and references in this Part to doing anything with, or without, the licence of the copyright owner shall be construed accordingly.

Prospective ownership of copyright

91.–(1) Where by an agreement made in relation to future copyright, and signed by or on behalf of the prospective owner purports to assign the future copyright (wholly or partially) to another person, then if, on the copyright coming into existence, the assignee or another person claiming under him would be entitled as against all other persons to require the copyright to be vested in him, the copyright shall vest in the assignee or his successor in title by virtue of this subsection.

(2) In this part–

'future copyright' means copyright which will or may come into existence in respect of a future work or class of works or on the occurrence of a future event; and 'prospective owner' shall be construed accordingly, and includes a person who is prospectively entitled to copyright by virtue of such an agreement as is mentioned in subsection (1).

MORAL RIGHTS

Moral rights not assignable

94. The rights conferred by Chapter IV (moral rights) are not assignable.

Transmission of moral rights on death

95.–(1) On the death of a person entitled to the right conferred by section 77 (right to identification of author or director), section 80 (right to object to derogatory treatment of work) or section 86 (right to privacy of certain photographs and films)–
  (a) the right passes to such person as he may by testamentary disposition specifically direct,
  (b) if there is no such direction but the copyright in the work in question forms part of his estate, the right passes to the person to whom the copyright passes, and
  (c) if or to the extent that the right does not pass under paragraph (a) or (b) it is exercisable by his personal representative.

CHAPTER VI REMEDIES FOR INFRINGEMENT

RIGHTS AND REMEDIES OF COPYRIGHT OWNER

Infringement actionable by copyright owner

96.–(1) An infringement of copyright is actionable by the copyright owner.

(2) In an action for infringement of copyright all such relief by way of damages, injunctions, accounts or otherwise is available to the plaintiffs as is available in respect of the infringement of any other property right.

Provisions as to damages in infringement action

97.–(1) Where an action for infringement of copyright it is shown that at the time of the infringement the defendant did not know, and had no reason to believe, that copyright subsisted in the work to which the action relates, the plaintiff is not entitled to damages against him, but without prejudice to any other remedy.

(2) The court may in an action for infringement of copyright having regard to all the circumstances, and in particular to–
  (a) the flagrancy of the infringement, and

(b) any benefit accruing to the defendant by reason of the infringement, award such additional damages as the justice of the case may require.

REMEDIES FOR INFRINGEMENT OF MORAL RIGHTS

103.–(1) An infringement of moral rights is actionable as a breach of statutory duty owed to the person entitled to the right.

(2) In proceedings for infringement of the right conferred by section 80 (right to object to derogatory treatment of work) the court may, if it thinks it is an adequate remedy in the circumstances, grant an injunction on terms prohibiting the doing of any act unless a disclaimer is made, in such terms and in such manner as may be approved by the court, dissociating the author or director from the treatment of the work.

PRESUMPTIONS

Presumptions relevant to literary, dramatic, musical and artistic works

104.–(1) The following presumptions apply in proceedings with respect to a literary, dramatic, musical or artistic work.

(2) Where a name purporting to be that of the author appeared on copies of the work as published or on the work when it was made, the person whose name appeared shall be presumed, until the contrary is proved–

(a) to be the author of the work;

(b) to have made it in circumstances not falling within section 11(2), 163, 165 or 168 (works produced in course of employment, Crown copyright, Parliamentary copyright or copyright of certain international organisations).

(3) In the case of a work alleged to be a work of joint authorship, subsection (2) applies in relation to each person alleged to be one of the authors.

(4) Where no name purporting to be that of the author appeared as mentioned in subsection (2) but–

(a) the work qualifies for copyright protection by virtue of section 155 (qualification by reference to country of first publication), and

(b) a name purporting to be that of the publisher appeared on copies of the work as first published.

the person whose name appeared shall be presumed, until the contrary is proved, to have been the owner of the copyright at the time of publication.

(5) If the author of the work is dead or the identity of the author cannot be ascertained by reasonable inquiry, it shall be presumed, in the absence of evidence to the contrary–

(a) that the work is an original work, and

(b) that the plaintiff's allegations as to what was the first publication of the work and as to the country of first publication are correct.

Index